Revolution and Economic Transition

Revolution and Economic Transition

The Iranian Experience

Hooshang Amirahmadi

STATE UNIVERSITY OF NEW YORK PRESS

Published by
State University of New York Press, Albany

© 1990 State University of New York

Printed in the United States of America

For information, address State University of New York
Press, State University Plaza, Albany, N.Y., 12246

Library of Congress Cataloging-in-Publication Data

Amirahmadi, Hooshang, 1947–
    Revolution and Economic Transition: The Iranian Experience /
Hooshang Amirahmadi
        p.   cm.
    Includes bibliographical references.
    ISBN 0–7914–0509–5 (alk. paper).—ISBN 0–7914–0510–9 (pbk. :
alk. paper)
        1. Iran—Economic conditions—1979–   2. Iran—Economic policy.
I. Title.
HC473.A48   1991
330.955'054—dc20   90–33035
                                                              CIP

10 9 8 7 6 5 4 3 2 1

Contents

Tables

Figures

Abbreviations

ABB	Asea Brown Boveri
AWACS	Airborne Warning And Control System
BASF	The Biggest West German Chemical Firm
BCFND	Basic Conceptual Framework for National Development
CASRP	Collective Approving Sectoral and Regional Plans
CCSRP	Collective Coordinating Sectoral and Regional Plans
CIA	Central Intelligence Agency
CIRA	Center for Iranian Research and Analysis
CPP	Council of Provincial Planning
CPS	Corrected Planning System
DPAS	Detailed Plan of *Amayesh-e Sarzamin*
DRA	Deputy for Regional Affairs
FLI	Front for Liberation of Iran
FRG	Federal Republic of Germany
GCC	Gulf Cooperation Council
GDE	Gross Domestic Expenditures
GDFCF	Gross Domestic Fixed Capital Formation
GDP	Gross Domestic Production
GNP	Gross National Product
HEM	Headquarters for Economic Mobilization
IACI	Iran Aircraft Industries
IEA	International Energy Agency
IEO	Islamic Economic Organization
IFLF	Interest Free Loan Funds
IHI	Iran Helicopter Industries
IHO	International Health Organization
IP	Intermediate Provinces
IRP	Islamic Republic Party
JCSP	Joint Councils of Sectoral Planning
LDP	Less Developed Provinces
MDP	More Developed Provinces

MENAS	Menas Associates, publishers
MESA	Middle East Studies Association
MFMTSDP	Macro Framework for Medium-Term Socioeconomic Development Plan
MIO	Military Industries Organization
MLTNGS	Macro Long-Term National Goals and Strategies
MTNSSDP	Medium-Term National Sectoral Socioeconomic Development Plan
MTSDPR	Medium-Term National Sectoral Socioeconomic Development Plan of the Regions
NATO	North Atlantic Treaty Organization
NBC	National Broadcasting Company
NCTR	National Cooperation Tax for Reconstruction
NIOC	National Iranian Oil Company
NPS	New Planning System
NSSP	National Spatial Strategy Planning
ONDS	Overall National Development Strategy
OPEC	Organization of Petroleum Exporting Countries
ORP	Office of Regional Planning
ORPs	Office of Revolutionary Projects
OSCP	Organization Supporting Consumers and Producers
PBO	Plan and Budget Organization
PH	Planning Headquarters
PPBO	Provincial Plan and Budget Organization
PPC	Provincial Planning Committee
PPO	Public Prosecutor's Office
PRG	Provisional Revolutionary Government
PSBR	Public Sector Borrowing Requirements
PUCE	Public Consumption Expenditures
RC	Revolutionary Council
RC	Reconstruction Crusade
R&D	Research and Development
RGC	Revolutionary Guards Corps
SAVAK	Iranian Secret Police under the Shah
SCP	Supreme Council of Provinces
SKF	Swedish Ballbearing Company
SSP	Spatial Strategy Planning

Note on Iranian Calendar Year and Transliteration

The Iranian solar *(shamsi)* calendar year, which starts on March 21, has been converted to the Gregorian calendar by adding 621 to the solar year. Thus, the Iranian year 1355, which corresponds to the period 21 March 1976 through 20 March 1977, is equated with 1976, and so on for other solar years.

The system of transliteration employed in this book is a somewhat modified version of the system recommended by the *International Journal of Middle East Studies*. All the diacritical marks are deleted, with the exception of the *ayn* (ᶜ) and the *hamzah* (ʾ) when they appear in the middle of a word. Persian and Arabic words are spelled in accordance with the *Webster's Third International Dictionary*, *Webster's New Geographical Dictionary*, or as they commonly appear in ordinary English usage. I have used O for short vowel and OU for the long vowel. Keen-eyed readers will note random inconsistencies, but such is the character of transliteration format and language.

Preface

This book offers an empirical and theoretical analysis of the relationship between revolution and economic transition using the case of the Iranian economy since the Revolution in 1979. It focuses on major macroeconomic, sectoral and territorial trends, problems, and policies; and explains factors influencing the economy including various domestic and international constraints. The book also presents a framework for the postwar reconstruction and examines the Islamic Republic's experiences and options. Further, the study gives policy recommendations and advances a few theoretical generalizations about postrevolutionary societies in the Third World. Although much has been written about the politics and ideology of the Iranian Revolution, the same can not be said about the postrevolutionary economy. There has been considerable speculation about the economy but very little hard data and analysis of economic trends, problems, and policies. Among the major shortcomings has been the lack of a deeper, more theoretical understanding of the nature and teleology of the Iranian Revolution. But, the gap is also felt beyond Iranian studies as, without exaggeration, the Iranian Revolution marks a turning point in contemporary world history. The country also has a large oil-dependent economy that is well integrated in the world market; this should make its economic experimentation and transformation relevant for a good number of Third World countries, postrevolutionary societies in particular.

Among the specificities of the Iranian Revolution is the contrast between its political, cultural, and ideological radicalism and fundamentalism (e.g., dislike for superpowerism, the West, East, and the "American Islam") on the one hand, and its economic and social pragmatism and conventionalism on the other. In the economic sphere, this has resulted in a major gap between the vision of the Islamic Republic and its actual achievements. Why has one of the most popular and radical revolutions in contemporary world history had such a limited positive effect on its economy despite a drastic change in politics and culture? Many in the social sciences must also be interested in pondering this question that touches on the domestic and international factors influencing the postrevolutionary Iran. I am hoping that the reader will find this book helpful in formulating a better informed response.

Intellectual curiosity aside, in writing this book I am also motivated by the urgency I feel for social change in the Third World, including Iran. However, what is even more needed is to explicate the main obstacles to social change in the Third World in order to determine what actually is possible under the given conditions in which the revolutionary societies find themselves. Otherwise, we risk the danger of promoting utopia and will fail to advance and implement more informed and workable development strategies and policies. This may in turn lead to a gradual discreditation of "revolution as a vehicle of social change," both in academia and in the world of practice. Additionally, I hope to draw attention to the national crisis that almost all postrevolutionary societies come to face and the need for a common front for building a new society. My prospective audience, therefore, includes a vast variety of individuals and institutions in and out of Iran, more notably, academic communities, policy makers, political groups, and practicing technocrats. It is in the spirit of these goals that my explanations and criticisms are complemented, at times, with policy recommendations.

I am under no illusion concerning the complex nature of the tasks involved in rebuilding postrevolutionary societies. Yet, this is no time for being a purely pessimistic critic or an overly enthusiastic supporter. The experience with social change in the last several decades should have taught us an important lesson: building a new society requires constructive dialogue and cooperation among otherwise antagonistic forces within a democratic framework governed by the role of law and justice. Without such an approach much energy will be wasted, as vividly indicated by the experience with the socialist reconstruction so far and by the ongoing upheaval and restructuring in Eastern Europe. What is needed, above all, is elaboration of a national interests agenda as a rallying point and pivot for social change. Blaming the opponent and waiting for it to move first for national reconciliation is part of an obsolete political culture that must be rejected, for it is the root cause of all national discords.

A book, after all, reflects the social biases of its author no matter how objectively it may have been researched and written. This book is no exception. Within my value system, national independence and development, peace, social justice, and democracy are ranked the highest. This is reflected in my analytical framework, evaluative criteria, and the analyses throughout the book. Understandably, my conclusions are based largely on my particular paradigm. Others, using a different framework, may or may not have arrived at the same results. However, my readers should be assured that in choosing this approach, I was not guided by some abstract hypotheses or speculative deductions. Rather, I let the facts, along with values, take the lead in the choice of both my organizing ideas and the larger analytical framework. Moreover, I have focused on the process to assess the outcome, and the outcome is not confused for the ultimate result. The reverse approach, which has been the basis for most postrevolutionary Iranian studies, equates the immediate result with final outcome and takes it as a point of departure for the analysis. Data and information is then sought to support the immediate outcome that is arrived at with little respect for the process that generated it. This method, which confuses process for the outcome and the immediate for the ultimate, has led to an abundance of hasty conclusions and ideologically and politically inspired literature on the postrevolutionary Iran.

An even more formidable problem involves incorporating the "feelings" of the ordinary people on the evaluation of a revolution that has touched their lives most deeply. Regardless of how hard we try, only an insignificant portion of such feelings get incorporated into a book of this nature. The problem arises primarily because most of these feelings are normative and thus incomprehensible outside their value context. Similarly, a revolution generates too many consequences for its economy, registered and otherwise, to be detected by any number of researchers, particularly by those focused on the macro picture, as with this study. Rapidity of change is another constant characteristic of young postrevolutionary societies that restrict the researcher in introducing a reasonable degree of detail or stability in his or her analyses and results. These and other shortcomings make any claim to comprehensiveness and consistency only relative. My extensive "on-site" research and discussions with many in Iran could not be expected to have resolved the problem either. Such contacts did, however, give me more insight into some of the finest aspects of the economic society. This brings me to a methodological observation: generally speaking, writers on postrevolutionary Iran may be grouped into three categories: those who have been totally detached from the society though not necessarily from the events; those who have remained on the periphery, and thus have maintained some contacts; and those who have lived in the society with a keen interest in its developments. This book could produce a more informed and touching analysis if I had spent more time in postrevolutionary Iran. However, although not an "insider," I have been fortunate to have remained on the periphery of the society.

Lastly, we still face the dilemma of how long a time should lapse in the life of a revolution before a more or less definite assessment may be made of its results. To be sure, ten years is not a terribly long time in the life of the historic Iranian Revolution to allow for a definitive assessment of its experience, particularly where the Revolution's teleology, that is, its direction and future consequences, are concerned. The temporal dimension aside, the spatial and structural impacts of the Revolution may not fully reveal themselves within the relatively short time that has lapsed since its inception. The long-term is not simply the sum total of the short-term, the real impact of a policy could well be different from its anticipated result, and surprises are always to be expected. It is with these qualifications in mind that I have attempted to initiate this research, hoping that it will facilitate future studies of a similar nature.

Although the book is an extended discussion of the economy, I have attempted to avoid economic reductionism by including historical, social, political, cultural, ideological, and territorial factors in the analysis. The study also incorporates both domestic and external factors and makes no a priori assumption about the primacy of one over the other. Comparisons are offered with the immediate prerevolutionary years, but for a more complete assessment of the economy's performance, such comparisons should be extended to include other Third World economies with similar conditions. Such an approach recognizes the enormity of issues involved in the Revolution, the complexity of the global environment, and the need for a cross-disciplinary and cross-ideological analysis.

The book is organized into five chapters. The first chapter, or the Introduction, outlines the analytical framework I have employed to explain the relationship between the economy and the revolution. This chapter also provides information about the research method and sources used in this research. The second chapter focuses on the factors of varying origins and nature influencing the postrevolutionary economy. Both domestic and international factors are given. The focus is on a set of constraining factors. Chapter Three then details the postrevolutionary economic trends, problems, the policies at macroeconomic, sectoral, and territorial levels. In this way, analysis precedes description and causal-consequential relations involved in the economy become evident. The largely critical evaluation in this chapter is, at times, complimented with policy recommendations. Chapter Four concentrates on the postwar reconstruction. A framework is given along with the experience and options of the Islamic Republic, including major obstacles to the reconstruction. The concluding chapter sums up the findings, updates the analysis to 1989, and advances a few generalizations about postrevolutionary societies in the Third World.

I began work on this book in 1986, immediately upon my return from Iran, where I participated in an International Conference on the Reconstruction of the War Damaged Areas of Iran, sponsored by Tehran University and the Headquarters for Reconstruction of War-Damaged Areas. During the trip, I collected a significant amount of data and information about the economy. By the time I returned to Iran in May 1988, to participate in the conference on the Persian Gulf, sponsored by the Institute for Political and International Studies, and again in August of the same year to participate in the International Conference on Aggression and Defense, sponsored by the War Information Headquarters, I had already completed most of the manuscript. The last two trips, however, made it possible for me to update my research and analysis and gain additional and new insights about the economy that had been experiencing a totally different condition since the fall of oil prices in 1986. In November of 1989, I again returned to Iran to participate in the International Conference on the Persian Gulf, sponsored by the Institute for Political and International Studies. Although the book had been completed by that time, the trip made it possible for me to update a few statistics for 1988–89—mostly incorporated in the concluding chapter—check on certain information about the most recent policy changes and the reconstruction plan, and improve on my observations about the economy and the society since the death of Ayatollah Khomeini in June 1989. Writing about postrevolutionary Iran requires continuous rewriting and updating as rapid change and fluid conditions in the political economy make it impossible for the researcher to create a finished product, particularly one that aims at a comprehensive analysis of the economy.

The writing of this book would not have been possible without the research I undertook during these trips. I remain greatly indebted to the organizers of the conferences and their institutional sponsors. But such research would have remained circumscribed and thus less inclusive if it were not for the constructive counsel and valuable assistance of many in the Ministry of Plan and Budget including my friends in the Office of Regional Planning, of whom Mohammad Hasan Fouladi deserves a special mention. While in the country, I also benefited from my discussions with a good number of lay people, deliberations with economic experts, and consultations with a few good friends and colleagues. They are too many to name and some were too modest to allow me to acknowledge them by name here. I am grateful to all of them particularly to Professor Gholamreza Vatandoust, Dr. Farhang Raja'i, Mahmoud Hosaini, Hamid Reza Sepehri, Bahram Chahardehi, and Mohammad Hakimi.

I also wish to thank those who helped in a variety of ways to make the publication of this book possible. I would like to thank Dr. Zahra Beheshti for her support and intellectual contributions to my research. Special thanks are particularly due to Dr. Paul Sprachman for reading an early draft of the manuscript and allowing me to benefit from his valuable suggestions and editorial assistance. Professor Abbas Alnasrawi, Professor Cyrus Bina, and Dr. Val Moghadam also read an early draft of the manuscript and gave me in depth analyses and valuable suggestions for changes, thereby contributing much to the improvement of the book. I am grateful to these good friends. Equally helpful were the anonymous reviewers of the manuscripts, Peggy Gifford and Dana Foote of the State University of New York Press, and Samy Amer, who assisted in producing the tables and the figures. Finally, I am indebted to Mohammad Razavi, Freydoun Nikpour, Mehdi Khajehnouri, Dimitri Ioannides, Edward Ramsamy, and Jong Hwa Park, all my students, for their research and technical assistance.

I am also grateful for the moral support I have received from my colleagues in the Department of Urban Planning and Policy Development and for secretarial assistance from the staff including Sonia Hamberg, Chris McLaughlin, and Beverly Edenzon. Finally, I wish to acknowledge financial and moral support from the following offices at Rutgers, The State University of New Jersey: Office of the Dean of Faculty of Arts and Sciences, International Programs, and Office of Research and Sponsored Programs.

Needless to say, none of the individuals or institutions named above, or throughout the text as sources of data and information, bear any responsibility for the ideas and opinions expressed in this book, or for its errors and shortcomings. For these, I alone remain accountable. Writing this book has been a true learning process and I expect to learn even more from my ardent and critical readers.

1

Introduction: The Limited Transforming Potential of the Middle-Class Revolution

By the time of the 1979 Revolution, Iran had developed into a semi-peripheral country, following almost three decades of a dependent capitalist growth path. By *semiperipheral*, I refer to the middle sector in a trimodal world system in which *core* and *periphery* are the two extremes.[1] Semiperipheral countries are distinguished by, among other characteristics, their expanding, but limited, home and export markets, technological dependency, and integration into the world economy. Increasing politicization of the economic decisions on behalf of an expanding private sector, emergence of monopolistic and complex economic structures, uneven development, and speedy destruction of traditional cultures following rapid industrialization and urbanization are among other major characteristics of semiperipheral societies. Being in the process of a major transition, these societies also live through potentially explosive political conditions generated by a combination of domestic and external factors. Iran earned its semiperipheral status through import-substitution industrialization and export-promotion strategy back in the 1960s and 1970s. The process was aided by increasing integration into the world system through the oil sector, an industry that has become vastly internationalized since the 1970s.[2] The foundation for the country's semiperipheralization had been laid down in the nineteenth century when the British and the Russian first penetrated and then dominated Iran's political economy.[3]

As I have argued elsewhere,[4] the Iranian Revolution reflected the failure of this model to benefit the majority, a cultural and nationalistic reaction to imperialism, a popular desire for political participation and social justice, and a strong will to alter the status quo and rebuild the society after an ideal homegrown model based on recreation of the forgone cultural values and ways of life. Factors contributing to the Revolution not only included the Shah's illegitimate return to power through a CIA-sponsored coup in 1953, and his despotic rule for over thirty years, but also influential were memories of the failed democratic movements, unmet expectations, a long and continued legacy of revolutionary political activism, and the presence of potentially liberating ideologies. Moreover, the limited industrialization had been accompanied with rapid urbanization in the late 1960s and 1970s, leading to a significant concentration of dispossessed social groups in major cities, particularly Tehran, where they later joined the revolutionary movement, the religious forces in particular. The Shah's rapid modernization strategy (a rather hasty Westernization program) had also led to the emergence of a two-culture nation in which there were hardly any mediating links between the so-called modern sector and the traditional society. Effective were also the changes in the larger world system of which Iran was a part. Fluctuations in oil prices in the 1970s had led to the 1973–75 economic boom and then to the unexpected 1976–77 economic bust. In the midst of the economic crisis, when the ruling class was divided on how to handle the situation and the dictator had to tighten his grip on the society to survive, President Jimmy Carter called for human rights and a limited democracy in Iran. Under these conditions, the Ayatollah Rouhollah Khomeini's strong-willed leadership of the broad-based coalition became a potent force in overthrowing the ancien régime, or more specifically, the "neopatromonial dictator."

A revolution may be characterized by the class nature of its leadership as the state that emerges from it becomes, somewhat inevitably, the major agent of immediate postrevolutionary change; it participates in political struggles as a distinct social strata with specific interests. Thus, just like most other revolutions in the Third World today, the Iranian Revolution can be defined as a "middle-class revolution" because it was *led* by the middle-class intelligentsia, although a broad coalition of the people participated in the movement. However, what distinguishes a middle-class revolution from, say, a socialist revolution is the *cross-class* ideology that its leadership brings into the postrevolutionary state. Religion, nationalism, regional socialism (e.g., Arab Baʿathism and African socialism), and populism are among such ideologies.

By the *middle-class,* I refer to those people who do *not* fall in either of the following two categories: (1) owners of major means of production be it money, machinery, patents, land or any other type of asset, including commodities, who garner significant profit, interest, or rent, and whose primary income source is nonwage-nonsalary earnings; and (2) nonowners of means of production who primarily subsist on wages or income earned through manual and productive labor, are unemployed, or live in welfare. I shall refer to (1) and (2) as the upper class and the lower class, respectively. The middle class, therefore, comprises a variety of social strata who live on their own mental or manual labor or on the labor of others. These include small proprietors, the self-employed or small employers, nonproduction salaried personnel (e.g., bank clerks, and salespersons), professional in the service of business and government including the military, and the intelligentsia. The last group includes the intellectuals, university professors, clergy and religious leaders, teachers, students, lawyers, physicians, and literary people. The intelligentsia tends to take a vanguard position within the middle class.

In so far as the middle class occupies an intermediate position between the upper and lower classes, it tends to share a common, though loosely defined, economic interest. Moreover, as the middle class does not own any major means of production, it finds economic nationalization a precondition for holding on to the political power and controlling the economic society. Monopolization of the political society thus becomes a necessity for the middle-class leadership. The class is, however, divided into various strata with differing economic positions and prospects. The internal heterogeneity of the middle class is further exacerbated by divisions along ideological and political stands. The class, for example, includes secular and religious tendencies, highly literate and illiterate people, modernists and traditionalists, and Leftist, Rightist, and Centrist groups. This *extreme internal heterogeneity* is a major source of *interstrata conflict* within the class. It is also the main reason why the middle class lacks a coherent and strictly middle-class ideology (i.e., a system of ideas) or a reasonably stable political stand. Lacking its own ideology (instead, the class has a lot of ideas!), the middle class employs an existing ideology and in so doing creates *dislocation*, that is, *noncorrespondence*, between its class interest and the borrowed ideology, a situation that leads to ideological factionalism and practical difficulties for the postrevolutionary leadership.

What ideology is borrowed is a conjunctural matter and depends on the relative strength of the various strata, their authenticity and ability to legitimize their drive for hegemony in the larger society, and the nature of the political movement. As this dislocation takes place in the context of a highly politicized revolutionary society, its effect is to exacerbate the intraclass conflict that, in turn, becomes the main source of opportunistic radicalism and aimless policy pronouncements. In cases where the middle-class leadership of the revolution adopts a cross-class ideology, additional difficulties may be expected to emerge including the leadership's inability to formulate a coherent and unified development strategy for reconstruction of the postrevolutionary society. However, as most within the middle class tend to look upward (i.e., in the direction of the upper class) and are motivated by advancing their socioeconomic and political position, they eventually, and after a long period of political vacillation, move toward moderation, pragmatism, and reformism, away from radicalism and strictly ideological considerations. The length of time this may take will depend on many factors including the leadership's ideological strictness and the amount of pressure exercised on the Revolution by its international and domestic opponents. The shift indicates that the leadership is willing to give up the utopia in favor of realism and what is actually possible.

These shortcomings aside, among the forces contending for the leadership of the Iranian Revolution, the middle class, its vanguard intelligentsia in particular, was most prepared and able to lead the Revolution. They were quantitatively and qualitatively superior to other social groups: they included both religious and secular tendencies, were active in criticizing the Shah's policies, and adhered to the nationalistic, culturalistic, and democratic aspirations of the Revolution. In sharp contrast, the upper-class intelligentsia lacked authenticity, for they were identified with the largely discredited ancien régime, and the relatively small vanguard of the lower class (Left intellectuals) had neither a unified leadership nor a popularly understood alternative to the ideals of the crowds in the streets. The Left had particularly suffered from the Shah's dictatorship and anti-socialism.

Middle-class revolutions often adopt an *indigenous* ideology and are largely *nationalistic*. In the case of Iran, a revolution that sought to dispel foreign influences would only naturally rely upon a native ideology such as shi'ism. The cross-class and universal character of the ideology and its identification with Iranian nationalism made it particularly attractive to the ordinary Iranians. Islamic ideology, which had already been revived by the uprising against the Shah led by the Ayatollah Khomeini in 1963 and through the extensive religious educational programs in the 1960s and 1970s, also promised reintegration of most dispossessed social groups into mainstream society.[5] This perceived reintegrative capability of Islam provided the religious middle-class intelligentsia, including the clergy, an added opportunity for the leadership of the Revolution. It is this particular Islamic strata of the middle class, not to any particular individual, whom I refer to as the *middle-class leadership* throughout this book.

The distance between choosing Islam and accepting the leadership of the charismatic Ayatollah Rouhollah Khomeini was only a short one. He had remained uncompromising to the Shah and was able to articulate the various ideals of different social groups both in his speeches and through the practical leadership of the Revolution. The Ayatollah's ordinary life-style and spirituality were additional sources of attraction for a people whose political leaders lived a spiritless material luxury. This Islamic leadership was also able "to rally behind him a wide spectrum of political and social forces" convincing them that their demands for national independence, social justice, and democracy would be realized in an Islamic Republic.[6] Nothing significant in the historical memories of the Iranian people had suggested that this promise would be broken.

For the purpose of this book, I distinguish between a *political* revolution and a *social* one. By the former, I mean a transfer of state power, by whatever means, from the class holding it to a class below it in the social hierarchy. A social revolution, on the other hand, has its object in transforming the inherited socioeconomic, political, territorial, cultural, and ideological structures on the basis of the revolution's stated objectives. It is my assumption that the political revolution was successfully implemented by the overthrow of the Shah's regime. This book, therefore, concentrates on the social revolution, primarily on transformations in economic structures and policies, and forces that constrained such changes. Moreover, as the stated aim of the Islamic Republic was not to create a socialist economy, I shall use what I call the *Islamic vision* of the postrevolutionary state as a criterion for assessing the performance of the postrevolutionary economy. But such an evaluation is objective only if it accounts for both opportunities and constraints facing the Revolution and is placed within a framework of analysis that allows for criticism, comparison, and policy recommendations.

Among the widely proclaimed aims of the Revolution was to achieve economic development, sovereignty, and justice. This aim was subsequently translated into an Islamic vision reflected in the new Constitution (see especially Articles 43 and 44) and in the First Socio-Economic and Cultural Development Plan of the Islamic Republic among other official documents. The economy had grown fast under the Shah but had become increasingly dependent on the capitalist world economy and had developed unevenly among economic sectors, social classes, and territories.[7]

The main purposes of this book are to examine the relationship between revolution and economic transition, develop a balanced analysis of economic transformation under the Islamic Republic, indicate the forced responsible for the gap between the vision and the actual performance, and assess the prospects for the postwar reconstruction.[8] I also wish to use this case study of Iran to reflect, in my conclusions, on the larger issue of postrevolutionary social change in the Third World.

Writers on revolutions as vehicles of social transformation may be grouped into three categories.[9] First, there are scholars who argue that revolutions bring about only negligible or fleeting changes in societal structures aside from a change in the ruling elites. Standing in sharp contrast to this view are scholars who believe that revolutions are among the most effective means for durable and pervasive social transformation including redistribution of power and wealth. Between these two extremes is the moderate view that maintains that revolutions have variable impact in different societies and on different aspects of a given postrevolutionary country, and that revolutionary governments face problems similar to most governments and are forced to make policy choices and compromises that result in the less than perfect achievement of initial goals.

This book supports a modified version of the moderate view. Specifically, accepting the variable nature of revolutions' impact, I argue that the transforming potential of revolution is determined by (1) the social basis of postrevolutionary leadership, the geopolitical importance (or position) of the country, and the hegemonic ideology of the revolution; and (2) the nature (and extent) of compromises (and policy choices) dictated by such diametrically opposing forces as what I call *opportunity* (enabling) *factors* and *constraining factors,* either generated along with revolutions or inherited by them. In most cases, such compromises generally take the form of a movement away from initial ideological commitments toward pragmatism (i.e., realism), moderation, and conventional policies. Whereas some of these determinants exist in all postrevolutionary societies, others are specific to given contexts or conditions. Equally variable is the impact of these determinants on different revolutions: whereas some are heavily influenced by the first set of the determinants, others are largely checked by the second set.

In the particular case of Iran, the middle-class basis of the leadership, Islamic ideology, and the proximity to the Soviet Union and the Persian Gulf became major determinants in the extent of the Revolution's impact on postrevolutionary social change. Whereas the geopolitical factor reduced the possibility of the semiperipheral

Iran to live a more autonomous life within the world system, the contradiction between the cross-class and universal Islam and the narrow interests of the middle-class leadership prevented a systematic view of social transformation from emerging. However, postrevolutionary transformation was also determined by a number of opportunity (or facilitating) factors and, to a greater extent, constraining factors. Specifically, at the outset, the Revolution had generated enormous opportunities in terms of national unity and purpose, massive energy and enthusiasm, new and creative ideas, innovative means of cooperative social change, new institutions and tremendous volunteer forces. It had also generated significant international support particularly among Third World and socialist countries, national liberation movements, and progressive forces in the Western world.

But, before these facilitating forces could be translated into purposeful practices for the realization of the vision (or goals of the Revolution), equally powerful constraints began to develop. Added to the burden of the Shah's economic legacy were the Revolution-induced expectations, unrealistic promises by the new regime, and increasing pressure from imperialism and domestic politics. The war with Iraq and dependency on oil and international markets were particularly damaging to the economy. Other constraining factors included infrastructural, material, managerial, and institutional bottlenecks. Struggles over state power and the social question of the Revolution (including workers councils, regional autonomy, land reform, housing for the poor, and a new international policy) and factional contests within the ruling power bloc created additional obstacles. Equally harmful were the state's inability to formulate a coherent economic policy and regulate its relations with the domestic opposition and the international community. Each of these economic, political, ideological, cultural, institutional, and international factors had its specific impact, and their intensified interaction in the postrevolutionary environment created additional powerful and complex obstacles. Finally, among these constraining factors, the war, fluctuations in oil revenue, the lack of a coherent development strategy, and the fractured domestic politics have been the most destructive.

These factors have hindered economic transformation in both production and policy areas, and only moderate changes have resulted. Most postrevolutionary economic indicators are characterized by wide fluctuations, tenacious problems, and variable but largely negative trends particularly with respect to such objectives as growth, stability, self-sufficiency, and equity. The real quantitative decline of the economy may indeed be greater than what is revealed by the rial figures, as the Iranian currency has greatly depreciated in value relative to foreign currencies, notably the U.S. dollar, since 1979.[10] At the risk of oversimplification, I maintain that the major economic cycles in the postrevolutionary period and its corresponding major determinants may be conceptualized as depicted in figure 1.1. Note that the economy has experienced three distinct periods: sharp decline (1977–80), strong growth (1981–83), and sharp decline (1984–87). Note also that the sharp decline had begun in 1977, the year preceding the revolutionary movement, and that impact of the oil factor, war with Iraq, and domestic politics has been the most devastating to the economy. However, the correlation between the economic cycles and the movements in oil prices or revenue is the most striking.

The transformation of the state's economic policies (fiscal and monetary) has been equally frustrated by the constraining factors including factionalism within the leadership. The result has been eccentric economic objectives, major policy reversals, and the Republic's gradual move away from its initial ideological commitments and radicalism (i.e., its Islamic vision) toward pragmatism, moderation, and conventional policies. This change in direction has

Figure 1.1

Three Major Economic Cycles and Their Determinants, 1977–88

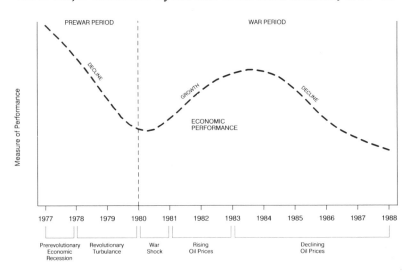

also come about because of avoidable and inevitable compromises that the middle-class leadership has had to make with its powerful domestic and international rivals and enemies. The urgent need for speedy adaptation to mostly unconventional and surprising movements in the economic and extraeconomic spheres was also responsible for the change. The middle-class leadership also faced the dilemma of reconciling its vision with the cross-class and universal ideology of Islam; and this tension, along with the internal heterogeneity of the middle class, prevented the leadership from maintaining its coherence and the coherence of its initiatives. Factionalism, in turn, opened the door wide for the political influence of the big bazaaris such as the profit-hungry merchants and their increasing ability to shape, change, paralyze, or neutralize major policies of the Iranian government.

However, trends in production and policy areas mask significant changes in the structure of the economy, redistribution of resources, and redefinition of national priorities and the states objectives and policies. Significant changes have also been introduced in societal relations and institutions. For example, defense-related industries have experienced significant growth, most large-scale economic units (industries and banks) have been nationalized, almost all basic needs are subsidized (or were at some point); the less privileged places, rural areas and deprived regions in particular, have received added attention, and various grass-roots organizations have been established. Moreover, although the vision has not been fully realized, the Republic has been able to muddle through without accumulating any significant amount of long-term foreign debt despite the war, reduction in oil revenue, and economic decline, a rather remarkable achievement. It should be also pointed out that the 1980s have been the worst post-WWII years for most Third World economies (including socialist postrevolutionary societies). Given this fact, although Iran lost tremendous opportunities in these years, the Iranian economy under the Islamic Republic is not the only case of disappointment for economic development.

The preceding analytical framework offers a far more complex analysis of the forces that face the Islamic state in transforming the society than those proposed by various Iranian Left groups and scholars in the mainstream tradition. In particular, although the majority among the latter group concentrate on religious "fundamentalism" of the new state as the main reason for its inability to continue in the path of "modernization," most, if not all, Left organizations focus on the class nature of the new state to predict its teleology.[11] A few small leftist groups considered the new state another "bourgeois state," thus arguing that no social change may be expected. They called for the overthrow of the Islamic Republic in favor of a socialist state. Most Left organizations, however, regarded the new state as dominated by the "petty bourgeoisie," but were divided on what it could actually achieve. Overstating the detrimental effect of imperialism, some believed that the "petty bourgeois democrats" had ideals similar to socialists and if supported in its struggle against imperialism and domestic reaction, and further radicalized, they could lead the society in the direction of a "noncapitalist way of development."[12] Others, however, were less optimistic, arguing that the petty bourgeoisie suffers from inherent limitations that would prevent it from making major strides in the direction of radical social change. They called for a protracted two-stage revolution, where the second, socialist stage, would take place at the end of a long road.

My analytical framework is also informed by what I wish to call a *modified world-system perspective*. According to this perspective, the self-contained, trimodal capitalist world system has a single division of labor (capitalist mode of production) and exists on the basis of an asymmetrical interdependence between the core, the semiperiphery, and the periphery. To me, the most significant contribution of the perspective is its emphasis on what Immanuel Wallerstein has called "the limited possibilities of transformation within capitalist world economy."[13] The core, which has the most complex economic system and the strongest state, dominates other areas and is able to constrain their development. A revolution in either the semiperiphery or the periphery will not lead to an automatic liberation from the constraining forces of the core as such forces are essentially economic in nature. However, they could make a difference in lessening the extent and impact of such core-imposed constraints, if the leadership followed a more prudent and planned strategy. Moreover, although active support from progressive states and other noncore capitalist nations can also be expected to mitigate certain limitations faced by the postrevolutionary societies, they are not guarantees for a successful social transformation.

The impact of structural constraints could also vary depending on the behavior of the leadership, which is why the role of personality is so important in historical episodes. From the present case study, it also appear that such structural limitations are particularly powerful in postrevolutionary societies led by the middle-class intelligentsia. At least initially, this leadership is hostile to both socialist and capitalist blocs and thus faces added pressure to demand increased functional autonomy and independent development within the world system. It is also shown that such limitations are imposed not only from the "outside," as indicated by most dependency theories, but also through the "domestic" arena and the interrelationships between the two contexts are structural and functional in nature. It must be noted, however, that world politics is in transition toward multipolarity of powers that, along with the current global economic and territorial restructuring, is providing new opportunities for social change in the Third World.[14]

I am further guided by a dialectical methodology that combines inductive and deductive approaches for investigation and presentation of the research materials. I begin with a number of what I call *fact-informed hypotheses* to guide data collection and my arguments. Such guiding principles are developed following a preliminary investigation of the research materials. The statistics and information are then organized and analyzed to identify recurrent patterns, relations, and trends, on the basis of which empirically-based generalizations are made for grasping the essence of the phenomenon including its inner laws of motion. The focus here is on the process and the interconnections of the various parts, which give birth to the outcome. Comparisons are also made with the corresponding patterns, relations, and trends in the immediate prerevolutionary years. Only then is it possible to establish the meditations and links between the essence and the appearance of the phenomenon under investigation, establish its uniqueness if any, and draw theoretical and policy-relevant conclusions. Finally, presentation of the findings follows a logical-historical sequence; that is, the empirical and theoretical materials and events are presented chronologically *and* in terms of their cause and effect relations.[15]

The arguments and analysis are supported by specific data, examples, information, and policy statements largely obtained from a number of published and unpublished government economic reports.[16] Unofficial sources, including my interviews[17] and publications by international and commercial organizations and scholarly communities inside and outside Iran, have also been consulted for a more balanced presentation of the materials.[18] On policy matters, I have also relied on Iran press digests in English, available through Echo of Iran and MENAS among other publishing houses,[19] Iranian newspapers and journals,[20] published books and articles, my interviews with the officials of the Islamic Republic, and discussions with friends and colleagues in the country. Systematic statistics on most aspects of the economy are not available to the public beyond 1986. The statistical secrecy was imposed by Iraq's war against Iran. To update the trend analysis, I have made cautious and limited use of the government's projections and extensive use of actual figures cited by the government officials and representatives of the Parliament (Majles) in their speeches and interviews, or reported in various daily, weekly, monthly, and occasional publications. Keen eyes may, therefore, detect inevitable inconsistencies in reported data here and there as various sources give differing figure or accounts of the issue.

Although the paucity of independently produced data makes it impossible to verify every officially published statistic, in a number of cases where I was able to cross-check my data their accuracy and internal consistency were established.[21] This is particularly true of statistics on trade, sectoral production, national income, investment, and the main items in the government budgets. Less reliable or inconsistent are statistics on military expenditures, war damage, inflation, unemployment, and income distribution. Another major problem with certain statistics, particularly government revenues and expenditures, concerns the huge gap between the official and free market exchange rates. I have assumed official rates throughout unless otherwise indicated. A more reasonable exchange rate would have given a better picture of the economy. The problem, however, is that no one has been able to establish such a rate in a volatile economy.

Clearly, such deficiencies along with other impeding factors tend to cripple a more comprehensive and accurate analysis of the economy. Included in such impeding factors are many unknowns about the complex forces influencing postrevolutionary Iran, the inner mechanisms of the Islamic government, the state's eccentric objectives and policy pronouncements, and information about the minute transformations that have occurred in small-scale operations and in the social relations at the class, family, and individual levels. As we shall see, a number of these influences have been imposed on the Revolution and are more or less beyond the control of the leadership, whereas others result from or because of the Revolution or its leadership. The postrevolutionary economy also eludes the existing theories or models of economic analysis as it has strongly been influenced by a variety of economic and extraeconomic forces originating from international and domestic sources. Nevertheless, I have, more or less, followed a Keynesian national income accounting framework and macroeconomic growth models, including the "Three-Gaps model," to organize and interpret my economic data and policy arguments.[22]

As for the remaining part of this book: Chapter 2 focuses on seven categories of influences on the postrevoutionary economy.

They include (1) the economic legacy of the Shah, (2) the struggle over state power and the social question of the Revolution (i.e., social justice), (3) the Iran-Iraq war, (4) the oil and Saudi factors, (5) struggle for national sovereignty, (6) major bottlenecks and underutilization of the existing productive capacities, and (7) ideological dislocation and systemic indirection including the lack of a development strategy and planning and the state's eccentric policies and pragmatic solutions. The origin, nature, complexity, and tenacity of these factors are explained for a better understanding of their specific impacts on the economy. Chapter 3 then concentrates on such major economic indicators as production and sectoral shifts and policies, investment and consumption patterns, general budget and budget deficit, prices and antiinflation measures, employment and its sectoral shifts, per capita income and income distribution, provincial development and policies, and international trade and balance of payments. For each of these indicators, I identify and explain major trends, structural changes, obstacles, and the state's policies. My assessment of these indicators is offered in the light of specific determining factors. Chapter 4 outlines a framework for postwar reconstruction and then focuses on the ongoing debates among the three main political factions and options that are actually available to the Islamic Republic. I also evaluate the Republic's experience and the most intractable obstacles to the reconstruction including a shortage of foreign exchange and the existence of an obsolete political culture. The book is concluded in Chapter 5, where I give a synthesis and update (to 1989) of the empirical findings along with a discussion on the Islamic Republic's gradual movement away from ideology toward pragmatic and conventional policies. A few generalizations are also advanced about postrevolutionary societies in the Third World, focusing on the relationship between revolution and economic transition.

2

Forces Influencing the Economy

The postrevolutionary economy has been influenced by both constraining and facilitating or enabling forces of varying origins, natures, complexities, and tenacities. These were listed in the foregoing Introduction. In this chapter, I focus on some major aspects of the most important such forces. A number of them had their origins in prerevolutionary political-economic discourse, whereas others were generated by or because of the Revolution. There were also forces that were created by the larger world system and others that resulted from specifically domestic discourses. Therefore, some of these forces developed independent of the middle-class leadership and remained outside its control or influence. Others, however, were not spontaneous, incidental, or imposed; rather they resulted from the state's actions and policies or lack of them.

Moreover, the constraining and enabling forces were of different natures, ranging from economic and social to political and ideological, to name only the four fundamental categories. They were also of varying complexities and perseverance, some concerning local issues and lasting for a few months or years, others involving national and international issues and enduring right up to the present. Finally, the balance between the forces of constraints and opportunities, which earlier in the postrevolutionary period favored the latter, rapidly changed in favor of the former. As a result, the impact of the constraining forces has gone well beyond neutralizing the progressive effects of the enabling forces; they have caused considerable regression in the political economy. Thus, a better understanding of these forces constitutes the main precondition for an in-depth and balanced examination of the postrevolutionary economic trends, problems and policies. Development of a more appropriate strategy for the postwar reconstruction is equally contingent upon such a comprehension.

THE SHAH'S ECONOMIC LEGACY

The Islamic Republic inherited a semiperipheral economy that had been in crisis and decline since 1976. The economy was also heavily dependent on oil and the capitalist world economy for both industrial inputs, including technology, and food items. Additionally, the economy had developed unevenly across social classes, regions, and economic sectors and was largely directed toward production and imports for consumption by a tiny minority of the rich and the upper middle classes.[1] Aspects of the lopsided development under the Shah are discussed in the subsequent sections. The crisis aspect needs emphasis at this point as it had a powerful impact on the post-revolutionary economy.

To begin with, the CIA-led coup of 1953 against the nationalist government of Mossadeq marked a turning point in modern Iranian history. For the next decade, the restored regime of Mohammad Reza Shah (1941–78) used the increasing oil revenue and financial-military support from the United States to build up its reppressive state apparatuses, including the notorious SAVAK. Political stability was also improved by the 1963 White Revolution, which included, among others, a Land Reform Program and a Profit-Sharing Scheme for the industrial workers. In the meantime, the Second Five-Year National Development Plan (1957–62) was implemented concentrating on infrastructure and institution building. Application of a "growth first, redistribution later" strategy of economic development then became the basic philosophy of the regime for the next fifteen years. Industries and urban centers were to gain at the expense of agriculture and rural areas.

Accordingly, the Third Plan (1963–67) and the Fourth Plan (1968–72) focused on economic growth measured by the GNP (Gross National Product) growth rate. A remarkable 11 percent-plus annual growth rate (on the average) was sustained for the entire 1963–72 period. This was achieved primarily by pumping more oil and establishing more new consumer goods industries in and around major cities, Tehran in particular—a policy that soon exacerbated regional disparity in the country. Initially, an import-substitution industrialization strategy was followed but later export-promotion also became an essential goal of the government. The import-substitution strategy had led to scarcity of foreign exchange and had become a barrier to expansion of business by multinational corporations in the country. With the change to an export-promotion strategy, the role of foreign sector and private domestic capital became increasingly important in the economy. However, the expanding investments were financed largely by the increasing oil revenue rather than domestic or foreign savings. The state, therefore, did not need to raise investment capital by reverting to regressive taxation or reliance on foreign savings. Availability of cheap loans from the state made a repressive wage policy unnecessary for boosting profitability of the private sector. Nonetheless, by 1972, disparity in income distribution had widened as had reliance on the capitalist world market for sustaining the growth momentum.

The turning point in the country's economic development, however, came with the so-called first oil shock that resulted in a quadrupling of oil revenue in 1973–74 period. Initially, this development generated a major economic boom in 1973–75 years. But soon the 1976–77 economic bust arrived, creating a real economic mess. The Iranian oil revenue increased substantially, to U.S. $18.5 billion in 1974, eight times larger than the 1972 revenue. The Fifth Plan (1973–77) was then hurriedly revised upward to spend the windfall. The decision was made by the Shah despite warnings from the planners about the probable consequences of overspending. Economic decisions under the Shah had long been politicized, as has been the case with most semiperipheral states. The general budget was affected first and foremost. Indeed, the government revenues quadrupled in 1974 compared to its 1972 level.

The money was spent on a variety of items but most notably on material and human expansion of the civilian and military bureaucracies. The number of government employees doubled between 1972 and 1974 and its expenditures for construction and military hardware reached legendary proportions. The country's defense budget rose from $1.4 billion in 1972 to over $9.4 billion in 1977. At constant 1974 prices, the increase amounted to an average annual growth rate of about 26 percent. A sizeable portion of the defense budget went to pay for imported military hardware, primarily from the United States. Indeed, over the 1972–77 period, Iran's military imports from the United States amounted to well over $16 billion. Sharp increases in wages followed as personnel shortage became a serious bottleneck. The government also adapted an expansionary monetary policy to stimulate private accumulation. The consequent increase in demand led to shortages of producer and consumer goods and to a sharp rise in prices. Only an open door policy toward imports brought the situation under control. In 1974, sharp cuts were made in import duties, taxes, and fees; and the rial was revaluated by 10.38 percent to make foreign commodities even cheaper. By the end of the year, Iranian imports had reached the all-time high of U.S. $10 billion, and it increased by another 60 percent in 1975. A 1975 economic accord with the United States obligated Iran to purchase $15 billion worth of American goods and services over the next five years. Over 80 percent of the imports were among capital and intermediate goods, two-thirds of which was used in manufacturing. The open door policy particularly enabled the private sector to expand its investment, by 117 percent in real terms in 1975.

As a consequence of the boom and the open door policy of the government, dependency of the economy on the capitalist world market increased significantly. For example, Iranian industries soon came to depend on the West for more than 65 percent of their inputs, including technology, intermediate goods and raw materials. Participation of foreign capital in Iranian banking and production also increased substantially. The amount of direct foreign investment from 1973 to 1976 was larger than the amount for the entire preceding two decades. Most such investments took the form of joint ventures with the government or the private sector and were financed largely by the Iranian banking system. Between 1973 and late 1974, some $12 billion worth of contracts and joint ventures were signed with the American firms alone. The boom also changed the sectoral composition of GNP in favor of construction and service, despite huge industrial investments. Financial institutions and real estate speculators were among the main beneficiaries of the boom. The urban land prices increased by more than seven times in most cities over the 1972–76 period. In the industrial sector, the boom produced unprecedented concentration. In 1976, for example, the large-scale industries (units with ten workers or more) produced 90 percent of industrial value added while employing about 18 percent of the industrial work force. Agriculture was the least affected by the boom as the state's subsidies for imported food prevented any significant amount of the oil revenue to trickle down to this economic sector.

The boom also extended the economy beyond its material, human, institutional, and infrastructural capacities. Inventory of goods declined by about 130 percent over the 1974–75 period as economy reached its maximum capacity utilization in the face of an ever-growing demand. Shortages also developed for both the unskilled and skilled labor force, resulting in substantial wage increases in some sectors; for example, over 35 percent in construction. Attempts to substitute capital for workers led only to increased demand for the highly scarce skilled personnel, who had to be imported at exorbitant wages. The salary payment to legal foreign workers amounted to U.S. $3.8 billion in 1977 alone. The bottleneck caused by the shortage of capital and intermediate goods was initially resolved by increased imports, but soon ports, storage, roads, and means of transport became severely strained. In 1975, the government paid over $1 billion to ships waiting to be unloaded. Attempts to use more expensive means for faster delivery of imports to private customers only increased imports cost. To these bottlenecks was added the frequent power blackouts starting in 1975. The economic over-extension, in turn, strained the public administration and led to increased corruption. The combined effect of these bottlenecks led to a substantial reduction in institutional efficiency and in the utilization rate of the existing capacities; for example, by over 50 percent in textile and automotive industries.

The strains on supply, in the face of a rising demand, led to hyperinflation and rapid rise in interest rates. The sharp decline in the oil revenues in 1975 could reverse the trend but the government's decision to maintain the level of its expenditures through deficit spending further exacerbated the situation. The sharp rise in prices and interest rates, in the face of an already high wage bill, significantly reduced profitability of the private sector, including foreign capital, which responded by holding back on new investment. The amount of private investment in 1977 fell by over 65 percent relative to the preceding year, leading to the 1976–77 recession.[2] The GDP (Gross Domestic Production) growth rate dropped from 17.8 percent in 1976 to 7.2 percent in 1977. All economic sectors experienced significant decline, but the hardest hit were oil and industrial sectors, real estate, and construction. Decline in industrial production reflected a 19 percent drop in growth of private investment in machinery and a 9 percent drop in the growth of the economy's fixed capital formation. Although growth rate of services as a whole had also declined, a few subsectors, notably hotel and restaurants, financial institutions, and housing rental, continued to prosper.

Public revenue was among the immediate casualties of the drop in oil revenue. The government had to scale down its development activities to pay its operating expenses. Already in the late 1975, the government owed its various contractors $3 billion in delayed payments. By 1977, the state could hardly pay its employees on time and at the end of the year it had a budget deficit of some 20 percent of the general budget. The private debt to the banking system also rapidly increased reaching the alarming level of 52 percent of the non-oil GDP, or $19 billion. By the beginning of 1978, the banking system had accumulated a deficit of some $3 billion, of which $2.6 billion had been given in loans to the Iranian and foreign capitalists who were fleeing the country even before the Revolution was fully underway.[3] For example, already in 1977, most large multinational corporations, including B. F. Goodrich and Allied Chemical, had sold their investments and left the country. The domestic capital waited a little longer, but when it began to flee it panicked and moved massively. Indeed, some $5 billion in foreign currencies may have left the country in 1978 alone. For example, on 27 November 1978, the striking employees at the Iranian Central Bank published a list of 177 persons of the ancien régime who had organized the transfer of $2,500 million abroad. Among them was Houshang Ansari, the Shah's Minister of Economic and Finance for over a decade and director of National Iranian Oil Company (NIOC) in 1978, who fled to the United States, taking $68 million of NIOC money with him.[4] Indeed, the new Government inherited almost as much foreign reserves as foreign debt (around $11 billion).

The political movement had begun in the late 1977 but its economic impact remained insignificant till November 1978. Thereafter to February 1979, when the Shah's regime was replaced by the Provisional Revolutionary Government (PRG), the mass demonstrations increasingly were coordinated with the growing strikes by the industrial workers, bazaaris, and civil servants for maximum disruptive effect and economic pressure on the regime. Strikes by the oil workers and bank employees proved particularly damaging to the regime's economic well-being and credibility in the capitalist world economy.[5] By the end of 1978, the revolutionary movement had helped to bring the crisis-ridden economy to the point of collapse. Indeed, by January 1979 most major economic sectors had come to a complete halt: oil exports had practically stopped, the banking system was nonfunctional, only a few large industries remained operative, channels of distribution were clogged, and services had dropped significantly. The government efforts to bribe the workers and the civil service employees through an increase in wages only worsened inflation and further reduced profitability of that section of the private sector still active.

Consequently, the 1978's GDP (Gross Domestic Expenditures) and per capita income each declined by 17 percent and gross fixed capital formation by 14 percent following a 32 percent decline in the oil revenue. This reflected the economy's heavy dependency on oil and, through this single-commodity export, on the capitalist world market. In 1978, over 83 percent of the government's foreign exchange payments and 60 percent of its revenues were drawn from the oil sector alone. Decreased oil revenue resulted from both reduction in production and decline in oil prices in international markets. In 1978, agriculture was the only sector of the economy that managed to grow moderately. This reflected the lesser revolutionary activities of the peasantry and the lesser dependency of the sector on the world economy.

With the decline in investment and capacity utilization, unemployment remained high, at 9.4 percent. The government, trying to deflect public discontent, managed to maintain the level of its current consumption expenditures despite the drop in its income by 25 percent and paid for the difference by an all-time high deficit spending of $7.2 billion. The private sector's consumption expenditures, almost 50 percent of Gross Domestic Expenditures (GDE), on the other hand, had declined as inflation had remained high, at 10 percent, and real wages and income had dropped. The foreign trade sector was not doing well either. Although value of imports had declined by 36 percent in 1978, it was more than offset by a 67.2 percent decline in exports for the year, leaving a $0.5 billion trade deficit. Although this economic crisis helped bring down the Shah's regime, it subsequently became a barrier to policies aiming at socioeconomic change under the Islamic Republic. The crisis was, however, symptomatic of an economy characterized by deep dependency on oil and imports, lopsided development across its social, sectoral, and spatial components, disarticulated relationship between its consumption and production systems and among economic sectors, and asymmetrical integration with the capitalist world system.

STRUGGLES OVER STATE POWER AND SOCIAL QUESTIONS

Nothing is perhaps more damaging to sustained economic growth than political instability, a sign of which is aimless and undesirably frequent leadership change. The destructive impact of political chaos is particularly severe in the case of postrevolutionary societies with a dependent capitalist economy where the business community rapidly loses its sense of security and patriotism. The Iranian case was no exception. Political instability and the lack of enthusiasm on the part of the business community has been among the major constraints on the economic growth in the postrevolutionary Iran.

To return the economy to a growth path, the new regime needed to regain immediate political stability and make bold and unmistakably clear decisions and policies. Instead, the postrevolutionary governments found themselves competing with many centers of power and they adopted a gradualist and confusing approach to major domestic and international problems, including economic policy. In what follows, I shall detail the two main phases of the struggles over

the state power and the accompanying contests over the social reform question of the Revolution. These struggles, as we shall note,
had many complex causes. One, however, deserves to be underlined:
the "Iranian obsolete political culture." (This will be discussed later
in this chapter and then in Chapter 4 in some detail.)

Two phases of struggle over state power may be identified. The
first phase was the most fervent and took place during the 1979–80
period, earlier, between the Provisional Revolutionary Government
(PRG) and the Revolutionary Council (RC), and later, between President Aboul Hasan Banisadr and the Islamic Republic Party (IRP).
Prime Minister Mahdi Bazargan, head of the PRG, and President
Banisadr controlled the remnants of the Shah's institutions and were
often dismissed as "liberal-bourgeois" by their "fundamentalist" and
leftist opponents. They were religious intellectuals with bases among
the national bourgeoisie and the new middle class (schoolteachers,
white collar service workers, government employees, students, lawyers, and like groups). The RC and the IRP, on the other hand, were
considered more Islamic and revolutionary. They consisted of various religious groups, the traditional middle and upper classes (merchants and traders of the bazaar, shopkeepers, and the like) and the
lower-class strata particularly the urban poor and dispossessed
groups. They controlled the grass-roots organizations established in
all levels of society during and after the Revolution. The RC-IRP top
leadership was, however, composed of the traditional middle-class
intelligentsia (clergy and nonclergy), although elements from such
diverse social groups as the merchants and dispossessed people were
also included in the coalition.

This first phase ushered in the victory of the Islamic forces.
They consequently incorporated certain groups of the new middle
class and national bourgeoisie among their supporters. The price
they paid for the victory was, however, extremely high, indeed no
less than the life of many hundreds, among them some of the most
able leaders of the Islamic movement. They included Ayatollah
Morteza Motahhari, Hojjat ol-Islam Mohammad Mofatah, Ayatollah Mohammad Hosain Beheshti along with over one hundred
prominent members of the IRP (among them some ministers and
Majlis representatives), President Mohamad Ali Raja'i and his prime
minister, Mohamad Javad Bahonar, Ayatollah Ali Qoddosi, and
Ayatollah Asadollah Madani. The Islamic forces coexisted within the
IRP in relative harmony until late 1983 (the RC had already been
dissolved in 1980 following the first presidential election). Around
this time, a stalemate in the war with Iraq and socioeconomic policies began to widen the conflict between the two principal Islamic

factions within the ruling power bloc, popularly known as "radicals," representing the traditional middle class, and "conservatives," standing for the age-old alliance between the merchants and the top religious hierarchy. Each of the two factions, however, comprised different political shades, ranging from moderates to extremists.[6] Over time, a "pragmatist-centrist" group also emerged and was able to gradually attract the new middle-class segment as well as sections of the liberal or bourgeois tendency. The radicals, however, continued to remain dominant until the presidential election in July 1989, for they controlled the executive, legislative, and the judicial branches. Dissolution of the IRP in June 1987 did not terminate the factional conflict; it simply placed it within the society at large. Following the cease-fire with Iraq in 20 August 1988, the contest among the three factions intensified, a major cause being the debate over a strategy for the reconstruction of national economy and the war-damaged areas. Although the radicals continue to remain a significant force, particularly in the Majils (Parliament), the 1989 leadership change, presidential election, and constitutional revisions all indicate that the pragmatists along with the conservatives have won the second phase of the struggle over state power in the Islamic Republic.

Although ideological-political motive has been the prime cause of the struggle over state power (and remains so for all Iranian political groups), the unresolved socioeconomic and national problems of the Revolution (i.e., the social question) provided additional encouragements or pretexts. The political chaos, in turn, became a source of incitement for sometimes bloody struggles over the social reform question. The PRG and Banisadr both sought to maintain the status quo by demobilizing the masses and reviving the old damaged institutions. The PRG opposed execution of the Shah's officials, banned strikes, abolished the workers' profit-sharing scheme (introduced back in 1963), announced amnesty for the fugitive capitalists, and initiated a loan program for reopening private factories.[7] It also initially resisted nationalizing any section of the economy. Soon, however, the banking system, which had accumulated huge foreign and domestic debts, was found in imminent danger of bankruptcy. Moreover, the large private banks, half of them joint ventures with international financial capital, continued to assist the wealthy Iranians to transfer huge sums to foreign banks, draining the country of its much needed foreign reserves. Most major insurance companies were also joint ventures and in a state of imminent collapse. Equally critical was the situation of major industrial establishments, which were closed down by the owners, who had borrowed huge sums from the banking system and fled the country. Under these circumstances and because of the increasing pressure from the grass roots movements, the PRG went along with the RC in announcing a series of laws nationalizing the country's banks, insurance companies, and major industries in the summer of 1979. The PRG, however, remained cool to increasing demand for changes in a number of areas including foreign policy, existing land tenure, housing policies, working condition, and national minority problems.[8]

In sharp contrast, the RC-IRP coalition, along with the Left and other "progressive forces," supported the execution of the Shah's officials, encouraged mass mobilization, and propagated nationalistic politics among the crowds in the streets. They supported the takeover of the American Embassy, organized demonstrations against "U.S. imperialism," and stepped up pressure on the government for speedy clean up *(paksazi)* of the public offices from the so-called antirevolutionaries. They also demanded quick resolution of the social question of the Revolution and for nationalization of major economic sectors including foreign trade. In retrospect, for some among the religious forces within the RC-IRP coalition, demand for structural change was a tactic to advance their political aim of dislodging the "liberals" from power and disarming the Left of its radical slogans. The Islamic forces used every opportunity to achieve their aim. Indeed, the American hostage drama ended the rule of the PRG in November 1979 and Iraq's invasion of Iran helped the ouster of Banisadr in June 1980. Thereafter, a bloody struggle began between the Left (including the Islamic Mojahedin and various Marxist and socialist groups) and the IRP, which had come to dominate state power. The bombing of the IRP's central headquarters on 28 June 1981 and the office of the prime minister on 30 August 1981 were the two major turning points in the struggle between the Left opposition (Mojahedin in particular) and the regime. The events eliminated many of the most powerful leaders of the Islamic Republic and led to mass executions, arrests, and imprisonment of the Left groups.

From the inception of the Islamic Republic, "the Left was faced with the difficulty of coming to grips with the new regime and formulating a policy of coexistence or confrontation."[9] During the PRG rule in the first stage of the struggle over state power, most Left organizations had supported the RC-IRP coalition. Under Banisadr's presidency, however, only two Left organizations remained with this coalition; namely, the Tudeh Party (the traditional Communist party) and the People's Feda'ian Organization (majority faction), whereas others either supported Banisadr (e.g., the People's Mojahedin Organization) or opposed the new regime in its totality, such as the People's Feda³i Organization (Minority faction), Paykar, and other smaller Marxist groups. The autonomy-seeking political organization, including the Kurdish Democratic Party and the Marxist Kumaleh, were also hostile to the regime. By the beginning of the second stage, the Left organizations had already been stripped of any significant organizational existence or political influence inside the country. Although sporadic clashes had already occurred between the government and the Left, the bloody confrontations began when the People's Mojahedin Organization called for demonstrations in protest over the killing of its members by the Hezballah (Party of God) groups or in support of Banisadr, beginning in early months of 1981.[10] Thereafter, in less than two years, the IRP-dominated regime eliminated most Left opposition groups by a combination of mass imprisonment and executions. The last organizations to be attacked were the Tudeh Party and the People's Fada³ian Organization (majority faction). By the end of 1983, the middle-class leadership had eliminated both the Right and the Left opposition and completed its drive for the total monopoly of state power.

The middle-class leadership's drive for political monopoly is rooted in the class's essentially well-founded fear of practices and intentions of the upper and the lower classes as well as its own unstable coherence. The middle-class leadership attempts to reform the postrevolutionary society after the image of the class it represents the most. The upper class, supported by the Right and its huge wealth and imperial powers, on the other hand, attempts to block unconventional changes and return the society to its prerevolutionary status quo. As it happens, sections of the upper class continue to play a key role within the ruling power bloc long after the revolution. If the upper class succeeds, the middle class will loose its newly acquired economic privileges and political autonomy. In sharp contrast, the lower class, agitated by the Left and motivated by its own desire for social justice, attempts to further radicalize the society in the direction of realizing its demands and expectations. They are involved in "illegal" seizures of factories, agricultural lands, and empty houses; they organize themselves in councils, unions, and parties to fight resistance to their actions. The Left particularly frightens the middle class by calling for the elimination of private property and the conventional army while resisting delivery of its machine guns to the state and dismantling its militia organizations. The politics of the Right and the Left also has the effect of destabilizing the middle class from within, leading to heightened factionalism. All this leads the middle-class leadership (or a particular faction of it) to quickly monopolize political power as a result of which the postrevolutionary society begins to polarize almost immediately after the revolution. The political monopoly is achieved primarily by means of partial economic nationalization and extended political repression. In the Iranian case, the middle-class leadership also has used politicization and radicalization of the Islamic ideology to neutralize its political rivals.

In retrospect, the Iranian Left failed to anticipate this monopolizing behavior of the middle-class leadership or its root causes and make democracy a major postrevolutionary project. Instead, it more or less espoused following a confrontationalist approach to the standing issues between itself and the regime. Those who wished to coexist (e.g., the Tudeh Party) were forced to pay dearly for the extremism of the others. From the beginning, the Left failed to realize that creating a state within another state would be unacceptable under any kind of government regardless of how democratic it was. The Left organizations, for example, insisted on preserving their arms and militias long after the Revolution, occupied the universities and fortified them, and ignored the government's repeated calls for a halt to increasing street demonstrations, some of which were carried by armed young radicals *(tazahorat-e mosalahaneh)*. They frequently cited their active participation in the Revolution as giving them the right to such demands and actions. While true, they failed to realize that such participation could hardly legitimize unthoughtfulness in political process and disruptive behavior. In the meantime, they enticed largely self-motivated grass-roots movements over the social question of the Revolution to further their political aim of taking over state power. These included struggles for the workers' councils, housing for the urban poor, land reform, regional autonomy, and national sovereignty particularly vis-à-vis the United States.[11] It needs to be emphasized that, although the Left acted as a catalyst for these movements, it was encouraged largely by the Revolution-induced expectations and the inability of the government to act in a centralized manner.

The industrial workers' councils' *(shuraha-ye kargari)* movement was largely spontaneous and aimed at introducing workplace democracy and legislation for better working conditions.[12] Specific demands included a share in management of the workplace, legislation of strikes, higher wages, a share in profit, unemployment funds, a forty hour work week, affordable housing, and job security. The workers had participated in the Revolution with devotion and strength and considered these demands just and legitimate. However, the government and the factory owners would not accept these demands, arguing that they were disruptive and political. At times the conflict turned violent as the state tried to intervene in behalf of the old owners and managers and the state appointees in public industries, who at times had been expelled or taken hostage by the workers. The state used a combination of force and persuasion to break workers' strikes and street demonstrations. The frequent clashes resulted in repeated work stoppage and disruption in production. The councils survived until mid-1981 when the then IRP-dominated government abolished them in favor of the now-existing Islamic workers-administrators councils.

The housing movement for the urban poor had its origin in a speech by Ayatollah Khomeini in which he promised to "build homes for the poor all over the country."[13] The urban poor had participated in the Revolution fervently and was considered the most reliable base of power for the new Republic. A Housing Foundation was subsequently established to carry out the task by means of private contributions. It started promoting self-help housing via interest free loans, provision of construction materials, and technical assistance. In the meantime, however, the foundation encouraged the poor to occupy empty houses, nonfunctioning luxury hotels, and unoccupied public buildings. This led to disruption and uncertainty in the private housing market and construction sector. Soon pressure from the private sector, the PRG, and the conservative religious groups forced the RC to limit the excesses of the foundation by nationalizing certain categories of urban lands and regulating the housing market.[14] Thereafter, all unauthorized housing takeovers were violently crushed by the IRP-dominated government.

The most violent struggle, however, took place over the land question in rural areas particularly in places where large mechanized farms existed or where the 1963 Land Reform had not been fully implemented.[15] These included most ethnic areas (notably Kurdestan, West Azarbaijan, Turkoman Sahra, and Baluchestan) and the provinces of Gurgan, Khurasan, and Fars, among others. Moreover, where land had been redistributed during the 1963 Land Reform program, the previous landlords reclaimed their lands, arguing that the Shah's reform was un-Islamic. The peasants, however, resisted eviction and along with the landless peasants began expropriating large holdings, justifying their action by citing Islam's concern for equity and social justice. The clash between the landlords and the peasants soon developed into large-scale bloody struggles as both sides were organized into respective unions and councils. As we shall shortly see, the consequence for agriculture was far-reaching because a good amount of disputed land could not be cultivated. The PRG took sides with the landlords citing illegality of the peasants' actions as the reason. The RC-IRP, however, supported the peasants except in places where political groups were demanding regional autonomy. Although the peasantry had not actively participated in the Revolution, they were considered a significant source of recruits in the newly created Islamic organizations such as the Revolutionary Guard Corps and Mobilization of the Oppressed. The peasant movement lasted until the end of 1981 when the IRP-dominated government brought it under control using a combination of repression and the promise of reforms, most of which remain to be implemented.

The revolution also became a source of encouragement for the ethnic peoples who had participated in it and expected rewards specifically in terms of regional autonomy and redress in interethnic disparity. The ethnic political organizations were also motivated by the fact that the central government was weak and could not use its repressive apparatuses effectively.[16] The government was not, however, sympathetic to demands for autonomy, which it considered a ploy for separatism. Not having the necessary force to repress the demand, the PRG recruited the landlords and their retainers to fight ethnic collective movements. But this policy made it easier for the ethnic political organizations to attract an increasing number of the landless peasants. Subsequently, the autonomy movements became entangled in the struggle over the land. The use of force against these movements was among a few other policies (e.g. anticommunism) that the RC-IRP shared with the PRG. Except for the Kurdish movement, which has been surprisingly tenacious, though not effective, all other autonomy movements were crushed before they could make any significant lasting impression on the national politics. Their impact on the economy of the period must have been significant as economic activities in the ethnic areas were largely disrupted and the state had to divert significant resources and energy to suppress them.

THE STRUGGLE FOR NATIONAL SOVEREIGNTY

The impact of external forces on postrevolutionary Iran has been also significant. Iran has in the past paid dearly for its geopolitical importance to both, the West and the East. Proximity to the Union of Soviet Socialist Republics, the Persian Gulf, and the country's control of the Strait of Hormoz has meant that revolutionary

Iran would be watched most closely by both the United States and the Soviet Union.

Iran was also a big market for Western goods and a country with huge gas and oil reserves. For example, the March 1975 economic accord between Iran and the United States "committed Iran to the expenditure of $15 billion on American goods and services over the next five years" and had set the stage for an "Iranian-American nonmilitary and nonoil trade" that, according to James Bill, "could reach $23 to $26 billion" by 1981.[17] Already in 1978, the United States was exporting some $12.7 billion worth of such goods and services. yet, the United States was Iran's second largest supplier of nonmilitary imports, the number one being West Germany. In 1978, Iran also purchased some $12 billion worth of military equipment from the United States, a deal that led the United States to purchase some 16 percent of Iran's total oil exports.[18] To get a better picture of Iran's importance to the West, one also must account for its multibillion dollar trade relations with Western Europe, Japan, and Canada. The Islamic Republic's geopolitical and economic importance increased in the face of a popular Revolution that sought to propagate its revolutionary Islam in the neighboring states where most of world oil energy is produced. Concern for the Republic's behavior multiplied because of a significant politicization of Islam (Islamic Revivalism) in the Arab world following the Revolution in Iran, the American hostage drama, and the Soviet intervention in Afghanistan. There was also the old concern with security of Israel and the new anxiety with the growing strength in Lebanon of the Palestine Liberation Organization and Muslim militia forces including Amal and Hezbullah. For the United States government, the Middle East became a region of "vital interests" by the early 1980 (the Carter Doctrine). The American administration was also determined to "retrieve" the strategically important Iran, which it had "lost" because of the CIA "intelligence failure."[19]

In addition, imperial powers and their lackeys have never lived in harmony and peace with revolutions. This imperial hostility increased in the face of a Revolution that demanded national independence, respect, and equal treatment within the world system. But the dominant core nations, the United States in particular, were hardly prepared to let an important semiperiphery break out of the chains of the capitalist world economy. Being also unhappy and disgusted with adventurism of the Islamic Republic, they used a variety of methods and means, violent and peaceful, covert and overt, diplomatic and economic, to undermine the Revolution and moderate the Islamic leadership. These measures were specially destructive for a

war economy that remained dependent on the single-commodity export of oil and on the capitalist world economy for the volume,
flow, and prices of it exports, foreign exchange, industrial inputs,
technology, and food items. It is unfortunate that the middle-class
leadership of the Islamic Republic, lacking a theory of foreign policy
beyond the general principle of "No East, No West," would use the
same model of force used against it by the imperial powers to respond to their destructive measures. A further problem with the Republic's international diplomacy concerned its inconsistencies and
vacillation between rapprochement and hostility toward the West in
general, and the United States in particular. The pressure of economic hardship dictated a more conciliatory relationship, while
distrust of the West remained the source of an unyielding foreign
policy conduct. This tension was further exacerbated by the factional politics within the state. A nonconfrontational, congruous diplomacy, *a la Sandinista* (Nicaragua), I suppose, would have been
more suitable in the given situation of Iran, even though such a policy would have not made the American administration content with
the Revolution either.

The struggle for national independence was fought on several
fronts but most notably against the United States's domination of
the Iranian politics and economy. To begin with, "the Great Satan,"
as Ayatollah Khomeini preferred to call the American government,
refused to recognize the Revolution; this policy was unacceptable to
most Iranians and their leaders. They recalled the Americans' unequivocal support for the dictatorial role of the Shah since the CIA-
led coup in 1953. Instead, the administration in Washington tried to
infiltrate the Revolution and change its course by means of a well-
orchestrated CIA intelligence operation. According to James Bill, the
Agency even used "visa weapon" for the purpose:

> By the fall of 1979, U.S. officials in Iran were using the visa
> weapon as a means of gathering intelligence information about
> revolutionary Iran. Most of the high-ranking members of the an-
> cien régime had been assisted, and now most applications origi-
> nated from middle-class Iranians. Their only hope for a visa was to
> provide valuable information to American authorities. This proce-
> dure was summarized in a September 18, 1979, memorandum
> from the U.S. defense attache: "Visa referrals will only repeat *only*
> be handled to gain intelligence information useful to the United
> States government."[20]

The CIA also attempted to recruit the new Republic's top administrators into its service. They included the Prime Minister Bazargan,

his deputy, Abbas Amir Entezam, President Banisadr, and Ebrahim Yazdi, minister of Foreign Affairs, among other "moderates."[21]

In the meantime, acting suspiciously slow in renegotiating major treaties and contracts involving the United States, the PRG invited mass protests and harsh criticism against itself. The secret meeting of Premier Mahdi Bazargan and his minister of Foreign Affairs, Ebrahim Yazdi, with Zbigniew Brzezinski, then national security advisor to President Jimmy Carter, on 1 November 1979, in Algiers, provided the opposition with additional pretext to accuse the liberal PRG of pro-Americanism. The meeting had followed the crisis that had been created by the Carter administration's admittance of the Shah to the country on 22 October 1979. He was said to have been admitted on "humanitarian grounds," more specifically for admission to Cornell University Hospital in New York City, where he later underwent surgery for cancer. For most Iranians, however, the Shah's presence in the United States meant more trouble for the Revolution. Looking for a pretext to force the Shah out of the United States and to oust the liberals from the revolutionary government, the ·Students of the Imam's Line, a heretofore unknown radical Islamic group, occupied the American Embassy in Tehran on 4 November 1979.[22] Ayatollah Khomeini, the RC-IRP coalition, the Left, and almost every progressive force in the country declared their support for the action. The day after, the Iranian government cancelled the 1957 Treaty of Military Cooperation with the United States, who retaliated on November 9 by halting shipment of $300 million worth of spare parts purchased by Iran.

The Students' immediate demands included the return of the Shah to Iran to stand trial for his "crimes against the people" and transfer of some billion dollars of his family's wealth to the country. However, as it subsequently became clear, the Students' true (and initially hidden) demand went well beyond the Shah. Specifically, they used the episode to expose the United States's past involvements in Iran (and the Third World) and to discredit those in contact with the American Embassy in Tehran, mostly the moderates associated with the PRG and with a few liberal organizations including the Liberation Movement *(nehzat-e azadi)*. Publication of some sixty plus volumes of documents captured from the Embassy was meant to help realize these aims.[23] In the meantime, the RC-IRP coalition used the episode to drive the liberals out of the government and destroy the Left and other potential opponents. The hostage episode occurred in the midst of the struggles over state power and the social question of the Revolution and signalled a shift to radical politics against "imperialism," the United States in particular.

The American government's response was initially cautious an diplomatic: It attempted to use the event to open direct talks with the new radicals in power, hoping to nurture moderation in the middle-class leadership and renew old ties of friendship. In the meantime, the American administration continued to infiltrate revolutionary posts and positions. Failing to achieve these aims, the United States sought to pressure or indirectly negotiate with the Islamic Republic through friendly states, influential individuals, and the United Nations. At the same time, however, it imposed trade embargoes on Iran, coordinated such actions with its allies throughout the world, Western Europe and Japan in particular, froze some $8 billion in Iranian assets held in the United States, introduced a more restrictive immigration policy against Iranian nationals, and banned the travel of Americans to Iran. Although not completely successful, the Carter administration was able to line up enough support for its policies to inflict significant damage on the Iranian economy, which remained dependent on the capitalist world economy for most of its industrial inputs and food items. Most major U.S. allies were also unhappy with the Revolution and its Islamic leadership and thus more or less cooperated with the Carter administration.[24] As we shall see, among other measures, the administration's economic punishment included manipulation of the international oil market largely through the Saudi leverage, which resulted in a significant fall in oil prices by 1986.

The United States also sought to destabilize the Islamic Republic by inciting division within the revolutionary movement, authorizing the CIA to finance activities of certain Iranian exile groups, and instigating military coups, the most ambitious of which was centered in Nuzheh air base near Hamadan in July 1980. The coup attempt had followed President Carter's decision to break diplomatic relations with Iran, on 7 April, and the failure of hostage rescue mission, on 24–25 April (see later). To give one example of such attempts, according to James Bill:

> U.S. intelligence agencies hired a private Texas firm known as Peregrine International Associates to carry out clandestine activities abroad. One of Peregrine's plans involved a 1982 plot to support a military coup against Iran that included the planned assassination of Ayatollah Khomeini. When the key Iranian military operative failed to appear in New York with the $120 million promised to finance the project, the plot died prematurely.[25]

Mansour Farhang (quoting *Washington Post*, 19 November 1986) indicates that: "In 1981, President Reagan's first act on Iran was to issue a secret presidential order, called "findings," authorizing the CIA to support pro-Western Iranian exiles opposed to the Khomeini regime." He then gives the following specifics:

> This order included the payment of nearly $6 million to various royalist Iranians based in Europe and financing an anti-Khomeini exile group radio station in Egypt. A Paris based group, Front for the Liberation of Iran, headed by Ali Amini, the man who negotiated the first post Mossaddeq oil agreement with the U.S. and British oil companies, received $100,000 a month. In 1983, Oliver North became involved in supervising the FLI after hearing allegations of corruption within the group.[26]

The list of those who received money from the CIA also includes such "nationalist" leaders as Rear Admiral Ahmad Madani, the first defense minister of the Islamic Republic, and Shahpour Bakhtiar, the last prime minister of the Shah. Bakhtiar and exile groups are also alleged to have received money from Iraq. In addition, a notorious "Tribal Alliance of Iran," formed by a small group of exiled Iranian tribal leaders continue to receive support from the CIA.[27]

The Reagan administration also encouraged its friends in the region to take a conflictual stand toward adventurism of the middle-class leadership in Iran and cooperated with certain plans designed to overthrow the Islamic regime. In the Middle East, the "Reagan Doctrine" was to be operationalized by Saudi Arabia, Iraq, and Israel, and other less important regional allies (e.g., Sudan under Ja'far Numeiri). In return, these governments would receive special favor from Washington.[28] Such cooperations with Iraq and Saudi Arabia are explained in a following section. Here I shall give two examples of such plans that involved Israel, among other nations. Example one, according to Samuel Segev (a former Israeli intelligence official), at least four governments were cooperating on a sophisticated plan to overthrow the Islamic Republic in 1982. The plan, which aimed at restoring the throne for the Shah's son, was organized by Israeli arms merchants and then defense minister Ariel Sharon, financed by the Saudi government (at some $800 million), backed by the CIA (under the directorship of William Casey), and based in Sudan under the leadership of Ja'far Numeiri. The plot was killed by the change in government in Israel after the massacre at the Sabra and Shatila Palestinian refugee camps.[29]

Example two, Stuart Schaar, in search of the main reason for the joint U.S.-Israeli arms sales to Iran as was disclosed during the Iran-Contra scandal, finds that the real motive laid in a plan to overthrow the Islamic Republic by means of a military coup. According to Schaar, Israelis had convinced the Reagan administration that more arms for the Iranian army would boost the morale of the moderate officers and assist them in defeating Iraq. In that case, according to Israelis, the officers would become national heroes, a position that would increase their chance for a successful coup against Ayatollah Khomeini. He quotes extensive Israeli and American sources to substantiate this thesis. To give one example, Schaar, quoting the *Report of the Congressional Committee Investigating the Iran-Contra Affairs,* writes that by 14 November 1985, National Security Council advisor William McFarlane told CIA director William Casey of the "Israeli military plan to move arms to certain elements of the Iranian military who are prepared to overthrow the government."[30] Mansour Farhang also suggests a somewhat similar scenario. Quoting the *Washington Post* (16 August 1987), he notes that Israeli defense minister Ariel Sharon had convinced the Reagan administration (back in 1982?) that arms sales to Iran would assist the United States and his country "to cozy up to some of these army generals because they are the ones that will knock off these madmen."[31] Quoting those involved in the "plots," *Newsweek* (19 June 1989, p. 4), gives the following details:

> Before their disastrous secret decision to sell arms to Iran, senior Reagan administration officials considered plots to overthrow—and perhaps take the life of—Ayatlloah Ruhollah Khomeini. In their 1985 discussions, former CIA director William Casey and top National Security Council officials raised the possibility of Israeli arms deliveries to Iranian dissidents who would then stage a coup. Another plan that was discussed involved an Israeli commando assault on Khomeini's stronghold, participants in the planning say.
>
> Casey was "100 percent behind" the anti-Khomeini plots, a U.S. intelligence operative says. But he and the other plotters eventually decided dropping in Israeli commandos would lead to a "bloody massacre" and considered poisoning Khomeini instead.

The plan to overthrow the Islamic Republic, according to Schaar, was "side-tracked by major shifts inside the Iranian armed forces by July–August 1986." Following the Iran-Contra scandal in November 1986, the Iranian government arrested some 200 officers including the army counterintelligence chief, Colonel Mehdi Katibeh, who was subsequently put to death along with many more.

There is as yet little verifiable evidence directly connecting the American administration to the origins of Iraq's war against Iran, which began in 22 September 1980. As Shahram Chubin and Charles Tripp have rightly noted: "In Iran's view the war launched by Saddam Hussein in September 1980 could only be explained by US complicity and encouragement."[32] Almost two weeks after the war had began, Banisadr, then president, gave an interview to *Newsweek* (6 October 1980, p. 24) in which he charged that the war was "a plan prepared by the Americans and the Iraqis." Similar views have also been expressed by other leaders of the Islamic Republic, including President Khamenei in his United Nation's address in 1987.[33] The war had followed a growing cooperation, since 1979, between the United States and the Persian Gulf states, Iraq and Saudi Arabia in particular, the hostage drama, the failure of the coup plot at Nuzheh, and the aborted military rescue mission inside Iran on 24–25 April 1980. Ordered by President Jimmy Carter, the mission was to use Tabas (in Khorasan province) as a first staging point to rescue the hostages in Tehran (almost 500 miles away). The operators were supposed "to kill all Iranian guards" in the Embassy and if necessary, "hose down the streets" of Tehran.[34] During the operation, several American transport planes and military helicopters crashed in the desert around Tabas, killing ten American servicemen. In retrospect, the Tabas episode had almost no chance for success and it must have been ordered out of a deep frustration on the part of the American leadership to resolve the hostage drama or moderate the Islamic leadership. Also other indications reinforced Iran's view that Americans must have, at the least, signaled a green light to Sadam Hosain for the invasion. For example, writing in June 1980, almost three months before the war began, the usually well-informed journalist Paul-Marie de La Gorce indicated that "a conflict between Iraq and Iran is the favourite hypothesis of certain Washington specialists."[35]

Regardless of Iran's view, from what is already known, it appears that the administration's regional policy after the Shah's downfall may have, at the least, been a source of encouragement for Iraq to invade Iran. To begin with, according to a Pentagon report, disclosed in May 1980, the Carter administration was working toward "improving relations with Iraq because of its military strength."[36] The new policy began in 1977 when the Iranian Revolution was just about to take shape. Indeed, as made public in a report by the Joint Economic Committee of the United States Congress in April 1980, over the 1977–80 period, some ten Pentagon officials along with thirty to forty other government officials visited Iraq.[37] This is while there were no diplomatic relations between the two nations and Iraq was still on the President's official list of "terrorist states." The new policy was given a more concrete purpose in the President's State of the Union Address in January 1980. In the address he had noted that the United States was ready to cooperate with the states in the Middle East to meet "this new threat" (meaning Iran) to the security of the Persian Gulf.[38] In November 1980, two months after the outbreak of the Iran-Iraq war, Saudi Arabia along with Kuwait, Bahrain, Qatar, United Arab Emirates, and Oman agreed to sign a mutual security pact. This was realized on 4 February in the form of the Gulf Cooperation Council, an organization that later on became known for its unequivocal support of Iraq in the war. Already in 1979, following the "second oil shock," the Pentagon had announced the establishment of a "rapid deployment force" of some 100,000 soldiers, ostensibly to protect oil shipments from the Persian Gulf.

Strangely enough, the first Iraqi intensive artillery shelling of Iran's border towns took place around the time of the aborted Tabas rescue operation. On 17 September 1980, when Sadam Hosain unilaterally nullified the 1975 Algiers accord defining the border between Iran and Iraq, the Carter administration remained approvingly silent. On 22 September 1980, when Iraq invaded Iran, President Carter was quoted as saying: "The fighting might convince Iran that it needs friends."[39] But not only did the President's anticipation that Iran would soon yield to the new pressure not materialize, but also the relations between the two nations became further strained in the course of the war even though the hostages had been released on 20 January 1981. The United States did not support the initial Iranian diplomatic attempts to end the war, refused to condemn Iraq for the invasion, and continued to remain silent on the issue of who was the aggressor in the war. Moreover, when in 1982, the Iranian military took the upper hand in the war, the American government increased its support for Iraq. As a first major step, the administration removed Iraq from its list of terrorist states in 1982. Then followed high-level official visits to Baghdad and announcement of some $2 billion in trade credit to Iraq in 1983.[40] It was also on 14 December 1983, that the United States launched the "Operation Staunch," to prevent the flow of arms to Iran, particularly from its western allies. In the meantime, Iraq's military received vital target data from the American intelligence sources in the region, and by 1984, the United States's AWACS planes in Saudi Arabia were directly involved in the war intelligence operations on the side of Iraq. In the meantime, the suicidal bomb attack by a Lebanese Shia on U.S. Marines stationed in Beirut, which killed 259 American servicemen, had further increased the tension between the Islamic Republic and the American administration. This course of events culminated in the establishment of full diplomatic relations with Iraq on 26 November 1984 and laid the foundation for the subsequent direct involvement of the United States in the war against Iran.[41]

It was, however, following the Iran-Contra scandal that the United States intensified its involvement in the war.[42] Ostensibly, the scandal involved sales of arms to Iran in exchange for American hostages in Lebanon and diversion of profits from the deals to Nicaraguan Contras. However, as we saw, Americans and Israelis were also motivated by their desire to overthrow the Islamic Republic, as well as other economic and strategic goals. In its part, the Iranian government must have been drawn into the scandal because of its growing need for arms and ammunition. Whatever the motivations, a covert operation of the sort could hardly remain secret for any length of time in an age of instant global communication and information flow; when the scandal was disclosed, it was so shocking that it left a devastating impact on the United States's international credibility.[43] Particularly disturbed were the U.S.'s Middle Eastern Arab allies. In this context, the Reagan administration decided to escalate hostilities in the Persian Gulf.

The turning point was the American decision to escort "reflagged" Kuwaiti oil tankers in the Persian Gulf on 7 March 1987. This decision led to a tripling of the American (and NATO) military presence in the Persian Gulf and to the direct participation by the United States in the war. According to Jochen Hippler:

> In the last half of 1987, some 75 US, French, British, Italian, Belgian and Dutch warships steamed into the Persian Gulf in what became the largest peacetime naval operation since World War II . . . Officially, this unprecedented peacetime buildup was to "protect the freedom of navigation" from Iranian and Soviet threats. On the face of it, this rationale was rather remarkable, since Iraq, not Iran, had initiated attacks on ships in the Gulf and had been responsible for some 65 percent of all attacks.[44]

To enumerate a few major events, only ten days after the reflagging decision, Iraqi Exocet missiles destroyed part of the US *Stark,* killing thirty-seven marines on board. The Reagan administration, however, blamed Iran for the disaster and accepted an apology for the "mistake" from the Iraqi government. Then, on 11 May 1987, Assistant Secretary of State for Near Eastern Affairs Richard Murphy visited Sadam Hosain and, according to Sick, "reportedly promised Saddam that the United States would lead an effort in the UN Security Council for resolutions calling for a mandatory halt of arms shipment to Iran." Subsequently, writes Sick, the United States introduced a draft resolution on the war "deliberately written in a form that Iran could not accept and included a provision for mandatory sanctions against any party that rejected it."[45]

Between August 1987 and July 1988, when Iran accepted the Security Council Resolution 598 for an immediate cease-fire, the *Joint Middle East Task Force* (established on 21 August 1987) carried several attacks on Iranian targets in the Persian Gulf, some indeed devastating for Iran's economic and military well-being; one was, however, the most provocative. On 21 September 1987, only hours before President Khamenei was due in the United States to present Iran's case to the U.N. General Assembly, U.S. helicopter gunships attacked an Iranian ship *(Ajr)*, which some unidentified Americans had seen laying mines in the Persian Gulf. As we shall see later on, Iraq also intensified its military operations during the same time period. The task force's operations included destruction of three major offshore oil platforms including the Rashadat drilling station, six Iranian naval vessels including two frigates, several speedboats, and finally, a civilian airliner that was shot down by a US Navy cruiser, *Vincennes,* on 3 July 1988 killing all 290 civilians on board, including 60 children.[46] In the meantime, Americans were finding more mines in the Persian Gulf shipping lanes, for which Iran was blamed. At least one US frigate, *Roberts,* was damaged by such mines. During this critical period Iran began to loose control on the war front. Iraq retook Majnoon oilfield from Iran on 26 June 1988 and then retook Halabcheh on July 11. Seven days after, Iran accepted the cease fire.

Publicly, the administration defended the reflagging policy, which it said was necessary for safe shipment of oil from the Persian Gulf and for reduction of the level of violence in that part of the world. But, as Jo-Anne Hart documents, "less than 1% of all transits through the Straits of Hormuz were effected."[47] Moreover, according to the *New York Times,* quoting Brian McCartan, a specialist at the Center for Defense Information:

> there was a 61 percent increase in the number of attacks on commercial vessels in the gulf since the United States began protecting Kuwaiti tankers there last July. From July 22, 1987, until today [July 20, 1988], he said, there were 188 such attacks, compared with 117 the previous year. In that period, Mr. McCartan said, the number of attacks by Iran almost doubled, to 106 from 54, even though American policy in the gulf was intended mainly to end attacks by Iran at sea.[48]

It is unrealistic to assume that the Reagan administration could not anticipate an escalation of hostilities with Iran in the wake of the reflagging decision. A more objective proposition is that the administration wanted to engage Iran in a new front so that its limited resources would be diverted from the war with Iraq. This would weaken Iran and encourage Iraq to prolong the war until that time when a cease-fire could be imposed on Iran.[49] The administration did indeed take credit for the cease-fire, which it believed would have been unimaginable in the absence of the American military operations in the Persian Gulf. In an editorial on 19 July 1988, the *New York Times* echoed the administration's view:

> An end to the Iran-Iraq war, with no victor, has been long a major goal of American policy. The increased deployment of the U.S. Navy in the Persian Gulf incurred many risks, as was underscored by the tragic shooting down of an Iranian airliner on July 3. But that deployment, combined with tough diplomacy, has contributed to Iran's failing fortunes on the battlefield and hence to its apparent decision to end the war.[50]

The hostage episode became a turning point in the relationship between the two countries gradually leading to extremely costly events for Iran and loss of prestige for the United States. The economic and financial cost of the episode to Iran was estimated at some $10 billion in a March 1981 study by the Iranian Central Bank.[51] The episode's indirect costs could add up to several billion more considering the damage the United States inflicted on several expensive Iranian targets in the Persian Gulf and support for the Iraqi war efforts leading to reversal military balance in the war. The U.S. administration also harmed the Islamic Republic by its frequent economic sanctions and manipulation of the oil market through the Saudi leverage. Although it is true that the Islamic middle-class leadership's adventurism was responsible for the hostage drama and the subsequent American violent reaction, it is not true that the United States would have let the popular Revolution alone in the absence of the episode. To the extent that the nationalist leadership was rejecting a subservient position in the world system and was engaged in radical politics at home and abroad, it was inevitable that the United States would inflict damage on the Revolution in the hope of moderating the leadership or replacing it with a more acceptable alternative. It is instructive to recall that the Sandanista leadership has from the start been the one least confrontational to the American administration. Nevertheless, they have also paid a heavy price for the administration's war against their Revolution through the *Contras*.[52]

The U.S.-Iran relations continue to remain tense and unfriendly one-year-and-a-half after the war and more than nine years after the hostage drama. By May 1990, American economic sanctions remained in place. They included a near total ban on imports and extensive controls on exports with military applications particularly technology that could contribute to chemical or nuclear proliferation. The postwar attempts by the two governments to mend their relations have been particularly marred by the hostages in Lebanon. The only area where some progress has been made concerns the settlement of numerous financial disputes between the two nations via negotiations led by the Iran-U.S. Claims Tribunal in the Hague. The last of such agreements was announced in May 1990 following the release of two American hostages in Lebanon. The U.S. government also continues to discourage its allies in restoring their economic and political relations with Iran. In the meantime, Operation Staunch, the name for the United States's systematic practice of discouraging other states from supplying Iran with weapons, also remains in effect. The Islamic Republic's contradictory position on this issue has particularly harmed the Iranian international interests.

In retrospect, a few rapprochements between Iran and the United States since the Revolution have ended in stalemates, standoffs, scandals, and major conflicts. No doubt we shall continue to witness cycles of intense diplomatic initiatives (covert and overt) followed by hostility and belligerence between the two states in the immediate future. Insofar as the United States remains unhappy with the behavior, demands, and policies of the Islamic Republic and to the extent that its policy toward Iran is guided by shortsightedness and plans for immediate gains, it will continue to create difficulties for the regime in the hope of moderating its middle-class leadership (i.e., making it pro-American) or prompting its downfall. Similarily, the Islamic leadership is bound to remain confrontational toward the United States in the immediate future insofar as it distrusts the administration in Washington and considers it a "world devourer" and an "illegitimate satanic player" in world politics. This behavior indicates that the Islamic Republic, too, lacks a more subtle policy toward the United States. If past experience is any indication, these approaches to international relations could be expected to be effective in inflicting damage on the adversary but not in producing the intended results. This conclusion is particularly relevant in an age of growing globalization of human relations, (asymmetrical) interdependence of nation-states, and ineffectiveness of political-military force in changing international relations.

The American administration on many occasions has indicated that it bears "no hostility toward the system of the Islamic Republic as a form of government.[53] If this is to be taken as true, then a more subtle American policy toward Iran should be based on the long-term tendencies of the middle-class leadership in Tehran rather than on its immediate and spontaneous reactive behaviors. The United States seems to be particularly concerned with the Islamic Republic's support for anti-Americanism in the Middle East and, of course, for hostage taking. As indicated by the past experiences, over time such leadership becomes pragmatist and more inclined toward peaceful coexistence and a fairly well-regulated relationship with the West, including the United States. The process, however, will have to go its natural course, as any pressure will only delay manifestation of such outcomes. Equally displeasing to the leadership in Tehran is the now obsolete U.S. policy of considering Iran in terms of American strategic interests, anti-Sovietism, concern for world oil supply, and concurrence with Israeli policies in the Middle East. The American administration should also realize that a more functional policy in the emerging multipolar and interdependent world system must be based on mutual respect, cross-cultural understanding, and international cooperation.

Similarly, a more intelligent Iranian foreign policy will not underestimate the U.S. ability to help or hurt a dependent semiperiphery, particularly one that is in revolutionary turmoil. The Islamic Republic must also take a hard look at its adventurist foreign policy and subject it to candid evaluation and criticism. This seems to be underway under the leadership of President Rafsanjani, but results so far are not significant. Both governments must realize that any improvement in their relations would have to be planned in stages and that at each stage a particular issue would have to be taken up for detailed and candid evaluation. The road ahead will be difficult and long, needing considerable patience and flexibility. It is also imperative that the least significant (that is the more easily negotiable) issues be considered first and that the principle of reciprocity should govern such negotiations. The U.S.-Iran Claims Tribunal in The Hague is an example of such an area. Iran can use the same businesslike approach as in the tribunal in dealing with the United States on other matters of mutual concern. A series of conferences or symposia also can be planned with participation of the academic community and policy makers from both sides to help in evaluation of such issues and the overall relationship between the two nations. But for such a dialogue to produce results, Iranians must first formulate a more coherent approach to their relations with the United States. The key to a more successful international policy in the present pluralistic world community is the ability to strike a balance between national interest and independence, on the one hand, and the interest and concerns of the competing nations, on the other. The fact that a nonconfrontational policy would not be enough for the imperial powers to accept the legitimacy of a revolution is no pretext for an agitational and adventurist foreign policy.

THE IRAN-IRAQ WAR

While the struggles for state power, social question of the Revolution, and national independence were in process, the Iran-Iraq war began on 22 September 1980. The war, as we shall see, complicated the socioeconomic and political problems as never before in contemporary Iran. An important observation concerning postrevolutionary societies is that almost all of them, middle class or otherwise, experience civil or international war during their formative years. This observation suggests that the postrevolutionary war has little positive correlation with the revolutionary leadership's class origin or ideology. Rather, the correlation is between the war and the revolution. On the one hand, revolutions tend to set in motion social changes unacceptable to beneficiaries of the status quo at domestic and international levels. To prevent radical changes, the reform resisters use a variety of means including civil and international wars, which are hoped to overthrow the radical leadership or force them into moderate and accommodative behavior. On the other hand, aggressive states find opportunities in revolutions for settling old accounts with the revolutionary societies, impose new demands on them, or gain a favorable relative political position. Again, wars are considered desirable alternatives particularly by states that subscribe to the philosophy of use of force in their international diplomacy. In other words, most, if not all, postrevolutionary wars primarily are *imposed* on postrevolutionary societies. However, this does not mean that the postrevolutionary leadership plays no role in creating the conditions for the war or its continuation, which it does to varying degrees. In addition, other generally case-specific factors tend to play a role in the postrevolutionary war. Earlier, we examined the American involvement in the Iran-Iraq war. In what follows, I first review some of the most important factors that contributed to the initiation and continuation of the war, and then focus on the impact of the war on the Iranian economy.

Roots of the War and Prospects for Peace

Iraq invaded Iran in September 1980, five days after Sadam Hosain had unilaterally abrogated the 1975 Algiers Treaty and had torn the document on Iraqi Television.[54] Incidentally, Sadam Hosain himself had negotiated and signed the treaty with the Shah, who, back in 1969, had also unilaterally abrogated a 1937 treaty between the two nations and had imposed acts of aggression against the new revolutionary regime in Baghdad until 1975. The Algiers Treaty had been concluded on the basis of "the principles of territorial integrity, the inviolability of borders and noninterference in internal affairs,' all of which were declared, in Article 4, as "integral" to the treaty. It demarcated their land frontiers on the basis of the 1913 Constantinopole Protocol and determined their fluvial frontiers (the Sahtt-al-Arab waterway) according to the Thalweg Line. In other words, sovereignty over the waterway was to be shared between the two states. All these agreements and the related documents were then duly registered with the Secretariat of the United Nations and, at the time, Iraq admitted that it had no more claims and that the disputes were ended.

The Iraqi president told his people that he was justified to abrogate the treaty because Iran had violated the treaty by its interference in Iraq's internal affairs. "Thus, the legal relationship concerning Shatt-al-Arab should return to what it was before 6 March 1975," he asserted and continued, "This Shatt shall again be, as it has been throughout history, Iraqi and Arab in name and reality, with all rights of full sovereignty over it." He also let the Iraqi people know that his army had already (on 13 September) captured certain Iraqi territories in Iranian occupation. He was referring to three small parcels of land, some 200 to 400 sq kms, in the region between Qasr-e Shirin and Naft Shahr (see Figure 2.1), awarded to Iraq by the Algiers Treaty.[55] Iran in its part, notified the United Nations (on 26 October) that it still considered itself bound by the treaty's provision. Iran also reminded the United Nations that the treaty provided a mechanism for resolving disputes between the two nations. Sadam Hosain, however, insisted in his reply to Iran's position, sent also to the United Nations (26 November), that the treaty was void and invalid.[56]

Sadam Hosain was in a sense right concerning the Islamic Republic's interference in the internal affairs of Iraq. After all, the Republic was supporting the Kurdish struggle in Iraq and the Islamic Al Daʿwa Party determined to overthrow the Baʿathist regime in Iraq. In the meantime, Ayatollah Mohammad Baqir Sadr, an eminent Shia leader based in Najaf and a close friend of Ayatollah Khomeini, was also calling for an Islamic revolution in Iraq. Al Daʿwa was at the time carrying underground operations against the regime including bombing of the Government buildings and assassination attempts against the Baʿathist officials, including deputy pre-

Figure 2.1
Iranian Provinces and Major Cities, 1976

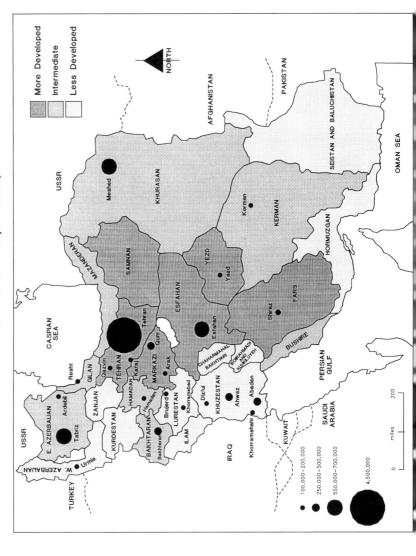

mier Tariq Aziz (on 1 April 1980). Moreover, Ayatollah Khomeini himself in several occasions (e.g., on 8 April) had called on the people and army of Iraq to overthrow Sadam Hosain's "non-Muslim" regime. Similar calls were also made by Tehran Radio's Arabic service and newspapers that had stepped up their virulent anti-Sadam Hosain propaganda following the execution of Ayatollah Sadr by the Iraqi regime in early April 1980.[57]

Such interferences, however, had not gone without a response, and one may safely assert, that Iraqi regime might have indeed prompted the Islamic Republic's unfriendly behavior. To begin with, it took about three months for Iraq to recognize the Iranian Revolution.[58] In the meantime, Iraq had begun supporting the separatist movement in Khuzestan, which the Iraqi government continues to call *Arabistan*. In May 1980, *Al-Thawrah* (Baghdad) published Tariq Aziz's statement on Arab-Iranian relations where he had noted that: "Some might say that Iraq brought up the question of the three islands, of Arabistan, and of the Shatt-al-Arab agreements, prompting Iran to respond in this fashion. Yes, Iraq did indeed bring up these issues . . ." He then went on to reaffirm Iraq's support for the "Arab people of the Ahwaz area" and denounced the "racial Persian domination" of the "Arabistan region."[59] Note also that all Iraqi maps show Khuzestan as "Arabistan" and as part of the "Arab Land" and that it is no secret that the Persian Gulf is renamed as "Arabian Gulf." According to Dilip Hiro, quoting *Observer* (24 June 1979) and *Guardian* (6 July 1979): "The Iraqi government responded [to Tehran's anti-Baʿathist propaganda] by smuggling among other things 170,000 AK-47 submachine guns to the Arab dissidents of Khuzistan."[60]

Iraq also allowed the Iranian opposition in exile, namely, Shahpour Bakhtiar, the last prime minister of the Shah and General Gholam Ali Oveissi, a prominent leader of the royalists, to establish a broadcasting station each on Iraqi territory. Reportedly, the two men were instrumental in getting Iraq to invade Iran with a view to overthrowing the regime in Tehran.[60] Among other early Iraqi responses to Tehran's hostility included several military operations, the most important of which were bombing Qasr-e Shirin (8 April 1980), shelling Mehran (29 May, 3 September), and attacking the Musian region (7–13 September). Also, Iraqis supported the Iranian Kurdish movement and deported "any Iraqi who had even the remotest connection with Iran, by birth, marriage or name."[62] Some 60,000 Iraqis of such definition had been expelled from their home by the beginning of the war in September 1980.[63] Iraq had equally retaliated Tehran's war of words with the harshest denounciation of

the Islamic Republic. In early April 1980, Sadam Hosain characterized the Ayatollah Khomeini as "turbanned Shah" and "madman of
Qom."[64] He later even threatened to "cut off the hand" of those
interferring in Iraqi internal affairs (meaning Ayatollah Khomeini),
and declared Iraq's readiness "to enter into any kind of battle to
defend its honour and sovereignty."[65]

Even accepting Iraq's position as cogent for abrogating the
treaty, the following question still remains valid: Why should abro-
gation of the treaty lead to a full-scale invasion of Iran? Since Iraqi
leaders well know that "interference" cannot justify "invasion,"
otherwise the Soviet Union and the United States, for example,
would have engaged in several wars during the "cold war" period,
they have tried to exonerate themselves by putting forth a "self-
defense" argument. It then cites the well-known *Caroline* (1837)
clause, as justification: "A necessity of self-defense, instant, over-
whelming, leaving no choice of means and no moment of deliberations."[66] According to Gary Sick: "The reality appears otherwise."
He continues:

> Iraq claims that Iranian aircrafts violated Iraqi air space on 69
> occasions between April and September 1980 and that on Septem-
> ber 4 Iranian artillery opened fire across the Iraqi border from the
> three small parcels of land that were supposed to be returned to
> Iraq under the 1975 treaty. Assuming the accuracy of these
> charges, the subsequent Iraqi attack, which bombed targets
> throughout Iran and captured more than 4,000 square miles of
> Iran's Khuzistan Province, would appear to be disproportionate to
> the provocation. Iraq never claimed that Iran was massing forces,
> and the total absence of any Iranian military preparation was un-
> mistakably obvious in the first few weeks of the war.
>
> The available evidence suggest that Iraq conducted a system-
> atic buildup of its military forces between April and September
> 1980 in preparation for a lightning offensive.[67]

Moreover, as we have noted earlier, by the time of its massive invasion of Iran on 22 September 1980, the Iraqi military had undertaken several operations against civilian and military targets inside
Iran, which were more devastating than any Iranian military operations against Iraq before the war. Therefore, and according to
Sick, "Iraq's claims of urgent self-defense are less than totally
convincing."[68]

Why then did Iraq invade Iran? Territorial gain was obviously a
major motivation. Of particular importance for Iraq was to gain full
sovereignty over the Shatt-al-Arab river.[69] This intention had already
been spelled out by Sadam Hosain in his 17 September television

statement and had become the stumbling block in the postwar negotiations. But this tells only a part of the story, as otherwise one cannot understand Iraq's attempts to occupy the whole of Khuzistan
province. Evidence suggests that the Iraqi regime was also determined to overthrow the Islamic Republic and replace it with a government inclined to friendly ties with Iraq. In view of the chaotic
political and economic situation in the country and the lack of an
effective military force (which had been noted in Tareq Aziz's May
1980 statement),[70] the Iraqi government had hoped for a quick victory. This proved illusory as it was based on misleading intelligence
from the Iranian exile groups and the United States. According to
Pierre Terzian, quoting *Le Monde,* Iraqis:

> hoped that within a week they could occupy much of Khuzistan,
> the region where 90% of Iran's oil reserves are situated, to estab-
> lish a link with Kurdistan to the north and finally to install an
> Iranian "free government" presided over by ex-premier Bakhtiar in
> Ahwaz, the old capital of Khuzistan, by 5 October [1980]. The
> whole operation was to succeed thanks to total disorganization
> of the Iranian Army and the information Baghdad had received
> from the Americans, from General Oveissi and obviously from
> Bakhtiar himself.[71]

As noted by Tariq Aziz in his May statement and then Saᶜdoun
Hamadi in his address to the United Nations in October 1980, the
Iraqi government was unhappy with the "Islamic Revolution" and
the Republic's attempt to export it. Aziz had argued that what has
happened in Iran "is not a revolution" and Hamadi had made it
known that: "We in Iraq refuse such a mediaeval ideology."[72] Rejecting the "Iranian experience" as a nonrevolutionary model unable to "uproot corruption, alter the negative aspects of society and
. . . erase the effects of zionism and imperialism in the Arab home-
land," Aziz had claimed that Iraq offered "the outstanding model of
complete patriotic and national independence, economic independence, political independence and free will."[73] In other words, the
pan-Islamism of the Islamic Republic was considered inferior to the
pan-Arabism of the Baᶜathist Iraq.[74] Ideological competition aside,
the Iraqi regime was also motivated in its struggle against the Islamic Republic by the new opportunity for regional leadership after
the fall of the Shah. This required, in the Iraqi leaders' view, establishing Arab hegemony over Persian "colonialism" and "territorial
expansionism" which, they argued, was responsible, for the "imposed" 1975 Algiers Treaty.[75] In view of this, the Iraqi leadership
used to call the war *Saddam's Qadisiyeh* in the early stages—in

memory of the battle in 635 that led to the defeat of the Persian Empire from the Arab (Islamic) invaders. A quick victory, the Iraqi leadership supposed, would also secure Iraq's leadership in the Arab world, a position that remained vacant since Egypt's expulsion from the Arab League following the Camp David Accord.[76] Finally, Iraq had its eyes on Khuzistan, which it continues to call *Arabistan*. In such an eventuality, Iraq would become the largest oil producer and exporter in the Middle East, something it needed to back up its claim to regional political leadership.

Thus, territorial gains, ideological rivalry, domination of Khuzistan, and regional hegemony were among the major motivations behind Iraq's invasion of Iran.[77] These motivations were reinforced by the historical roots of the conflict, a fact acknowledged by Hamadi in his October 15 statement in the United Nations. Other reinforcing factors included the unpatriotic politics of the Iranian exile groups, the hostage drama and the American support for Iraq (explained earlier), Saudi Arabia's malicious policies within OPEC (see later), Iran's chaotic political, economic, and military conditions, and above all, Iraq's growing economic and military strength since the late 1970s. The personal rivalry between Ayatollah Khomeini and President Sadam Hosain contributed to the continuation of the war but did not constitute a cause or motivation for it.[78] Equally critical for the continuation of the war was the significant financial and material support given to Iraq by the Arab states. According to Youssef Ibrahim, such financial support amounted to "more then $50 billion since 1982." He then quotes a "Palestinian official" as saying that: "All the Arab aid to Egypt, Syria, Jordan and the Palestinians in 40 years of war against Israel is a fraction of the aid they have given Iraq in the six years."[79] The U.S. role in prolonging the war after 1987 has been noted already. The Israeli role should be also underscored. According to Joel Brinkley, writing in the *New York Times* (24 July 1988, p. 2E): "With the exception of the world's arms merchants, hardly anyone has been happier than Israel that Iran and Iraq have spent the last eight years at war." And "For years Israel did all it could to keep the war going in the Persian Gulf."

Another factor that helped sustain and prolong the war was international military sales. According to *Business Week* (December 29, 1986), "military sales, both open and illicit, [were] big business: about $70 billion" in the first six years of the war. Of this, "Iraq [had] acquired some $40 billion," the rest going to Iran and other countries in the region. According to a 1989 study on weapon sales to the Third World by Richard F. Grimmett, a specialist in national defense at the Congressional Research Service, reported in the *New York Times* (1 August 1989, p. A1-A8):

> Sales to Iran and Iraq accounted for 21.5 percent of arms sales by all suppliers to the third world in the last eight years. In the period, Iran bought a total of $17.5 billion worth of arms, Iraq bought $47.3 billion worth and the third world as a whole purchased $301.4 billion worth of arms.
>
> ... Arms sales to the Middle East by all suppliers totaled $95.3 billion from 1985 through 1988, as against a total of $113 billion in the previous four years.

Western Europe was the largest supplier of Iran and Iraq over the 1981–1988 period, providing 31 percent and 21 percent of all weapons purchased by the two countries respectively. Soviet Union and the United States accounted for 34 percent and 16 percent of all arms sold to the Middle East over the 1985–1988 period. Of the Soviet sales between 1985 and 1988, $4.7 billion went to Iraq and zero to Iran. Among the largest Iran's suppliers were China and North Korea, whereas Iraq made most of its purchases from France, the third largest supplier of weapons to the Third World after the USSR and United States.

Among the factors that reinforced Iraqi leaders' motivations, the country's growing economic and military sttrength also provided the precondition for the war. Although the Baʿathist leadership had built a reasonably strong state over the 1968–78 period, Iraq remained cagey in its oil and trade policies until about 1978. With the onset of the Iranian Revolution, however, Iraq began rushing to produce and export more oil, import more military and consumer goods, and increase the size of its armed forces (see Table 2.1 and Figure 2.2). The shift, some have suggested, might be considered a first major step in planning for the war. Quoting American and Iraqi sources, Pierre Terzian gives the following assessment:

> Right from the fall of the Shah in early 1979, Iraq had been preparing for this eventuality [war] by building up substantial stocks of arms and spare parts, as well as monetary reserves amounting to $35,000 million just before the war. It was to finance this war that, according to James Akins, ex-US ambassador to Saudi Arabia, Baghdad decided to increase its oil production in 1979 and 1980. In fact, on 10 October 1980, just three weeks after hostilities broke out, the Governor of the Iraq Central Bank, Hassan Najafi, declared "We can maintain the war effort for a year without exporting any oil at all."[80]

As indicated in table 2.1, in 1979, Iraq's oil production increased by 35 percent compared to the previous year, but declined

Table 2.1 Iran and Iraq Compared: Total Oil Production, Exports, Imports, Military Expenditures, and Number of Armed Forces, 1977–82 (formative years of the Iran-Iraq war)

Year	Oil Production (million barrel/day)		Total Exports (billion $)		Total Imports (billion $)		Armed Forces (thousands)		Military Expenditures (billion $)		Military Expenditures Per Capita ($)		Armed Forces per 1000 People (soldiers)	
	Iran	Iraq	Iran	Iraq	Iran	Iraq	Iran	Iraq	Iran	Iraq	Iran	Iraq	Iran	Iraq
1977	5.9	2.3	21.4	10.4	16.6	4.5	350	140	11.9	4.7	336.4	398.0	9.9	11.8
1978	5.7	2.6	18.4	11.9	13.6	4.2	350	362	14.5	6.1	397.0	499.6	9.6	29.5
1979	5.3	3.5	20.1	20.3	11.5	9.9	415	444	9.1	7.0	240.3	548.6	11.0	34.9
1980	3.2	2.6	12.3	28.6	15.7	13.9	305	430	7.7	12.2	197.1	921.2	7.8	32.6
1981	1.5	0.9	12.8	9.4	15.3	20.8	260	392	8.5	15.1	209.3	1102.2	6.4	28.6
1982	2.4	0.9	20.3	11.2	13.4	21.5	240	404	9.6	15.4	227.3	1083.1	5.7	28.5

Sources:
Tables 2.4, 3.20, and 3.22; *IMF Directory of Trade Yearbook* (Washington, DC: International Monetary Funds, 1983); OPEC, *Annual Statistical Bulletin* (1979–84); *World Military Expenditures and Arms Transfers 1987* (Washington, DC: US Arms Control and Disarmament Agency, 1988); and *Petroleum Economist*, 50, no. 3 (March 1983).

Figure 2.2

Iran and Iraq Compared, 1977–82
(formative years of Iran-Iraq war)

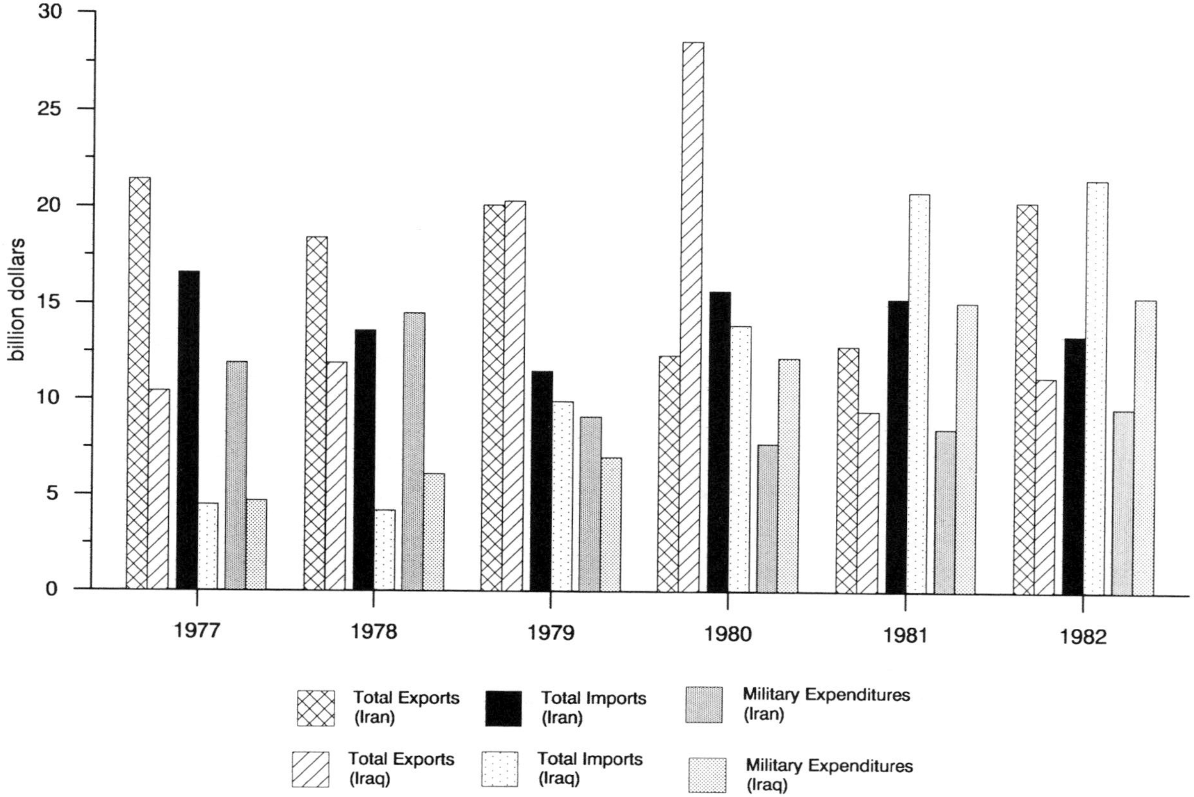

after the war began in 1980. The most significant change, however, occurred in Iraq's exports and imports. Over the 1978–80 period, they increased by 140 percent and 231 percent, respectively. The huge increase in imports was paid from an estimated foreign exchange reserve of some $35 billion. Note that over the same period, Iranian oil production and exports had declined while its imports had increased only slightly. Commenting on the sudden increase in Iraq's imports, Abbas Alnasrawi suggested that it "may be considered as a precautionary measure by Iraq should a war actually break out."[81] Equally immense were increases in Iraq's military expenditures and number of armed forces. Between the years 1978–80, they increased by 100 percent and 19 percent, respectively. The corresponding figures for Iran indicated a decline of 47 percent and 13 percent, respectively. Note that the Iraqi armed forces had already been increased by 150 percent between 1977 and 1978. (These changes become the most meaningful when they are considered in the light of the fact that Iran's population is about three times larger than that of Iraq.) Thus, in per capita terms, Iraqi military expenditures in 1979 and 1980 were 2.3 times and 4.7 times larger than those of Iran. In the same years, Iraq's armed forces per 1000 people were also 3.2 times and 4.6 times larger than those of Iran. Figure 2.2 shows the gap that developed between Iraq and Iran over the given indicators beginning in 1978.

Fighting a nation in total disarray and largely weakened by the Revolution of 1979, the Iraqi army occupied some 14,000 sq km. of Iran in less than two weeks, including Khorramshahr, a city of 300,000 people on the bank of Shatt-al-Arab waterway. Believing that offensive force could be used to overthrow or at least impose political conditions on the Islamic Republic, the Iraqi government paid only lip service to several peace proposals in the first two years or so until the city of Khorramshahr was liberated in June 1982. This Iraqi attitude was also promoted by what Gary Sick has called the "lackadaisical approach" of the UN Security Council in the first six years of the war. For example, on 28 September 1980, the council adopted Resolution 479, which was almost totally one-sided to the benefit of Iraq. It did not refer to the conflict as a war, "thereby evading the Security Council's responsibility under the UN Charter to determine if an aggression had occurred," and called for a cease-fire that did not require withdrawal of Iraqi forces from the Iranian territories. This Council's attitude, again according to Sick, "was more than oversight." At the time, the hostage drama was in progress, Arab states were reluctant "to chastise an Arab government," and more important, "the superpowers and others concluded that their interests could best be served by letting the two regimes exhaust themselves on the battlefield."[82] Iran rejected the Resolution and thereafter associated the Security Council, the superpowers, and most of the Arab states with Iraqi war aims, leading to its apathy for the subsequent peace movements.[83] Moreover, by 1982, Iran had made major advances in the war, while Iraq's inability to overthrow the Islamic Republic or impose political conditions on the regime in Tehran had become increasingly apparent. These developments, among others, had made Iran both uncompromising and disenchanted with several peace initiatives. It was also around this time that Sadam Hosain, with assistance of his friends, launched a well-orchestrated peace propaganda offensive that successfully isolated the rejectionist Iran until it agreed to the U.N.-sponsored cease-fire on 17 July 1988.

In particular, Iran missed several opportunities to settle the war peacefully. These included the 12 July 1982 UN Resolution 514, and a few useful attempts by the Islamic Conference Organization (in 1980–82 and 1985), the Non-Aligned Movement (1981), the Gulf Cooperation Council (GCC) (1982–85), and by the Arab League on 11 September 1982 (at the summit conference in Fez, Morocco). The Arab League "peace plan" was the first real opportunity for a cease-fire if not a comprehensive peace. It included provisions for an immediate cease-fire, "complete evacuation of the Iranian territories by Iraq, and compensation of US $70 billion to Iran through the Islamic Reconstruction Fund."[84] Iran should have accepted the league's proposal and this is a view almost universally held in Iran today, even within the high ranks of the government. The Islamic Republic rejected the proposal for several reasons, but three were critical: first, the Iranian economy was in its best shape in the postrevolutionary period and the oil revenue had reached $20 billion in 1982—indeed there was no economic pressure; second, a majority of the Islamic leadership believe that force could be effectively used in exporting the Revolution and reshaping international relations; and third, consolidation of political power and military forces had not yet been fully achieved.

Another major opportunity was missed in May 1985 when the Saudi foreign minister traveled to Tehran on the behalf of the Islamic Conference Organization and the GCC. His mission was also dismissed as unacceptable and received no serious consideration. Although the Iranian economy was not doing well at the time, it was not as bad as it became after the 1986 oil price crash. More important, political (military) force seemed to be working, although the Islamic Republic had encountered difficulty in taking Basra, a city of

1 million bordering Iran in northern Iraq: Iran was fighting inside Iraq and had occupied several strategic sites including the Fao Peninsula. The possibility of exporting the Revolution and overthrowing the Iraqi regime seemed real and at hand. Also around this time the Iran-U.S. rapprochement was underway. The Islamic leadership, too upset with the Iraqi leadership for the invasion and its subsequent unprincipled conduct of the war, was incapable of rationalizing a peace with Iraq under the same Sadam Hosain leadership.

The last major opportunity occurred in July 1987 with Resolution 598. Although Iran did not reject the resolution, it conditioned its observations of the terms of the resolution to the formation of an impartial international committee to look into the question of who started the war. In retrospect, the Islamic Republic should have accepted the resolution without the condition and for a number of good reasons: (1) the economy was in its worst shape ever; (2) the oil revenue had dropped from a projected $15 billion to an actual $5.8 billion forcing the government to adopt an austerity Plan for New Economic Conditions; (3) international isolation had left Iran with only a few friends; (4) support for war was waning at home and abroad; and (5) thanks to the superpower diplomacy, the war had been locked up in a virtual stalemate for almost three years—offensive force did not seem to be working for the either side. Additionally, in the aftermath of the Irangate scandal, the American government had moved further away from the Islamic Republic toward its Arab friends including Iraq. As we have seen, already in May 1987 the United States was attempting to impose a total arms embargo on Iran through a UN-sponsored resolution.

Yet, the most important reason why the Islamic Republic should have accepted Resolution 598 was to show the whole world that Sadam Hosain was not sincere in supporting the UN resolution. It was obvious that Iraq would not accept conditions set in the resolution if it did not have to: The international committee of inquiry would have named Iraq as instigator of the war and Sadam Hosain would have had to accept a return to the status quo that existed prior to the invasion of Iran. The Iraqi leadership would also have difficulty in explaining such an outcome to the people; this is why Iraq began setting preconditions for the peace process almost immediately after Iran accepted the resolution.

Unfortunately, however, the Islamic Republic missed the opportunity not only because it was unable to predict Sadam Hosain's behavior, but also because the middle-class leadership in Tehran was not yet totally convinced that force could not be effectively or gainfully used in today's world politics. The stalemate on the war front was publicly attributed to superpower's designs for destruction of the Islamic Republic and, privately, to the uncovering of the Irangate scandal that had deprived Iran of military machines from the United States and elsewhere. They were also strangely ignorant of Iraq's successful campaign to revive its army by new recruits and military purchases. The worsening economic situation was also believed to be manageable as the 1986 drop in oil revenue was considered temporary. They were only superficially aware of the changing world oil market and the strategic designs of the Saudis oil policy (see later). The conviction for the export of the Revolution had not diminished either, despite setbacks for the Islamic Republic in its confrontation with Saudi Arabia and the diminishing influence of the Lebanese Hezballah in that country's politics.

Iran at last accepted the UN Resolution 598 on 18 July 1988, almost a year after it was adopted by the Security Council. During the year from the adaptation of the Resolution to its acceptance by the Islamic Republic, many things changed in domestic and international conditions. The worsening economic situation forced the Islamic Republic to adopt a new Economic Policy for Survival and the growing pressure from and confrontation with the United States following the Irangate scandal became too costly in material and diplomatic terms. The United States was able to effectively control the flow of arms to Iran and used the Islamic Republic's refusal of the UN Resolution 598 to further isolate it internationally. Strangely enough, it took the downing of the Iranian Airbus by the United States for the Islamic Republic to realize how isolated it had become: despite serious attempts, the Islamic regime was unable to gain almost any international support to condemn the United States's overt violation of international law.[85]

As was noted earlier, Iraq had also intensified the war to coincide with the increased U.S. entanglement with the war following the Irangate scandal and after the meeting in Baghdad, on 11 May 1987, between Assistant Secretary of State for Near Eastern Affairs Richard Murphy and Sadam Hosain. Thus, between August 1987 and July 1988, when Iran accepted the Security Council's Resolution 598 for an immediate cease-fire, Iraq's conduct of the war became increasingly unprincipled and in total violation of laws and conventions governing the conduct of international wars. Mention should be made of Iraqi's "war of the cities," missile attacks on industrial and residential targets, use of chemical weapons at an expanding scale, and attacks on shipping in the Persian Gulf.[86] As has been noted by Gary Sick, Iraq had full support of the United States for these undertakings. For example, "The United States intervened twice at the United Nations, first to prevent an emergency meeting to end the war of cities and later to oppose a formal condemnation of Iraq for its use of chemical weapons."[87] Because of the United States's direct involvement and support from Arab states, Saudi Arabia and Kuwait in particular, these Iraqi tactics earned it a series of victories beginning with retaking Fao on 17–18 April 1988, followed by capturing Shalamcheh, Mehran, and Majnoon, among other areas. Iranian response to these episodes was also hampered by the conflict between the Revolutionary Guard Corps and the Army, and did not help to reduce the increasing domestic opposition to the war. The war of the cities also brought the war home to Tehranis (who control both wealth and power in Iran) as never before and thus created a tense situation in the capital. Around this time (May 1988) Mehdi Bazargan (leader of the Liberation Movement of Iran) made public a letter to Ayatollah Khomeini in which he brutally criticized the government's policy of continuing the war.[88] The Iraqi tactics were also instrumental in convincing the leadership that offensive force was not working and a whole new strategic outlook had to be developed for the war and international relations.

Whatever the reason, Iran accepted Resolution 598 only to find out that Iraq was not ready for it. Intoxicated by a series of military victories, Sadam Hosain regained confidence and began to revive his earlier view of force as an effective means of settling international disputes. Almost immediately after Iran accepted the resolution and its cease-fire conditions, Iraqi regime began to sabotage the peace process. First, it tried to categorize Iran's move as "tactical" and "deceptive" and vowed, in a statement by Tariq Aziz included in a letter to the UN, "to go on with the war," which it did.[89] Yet, Ayatollah Khomeini had declared in his statement accepting the UN Resolution that: "We formally announce that our objective is not to have a new tactic for continuation of the war."[90] Thus, Iraq "resisted accepting a cease-fire while continuing its mopping-up operations. Iraq also continued to demonstrate a contemptuous disregard for the Security Council and for world opinion on the use of chemical weapons."[91] The Iraqi army penetrated deep into Khuzistan province one day after Iran accepted the resolution, taking large tracts of land and some 20,000 POW's. In the meantime, the National Resistance Army of the People's Mojahedin Organization, stationed in Iraq, began its major assault on Iran under the code name "Eternal Light" *(Frouq-e Javidan)*. The organization, which had upheld the theory that the Islamic regime would not survive if it were to accept a cease-fire, felt that the opportune moment had arrived to overthrow the Republic. As it happened, the theory proved to be totally unfounded. Soon, however, the whole world knew that Iran's position was strategic and sincere. Yet, only under mounting "international pressure" did Sadam Hosain agree on August 6 to accept a conditional cease-fire. The conditions included "five practical steps" that were outlined in Tariq Aziz's letter to the UN Secretary on 18 July. The issues raised in that letter were not included in Resolution 598.[92]

Demand for "direct talks" was "step" number one. Iraq wanted the UN off the negotiating table in the hope of forcing Iran into accepting its conditions and ultimately moving the peace process to outside the framework of the Resolution. This was reflected in a fourth "step" demanding the UN help only if direct talks were to fail. Sadam Hosain particularly feared the Resolution's anticipated international committee of inquiry, which, if established, would most probably declare Iraq an aggressor with implications for reparation of war damage. Iran's response to direct talks, after some initial maneuvering, was positive.[93] As a second "step," Iraq demanded that the UN "immediately undertake the task of cleaning the Shatt-al-Arab waterway,' a task that could take about two years and, according to Ismat Taha Kittani, the chief Iraqi UN delegate, could cost "at least $1.5 billion."[94] Iran accepted the demand but argued that the task should be accomplished within the framework of the Algiers Treaty, a position that Iraq rejected. A third "step" was a demand for "Iraq's full rights in free navigation in the Arab Gulf waters and the Strait of Hormuz." Finally, Iraq called upon Iran "to refrain from intercepting or attacking ships and oil tankers operating in the territorial waters of the Gulf states"—acts that Iraq had itself initiated. These demands were also granted by Iran. Subsequently, Iraq raised its most critical demand, namely, total sovereignty over Shatt-al-Arab, a demand no government in Iran would be able to accept without endangering its existence.[95] In the meantime, Iraq threatened to dig a canal near the mouth of the waterway to the Persian Gulf, a threat that, if implemented, would have far-reaching consequences for Iran and for the Iran-Iraq relations for years to come. (The threat may well be a political bluff, as Iran can also take similar measures with even more damaging consequences for Iraq, but it at least indicates the Iraqi leadership behavior.)[96]

Iran continued to insist that the two nations return to the status quo as defined by the 1975 Algiers Treaty.[97] Iraq did not want that Treaty as the basis of its negotiations with Iran. After all, Sadam Hosain had abrogated the Treaty before he ordered the invasion of Iran. To rescue the peace process, a Four-Point Proposal was forwarded by Perez de Cuellar, the UN General Secretary, on 1 October

1988 after it became clear that the two nations may not continue the peace talks within the framework of Resolution 598.[98] The proposal demanded that (1) the two sides withdraw their forces behind their prewar borders and exchange prisoners of war; (2) Iran guarantee unimpeded shipping in the Persian Gulf for Iraq; (3) the two nations undertake a feasibility study to dredge Shatt-al-Arab waterway jointly, and (4) without reference to the issue of sovereignty. The proposal was intended to respond to some of Iraq's concerns and defer the issue of sovereignty over the river for a later time. Iran agreed to these principles but Iraq continued to raise the sovereignty issue. Toward the end of 1989, Iran came up with a new proposal calling for the simultaneous withdrawal of forces from the occupied territories and exchange of war prisoners. Iraq made no positive gestures in response to this new Iranian initiative.

As we have noted, Iran has made significant concessions but the peace process remains fragile and in a dangerous deadlock. In early 1990, after one year and a half of negotiations, the two sides were no closer to a settlement of their disputes than they were at the beginning of the cease-fire on 20 August 1988. Even the first article of the Resolution, calling on both sides to "withdraw all forces to the internationally recognized boundaries without delay," remained unaccomplished. Iraq continued to occupy some 1,065 sq km of Iranian territories, all captured after Iran had accepted the cease-fire. Additionally, the cease-fire had on many occasions been violated by both armies, which were only 20 feet apart in certain critical areas, and an initial attempt to exchange prisoners of war was suspended.[99] During the last days of 1989, Iran freed a number of Iraqi MIAs as a humanitarian gesture but the initiative did not draw much enthusiasm in Iraq, which continued to accuse the Islamic Republic of sabotaging the MIAs exchange process.

Given the situation as it existed between the two nations one year and a half after the cease-fire, can a comprehensive peace be negotiated? Answer to this question has two parts. To begin with, there is little possibility that the war will revive in the immediate future. There are several reasons for this, but major among them are, first, economic conditions in the two countries are extremely bad and war reconstruction must begin without delay; second, there is no support for the war among the peoples of the two nations; third, international support for the war is lacking; and fourth, a new climate of superpower relations has made use of force unacceptable, and the two nations are now well aware of this critical fact. These and other factors may provide the necessary conditions for the continuation of the cease-fire in the short run, but whether the two nations will settle their disputes in a comprehensive way soon is doubtful. In the absence of a major crisis in the Persian Gulf area, a situation similar to that between Syria and Israel today may persist between Iran and Iraq for years, despite the fact that the nature of the conflicts between the two pairs of nations are dissimilar. The unsettled situation may indeed politically benefit both governments in the short run as they need the tense environment to control their largely dissatisfied populations. Indeed, both governments used the cease-fire to further eliminate the political opposition as they used the war to do the same. Iraq also used the occasion to eliminate the Kurdish movement at a significant scale, reportedly using massive chemical agents.[100] In the long run, however, they both will lose from a no-war–no-peace situation as it will undermine their efforts to reconstruct the war damage and solve the urgent economic problems. Moreover, if the situation remains as tense and dangerous as in the present (early 1990), the war could revive in the distant future unless utmost restraint and care is exercised by both sides or Iraq finds a new victim. Indeed, these concerns make the two nations continue their discussions despite disagreements on many key issues.

On its part, Iran can still help reduce the tension between the two governments and improve its international standing by proposing to free all Iraqi MIAs without any conditions attached. It is true that Iran has more Iraqi MIAs than Iraq has Iranian MIAs, but this has not improved Iran's negotiating position. Sadam Hosain cares little about the Iraqi MIAs in Iran except that they have provided his government with a lot of propaganda at the international level. The Islamic Republic may also agree to hold direct talks with Iraq at the top leadership level (e.g., between the two presidents), for the purpose of peace formula discovery, but such talks must be held within the framework of Resolution 598 and under the auspices of the United Nations. The peace process must be considered a long, arduous, and incremental trust-building or perception changing process that must go through all its stages and reach a comprehensive settlement target only by means of partial successes. Iran must also take steps to improve its international policy in the hope of gaining more support for its proper position in the negotiations with Iraq. In the meantime, Iran must strengthen its domestic economy and defensive capabilities. This will demand not only financial and material investments, but also, and more important, democratization of the society and encouragement of the citizens' participation in national integration and defense. The postwar reconstruction should become a major focus for national attention and the peace issues must be widely discussed at various public and private forums. It must be realized that, whereas the use of offensive force has lost much of its effectiveness in imposing conditions (at home or abroad), the show of force will continue to remain a major tool in national defense and international relations. The effective projection of defensive force, however, requires a well-developed economy that in turn can be built only on a solid basis of science, technology, and democracy. Thus, putting more resources into research and development (R&D) is a must for Iran, as is participation of its people in the management of their affairs. This is particularly so now that Iraqis are making significant progress in defense and space sciences and the so-called superpowers are experiencing decline in their ability to shape regional politics in an age of global restructuring. A healthy competition in scientific and technological research could make Iran, which is, population wise, already the largest country in the Middle East, into a major regional power and improve the chance for peace and stability in the region by counterbalancing a restless Iraq.

Impact of the War on the Economy

I now turn to the impact of the war on the Iranian economy, a subject of considerable importance for a more realistic assessment of economic trends, problems, and policies under the Islamic Republic. But first a few words on the nature of the war-damage data and the methods by which they have been created. As I am interested in the impact of the war on the economy of Iran, I shall refrain from making comparisons between the damage from this war to that from other wars. It suffices to indicate only that the Iran-Iraq war will be recorded as one of contemporary history's long and costly wars. Next, the data given here are primarily "official" not only because they are produced by the Iranian government but also because they are produced with a view on possible war reparation.[101] It is, therefore, reasonable to assume that the reported data tend to be inflated. The overestimation problem might have been compounded by at least four other factors: first, the government has thrown almost "everything but the kitchen sink" into the damage numbers; second, for the most part, the damage figures are calculated on the basis of current prices and thus reflect the postrevolutionary rampant inflation; third, the dollar figures (e.g., in the case of lost oil revenue) are based on official exchange rates between the rial and dollar, which happens to be some ten to fifteen times smaller than the black market exchange rates; and fourth, the huge loss reported for actual oil revenue and for the opportunity costs in the sector is based on oil prices higher than the average oil prices for the war years. The exact price figure used is unknown to this author.[102]

As opposed to this tendency for overestimation, the government has tended to exclude certain cost items from the war-damage figures, thus contributing to underestimation of the reported damage. These include (1) damage to the military-defense sector (hardware, software, personnel, expenditures), (2) monetary value of the damage to the population (e.g., lost earnings by killed, disabled, maimed, missing, POWs, war-related unemployed), (3) environmental and psychological demage, (4) the reconstruction costs of the war damage, (5) the postponement of important development and educational projects, (6) the cost of the war-related inflation, (7) the cost of oil given to Syria as gift and at discount for supporting Iran's war efforts (some $11.3 billion), (8) additional shipping charges for oil exports (about $3 billion), (9) the cost of imports of oil by-products (some $14 billion), (10) the cost of reorienting imports to ports outside the war zone ($3.5 billion), (11) the cost of shipping oil to outlaying terminals for exports and the insurance surcharge for oil tankers (some $3 billion), and (12) the cost for reversing an early policy of maintaining a lower defense spending ($84 billion).[103] Assuming that the underestimates are, more or less, compensated for by the overestimates, the total official damage figures, on the balance, may be considered reasonably accurate.

Finally, the methodology used in calculating the damage needs some explanations. Following issuance of the circular dated 27/3/1361 by the Prime Minister's Office concerning estimation of the war-damage, a number of meetings were held in the Ministry of Foreign Affairs, as a result of which four committees were established to take the responsibility for the task. They included the Military Committee, the Economic Committee, the News and Information Committee, and the Political and Legal Committee. The circular had also directed various government offices to undertake the task of estimating their respective war-damage. They were then asked to send their information to the respective committees for compiling and finalizing the estimates. To better coordinate and standardize the activities of the various offices, the Economic Committee developed a series of models, techniques, tables, questionnaires, and guidelines and published them in a book called *Raveshha va Olgouha-ye Lazem Bara-ye Baravourd-e Khasarat-e Jang-e Tahmili-ye Iraq Aleyh-e Iran* [Necessary Methods and Models for Estimation of Economic Damage of the Imposed War of Iraq Against Iran.]

Essentially, the method used for gathering data included "head counting and sampling," depending on the type of activities. Direct observation, mailed questionnaires, and interviews were used separately or in combination. Where appropriate, simple statistical techniques were also used to arrive at damage estimates. The damaged elements were grouped into four categories: (1) Iraqi POWs, (2) expelled Iraqis, (3) the private sector, and (4) the public sector. For the first two, monetary loss was calculated through multiplying the average expenditures per person by the number of such people. For the public and private sectors in economic realm, seventeen sectors were identified and for each sector from one to nine types of damage were identified.[104] Such damage was also divided into "direct" and "indirect" damage. Direct economic damage included damage to buildings and public establishments, machinery and equipment, material goods, and other similar national wealth including infrastructure, cash and in-kind assistance, and payment of wages and salaries to those sent to the war front (excluding regular military personnel), damage to machinery and vehicles sent to the war front, and welfare payments to war-inflicted population. Indirect economic damage, on the other hand, in large part, included opportunity costs (e.g., lost potential GNP and lost potential earnings from oil), reductions in capacity and delays in operation, and obstacles and difficulties resulting from the war. To arrive at the damage for each sector, the number of units damaged (or lost) was multiplied by the unit price (present or future). In practice, however, determination of units damaged or lost and proper pricing proved very complicated. In most cases, a percentage was assigned to represent the degree of damage a unit had sustained and damages of over 60 percent were considered total loss. "Average regional prices" were usually taken to represent the current price for the damaged items and only occasionally was inflation accounted for. To determine opportunity costs, assumptions were made about future prices, and care was exercised to prevent double counting.

To return to the impact of the war on the post-revolutionary economy. Iraq invaded Iran along a front of 1,352 km, penetrating at certain places as deep as 80 km into Iran. In less than a few weeks, over 14,000 sq km of the country were occupied in the five southern and southwestern provinces of Khuzestan, Bakhtaran, Ilam, Kurdestan, and West Azerbaijan (Figure 2.1). These provinces border Turkey, Iraq, and the Persian Gulf and comprise the Zagros Mountains and Lake Urmia. The total land area is 178,000 sq km, 10.8 percent of the country's total, and, in 1980 when the war began, some 6.3 million people, that is, about 16.7 percent of the nation's population, lived in these provinces. They were also more densely populated than many other parts of the country, with a density rate of 35.4 persons per sq km as compared to the national average of about 23.2 in 1980. The majority of the provinces' populations are ethnic minorities (Azaris, Kurds, and Arabs) and as much they are considered politically very significant, also economically important. Khuzestan, in particular, is the oil capital of Iran and home for major economic establishments including port facilities, steel factories, oil refineries, and petrochemical complexes. Other provinces adjoining the war zones and cities in different parts of the country have also suffered, particularly from repeated missile attacks on the civilian sectors.

The destruction caused by the war has been truly enormous particularly in the five provinces mentioned.[105] To begin with, out of a population of 50.6 million (in 1986), there have been some 300,000 casualties, including 61,000 missing in action, about 50,000 of which remain in Iraqi prisons (includes some of the MIAs), and at least another half million are disabled or maimed.[106] Moreover, some 2.5 million have lost their homes and jobs or are displaced, in various refugee camps, makeshift shacks, and temporary shelters in major urban centers. To this list of human damage one must add the millions of energetic and productive working people who served in the war in varying capacities as military personnel, paramilitary and irregular forces, technical experts, and volunteers.[107] It must be noted that the volunteer forces were primarily young and the most dedicated to the Revolution.

Equally devastating has been the impact of the war on the country's human settlements including population distribution, urban systems, and rural areas in the war zones in the southern and southwestern parts of the country. The 1986 (Iranian 1365) national census put the total population of the five war provinces at 7.6 million, or about 15 percent of the national population. The corresponding figures for 1976 (Iranian 1355) were 5.7 million and 17.2 percent, indicating that these provinces have lost a significant portion of their population.

A total of fifty-two cities have been damaged, all of them in the war provinces. Of these, six cities have been completely leveled (Hoveizeh, Qasr-e Shirin, Musian, Ozgoleh, Khosrawi, and Naft Shahr) and another fifteen have sustained between 30 to 80 percent destruction (Khorramshahr, Nosoud, Dehloran, Gilan-e Qarb, Abadan, Bostan, Mehran, Susangard, Shush, Dezful, Andimeshk, Baneh, Sar Pole-e Zohab, and Sardasht). The city of Khorramshahr, which had some 300,000 people in 1980 and was by far the most important of Iran's ports on the Persian Gulf, is presently a ghost town. Eighty percent lies under rubble and what is left is unusable. In addition, a number of major cities in other parts of the country, including Tehran and Esfahan, have also been hit by missiles and bombs on numerous occasions and have sustained substantial damage.[108]

Destruction of rural areas has been even more devastating. Well over 30 percent of the villages in the five war provinces, that is some 4,000 settlements, have been completely destroyed and many more villages have sustained heavy damage. The monetary value of total damage to the country's settlements (urban and rural) was put at about $13 billion for the September 1980–September 1985 period (of which 54 percent related to rural destruction). Statistics for the remaining war period (to August 1988) are not yet available to the public. The best educated guess is that some $5 billion worth of damage may have been inflicted during this later period, raising the total figure for damage to the settlements to around $18 billion.[109]

Yet, war-damage has been the most devastating to the country's economy. Table 2.2 and Figure 2.3 gives direct and indirect economic damage for nine sectors up to September 1985. The total damage amounted to over 24,707 billion rials or $309.1 billion, of which direct damage accounted for 35.5 percent or about $110 billion. To compare, the country's 1985 GDP was worth $176.6 billion (in current prices, at 84.9 rials to $1). Opportunity costs make up a sizable portion of the indirect costs, and direct costs largely include destruction to machinery, buildings, materials, goods, and similar national wealth. The 1988 official report on the war economic damage has not yet been released. Figures cited in unpublished documents and speeches by the government officials indicate a much higher total damage figure.[110] In particular, the direct economic damage to the end of the Iranian year 1365 (i.e., to 21 March 1987) is estimated at $189 billion.[111] Assuming that this represents, as in the previous report, only 35.5 percent of the total damage, we arrive at the staggering figure of $532.4 billion for direct and indirect war economic damage as of 21 March 1987.

The exact cost figures for the remaining war period (21 March 1987–20 August 1988) are not yet available. However, some $60 billion may have been added to the total damage ($21 billion as direct damage) assuming that the damage accrued at the same annual rate as during the 1985–87 period. Therefore, from the beginning of the war in September 1980 to the time of the cease-fire on 20 August 1988, some $592 billion in damage has been inflicted on the economy, of which some $210 billion relate to damage inflicted on the country's machinery, buildings, equipment, materials, goods, and similar national wealth.[112] This direct economic damage alone accounts for over 19.5 years of oil revenue (at the 1987 earning level

Table 2.2 Economic Damage of the War to September 1985 (million rials, current prices)(a)

Type of Damage

Sector (b)	Direct (c) Amount	% Total	Indirect (d) Amount	% Total	Total Damage
1	2,915,013	83.4	579,440	16.6	3,494,453
2	129,474	5.6	2,172,185	94.4	2,301,659
3	1,238,188	9.4	11,988,085	90.6	13,226,273
4	171,765	33.8	336,999	66.2	508,764
5	127,497	92.6	10,138	7.4	137,635
6	468,687	97.2	13,535	2.8	482,222
7	3,160,378	100.0	0.0	0.0	3,160,378
8	331,013	88.1	44,542	11.9	375,555
9	239,948	23.5	780,145	76.5	1,020,093
Total	8,781,963	35.5	15,925,069	64.5	24,707,032

Source and Notes:
Calculated on the basis of Table 2 in *Kholaseh-e Gozaresh*, #7.

(a) Numbers are rounded. To convert rial figures into US dollars, use the exchange rate $1 = 80 rials.

(b) The original table gives data for 17 sectors. These are combined here into 9 sectors:
   1. Agriculture (all subsectors).
   2. Manufacturing industries.
   3. Oil and energy (combines 3 and 4 in original table).
   4. Telecommunications: roads, transportation and customs (combines 5 and 9 in the original table).
   5. Education and Islamic guidance; health and welfare (combines 7 and 8 in the original table).
   6. Housing and urban development (structures constructed by the Ministry of Housing and Urban Development). Municipalities (including buildings and equipment belonging to municipalities and other buildings in cities; the damage also affected the properties, furnitures and the likes belonging to city dwellers) (combines 6 and 11 in the original table).
   7. Revolutionary foundations (the damage in this case affected the villages in the five war provinces and included the expenses incurred by the Guard Corps [e.g. expenditures for provisions of basic needs of its fighters and payments to families of those killed, disabled, and injured in the war], the expenditures relating to war migrants, the expenses incurred by war captives and asylums, and the cash and/or in-kind assistance contributed to the war fronts by the Imam's Assistance Committee, the Fifteen of Khordad Foundation, and the Foundation for the Oppressed) (listed as number 12 in the original table).
   8. Banks (including assets, buildings, bad debts, and opportunity costs); commerce and finance (combines 10 and 13 in the original table).
   9. Labor and justice; Red Cresent-Tehran Municipality; Prime Ministry and Ministry of Plan and Budget; Gendarmerie and Police (combines 14,15,16, and 17 in the original table).

(c) Includes damage to various buildings and public establishments; machinery and equipment; material goods and other national wealth; cash and in-kind assistance and payment of wages and salaries to those sent to the war front; damage to machinery and vehicles sent to the war front; assistance to expenses of war-inflicted population.

(d) Includes opportunity costs (in large part); reduction in capacities and delay in operations; obstacles and difficulties resulting from the war.

Figure 2.3

Economic Cost of the War, to September 1985
(current prices)

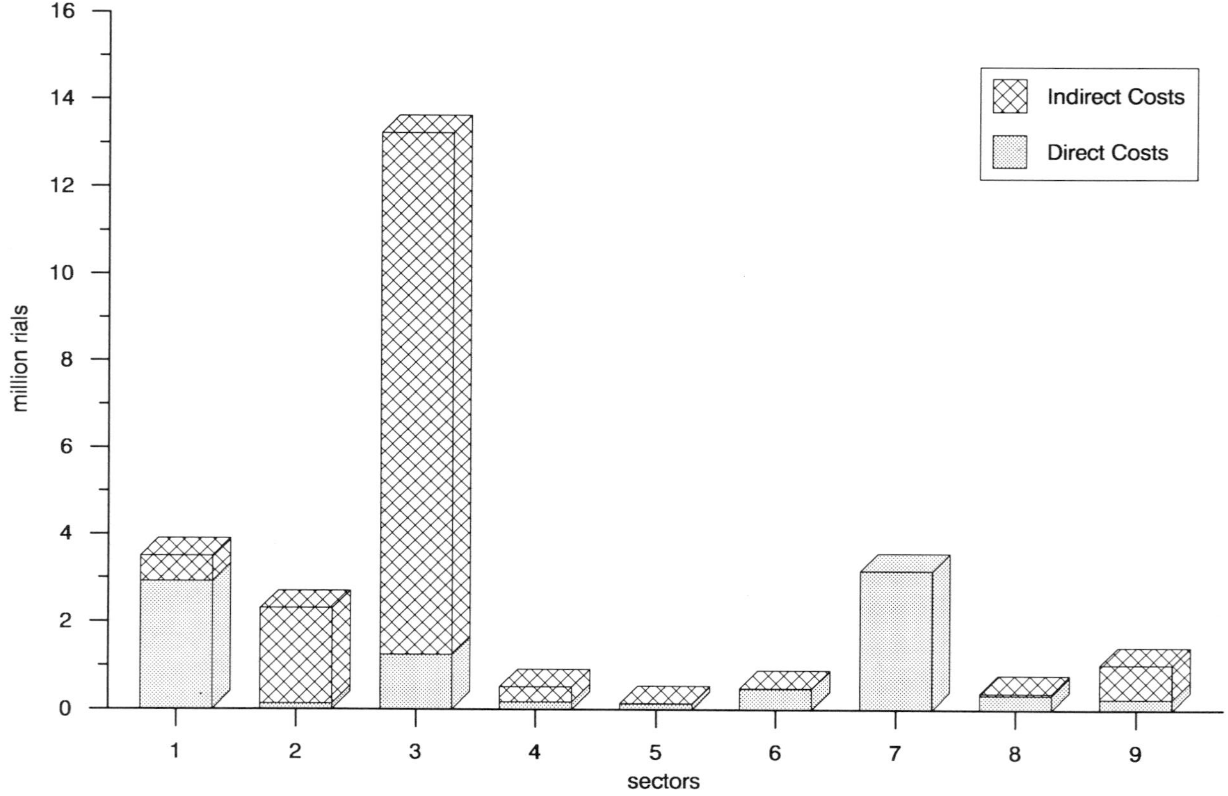

of $10.7 billion).[103] The June 1990 earthquake may have cost Iran an additional $10 to $15 billion in direct damage including 110,000 houses (*Kayhan-e Hava³i*, 20 Tir, 1369, p. 2).

To better appreciate the extent of the war's economic destruction, we now turn to investment losses and the sectoral disaggregation. To begin with, during the 1981–86 (Iranian 1360–65) period, on the average, some 43.7 percent of each year's investment in the country had been damaged.[114] The direct annual damage to the agriculture amounts to about 30 percent of annual value added in this sector, with damage to the sector's buildings and machinery amounting to 40 percent of the annual investments in the sector. The direct annual damage to the oil sector is estimated at 20 percent of the sector's annual value added and the damage to the sector's capital stocks stands at some 145 percent of total investments in the sector during the 1981–86 period. In other words, the war has destroyed all investments in the oil sector since 1981 plus some 45 percent of the sector's prewar capital stocks. The direct annual damage to the capital stocks in the industry and mines sector amounts to about 10 percent of the sector's annual investments. This sector has suffered from damage to such important industrial establishments as the Abadan Refinery (the world's largest), the Ahvaz Iron Work Factory *(Navard-e Ahvaz)* and the newly built huge petrochemical complex in Bandar-e Imam on the Persian Gulf coast. Estimates for the construction sector indicates that the total destruction in the sector is larger than the country's annual ability for construction of residential units. The direct damage to the education sector is estimated to equal the total credits needed to built 14,000 classrooms.[115] For a complete picture to emerge, damage incurred afterward (yet unavailable) should be also accounted for.

The financial and budgetary damage of the war have been equally significant. In a speech in July 1989, President Hashemi Rafsanjani, then speaker of the Parliament, revealed that: "during the war some 60 to 70 percent of the country's income was spent on the war."[116] Unconfirmed reports have indicated that in the first months of the war as much as $300 million a month was being spent on it. Table 2.3 and Figure 2.4 present the direct and indirect war expenditures over the 1981–86 period. The total war expenditures have amounted to 3,538.2 billion rials (about $41.6 billion at 84.9 rials to $1) for the period, accounting for 16.9 percent of all public expenditures in the period. Another $12 to $15 billion may be added to the total figure (for the remaining war period to August 1988) to arrive at the grand total of some $53.6 to $56.6 billion for the entire war period. About 88.7 percent of the war-related spending over the 1981–86 period have gone to direct expenditures, of which some 91

Table 2.3 The War Expenditures, 1981–86 (billion rials, current prices)

Expenditure Category	1981	1982	1983	1984	1985	1986	1981–86 TOTAL
Total War Expenditures (a)	391.4	532.0	674.0	521.8	538.0	881.0	3538.2
1. Direct (b)	380.9	515.0	594.0	449.0	425.0	781.0	3144.9
• Defense (c)	380.9	445.0	503.0	399.0	400.0	746.0	2873.9
• Reconstruction of War-Damaged Area	0.0	70.0	91.0	50.0	25.0	35.0	281.0
2. Indirect	10.5	17.0	80.0	82.3	112.0	100.0	401.5
• Foundation for Affairs of the War Migrants	0.0	0.0	40.0	39.3	63.0	45.0	187.0
• Martyrs Foundation	10.5	117.0	40.0	43.0	50.0	55.0	215.5
Total Public Expenditures (d)	2,861.0	3,367.0	3,895.0	3,631.0	4,135.0	4,050.0	20,939.0
The War Expenditures as Percent of Total Public Expenditures (%)	13.7	15.8	17.3	14.4	13.0	21.8	16.9

Sources and Notes:
Compiled from *Bazsazi*, (1366), pp. 10–11.

(a) These figures exclude the regular defense budget and therefore underestimate the total war expenditures. See Table 3.6.

(b) Direct expenditures include (1) payments for purchase of defensive equipment by the Ministries of Defense and Sepah (Revolutionary Guards Corps); (2) war-related expenditures of the Gendarmeri and the Islamic Revolutionary Committees; (3) expenses of engineering operations in the war fronts by the Ministry of Reconstruction Crusade; (4) payments to individuals for war damage; (5) payments for the reconstruction and renovation of the war-damaged areas.

(c) Excludes the regular defense budget, i.e., the part of the ministry's expenditures that would have been needed in the absence of the war.

(d) Figures in this tables are not comparable to those given in Table 3.6.

Figure 2.4
The War Expenditures, 1981–86
(current prices)

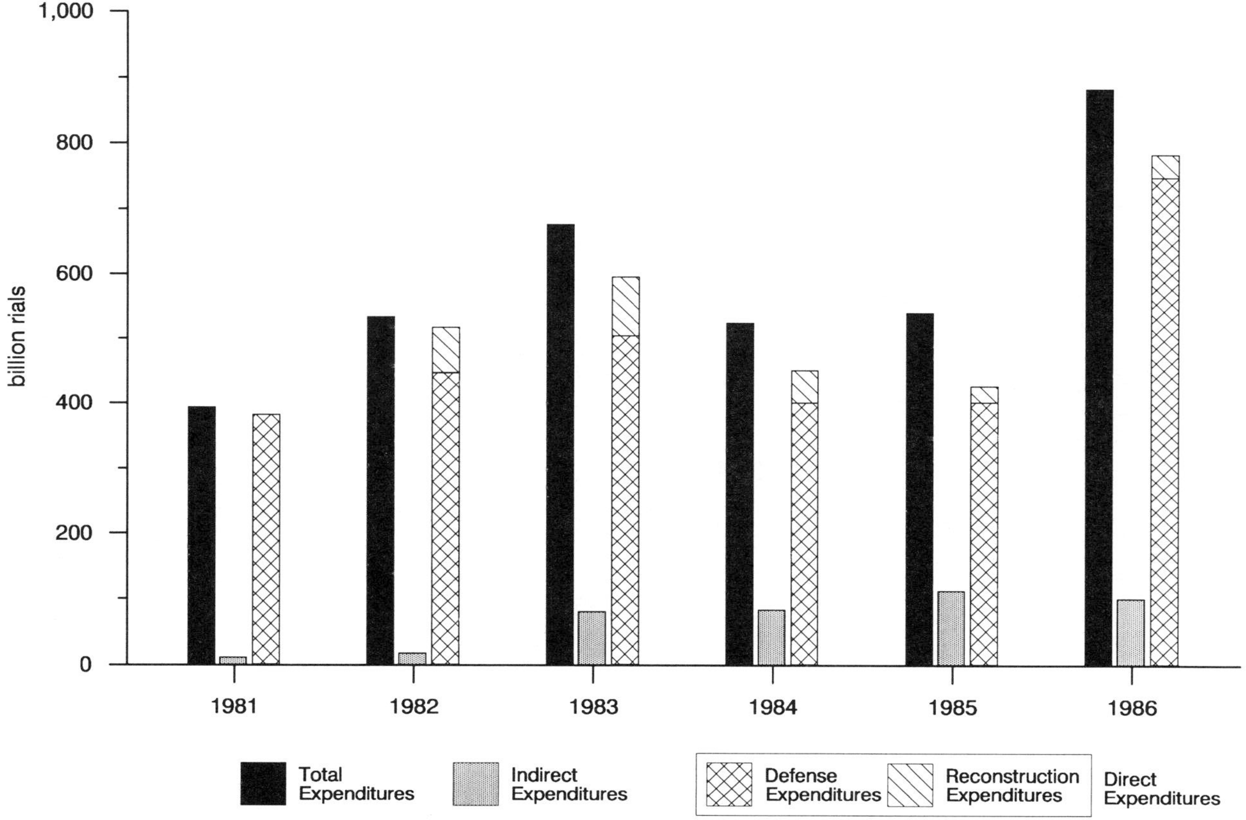

billion rials

1,000
800
600
400
200
0

1981   1982   1983   1984   1985   1986

Total
Expenditures

Indirect
Expenditures

Defense
Expenditures

Reconstruction
Expenditures

Direct
Expenditures

percent had been earmarked for the war-related defense spending. In sharp contrast, reconstruction of the war-damaged areas received only 8.9 percent of the direct spending. Equally meager was the share of the indirect costs in the total war expenditures, some 11.3 percent, paid to Martyrs Foundation and to the Foundation for the Affairs of the War Migrants.

THE OIL AND SAUDI FACTORS

The key to understanding the Iranian economy lies with comprehending the nature of various constraints on the country's oil revenue. This is so because the modern sectors of the Iranian economy all are dependent on earnings from oil. Some 90 percent of the state's foreign exchange earnings come from crude oil exports that pay for various kinds of Iran's ever-increasing industrial and food imports. It is also through this major export commodity that Iran is integrated into the world system and has achieved the status of a semiperipheral dependent state. The modern industries of Iran, for example, are dependent on the world economy for more than 65 percent of their inputs. Oil is, in short, the economy's real life line. Yet, Iran has only limited control over the production, export and price of its oil, for these are determined largely by the changes in the world economy and within OPEC. In other words, although oil is everything to the economy, it cannot, and should not, be considered a government economic policy tool. Dependency on oil also constrained Iran's budget and therefore its socioeconomic development policies. It had a further negative impact on the nation's international policy as the state's autonomous maneuvering in the field of diplomacy was significantly limited. Moreover, under such uncertain conditions, planning became very difficult in the postrevolutionary period when oil prices experienced wild fluctuations. To further complicate the picture, imperial powers retaliated against the Islamic Republic's demand for changes in the existing international order by manipulating the world oil market or through their oil companies and proxies in the OPEC, notably Saudi Arabia. Additional problems were created by the leadership itself as it remained inattentive to structural changes in the oil markets since the late 1970s and could not manage the oil revenues, much of which were wasted in the war. Tables 2.4 and 2.5 and Figures 2.5 and 2.6 reflect the extreme volatility of the oil production, export, and price.

Despite these constraints, the postrevolutionary leadership of the country did attempt to seize upon the opportunities generated by the Revolution to devise and adopt a new oil policy. Iran's foreign ex-

Table 2.4   Iran's Crude Oil Production and Exports, 1976–86 (million barrels/day)(a)

Year	Production	Share in OPEC Production	Exports (b)
1976	5.9	19.2	5.3
1977	5.7	18.2	5.0
1978	5.3	17.4	4.6
1979	3.2	10.0	2.8
1980	1.5	5.4	1.0
1981	1.3	5.8	0.8
1982	2.4	12.1	1.7
1983	2.5	13.8	2.0
1984	2.2	12.5	1.6
1985	2.2	13.7	1.5
1986	1.9	10.2	1.1

Sources and Notes:
Tahavvulat, pp. 545–47; *Gozaresh* (1363), vol. 2, Ch. 8, p. 17 and (1365), vol. 2, Ch. 5, pp. 18, 23, and Ch. 19, p. 18; *Majaleh* (1364), pp. 66–68; *Taraznameh* (1362), pp. 166–68 and (1363), p. 177; and Bank Markazi *Annual Report and Balance Sheet* [English version] (1985), pp. 138–39.

(a) Rounded.
(b) Crude oil and oil-related products.

change reserves on the eve of the Revolution exceeded $11 billion and most of the Shah's debts (of almost the same amount) were not due for a few years to come. Moreover, oil prices had had a major jump in 1979, reaching the historic peak of slightly below $40 per

Table 2.5   Official and Spot Prices for Iranian Light Crude Oil, 1978–87 (dollars/barrel)

Year	Official Prices (1 January)	Spot Prices (January Average)
1978	12.8	13.5
1979	13.5	30.0
1980	28.5	38.1
1981	37.0	39.8
1982	34.2	34.1
1983	31.2	30.9
1984	28.0	28.0
1985	29.1	27.5
1986	28.0	23.6
1987	28.0	17.6

Sources:
Tahavvoulat (1983); *Petroleum Intelligence Weekly,* (1981–88); *Oil and Energy Trends,* (1979–85); *OPEC Annual Statistical Bulletin,* 1982; *OPEC Bulletin,* (1980–88).

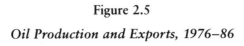

Figure 2.5

Oil Production and Exports, 1976–86

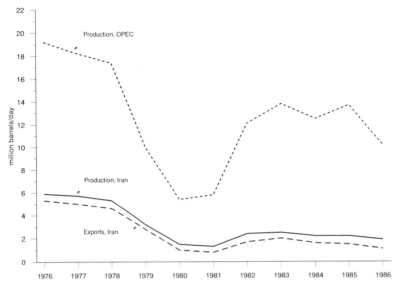

barrel. This so-called second oil shock had followed the Iranian Revolution and the subsequent panic in the world oil markets. In the
meantime, imports had declined significantly leaving the country
with a $5.6 billion balance of trade surplus. Additionally, enthusi-
asm for national sovereignty had created the needed political consensus for a major policy change. Oil production was also already at
a low level because of the workers' strikes and departure of the sector's foreign experts and many of its native technical staff. The new
policy would further benefit from the anti-import attitude of the
revolutionary leaders, initially leading to the cancellation of several
billion dollars of advanced import purchases from the West, including some $12.5 billion worth of military equipment from the United
States.[117]

The new policy began by terminating the oil consortium's control of Iranian oil production, export, and marketing. All such operations were transferred to the National Iranian Oil Company. The
consortium was comprised of the so-called majors and its national
ownership included the United Kingdom, 46 percent; the United
States, 40 percent; the Netherlands, 8 percent; and France, 6 percent. Next, all joint-venture oil companies, including those active in
exploration in various parts of the country, were nationalized and

Figure 2.6
Iran's Light Crude Oil Prices, 1978–87

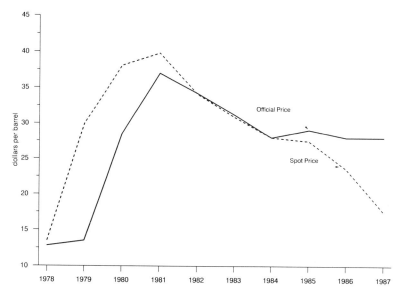

transferred to the NIOC. The organization was then combined with other oil and gas related national companies to create a new Ministry of Oil in mid-1979. The new policy was predicated largely on a lower level of export (below 3 mb/d), as compared to prerevolutionary level of some 5 to 6 mb/d. The new government wished to prolong the life of the country's oil reserves and gradually reduce its dependency on oil exports. The government also planned to increase its investments in downstream projects so that export of products would gradually increase at the expense of export of crude oil. Within the OPEC, Iran was to defend a policy of limited production and increasing prices. Other important policy measures included pruning the defense budget by 50 percent, promoting nonoil exports, pursuing an aggressive price policy, and broadening sales markets by utilizing spot sales (as opposed to contract sales), barter trade, and government buyers. Oil exports to Israel and South Africa had already been suspended. Among other measures, promoting the less-oil-dependent sectors (e.g., agriculture), and diversifying the economy and the country's trade partners were hoped to help realize the goals of the new oil policy.

As we shall see later in this book, some of these measures were implemented and steps were taken to implement others. But before the new policy could be carried through, obstacles began to develop. The economic recession that had started in 1977 continued through 1980. Although the price hike in 1979 had increased the state's foreign exchange revenue to about $19.3 billion, the domestic political struggles and the state's ideological limitations would not allow the government to devise a plan for rejuvenating the economy. in the meantime, Iraq invaded Iran and inflicted heavy damage on almost all sectors of the economy. The war also destroyed some of the most important Iranian oil installations, including the Abadan refinery, the world's largest. The consequent reduction in oil production and exports led to a sharp drop in the state's oil revenues in 1980 and 1981 ($11.6 billion and $12.4 billion, respectively). At the same time the state had to reverse its policy of pruning the defense budget and thus military spending began to rise. The government's operating expenditures also began to increase rapidly as the war dragged on; they were already rising because of the expanding size of the Revolutionary Foundations *(nehadha-ye enghelabi)* and increased subsidies for certain basic needs to offset inflation. All these factors led to an increased need for revenues, including foreign exchange. The revenue problem was further complicated by the government's inability to promote nonoil exports and collect taxes from the rich and by the gradual decline in oil prices and the value of the U.S. dollar beginning in 1981. Although oil revenues increased again in 1982 and 1983 (to $20 billion and $20.4 billion, respectively), the Republic's obsession with the war and its increased budgetary commitments made it impossible for the government to return to the new policy. Instead, the government followed a pragmatic and reactive policy, similar to the approaches it used to cope with other economic matters. By the collapse of oil prices in 1986, the new oil policy was permanently shelved and a new, somewhat *a la Shah*, policy began to take shape.

The most formidable constraints, however, had their origins in the world oil markets and within OPEC—the Saudi policy. To begin with, the Islamic Republic was surprisingly inattentive to the transformation in the world oil markets in the aftermath of the first oil shock in 1973–74. In 1986, for example, when the Iranian oil revenue dropped from a projected $15 billion to an actual $5.8 billion, the government was so unprepared that it had to introduce an emergency economic plan to cope with the shock's disastrous consequences. The 1973–74 oil-related events (Arab oil embargo and oil price hike under the leadership of OPEC) had made the West increasingly oil conscious. The United States led the crusade against OPEC, which began with the creation of the International Energy Agency (IEA) in 1974, with the participation of all major oil-consuming nations except France. This new "cartel of oil companies" was to create a surplus of energy by a combination of several means including reduction in demand, development of new energy sources, and engineering of occasional glut. In 1975, Henry Kissinger noted that the "most important" objective of the American energy policy was "to bring in alternative sources of energy as rapidly as possible so that the combination of new discoveries of oil, new oil-producing countries, and new sources of energy create a supply situation in which it will be increasingly difficult for the cartel [OPEC] to operate."[118]

In retrospect, the United States has been quite successful in achieving these objectives. According to James Jensen: "The 1985 demand for oil in the non-Communist world was 45.6 mb/d. At that level, demand was 5 percent lower than it was in 1973 at the time of the first oil shock."[119] For the OPEC, however, the decline in demand was disproportionately higher. In 1975, for example, the share of OPEC in the total non-Communist production was 68.2 percent; by the end of 1984, it had declined to 44.4 percent. By 1986, OPEC had lost some 20 mb/d of its potential production, of which 14 to 15 mb/d had been taken away by the non-OPEC producers.[120] The aggregate OPEC production declined by about 45 percent between 1979 and 1985. OPEC's share in world exports also declined, from just over 80 percent in 1981 to 65.5 percent in 1984. In the meantime, the world oil market was flooded by oil from the Saudi Arabia and the non-OPEC producers, resulting in a major oversupply or glut by 1985.[121] Within the OPEC, Iran was the biggest loser. Its share of OPEC production and exports of crude oil declined from 19.1 percent and 18.2 percent in 1976 to 14.1 and 13.4 in 1985, respectively.

The decline in world demand, including that for the OPEC oil, resulted from a number of interrelated factors. With the rise in oil prices, Western governments began to expand subsidies and promotional programs for oil substitutes. As a consequence, the relative prices of these products (gas, coal, nuclear energy) declined while demand for them increased leading to expansion in their production and use. The West also followed a policy of promoting energy conservation largely by means of discouraging consumption or changing their peoples' consumption habits (e.g., a shift to smaller cars in the United States, lower speed limits, fuel switching). The decade-old restructuring process in most residential, commercial, industrial, and transportation activities also led to invention of less energy-intensive materials and technologies. Reduction in production of steel and its use in production of automobiles is an example of such restructuring. In the meantime, the capitalist world economy has been unable to fully recover from the economic recession that began in 1974. Capitalist countries, which had sustained a GDP growth rate of slightly over 5 percent, average per year during the decade preceding the first oil shock, could not improve their growth rate much beyond a mere 2.5 percent since then. Last, although demand for OPEC oil shrank, the supply of non-OPEC oil increased in the world market since the mid-1970s. New exploration in the North Sea (England and Norway), Mexico, and smaller producers throughout the world was particularly damaging to OPEC.

Thus, ever since the second oil shock in 1979–80 period, prices of the OPEC oil have been strained by shrinking demand and expanding competition. Nevertheless, and as shown by Cyrus Bina, as long as the least efficient production in the United States remained the basis for the formation of world oil prices in a fully internationalized industry, the OPEC producers could manage to make a superprofit.[122] However, with the deregulation of American oil market, completed by the Reagan administration in the early 1980, and new incentives for private investment, most U.S. oil companies began to improve their productivity. In the meantime, short-term trading in spot and futures markets began to increase. This situation developed following the termination of the concession system, which was completed in 1980, and the emergence of the North Sea oil. The deregulation in the United States also strengthened the position of the large American firms in the spot and futures markets. Additional destabilizing influences on the oil markets came from the speculative and vacillating stockpiling policies of the Western oil companies. Their malicious practices became so threatening that even the Saudi Royal Cabinet could not remain silent and had to issue a stern warning to them, accusing them of "misconduct" and generating "an atmosphere of panic" in the world oil markets. The Saudis also plead, in vain, for the Western countries to put restrictions on their oil companies, making them behave more responsibly in the world oil markets.[123]

Influences of these forces on the OPEC process cannot be overestimated. They combined with at least two other influences on the oil market to bring about the 1986 crash, the "third oil shock," as a result of which oil prices declined from about $28 per barrel in mid-January 1986 to $10 per barrel by the first week of April 1986, with real, inflation-adjusted prices in the area of $4 to $5 per barrel.

These two other forces were the mistaken OPEC policies and what I shall call the "Saudi factor." The two were, however, closely related. Beginning in the early 1970s, OPEC gradually replaced the oil companies as oil price regulators, a function that it performed reasonably well in the initial years.[124] In the 1980s, however, OPEC has been reduced from a "price maker" to a "price taker," largely as a result of global restructuring and opportunism of the OPEC members. What proved disastrous for OPEC however, was the fact that it initially gave only lip-service to such transformations and did not adopt a long-term strategic perspective in pricing its oil. Instead, it went with the wind, assuming that the future would remain bright. Such a strategic mistake was already evident following the 1979–80 price hike. Instead of intervening in the market to regulate the price at a more stable level, OPEC decided to take the superprofit and allow the market forces to run their courses.[125] But the price hike had come about not on the basis of an imbalance between supply and demand but due to more deepseated changes in the capitalist world economy. Indeed, in 1979, the oil supply had not declined even if Iranian oil production and exports had at times come to a standstill. Saudi Arabia and Iraq had more than offset the drop in Iran's share. In 1979, OPEC production, at 30.9 mb/d was some 65 percent higher than its 1981 production, reported at 22.6 mb/d.

The Saudi factor is closely related to the growing importance of intra-OPEC power struggle for oil price level and stability, the increasing politicization of the organization in the last fifteen years, and the growing vulnerability of OPEC to the whims of its powerful members. The "struggle for the leadership of OPEC remained a dormant issue under the tight market of 1979–80. It was only in soft market periods (for instance 1974–1978 and 1981–1985) that this struggle created considerable intra-OPEC tensions."[126] After the Iranian Revolution, Saudi Arabia became the absolute "swing producer" of OPEC, a position that contributed to its growing power within the organization in the subsequent years. The kingdom used its new-found power to make economic and political gains and friends. In particular, it used its power within OPEC to regulate oil prices according to its economic needs and requirements of its Western friends, the United States in particular. The Saudi Royal Cabinet also used its economic power to help counterrevolutionaries throughout the world and undermine postrevolutionary regimes, including Iran. This Saudi policy was part of a larger mutual commitment that had developed between the kingdom and the United States beginning in the mid-1970s. In Terzian's words: "A new strategic triangle had emerged on the international scene—OPEC at the mercy of Saudi Arabia; Saudi Arabia aligned with the United States; the United States committed to the protection of Riyadh—and OPEC was to remain a prisoner of this triangle throughout the following years, escaping only thanks to exceptional—and ephemeral—circumstances."[127]

Thus, following the Iranian Revolution in 1979, according to Mohammad Farouk Al Husseini: "Saudi Arabia was called upon by the international community to increase its production in order to alleviate the adverse effect that might have been engendered by a world energy crisis. Production was accordingly increased to 9.5 mb/d in 1979, 9.9 mb/d in 1980 and 9.8 mb/d in 1981."[128] Aramco was already, in late 1978, producing some 2.5 to 3 mb/d more than its production earlier that year. As was later revealed by a U.S. Senate report, Aramco's maximum production capacity was about 9.3 mb/d and the overproduction had "caused irreparable damage and reduced ultimate recovery rate of oil in places."[129] Although the Saudis' overproduction policy had begun in the mid-1970s, it became a well-established practice only after the Iranian workers' strikes, which had interrupted the country's oil exports in 1978.

The kingdom also tried to keep the lid on oil prices. However, due to the soft market conditions prevailing in 1979–80 period, these Saudi malicious tactics proved largely ineffective. As noted by Fereidun Fesharaki and David Isaak: "In 1979, the Saudi initially kept their prices at $18/barrel—$4 barrel below similar-quality crudes—but spot prices rose to $45/barrel. The Saudi were *forced*, step by step, to raise their prices to $24/barrel, then $26, $28, $30, and finally to $32/barrel in December 1980. Still their prices were $3–4/barrel below similar-quality crudes"[130] (Italics added). According to Terzian, "this gap between Saudi prices and those of other producers represented a loss of over $23,000 million over the period February 1979 to September 1981."[131] The lower prices of the Saudi oil also led to widespread corruption among top-ranking Saudi figures including some members of the royal family. The two most important cases involved the notorious Prince Mohamed bin Abdul Aziz, King Khaled's elder brother, and Prince Bandar bin Faisal bin Saud. Both are reported to have approached oil companies, offering them lower-priced oil in exchange for multibillion-dollar commissions.[132]

Whatever the cost, by 1981, Saudi Arabia had "succeeded in imposing its will on the other OPEC members, forcing them to realign prices at the lowered Saudi scale."[133] In an interview with NBC television on 19 April 1981, Ahmed Zaki Yamani, then Saudi oil minister, said that the current oil glut was "engineered" by his government to stabilize the world oil price.[134] Another source also quoted the Minister for expressing a similar idea: "We engineered the glut and want to see it in order to stabilize the price of oil."[135] Following this policy, the Saudis found themselves in opposition to the other twelve members of OPEC during the organization's sixtieth meeting in Geneva on 25–27 May 1981.

While this Saudi policy was inflicting real wounds on OPEC (e.g., prices collapsed in February 1982), the kingdom introduced an even more malicious tactic in 1985. This new policy is known as "netback" deals, or as some have rightly called it, " a price war."[136] Under the netback pricing arrangements, oil companies buying Saudi oil were guaranteed profits at the refining stage by indexing the crude oil price to the market value of the products made from it. The netback mechanism, therefore, reduced risk in the volatile oil market. Under such a lucrative arrangement for the oil companies, Saudi Arabia had no difficulty increasing its production and export and flooded the oil market. Indeed, by the end of 1985 Saudi production and export more than doubled. Specifically, Saudi oil exports rose from 2.5 mb/d in the fall of 1985 to 4.5 mb/d in early 1986 and close to 6 mb/d in the summer of that year. As a result, "the potential world oversupply of oil, as earlier in the year, became an actual oversupply."[137] In the aftermath of this development, OPEC terminated its policies of fixing its oil price and restricting production to the level of world demand after accounting for non-OPEC oil. These changes then set the stage for the big crash of 1986, which had, strangely enough, occurred less than two months after Iran had taken the Iraqi port of Fao, following a surprise major offensive.

Generally speaking, although all OPEC members have suffered from the declining oil market and the Saudi policies, the Islamic Republic has felt the greatest impact. The republic was involved in a war for which it had no international support and had inherited an economy that was in deep crisis and highly dependent on oil revenue. Moreover, the Saudi policies were designed not just to "cripple the Islamic regime economically" but also to strengthen its enemy, Iraq. The Saudis were "financing Iraq's war effort" from the start and in a variety of ways including unilateral transfers in cash and in kind, credit arrangements, and loans.[138] In a single year, 1981, for example, Saudi Arabia along with Kuwait, Qatar, and the United Arab Emirates "provided Iraq with financial assistance, in the form of an interest free loan of $30,000 million."[139] To achieve the maximum destructive effect, the Saudi policy was also coordinated with the United States's destabilizing campaigns and economic sanctions against the Islamic government in the aftermath of the hostage drama. For example, on 5 June 1984, a Saudi F-15 shot down an Iranian F-4 phantom jet, an event that, according to Elizabeth Gamlen, happened as "a direct consequence" of the Saudi air cover by "the US operated and controlled AWACS."[140] Iran was perhaps fortunate that the crash of 1986 was equally harmful to the American oil industry in Texas. As a result, and according to James Bill, "Iran's and America's interests converged on this issue." The Saudis were then pressured to sign an agreement with Iran on lower production in late summer 1986.[141]

Saudi Arabia has continued to undermine the Islamic Republic in the postwar period, a fact that, at the least, indicates fundamental disagreements between the two regimes over such issues as religious conduct, regional security, and international alliances. As was widely reported in the New York Times,[142] along with Kuwait, the United Arab Emirates, Qatar, and Iraq, the kingdom stepped up its oil production almost immediately after the cease-fir on 20 August 1988. By early October, Saudi production had reached 5.7 mb/d, well above its OPEC quota of 4.3 mb/d. The Saudis claimed that they were protecting their market share from Iran's possible incursion, a pretext that soon became untenable. The Islamic Republic continued to produce at less than its OPEC quota of 2.4 mb/d throughout 1988. In the meantime, the Saudi government and its allies, other members of Arab OPEC, raised the question of production parity between Iran and Iraq as a condition for a new OPEC accord on price and production. This was rather an unfair demand as Iraq's share had always been lower. Iran, however, had a much bigger economy and a population four times as large as that of Iraq. Nevertheless, after an initial period of resistance, Iran gave in only to find that the Saudis had another plan in their bag: almost immediately the kingdom attempted to sabotage the OPEC agreement by conditioning its implementation to settling certain political disputes between itself and the Islamic Republic. To back up this new demand, the Saudis threatened to lower their oil prices, a position that led only to widespread protest by other members of the organization.[143]

Throughout the Saudi Arabian undeclared war against the Islamic Republic, the middle-class leadership in Tehran found it hard to take effective measures against the kingdom. Ayatollah Khomeini's call for the Saudi people to rise up against the Saudi leadership was not successful. Although in November 1979 a group of several hundred religious people seized the Grand Mosque in the Holy City of Mecca to force new changes on the Saudi king, they were quickly and mercilessly subdued and destroyed by the Saudi police and troops. The policy of making *Hajj* (annual Muslim pilgrim to Mecca) into a religious-political event also backfired: some 450 Iranian pilgrims were killed by the Saudi police during a political demonstration in July 1988 in Mecca, and after some political maneuvering, Iranians were banned from pilgrimage in 1989. The events also led to suspension of diplomatic relations between the two nations. But, certain of the Republic's measures against the Saudis proved quite effective. The policy of creating a united front with the "radical states" within OPEC (Algeria and Libya) against the Saudi royal government was one. The Islamic government was also successful in applying, at times, an aggressive pricing strategy in spot markets and in making extensive barter deals with Eastern European nations. In 1982, for example, Iran announced three successive price cuts in less than three weeks, and its oil price was $4 to $5 lower than the price for comparable Saudi oil. Even the United States, who had once boycotted Iranian oil, took advantage of the situation and purchased the cheap Iranian oil to build up its reserves. It seemed as if the Republic had a design to paralyze the "Saudi OPEC." In response, the Saudis surprised every one in the oil market when they offered to cut their production in order to boost prices. But, Iran did not give in, and as a result, the country's oil revenue increased to its postrevolutionary peaks in 1982 and 1983 ($20 billion and $20.4 billion, respectively). It must be noted, however, that, at the time, Iran was making advances on the war front, a development closely watched by the Saudi government.

It was not, however, until Iran had retaken the city of Khorramshahr from the occupying Iraqis on 24 May 1982 that the Saudis took the Islamic Republic seriously. The Saudis panicked, offering compensation for the war damage and cooperation in regional affairs. The Islamic Republic was, however, in a totally different mood. Confident of its military power and assured by its increased oil revenue, the Republic decided to continue the war until Sadam Hosain was overthrown and his allies punished. In the meantime, the Republic's policy toward Saudi Arabia, as declared by Mohamad Gharazi, then Iranian oil minister, would consist of "isolating Saudi Arabia, compelling her to behave as one member amongst others." But, he continued, "Our struggle with Riyadh will not take place on the oil market, it is a political struggle. Once Sadam Hussein has fallen, many problems will be resolved."[144] In retrospect, this proved wishful thinking on the part of the middle-class leadership in Tehran, who could not see the larger political economy of the Middle East and its place within the capitalist world system. As is well-known by now, the United States intervened in the war on the side of Iraq, initially creating a stalemate, then forcing the Islamic Republic into a situation that it had to accept a less than optimal conditions to end the war. The middle-class leadership had ended the hostage drama in an exactly similar fashion.

In conclusion, powerful forces, working together or in isolation, have influenced the postrevolutionary Iranian oil sector. Such forces were largely external and remained outside the Islamic Republic's control. As we shall shortly see, in the absence of a well-designed, active, thoughtful, and consistent policy to cope with these forces, their consequences proved the most disastrous. The rather erratic and reactive policies, which were followed most of the time, could hardly be expected to mend the problems. For example, in the first two years, the Islamic government tried to cope with the revenue problem by a policy of drawing from the existing reserves, raising taxes, increasing deficit financing, underselling OPEC, and making more barter deals (oil for imports). Soon, however, foreign exchange reserves were down to a critical level, inflation soared, the conservative bazaaris protested tax increases, and the oil price war became untenable. Already in 1981, the government was forced to give up its initial idea (the new oil policy) of reducing dependency on oil in favor of increasing production and export, diversifying dependency and redefining its expenditures priorities. In the subsequent years, the largely confrontationist policy was also reversed in favor of a more cooperative policy within OPEC, despite the Saudis' continued sabotage.

Since the cease-fire, the government has even tried to accommodate unreasonable demands by the Arab members of OPEC in the hope of strengthening solidarity within OPEC, an example of which was production parity between Iraq and Iran. The foreign exchange needs for the postwar reconstruction will impose additional imperatives for further lapse into the prerevolutionary oil policy, pragmatism in relations with the Persian Gulf states, and a more accommodative behavior within OPEC. The International Conference on the Persian Gulf, organized by the Ministry of Foreign Affairs in November 1989 (the author was among the participants), has exemplified the new conciliatory approach to relations with the Persian Gulf states. The main theme of the conference was regional solidarity; emphasis was placed on common interests and cultural heritage, and divisive issues were hardly raised. OPEC's meeting on 27 July 1990 gave another indication of Iran's growing cooperation with its former enemies, Iraq and Saudi Arabia. The meeting raised OPEC oil price to $21 per barrel and fixed its production ceiling for all 13 members at 22.5 million b/d. (See *New York Times*, July 28, 1990, pp. 1 and 30).

CAPACITY UNDERUTILIZATION AND THE BOTTLENECKS

The postrevolutionary Iranian economy has also suffered from significant underutilization of its existing capacities, itself a consequence of various constraining factors, some of which have already been explained. A more realistic assessment of what has happened to the economy should also account for this factor and its underlying causes. In what follows, I will first give an over-review of capacity underutilization and its relation to economic decline in the postrevolutionary period, and then explain a number of important infrastructural and superstructural bottlenecks that are at its root. Although most spheres of life in the country (economic, as well as social and political) remain underutilized in terms of actual and potential capacity, I shall focus on the economic sectors and on the existing capacity. (The Islamic Republic's performance in generating new capacities is further discussed in the next chapter in the section on fixed capital formation.)

In the absence of comparable statistics for the prerevolutionary years, it is hard to evaluate the performance of the Islamic Republic with respect to generation of new or utilization of the economy's existing productive capacity. The available estimates, however, do indicate significant capacity underutilization and a clear correlation between this problem and the crisis in the economy.[145] As reflected in Table 2.6, most economic sectors were underutilized in 1985 and the changes in the existing capacity and its utilization rate over the 1982–85 period (the only period for which comparable data are available) were mixed: increasing significantly in a few sectors, declining in a number of others, and remaining unchanged for the rest. Overall, however, the trends have been on the negative side, leading to underutilization of human resources, a factor that has had a tremendous detrimental effect on the postrevolutionary production.

In the agricultural sector in 1985, the rates of utilization of existing capacity were 60, 12, and 79 percent for cultivable lands, fishery production, and animal husbandry, respectively. Expansion of production on cultivable land remained constrained by the lack of irrigation networks, among other factors, while fishery suffered from the war, religious restrictions on certain products, and the troubled relations between the private fishermen and an industry that is totally nationalized. None of these subsectors experienced any significant change in their capacities or utilization rates over the 1982–85 period. The only exceptions were pasture production, which was overutilized (overgrazed) by 50 percent, and mechanization power in agriculture, expansion of which was 57.4 percent in

Table 2.6 Estimates of Existing Capacity and Rate of Utilization in Economic Sectors, 1982–85

SECTORS	Existing Capacities 1982	Existing Capacities 1985	Degree of Utilization 1982	Degree of Utilization 1985	Rate of Utilization (%) 1982	Rate of Utilization (%) 1985	Change in Capacity (%) 1982–85	Change in Utilization (%) 1982–85
Agriculture:								
Cultivable Lands (000 ha)	18,500	18,500	10,969	11,035	59.3	59.6	0.0	0.6
Irrigated (000 ha)	8,500	8,500	5,127	5,170	60.3	60.8	0.0	0.8
Forestry Production (m. m³)	4.0	4.0	1.3	1.7	32.5	42.5	0.0	30.8
Pasture Production (M tons)	10	10	15	15	150.0	150.0	0.0	0.0
Fishery Production (000 tons)	558	558	57	65	10.2	11.6	0.0	14.0
Beef Production (b.r.)	897.0	991.5	660.2	778.7	73.6	78.5	10.5	17.9
Mechanization Power (m.h.p.)	4,707	7,410	1,732	3,001	36.8	40.5	57.4	73.3
Water:								
Water Provisions (m. m³)	110,000	122,230	59,000	71,330	53.6	58.4	11.1	20.9
Irrigation and Drainage (000 ha)	6,890	6,890	3,350	3,375	48.6	49.0	0.0	0.7
For Cities and Industries (m. m³)	1,500	1,590	1,400	1,490	93.3	93.7	6.0	6.4
Manufacturing Industries (b.r.):	3,060	3,871	1,852	3,168	60.5	81.8	26.5	71.0
Mining								
Copper Production (000 tons)	15,160	16,000	8,080	8,800	53.3	55.0	5.5	8.9
Investment on Equipment and Operation (m.r.)	22,579	13,960	22,289	10,870	98.7	77.9	−38.2	−51.2
Power Plants (mega W):	8,758	11,323	4,998	7,055	57.1	62.3	29.3	41.2
Energy Production (MkW/h)	41,232	53,058	26,323	38,317	63.8	72.2	28.7	45.6
Electricity Production (b.r.)	169.0	218.8	107.9	157.0	63.8	71.8	29.5	45.5
Oil:								
Crude Oil Production (000 b/d)	3,159	3,159	2,686	2,300	85.0	72.8	0.0	−14.4
Refinery (000 b/d)	558.0	598.9	562.8	615.0	100.9	102.7	7.3	9.3
Gas:								
Production (m.m³/d)	78.4	72.8	48.0	38.7	61.2	53.2	−7.1	−19.4
Refinery (m.m³/d)	36.8	57.8	1.8	8.8	4.9	15.2	57.1	388.9
Housing Construction (m.m²):	32.5	39.0	21.0	25.0	64.6	64.1	20.0	19.0
Transportation:								
Via Roads (m.t/km)	92,280	125,032	61,520	100,026	66.7	80.0	35.5	62.6
Via Rail (Mtons)	16.3	17.1	7.9	12.0	48.5	70.2	4.9	51.9
Via Air (tons)	69,217	69,217	33,911	35,430	49.0	51.2	0.0	4.5
Port Capacity (Mtons)	15.0	26.4					76.0	

Source:
Compiled from and calculated on the basis of information given in *Zarfiyatha* (1365), pp. 7–36.

capacity and 73.3 percent in utilization rate, increasing from 36. 8 percent in 1982 to 40.5 percent in 1985. In 1973, there were 75,023 tractors in the country. The figure increased to 93,051 in 1982.

Equally underutilized was the capacity for water provision, manufacturing, power generation, and housing construction, with utilization rates in 1985 of about 58, 82, 62 and 64 percent, respectively. Among these, only manufacturing improved significantly in its utilization rate, by 71 percent over the 1982–85 period. This happened because of a significant increase in oil revenues in 1982 and 1983. The only economic sector with a comparable improvement in capacity or utilization was transportation via roads and rails. The sector's utilization rates were improved by 80 and 70 percent over the comparable figures in 1982 as war activities were expanded in the Iraqi territories. Finally, whereas changes in the existing capacity and utilization in mining seem to have been insignificant, oil and gas production capacity declined by over 14 and 19 percent, respectively, reaching the levels of 73 and 53 percent in 1985. The war was particularly responsible for the decline. The gas contract with the Soviet Union also remained suspended until summer 1989, when a new contract was signed between the two nations. The remaining oil refineries were, however, overutilized in 1985 and many of the existing ones were destroyed by the Iraqi missiles.

Systematic statistics beyond 1985 are hardly available. Given that the economy has declined further since 1985, it is more likely that the rate of utilization in most economic sectors has also reduced. Data sporadically reported in official interviews, parliamentary debates, and newspaper commentaries support this assertion. The most recent estimates put the utilization rate of industrial capacity at around 40 percent. In a speech in July 1989, President Hashemi Rafsanjani, then still Speaker of the Parliament, noted that "the existing factories are operating, on the average, at 40 percent capacity, while their expenditures have not declined accordingly."[146] Moreover, any addition of new capacities have been constrained by the austerity Plan for New Economic Conditions, devised in 1986 following the fall in oil prices. The plan aimed at preserving the level of capacity utilization in economic sectors, an objective that could not be maintained under a subsequent revision of that plan. The new Economic Plan for Survival, instead, aimed at minimizing the rate of decline in capacity utilization. It was not until after the cease-fire that the government again introduced an economic plan (a revised version of the first plan for reconstruction) predicated upon the maximum use of the existing capacity.

Underutilization, however, is a consequence before it is a cause. Factors underlying the phenomenon are many, complex, and often the most formidable to cope with. They include domestic factors and influences external to the economy and are composed of financial, functional, structural, and historical forces. Among these factors are also those inherited by or imposed on the Islamic Republic and others that have been created, or exacerbated, in the postrevolutionary period. Major examples include the war, decline in oil revenue, and dependency on external resources. As we shall see in Chapter 3 and 4, these factors in combination have produced significant fiscal, foreign exchange, and saving-investment gaps. Other important determinants of capacity underutilization have included technological, institutional, organizational, and infrastructural bottlenecks. Equally significant have been bottlenecks in the areas of management and control, planning and implementation, skilled human resources, and provision of social and private services, including housing, health care, and education.[147] (We have already discussed some of these constraining factors and bottlenecks. Others will be discussed here and in the subsequent chapters.)

Note that I am studying social sectors, infrastructures, and managerial issues as "bottlenecks" because I wish to underscore their importance to economic development. As is well known, these sectors are ordinarily considered "nonproductive" and carry a low priority in development planning. Because the latest revision of the first plan places a high priority on removing "bottlenecks," my new formulation of the so-called nonproductive sectors as bottlenecks should considerably help planners advocate a higher priority in implementation for these sectors. Although space does not permit a more elaborate presentation, an overview of these bottlenecks is indispensable for a better comprehension of the deep and complex roots of Iran's economic ills and development prospects.

A good number of the constraints, regardless of their origin and nature, indeed, are oil related. In particular, most institutional, organizational, financial, social, and infrastructural bottlenecks have been deeply influenced, if not primarily created, by the improper use of the oil revenues. Indeed, many Iranians think, I believe correctly, that their country would have been better off without oil. Specifically, oil wealth has been responsible for the country's wild economic fluctuations, dependency on the world market, and uneven development of the economy. Most significant, however, oil has had a corrupting effect on the Iranian rentier state. Considering the oil revenues as a windfall, plenty and durable, the rentier state did not feel the need for developing a sense of responsibility for a disciplined economic management and did not plan for the proper use of this exhaustible resource. For example, instead of being invested in alternative income-generating projects or in obstacle-removing programs and plans, oil revenues were lavishly spent on projects that largely generated expenditures and boosted consumption. The oil-financed investments also tended to create grandiose and modern capacities that had little base in domestic resources, technical capability, or managerial skills. These capacities remained the most underutilized in the postrevolutionary period when scarcity of foreign exchange constrained importation of the needed intermediate inputs. The "inappropriate capacities" problem was considered so critical that for a while the postrevolutionary leadership considered destroying some parts of them. This was extensively discussed during the revision of the original plan of the Republic.

The war was not only an expensive undertaking but also a destructive one. As was noted, it demolished the existing capacity and prevented building of new ones in all economic sectors, oil in particular. In the absence of technological development in the country, destruction inflicted on the existing machinery and equipment proved the most damaging to the dependent economy. The destructive impact of the war in the face of a volatile and largely sluggish oil market also led to serious foreign exchange shortages. As a result, it became increasingly difficult for the state to allocate enough foreign exchange to economic sectors (see next chapter). The most hard hit were large modern industries, which depended on a world market for some 65 percent of their input (intermediate imports in particular.) Technological dependency was even worse for most modern assembly plants, between 80 to 90 percent. The American-led trade embargoes further complicated the problem by making it both difficult and expensive for Iran to procure industrial and food items. In the meantime, value of Iranian rial relative to foreign currencies declined sharply, making industrial inputs even more expensive, particularly for the private sector. Moreover, speculation in foreign currency had become so lucrative a trade that even the state agencies did not want to spend their scarce foreign currency allocations on any activity but those with the highest return in the shortest turnover time. In such an environment, it was most natural for the service sector to grow despite an economy that was indeed declining rapidly.

The institutional bottlenecks have been particularly damaging to the economy. At the root of these problems is the lack of adequate legislations in many key areas of the economic and political spheres. To begin with, there has been an unclear relationship between the economy, on the one hand, and ideology and politics, on the other. Although the government was unable to play the role of an intelligent entrepreneur, it hardly allowed the private sector to blossom. The protracted factional politics in general and specific reforms in particular have been major sources of discouragement for expansion of any significant private initiative. In the meantime, a definitive view of private property could not emerge because of differing interpretations of Islam. The fate of the labor law, land reform, tax reforms, income distribution, women rights, political democracy, provincial administration, and nationalization of international trade, among other important issues, continue to remain indeterminate. The lack of a unified position on the ideology of the state also led to frequent policy reversals that had the effect of injecting increasing uncertainty into the private market, leading to capital flight and the transfer of existing investable funds to quick-return, high-profit services and trades, including speculation in foreign currencies. Islam's restriction for "forbidden" or undesirable economic activities (such as tourism and production of alcoholic beverages and services relating to them) put additional constraints on production. The new post revolutionary anti-luxury consumption patterned culture also tended to reject certain "unnecessary" production lines or methods, and the domestic market remained inadequate to create the dynamism for economic growth.

Other institutional bottlenecks emanated from structural cultural barriers. These included what some have called the *Iranian mentality*, which is characterized by such attributes as dogmatism, extremism, cynicism, and disunity.[148] Clearly, these attributes are also observable among peoples of other nations, and not all Iranians harbor such a "mentality." Indeed, Iranians have also been praised for being benevolent and gracious, brave and rebellious, selfless and magnanimous, and cooperative and dependable. The fact remains, nevertheless, that the Iranian nation suffers heavily from a number of centuries-old, deleterious sociocultural traits; and denying their existence for the sake of preserving national pride will only exacerbate their destructive impact. I prefer to use the terms "obsolete political culture" to refer to such traits that remain at the roots of the country's badly fractured politics. This obsolete political culture, I wish to emphasize, is distinguished by obsolete ideas, lack of political balance and tolerance for opposite views, extremism and obsession with the use of force, and rejection of political flexibility and compromise. These largely political bottlenecks proved even subtler and more destructive, first to the country's political order and then, through politics, to the economy (more on political culture in Chapter 4).

Equally significant were organizational obstacles. These included the existence of many parallel organizational and the lack of a few needed ones, particularly coordinating and consultative bodies at almost all governmental levels, existence of new offices with no clear governmental links, and lack of proper centralized control of the state's apparatuses, particularly at lower implementation levels.[149] Examples of parallel organizations include the Army *vs.* the Revolutionary Guards Corps, the police *vs.* Islamic Revolutionary Committees, the Ministry of Agriculture *vs.* Ministry of Reconstruction Crusade, Ministry of Housing and Urban Development *vs.* Housing Foundation of the Islamic Revolution and Housing Organization, interest-free loan institutions *vs.* the banking system, management of the universities *vs.* the Council for Cultural Revolution and other grass roots organizations, and most significantly, the Foundation for the Eighth Imam *(Astan-e Qods-e Razavi) vs.* the government. The most recent addition to this list is the Council of Policy Making for Reconstruction, which duplicates the government function in planning for reconstruction of the nation's economy. For example, following the cease fire, the council and the Ministry of Plan and Budget were each busy drawing its own plans, while the other ministries went ahead with their own projects and programs.[150]

Other organizational problems included ambiguity in the roles governing organizational links, lack of regulations concerning capital-labor relations, and absence of adequate intragovernmental coordination.[151] Yet, it is the excessive bureaucracy from which the public sector suffers the most. This problem is at the root of corruption, lack of a work ethic, and increasing inefficiency in the government offices. As reported by the Prime Minister Musavi in 1988, the average length of useful work in some public offices has reached one hour and thirty minutes a day.[152] The public administrative structure also is not responsive to the needs of the society, objectives of the Revolution, and circumstances in which the state has found itself in the wake of the war and other constraints. All of these have made the state unable to effectively discipline the private sector, particularly when it comes to using state subsidies or implementing its laws and policies.

No less significant has been the managerial bottleneck created by the lack of experience on the part of the new leaders, managers, planners, and policy makers to deal with complex organizations and policy issues they came to control or face. This situation, of course, seems to be natural to almost all revolutions as they initially alienate the established technocrats and replace them with inexperienced "revolutionaries." In Iran after the Revolution, the new regime fired, forced into retirement, or repurchased services of many of the country's managers and technocrats on the pretext that they were nonrevolutionary or cooperated with the ancien régime. The "cleaning" *(paksazi)* of the public offices became a major first step of the Islamic Republic. The new regime also alienated a significant number of the country's professionals, who were alleged to have expertise *(takhassos)* but not commitment *(ta'ahhod)* to the Revolution. For example, in 1976, 1,047 experts with a B.S. degree or above worked in the Plan and Budget Organization (PBO). Following the Revolution, the PBO was closed for a while and, when it reopened in 1981, the number working there had declined to 210.[153] The organizational and managerial bottlenecks have led to errors in planning, implementation, and administration and to the inefficient use of resources in the productive units and public offices.[154]

The shortage of skilled personnel has been even more damaging to the economy. In the prerevolutionary years, many experts were brought from abroad. Following the Revolution, not only did these people leave, but also many educated and professional Iranians also migrated, largely to the West. The Islamic Republic has not invited in any significant number of foreign specialists. The human resource problem was compounded as level of political repression increased, and the government closed the country's universities and colleges for about four years under the banner of Cultural Revolution and Islamization of education. Although a new generation of experts is emerging in all these areas and the old technocrats, who refused to cooperate or were discharged by the new regime, have returned to work at an increasing numbers, the situation continues to remain critical. Statistics indicate that the total number of graduates (skilled human resources) until the Iranian year 1365 were 542,228 (13.1 percent returnees from graduates of foreign institutions of higher education and 86.9 percent from domestic universities), among whom 50 percent were graduates in technical subjects. Of the total number of graduates since 1335, only 277,775 people have been employed in the public sector, and they account for only 4 percent of public sector's employees. The ratio of graduates in applied fields to the total population is very low, 300 per 100,000 population as compared to 5,500, 5,200, and 5,100 for Japan, the Netherlands, and the Soviet Union, respectively. The figure for technicians is even more disappointing, 600 per 100,000 population as compared to 25,000 in Japan. Finally, per 100,00 population there are only 300 students in higher education and 17 faculty members. The comparable figures for the United States, Japan, and England are 4,500 and 150, 1,700 and 90, and 550 and 78, respectively.[155] The most recent calls by the leaders of the Islamic Republic inviting the Iranians abroad to return and assist in the postwar reconstruction have to be considered as preliminary.[156]

The skill constraint is a manifestation of deeper problems within the Iranian educational system. These include a high level of illiteracy and a shortage of school space and teachers. In 1976, some 48 percent of the population six-years-old and over were literate; the figure ten years later, in 1986, was about 62 percent, indicating some improvement but still low compared to many Third World countries, for example, in Latin America. Moreover, in 1976, of 27.1 million population of six-years and over, only 28 percent were attending schools, of whom less than 2 percent were engaged in higher education. The proportion of school-enrolled to education-eligible population for this year is reported at 73.1 percent. The corresponding figures for 1986 were 38.7 million, 29 percent, 1.6 percent, and 88.7 percent.[157] In this year, the ratio of students to teachers in primary education was 13.9 in urban areas and 45.3 in rural areas. The same ratios in secondary education were 15.8 and 60.1, respectively. Because of space and teacher shortages, many primary and secondary schools in the country are open two to four shifts (A.M. and P.M.), and in some schools the population of students is so large that many must sit on the floor.[158] Given the present level of educational resources and the population growth rate, it will take no less than forty years for all Iranians to become literate.

The Iranian educational system also suffers from uneven distribution of resources across classes and territories, particularly in higher education; degree elitism; lack of correspondence between contents of higher education and the needs of the society; and insufficient resources for research. In 1976, level of illiteracy in rural areas was some 24 percent higher than in the urban centers; and in some underdeveloped provinces, illiteracy was, and continues to remain, as high as 60 to 70 percent.[159] In 1986, only 2.49 percent of the country's development budget and 2.55 percent of its current expenditures went to higher education and research. Even more disappointing is the money going into research and development. In 1988, for example, only 0.14 percent of the country's GNP was being spent on research as compared with 3.67 percent for the USSR and 2.7 percent for the United States. In the same year, Iran's per capita expenditures on research amounted to only $5 as compared to $450, $253, and $357 for the United States, Japan, and West Germany respectively.[160] Other problems include low level of teachers' salaries, insufficient institutional framework, and excessive bureaucracy, inadequate textbooks, outdated pedagogies, and lack of a clear definition for the private schools.[161] These deficiencies call for a total educational reform that must begin with substantive legislative changes.

Another bottleneck contributing to economic decline is the lack of adequate health care. We sometimes forget that production, of any kind, is dependent on the people involved in it. A society that does not provide its people with adequate health care cannot expect full utilization of its resources . After all, unhealthy people lack sufficient labor power to produce, perform services, or engage in reproduction of their kind. Above all is the shortage of physicians, dentists, physical therapists, midwives, nurses, paramedical personnel, medical schools and laboratories, hospitals and hospital beds, medical and hygiene equipment, drugs, and ambulances. Here are a few statistics reported by *Kayhan* daily, quoting a 1986 government census: for every 3,000 persons there was one physician (International Health Organization's standard is 1,000 per physician); for every 20,000 persons there was one dentist (IHO's standard is 10,000 per dentist); for every 18,000 women there was one midwife (IHO's standard is 500 per midwife); for every 700 persons there was one hospital bed (IHO's standard is 250 per hospital bed); and for some 50 million people there were less than 600 hospitals in the country.[162] These problems were all inherited from the ancien régime and further worsened in the postrevolutionary period; in 1976, for example, for every 2,246 persons there was one physician; for every 15,069 persons one dentist, and for every 602 persons one hospital bed.[163] Tremendous effort is needed to correct the problems. For example, to reach the world standard, Iran needs some 127,000 hospital beds, around 97,000 midwives, and about 50,000 physicians, of whom only 17,000 exist and the rest must be trained. To correct the shortage of physicians, some 7,000 medical students must be admitted to the universities each year until 1995, a rather impossible task given the experience: in the late 1970s, only 700 to 800 medical students were annually admitted to the universities; the number has been significantly increased in the postrevolutionary period, to about 3,000 a year on the average. Nevertheless, a gap of some 4,000 students a year still remains.[164]

The shortage is, however, unevenly distributed across classes and territories, with the lower classes, rural areas, and the outlying regions in the worst condition. Most medical resources of the country are concentrated in Tehran. For example, some 33 percent of all hospital beds, some 60 percent of urban hospitals, about 60 percent of dentists, and some 77 percent of midwives are located in Tehran. Further, statistics for 1983 indicate that there was one dentist for every 5,112 people in Tehran Province, while in Kohkiluyeh and Boyer Ahmadi Province, there was one dentist for every 138,650 people. The situation in Ilam, Kurdestan, Sistan and Baluchestan, Zanjan, and Lorestan, among other underdeveloped provinces, was no better. In Zanjan Province in 1976, for example, for every 8,065 persons there was one physician; the figure for 1986 was 7,634.[165] Yet, the country's rural areas had the worst health conditions. In 1986, for example, of 17,804 physicians in the country, some 93.3 percent practiced in urban centers. Yet, about 46 percent of the country's population lives in rural areas. In other words, the ratio of urban physicians to rural physicians was 12 to 1.[166]

Moreover, in the absence of a nationalized health system (less than 15 percent of the population is insured), the excessively high cost of medical care in the country makes it almost impossible for the poor to receive adequate treatment. This social group also suffers from malnutrition that further exacerbates the health problems. Finally, if curative medicine is insufficient, preventive medicine, including vaccination, remains largely undeveloped in the country. The problems are further exacerbated by inadequate sanitation facilitates, particularly in rural areas, and lack of adequate health education and information. The problems with health care services originate in the prerevolutionary years, and despite some efforts by the Islamic Republic to expand medical education, the problems remain unresolved to say the least.[167] The war and migration of a large part of the country's medical personnel to foreign countries were the two most damaging factors to the postrevolutionary health care services.

But, it is equally important to make sure that people, the working people in particular, are also provided with adequate shelter. A homeless individual or one who lives in a slum or a shack can not be expected to be productive. The housing sector in Iran suffers from many problems, all of which have their origins in the prerevolutionary period. Indeed, and as we have noted in the beginning of this chapter, one of the fiercest postrevolutionary struggles occurred over housing between the homeless people, the landlords, and the government. Although this struggle did not resolve the housing question, it did underscore its critical nature. Problems of the housing sector include the shortage of existing housing, high price of materials and lands, exorbitant rent, congestion, an unregulated market, and low housing quality.[168] For some poor Tehranis, rent accounts for as much as 80 percent of their income, and on the average Iranian tenants pay no less than 50 percent of their income for rent. These problems are further exacerbated by the country's excessive population growth rate (3.9 percent, average per year over the 1979–88 period), massive rural-to-urban migration, extremely skewed income distribution, a high level of absolute poverty, and excessive unemployment rates. The sector also suffers from dependency on foreign markets for materials and technology.

The housing shortage is, however, the number one problem of the sector at present as it has been for the last several decades. In 1976, for example, the country's housing deficit was estimated at 1.4 million units. By 1983, it had grown to 1.75 million units, of which 1.08 million units were needed in the urban areas where some 54 percent of Iranians live. The most conservative estimates would put housing shortage by the end of 1988 at some 2.2 million units. The war destroyed some 114,860 houses of which 74,456 had been reconstructed by the end of the war. To resolve the shortage, planners have indicated in the Islamic Republic's first plan that the country needs to construct some 360,000 units (each with 100 sq km of foundation) a year on the average over the next two decades or so. This may prove an impossible task given the past experience. During the fifth plan under the Shah, for example, some 810,000 housing units were to be built in cities; the actual numbers built, however, were 580,000 or 116,000 units per year. Similarly, housing production in the postrevolutionary period has remained sluggish. Available information suggests that, at best and on the average, some 120,000 houses might have been built each year in the urban areas over the 1979–88 period.[169] Note, however, that this figure includes the reconstruction of houses destroyed by the war. The earthquake in June 1990 destroyed an additional 110,000 units as reported by President Rafsanjani.

The shortage aside, most of the available houses are not in good condition or standard. For example, in 1976, some 51.8 percent of the country's housing was without electricity and 48.1 percent had no piped water. For the rural areas, the corresponding figures were 85.8 percent and 78.5 percent. The situation was equally bad in the underdeveloped regions. In Kohkiluyeh and Boyer Ahmadi, and Sistan and Baluchestan Provinces, for example, only 11.5 percent of houses had piped water and 26 percent had electricity.[170] Ten years later, housing quality has somewhat improved. For example, of a total of 8,217,375 houses in the country, some 84 percent had electricity and about 75 percent had piped water. The corresponding figures for the rural areas were 3,547,652, 63 percent, and 53 percent.[171] The improvement is largely a result of the rural electrification programs that the Reconstruction Crusade *(jihad-e sazandegi)* implemented in the initial postrevolutionary years. Nevertheless, the housing situation continues to remain critical and a major obstacle to economic development.

Finally, there are a group of infrastructures that might be considered critical for mobilization of human and material resources and thus for economic development. These include electricity and other energy sources, port facilities, roads and other transportation systems, communication and telecommunication networks, and basic industrial services. Needles to say, electricity is today the prime mover of economic expansion and technological progress including mechanization and automation, while communication and transportation are indispensable for distribution of production inputs and outputs, dissemination of political and economic information, and exchange of ideas, science, and cultural values among peoples and nations. The Iranian economy has been suffering for years from serious bottlenecks in these and other critical infrastructures. The bottlenecks have manifold dimensions: low per capita production; uneven social, sectoral, and geographical distribution; heavy dependency on foreign exchange and technology; and improper use of a substantial part of the existing capacity (e.g., for consumption of luxury goods.) These problems have many causes but a few deserve mentioning: (1) a relatively rough geography (mountain and desert terrain), (2) lack of comprehensive planning and spatial-temporal coordination with other economic sectors, (3) shortage of skilled workers to operate the sophisticated foreign technology that has been utilized in power-generating and telecommunication projects, (4) a need for huge investments with a relatively long turnover time, and (5) the undeveloped condition of Iran's heavy industry. This last is also a consequence of the country's infrastructural defects.

In 1978, just before the Revolution, the country's installed power-generating capacity was reported at 7,024 megawatts (MW). Despite the war, it increased to 12,369 MW by 1985, indicating an impressive 76 percent increase a year on the average. The increase was due to the new regime's attempts to electrify rural areas and smaller towns. The country's per capita electricity production and consumption has also increased in the last several years, from 513 kW/h and 348 kW/h in 1976 to 853 kW/h and 654 kW/h in 1986.[172] Nevertheless, per capita production and consumption of electricity remains low relative to many Third World countries, including neighboring Turkey. It was hoped that the Revolution would lead to higher investments in this area and remove a major part of the energy obstacle. However, the hope did not fully materialize and the war is partly to blame. It not only destroyed a portion of the existing power-generating capacity but it also left other portions unavailable to the civilian production for military needs had higher priority. Thus, just as before the Revolution, blackouts remain a fact of life for Iranian urbanites, Tehranis in particular. During the war, the length and frequency of such blackouts worsened as did the nonproductive use of the available electricity, an increasing amount of which continues to be spent in services and luxury consumption.

Equally deficient is the country's transportation networks, a bottleneck that has for years constrained Iran's economic expansion. Transportation involves movement of people, transferable factors of production, and final products; it connects economic poles in an otherwise geographically dispersed production site and market. Transportation is also critical for the proper functioning of the import-export sectors, particularly in such semiperipheral countries as Iran, where the economy remains highly integrated in and dependent on the world market. The networks include roads, railways, ports, and airports, and involve motor vehicles, ships, and airplane. In all these areas, Iran remains highly deficient. In 1979, there were only 63,000 km of roads, of which less than 14 percent were main roads. This increased to 139,368 km by 1985, of which main roads accounted for only 12.5 percent. Note also that the main roads are distributed very unevenly across the country, with developed provinces accounting for over 80 percent of the main networks. The more than twofold expansion of road networks in the postrevolutionary period occurred primarily because of a sizable increase in rural roads built by the Construction Crusade in the initial postrevolutionary years. Considering that the country is 1,648,000 sq km and in comparison with developed countries, Iran's road networks are extremely deficient. To give one example, in 1982, neighboring Turkey, at half the size of Iran, had some 225,000 km of roads, of which about 27 percent were asphalt.[173] Iran also remains deficient in the number of motor vehicles; most of the existing vehicles are used for personal transportation. Thus, of 2,758,404 registered motor vehicles in 1986, cars accounted for 68.4 percent, whereas buses, minibuses, trucks, and pickup trucks together accounted for 30 percent.[174]

Even more underdeveloped are Iran's railways, ports, and airports. In 1979, there were only 4,567 km of railroads, forty-two ships with 525,000 tons of capacity, and twenty-five Boeing aircrafts. By 1986, the corresponding numbers had increased to 5, 802, 76, 2,097, and 27.[175] To compare, England, with only one-seventh the area of Iran, has some 18,400 km of railroads; that is, 3.2 times as much as Iran. Iran's port facilities also remain limited even though the country is surrounded by the Persian Gulf to the south and the Caspian Sea to the north. Prior to the war, there were eight ports and in 1977 some 3,300 ships entered Iranian ports, with a crude capacity of 28 million tons. The war destroyed 60 percent of the country's port facilities and reduced the number of the usable ports to six. The two destroyed ports are Khorramshahr, by far the country's most important commercial port, and Bandar Khomeini (previously Bandar-e Shahpur). Khark Island, where most of the nation's oil terminals were located, was also damaged to a significant degree as was Abadan, the second largest port city in the nation. Moreover, over the 1982–86 period, on the average, only 1,316 ships entered the country's ports each year, with an average yearly crude capacity of about 12 million tons. Over the same period, the average waiting time for the ships in Iranian ports was 235 hours as compared to the world standard of 110 for commercial ships and thirty-six hours for oil tankers.[176]

Communication and telecommunication networks in the country also remain deficient in quantity and quality. Even after notable improvements, there were only 231 postal service facilities per 10,000 sq km in the country in 1986, and the provincial variation was very high.[177] As a result, mail delivery is extremely slow and mail congestion has reached a critical level. Ironically, Persia was a world pioneer in developing postal services twenty-five centuries ago. The postal service deficiency, in turn, makes it difficult for the country's managers and policy makers to remain in touch with new developments or transmit, on time, decisions and policy changes to their respective offices. The country's telegraph services have also improved in the postrevolutionary period, but not enough to remedy significant deficiency in this extremely important area. In 1986, for example, there were only 545 teletype, 9 telex centers, and 7,250 canals. The corresponding numbers for 1982 were 269, 9, and 3,641.[178] Equally inadequate is Iran's telephone services, which has indeed declined over the last several years in urban places. In 1982, 123 cities were equipped with an intercity microwave system; the number had declined to 113 by 1986. During the same time period, carrier centers and cordless intercity telephone centers also declined, from 543 and 47 in 1982 to 396 and 29 in 1986, respectively. This result has been caused in part by the war that damaged many urban centers in the country. As opposed to decline in cities, telephone services in rural areas have improved. For example, only 1,030 rural areas had intercity telephone service in 1982; the number increased to 2,077 areas in 1986.[179]

In sum, the country suffers from a significant underutilization of its existing productive capacity and from various bottlenecks that prevent Iran from improving its utilization rates or develop new capacity. Underlying such bottlenecks are formidable domestic and external factors of a functional, structural, and historical nature. Whether they were inherited or created after the Revolution does not change the fact a bit that unless they are removed by comprehensive planning and a well-designed policy, little can be done to change the country's economic situation. The Iranian planners should be given credit for recognizing these problems and making "bottleneck removing" a top priority, to be undertaken in the first stage of a three-stage economic development process. However, if experience is any lesson, a major gap could develop between the plan and its implementation. I trust that the planners also realize the need for a comprehensive solution. There could hardly be cures for these bottlenecks in isolation or without regard for the country's other socioeconomic and political dilemmas. A total approach, does not, however, mean that incremental improvements should be neglected or postponed. Moreover, as a good number of these bottlenecks are rooted in Iran's oil wealth and policy, a more realistic bottleneck-removing program must begin with a well-designed plan for this sector of the economy.

IDEOLOGICAL DISLOCATION AND SYSTEMIC INDIRECTION

As I argued in the Introduction, almost immediately after the Revolution, a *dislocation,* or *noncorrespondence,* developed between the leadership and its ideology, leading to ideological factionalism within the state. This dislocation occurred when the core middle-class leadership faction tried to present a *middle-class* interpretation of the *cross-class* and universal Islam. Others within the power bloc, however, disagreed and forwarded alternative radical (lower-class) and conservative (upper-class) perspectives. Coupled with political factionalism over the state power, the ideological dislocation and factionalism, as we shall shortly see, prevented the leaders from formulating a coherent development strategy with a definite direction, institutionalizing a suitable planning system, and designing consistent policies for economic growth and management. These short-comings, in turn, became powerful negative impacts on the country's economic performance. The ideological dislocation and *systemic indirection,* along with other constraining factors, also became causes for compromise and adoption of more pragmatic policies on several occasions. However, although such initiatives helped the state to muddle through serious crises at times, they also created more difficulties, and thus invited ideological pressures, and did not survive for any significant length of time. On the balance, however, ten years later, the Islamic Republic, compared to its formative years, has become less rather than more ideological with respect to social, economic, and political matters. As ideological and political factionalism within the state reflects deep-seated divisions within the society, its settlement would depend upon the resolution of such larger questions as national development and social justice.

In Search of a New Planning System

The new Constitution of 1979 makes "systematic and sound planning" a major tool of economic management (Article 44). It also accepts regional planning for balanced national development, contains several articles concerning justice and local participation, and makes sectoral and spatial councils pivotal in a new planning system. Thus, Article 2 obligates the government to establish "justice" through a number of measures including the "negation of all kinds of oppression, tolerance of oppression, dominance and acceptance of dominance," and Article 3 makes it a duty of the state to provide the necessary conditions for the "participation of all the people in determining their political, economic, social, and cultural destiny." Article 7 declares participation in decision making for administration of the country the most essential condition for establishment of a participatory system and identifies various types of consultative councils as organs where such decision should be made. A subsequent Councils Law has made the councils also responsible for a survey of needs and shortcomings of their constituencies, preparation of proposals and plans, supervision and control of projects, and coordination among various executive units.[180]

Two types of consultative councils are identified: spatial and sectoral. The former, according to Articles 7 and 100, are formed at block, district, city, village, county, and provincial levels, whereas the latter, according to Article 104, are organized within socioeconomic and administrative units. Members of the councils vary from three to seven persons and people only elect the members of the councils at the bottom of the council hierarchy; namely, the block, village, and factory (or other operating units) councils. Members of the higher-level councils are then chosen from among the members of the lower-level ones. The Constitution also anticipates a Supreme Council of Provinces to be composed of one representative from each provincial council. It is empowered, in Article 101, "to prevent discrimination and to gain cooperation in development planning and welfare programs for the provinces and to supervise their coordination." The council is also given the right, in Article 102, "to make plans within the limits of its duties and submit proposals to the National Assembly." Moreover, according to Article 103, "the governors, commanders, district chiefs, and other authorities that are appointed by the government are obligated to obey the Council's decisions as long as they fall within the limits of the Council's powers."[181]

Concern for balanced regional development is also pronounced in other articles in the Constitution. Article 15, which declares Persian as the official language of the country, allows for "the use of local and nationalities languages in their press and mass media," as well as in teaching of their literature in their schools." Article 19 declares that "the people of Iran, regardless of ethnic and tribal origins, enjoy equal rights"; it emphasizes that "color, race, language and the like will not be cause for privilege." Finally, Article 48 mandate that: "there should be no discrimination with regard to benefits to be gained from the use of natural resources, the utilization of public funds on the provincial level, and the distribution of economic activities among the provinces and various regions of the country. This is so that every region will have within its reach capital and opportunity to fulfill its needs and develop its skills."

These provisions, notwithstanding, the Constitution allows for a largely top-down, centralized management system. For example, provincial governors and councils are subordinated to the central administration (Article 100) and the centralization of the government budget is made mandatory (Article 53). The 1989 revisions of the Constitution are intended to make the system even more centralized. Nonetheless, if implemented, the Constitution would have provided planners with the ingredients needed to institute a participatory planning system. Councils would have acted as a cornerstone for this new approach. In practice, however, planning has become a dead intellectual exercise and despite resistance to centralism and sectoralism, both these forces have become dominant as in the past. Regional planning and councils play only peripheral roles in the new planning system. The first indication that the country's planning system will follow the old centralist and sectoralist line came with the limited emergency planning of the Provisional Revolutionary Government (PRG) in 1979. The PRG had set up the Office of Revolutionary Projects (ORPs) and invested it with the power to formulate the new government's general policy frameworks. The ORPs Program was published in the summer of 1979. Despite growing pressure from the provinces, the program focused its attention on economic sectors.[182] A second indication came, in November 1981, when the Economic Council established ten ad hoc committees within the Plan and Budget Organization (PBO) to work toward a draft of the first plan. None of the committees were led by regional planners or provincial interest groups.[183] However, not until the end of 1981 did the sectoralists take full control of PBO and the activities underway for the formulation of the aborted First Economic, Social, and Cultural Development Plan of the Islamic Republic (1983–87). Only recently have regionalists made some headway into planning procedures. A review of the debates over these issues and the procedures employed to formulate the aborted first plan demonstrates the nature and extent of this discrepancy between theory and practice of planning in the postrevolutionary Iran.

Initially, the new leadership was unanimous in its support for economic planning, but divided on the nature of a more suitable planning system. From a procedural perspective, the division occurred along the traditional sector *vs.* space line. More specifically, some advocated a centralized sectoral planning system, similar to one under the ancien régime, and others argued for a spatially based planning system. I shall refer to the first group as *sectoralists* and to the second group as *regionalists*.[184] The sectoralists favored a planning procedure whereby a national sectoral plan would be prepared first and then disaggregated into regional sectoral plans. In arriving at such a plan, argued the sectoralists, the objectives would flow from the national to regional level, whereas project proposals would run in the opposite direction (Interviews, 1986). This procedure differed from the old practice only in that it allowed for some regional participation in formulation of projects but, like the past approach, it did not provide for regional participation in formulation of development objectives. In defending the approach, the sectoralists were motivated by their growth-oriented development strategy and their concern for the rising regionalism.[185]

The regionalists, on the other hand, argued for a planning approach whereby comprehensive regional plans are produced first and then aggregated to create the national plan (Interviews, 1986). Initially, this position was quite underdeveloped and could hardly stand up to criticisms. For example, the sectoralists alleged that because project proposals come from the regional levels, the national plan is already regional in essence and that the approach produces regional plans anyhow. In the course of the debates, however, the regionalists were able to develop their perspective into a more coherent framework. Their new arguments went as follows: the project proposals received from the province for formulation of the first plan were not based on any spatial analysis or strategy and could not, therefore, replace regional plans. For the proposals to become meaningful they must be placed within the framework of a National Spatial Strategy Plan or *Amayesh-e Sarzamin* (see below). First, a unified national strategy must emerge, then spatial deductions made from such a strategy, leading to the basic design of *Amayesh-e Sarzamin*. Then, within this latter framework, the potential and responsibilities of each region would be identified, regional plans produced and then aggregated for arriving at the national plan (Interviews, 1986). This procedure, according to regionalists, is needed because any kind of national plan requires a specific type of regional plan. If, for example, national planning wants to emphasize economic growth, then a regional plan suitable for this purpose will emphasize efficiency and comparative advantage. On the other hand, a national planning concerned with balanced development will incorporate equity objectives in its resource allocation schemes and regional plans.

The struggle between the sectoralists and the regionalists reached a turning point in December 1981 when simultaneously with the approval of the Law of the First Plan and during the early stages for its organization, the Office of Regional Planning (ORP) was closed and its facilities and staff were distributed among other sections of the PBO.[186] Later, in January 1982, when a New Planning System (NPS) was approved by the Economic Council for Formulation of the First Plan, ORP's facilities and staff were placed at its disposal. The system, given in Figure 2.7 had been originally proposed by PBO back in September 1981. Although the NPS was designed to produce a sectoral national plan, it also incorporated some of the main spatial conceptions built into the Constitution. The regionalists remained unhappy, however, with the limits it placed on the role of provinces in national planning.

Then in May and July 1982 two important seminars were held on the yet nonexistent first plan and NPS (Interviews, 1986). In the first seminar in Tehran, all talks were sectoral, and no one was allowed to speak for regional planning, provinces, or councils. Following the May seminar, a few regional planners, primarily those residing in the less developed provinces, began to analyze the pros and cons of the NPS and were subsequently able to produce a proposal for a corrected planning system. The proposal was brought to the attention of other colleagues during the July seminar held in the city of Mashad in Khorasan Province. In accordance with the regionalists' perspective, the proposal sought to design a planning system that allowed for the formulation of comprehensive regional plans before preparation of sectoral plans. The proposal was sup-

Figure 2.7

The New Planning System, Approved by the Economic Council in 1982

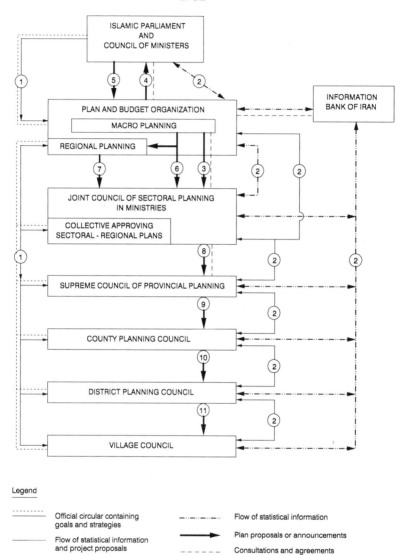

Legend

---------- Official circular containing goals and strategies

——— Flow of statistical information and project proposals

—··—··—·· Flow of statistical information

➤ Plan proposals or announcements

- - - - - Consultations and agreements

Source:
Amirahmadi, "Regional Planning in Iran: A Survey of Problems and Policies."

ported by a majority of regional planners present at the seminar and included in the Report on the Method of Determination of Quantitative Goals for Development of Agricultural Sector. The report was then presented at the important plenary session of the seminar. This was the first attempt to again raise regional planning as an issue. The proposal was not, however, included in the resolution of the seminar, which did not acknowledge the significance of regional planning for balanced national development (Interviews, 1986). Worse yet, the triumphant sectoralists undermined, in practice (see Figure 2.8), even the limited role that NPS had given to the provinces and the councils.

Thus, during the preparation of the first plan, no district or village councils were established and the few county councils that were formed did not participate actively in the plan-making processes. Moreover, the Supreme Council of Provinces (SCP) was not established and the formation of the Council of Provincial Planning (CPP) did not follow the procedures stipulated in the Law of Councils. Instead of its members coming from county councils, they were elected from among provincial heads of sectoral offices with the provincial governor as chair and the director of the provincial planning office as secretary. This body has also become known as the Provincial Planning Committee (PPC).[187] Consequently, and given that the ORP had already been closed, spatial planning suffered a tremendous setback. The implemented system also did not include the information bank stipulated in NPS and it downgraded the status of the Collective Approving Sectoral and Regional Plans (CASRP) by changing its function from approving to coordinating plans. With regional plans eliminated, approval of sectoral plans was delegated to the respective ministers.

The dominance of sectoral considerations in preparation of the first plan was also demonstrated in the procedures applied to the task.[188] The task began at the provincial level. Under the guidance of the CPP, local planning offices (various councils and committees) prepared reports concerning the past and present socioeconomic situation in their respective provinces, copies of which were then sent to PBO and the Joint Councils of Sectoral Planning (JCSP) formed within ministries. Using the reports and other information, the JCSP prepared its own reports and sent copies to PBO. On the basis of these reports and the Constitution, the PBO (with the assistance of representatives from other government organizations) formulated the socioeconomic development objectives of the Republic for a twenty-year period (1982–2002).[189] The document was then sent to the Economic Council for review and comment. The received reactions

Figure 2.8

The New Planning System in Practice, 1983–85

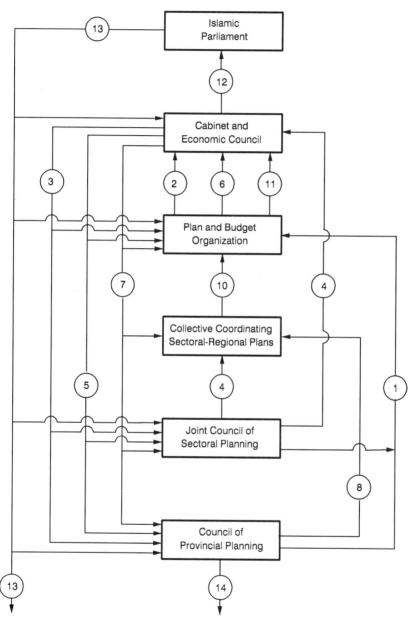

Source:
Mashayekhi, "Barrasl-ye Nezam-e Barnamehrizi-ye Keshvar Dar Amal Va Chand Pishnehad-e Eslahi" (original in Persian).

were then incorporated by PBO in a modified document, called "The Macro Quantitative Objectives and Policies for Socioeconomic and Cultural Development of the Islamic Republic in the Period 1361–1381."[190] The latter was approved by the Economic Council and returned, through the prime minister's office, to the PBO, CPPs, and JCSP. This last body then prepared the five-year macro quantitative objectives and policies of their respective sectors and sent them to the Economic Council for comment and approval. The modified and approved documents were again sent back to the PBO, CPPs, and JCSP. On the basis of all these documents, the PBO prepared the Five-Year Macro Economic, Social, and Cultural Development Plan of the Islamic Republic for 1362–1366 (1983–87). The plan was then sent up to the Economic Council, who, after few changes and approval, returned it to the PBO, CPPs, and JCSP for preparation of sectoral development plans.

The Councils of Provincial Planning, with the help of the planning committees and councils under their supervision and using the macro quantitative objectives and policies and the objectives and policies for sectoral development, prepared the provincial plans for various economic and social sectors and sent the sectoral plans to the Collective Coordinating Sectoral and Regional Plans (CCSRP) within the respective ministry. Similarly, each JCSP prepared its sector's plan on the basis of the macro quantitative objectives and policies, objectives and policies for sectoral development, and the approved macro plan. Such plans were sent to respective CCSRPs for coordination with provincial plans and for use in preparation of the sectoral provincial plans. After these latter plans were approved by the respective ministers, they were sent to PBO. The plans received from the CCSRP were, after investigation, summarized and integrated into a book called the *First Economic, Social, and Cultural Development Plan of the Islamic Republic of Iran, 1362–1366.*[191] The book was then sent to the prime minister's office and through it to various ministries for comment and critique. After agreements were reached between the ministries and the PBO over the changes made in the proposed sectoral plans during the course of summarizing and integrating the various plans, the first plan was approved by the council of ministers and then sent, along with the First Five-Year Plan Bill of the Islamic Republic, to the Majlis.

Thus, the procedures used for the formulation of the first plan were designed to produce a national plan composed of various sectoral plans. Provinces did not participate in setting the objectives or the policies built into the plan and provincial development plans were not produced for expressed purpose of provincial development.

The only two major tasks assigned to the provinces were the preparation of preliminary reports and formulation of sectoral plans on the basis of prespecified objectives and policies. The provinces were indeed looked upon as tools for national economic growth and locations for sectoral projects rather than as smaller societies with all the complexities and needs of the larger Iran. Sectoralist and centralist forces also undermined the councils' formation and participation of those that had been formed in the wake of the Revolution. These forces used the need for economic growth and efficiency in the aftermath of the ongoing economic crisis as the basis for their position. In reality, however, they were motivated by their desire to preserve the age-old dominance of the sectoralist and centralist forces in the Iranian political and socioeconomic systems.

Despite these early defeats, regionalists have endured in the Islamic Republic. In particular, the July seminar became a turning point for a new approach to planning that has gained increased attention in the postwar period. Following the seminar, the Group for Case Studies, one of many organized during the preparation of the first plan, had submitted a draft of a Corrected Planning System (CPS) to Prime Minister Mir Hosain Musavi along with its application in the form of the Plan for Organization of Industries in the Region under the Influence of Tehran Metropole (Figure 2.9). The prime minister's approval had been subsequently gained. He had then ordered Dr. Taghi Banki, then PBO chief and a sectoralist, to accept the draft and use it for the preparation of the first plan (Interviews, 1986). With Prime Minister Musavi's insistence, the need for spatial planning was also emphasized in the text of the first plan bill, which was being prepared for presentation to the Parliament.[192] Although nothing significant happened in practice at the time, the prime minister's support for spatial planning in general and the draft of CPS in particular was instrumental in the development of a new approach to planning in the Islamic Republic based on the concept of Spatial Strategy Planning (SSP) or *Amayesh-e Sarzamin*. [193]

According to the regionalists, SSP offers a system of comprehensive development planning in which space, time, and matter are articulated. Moreover, in SSP, sectoral and spatial planning are reasonably integrated, as are the functions of regional and national planning.[194] Specifically, *Amayesh-e Sarzamin* offers a methodology

> for ordering [or determining] the relationships between man, his activities, and space for logical [i.e., efficient] utilization of potentialities in the direction of improving the material and mental conditions of society in the course of time based on ideological values and with regard to cultural and ethnic traditions using science and experience.[195] (My translation.)

Figure 2.9

Draft for a Corrected Planning System: The Network for Preparation of a Tentative Plan for Metropolitan Region of Tehran (MRT), 1983

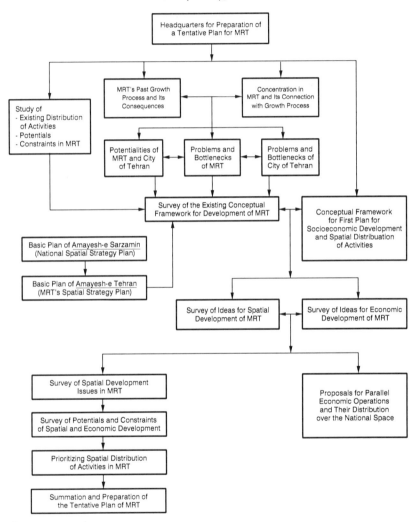

Source:
Plan Budget Organization, Office of Regional Planning, *Motl'at-e Tarh-e Paye-he Amayesh-e Sarzamin-e Islami-ye Iran* (original in Persian and in a different format).

The regionalists also claim that SSP can better assist planners and policy makers to develop spaces according to their comparative advantages or noneconomic urgencies (e.g., the Eastern Axis Project to control drug trafficking); promote balanced development of productive capacities, population, infrastructures, and social services; decrease regional disparities through faster growth of underdeveloped regions; form an integrated system of human settlement hierarchy and specialization; and preserve the environment and natural resources through their planned utilization and legal protection.

SSP is carried out in three stages as indicated in Figure 2.10. In the first stage, three major documents are produced; namely, the Basic Conceptual Framework for National Development (BCFND), the Overall National Development Strategy (ONDS), and the Basic Plan of *Amayesh-e Sarzamin,* or the National Spatial Strategy Plan (NSSP). The BCFND renders the main policy orientation toward national development with regard to long-term development goals and the country's capabilities and constraints. It focuses on the relationships between growth and development, exogenous and endogenous resources, and tradition and modernity. The ONDS is then formulated by translation of BCFND into policies for social, economic, and spatial development. It also determines the place and function of the main economic sectors in national development, identifies a framework for technology adoption, and sets criteria for such policy issues as foreign and domestic marketing, supply of investable funds and work force, level of centralization of decision making, and ways of decreasing regional disparities. The NSSP is then produced to reflect the long-term image of development over space, or the spatial organization of activities in the country (see Figure 2.11). The document specifies resource allocation patterns, sectoral distribution of population and employment, settlement patterns in urban and rural areas, and place and functions of each region in the development process and interregional relationships. Sectoral planners implement this stage with regional planners as their advisors.

In the second stage, two documents are produced: The Detailed Plan of *Amayesh-e Sarzamin* (DPAS) and the Macro Framework for Medium-Term Socioeconomic Development Plan (MFMTSDP). The latter sets the medium-term (five-year) targets for socioeconomic sectors on the basis of the medium-term goals and strategies for national development and with regard to mobile investment resources. The DPAS, on the other hand, is the country's comprehensive long-term image plan, reflecting the details of the spatial organization of

Figure 2.10

The Processes of Comprehensive National Development Planning

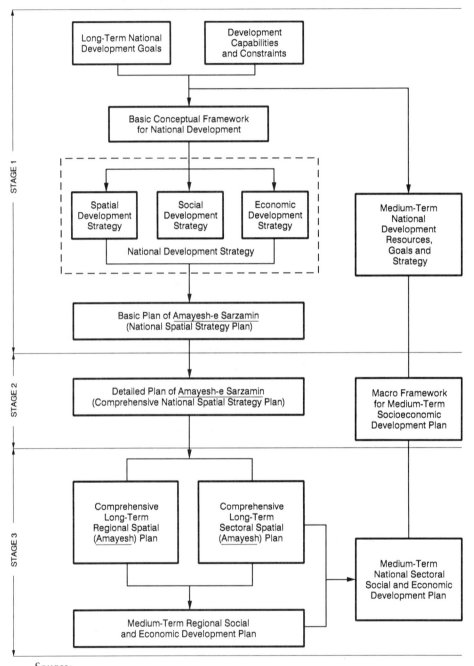

Source:
Adapted with modifications from Fouladi, "Comprehensive National Spatial Planning."

Figure 2.11

Deduction Process of National Spatial Strategy Plan (Basic Plan of Amayesh-e Sarzamin): First Stage for Arriving at the National Regional Comprehensive Development Planning System

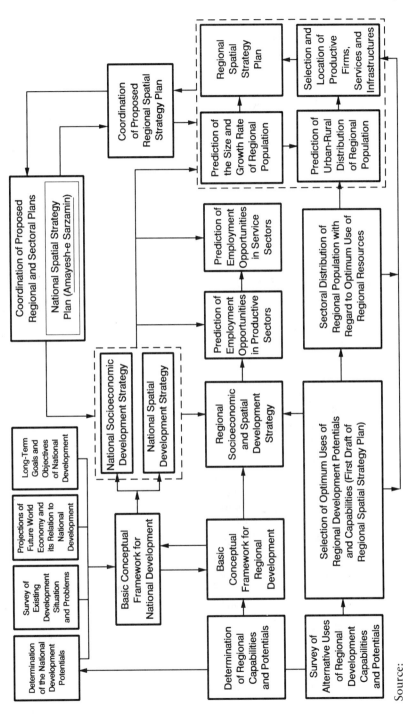

Source:
Adapted with modifications from Fouladi, ibid.

development. It focuses on regional comparative advantage and specialization, settlement scale and function, and geographic distribution of productive activities, social services, and infrastructural networks. This stage is implemented jointly by national and regional planners.

Finally, in the third stage, contents of the Medium-Term Socioeconomic Development Plan of the Regions (MTSDPR) and the Medium-Term National Sectoral Socioeconomic Development Plan (MTNSSDP) are detailed. The regional plans are prepared on the basis of the projects included in the region's *Amayesh* plan and with regard to the regional resources (indigenous or obtained from outside). The sectoral plans are then formulated on the basis of the regional plans and coordinated in terms of their input and output requirements at the national level. Regional planners implement this stage with sectoral planners as their advisors. By mid-1989, the first stage had been completed and the second stage was in progress. The results so far are considered as tentative and not binding except for two documents: the Macro Long-Term National Goals and Strategies (MLTNGS), which passed the Parliament in October 1985, and the National Spatial Strategy Plan, which passed the Parliament in October 1986. The MLTNGS specifies the goals and strategies of the first phase of development in the Islamic Republic, called the Preparation Phase in the Revised First Plan (see below).

Several observations may be made concerning the debates between the sectoralists and the regionalists. First, despite their provincial outlook, the regionalists were as much in favor of a centralized planning system as their sectoralist counterparts. Indeed, both groups failed to address the critical role of spatial and sectoral councils in setting development objectives for their constituencies and local participation in decision making. Although central planning and control may be urgently needed in postrevolutionary Iran, it does not need to be so rigid as to allow for only limited participation by local people. The need for a controlled decentralization is dictated not simply by popular desire for participation in their destiny but also by such objective factors as the country's large size, diverse ethnic composition and regional cultures, uneven regional development and resource distribution, and the differential needs and impacts of various development projects. The "advisory" position given the provinces by the regionalists' approach in the first stage seems inadequate to the extent that advice is sought in matters of plan preparation and local land uses. More important are decision making for setting objectives and policies that affect the local community, local fiscal policies, and budgeting resources allocation for local projects.[196]

Second, both groups so far have focused on the form rather than content of planning. Although it is important for a country to find the right procedure for formulating its development plan, attempts in this direction must be complemented by efforts to comprehensively analyze the reality and define developments in terms of national goals and the means to implement them. To the best of my knowledge, both groups took the Constitution as their only contextual basis and at times even ignored laws or specific policies that had already passed the Parliament. Although it was legitimate to focus attention on the Constitution, this was hardly enough. The goals, as well as the tasks, outlined in the Constitution are too abstract and too broad to serve as anything but a guide for such a specific task as planning for sectoral or regional development. For example, the Constitution obliges the state to implement the national goals of social justice, independence, freedom, and economic progress. What these mean in practice and how they are achieved is left for the law and policy makers, politicians, and planners to decide. Unless decisions on these issues are made in detail, debate over procedures may not produce the desired ends. Moreover, the Constitution is ambiguous or equivocal concerning certain important issues. For example, according to Article 44, "the economic system of the Islamic Republic consists of three sectors: government, cooperative, and private with systematic and sound planning." Yet in Article 43, the Islamic economic system is defined as one that "prevents profiteering from the labor of others." The two principles are contradictory: the private sector cannot exist without making profit from the labor it employs.

Finally, lack of attention to the content of planning led both sides, regionalists as well as sectoralists, to neglect the important issue of implementation. Specifically, mechanisms to account for changes and problems with projections were hardly incorporated in the plan-making procedures. Also absent was a feedback mechanism to allow for continuous adjustment of the first plan, anticipate unpredicted occurrences, and account for the impact of earlier decisions on objectives intended for a later stage. The debaters did not specify means and tools for implementation of the plan, including national resources and such policy instruments as control, incentive, taxation, and credit. Regionalization, which is normally a prerequisite for image planning, also received little attention. In 1983, the twenty-four provinces of the country were divided into ten planning regions, each with a regional center. The scheme was, however, soon revoked because of opposition from the sectoralists. As a result, the first plan was not grounded in terms of its locational and administrative requirements, making its implementation even more difficult.

In Search of a Development Strategy

The debate over procedural matters of planning continues and ten years after the Revolution a unified planning system has not yet emerged. Indeed, different planning offices in the country apply different procedures to their respective projects. The range varies from the bottom-up approach of the Ministry of Reconstruction Crusade to the top-down approach of the Ministry of Plan and Budget. The problem with planning in the Islamic Republic, however, goes beyond procedural matters. Equally unsettled remains the contextual issues of planning, primarily specification of a development strategy. The search for a "third way" based on Islamic principles has preoccupied the ideologues and policy makers of the Republic ever since its inception in 1979.[197] The existing socialist and capitalist models were dismissed for their inappropriateness in building an Islamic society, where concerns for traditions and culture are to be integrated into the political economy. Moreover, as noted by President Hashemi Rafsanjani, "Western capitalism" is "unjust and exploitative," while "Eastern Communism" "kills private initiatives" and "instigates antagonism between the state and the populace."[198]

An approximate vision of the Islamic alternative was incorporated into the new 1979 Constitution.[199] Article 43 specifies a number of "regulations" on the basis of which the Islamic Republic must "achieve independence in national economy, uproot poverty and impoverishment and fulfill growing human needs, while preserving its independence." These regulations include (1) securing basic needs for all (food, housing, health care, education, clothing, hygiene, and the like); (2) securing full employment for all; (3) securing opportunity for self-improvement of individual citizens and their participation in the leadership of the country; (4) preventing profiteering from the labor of others; (5) prohibiting monopolistic, speculative, and usurious dealings; (6) forbidding extravagance in economic matters; (7) learning from experts in science and technology; (8) preventing foreign economic dominance; and (9) achieving self-sufficiency in production of food and industrial products. Article 44 then specifies the "economic system" as comprising three sectors: "governmental, cooperative and private." The public sector "consists of all major industries, foreign trade, major mines, banking, insurance, power production, dams and major water-carrying networks, radio and television, postal, telegraph and telephone system, air, sea, land and railroad transportation, and other similar to the above, which in the form of public ownership are at the disposal of the government." The cooperative sector includes cooperative companies and organizations in urban and rural areas. This sector was recently defined by Hashemi Rafsanjani as "privately organized" units that bring "a large number of people together as private sector." Last, the private sector "consists of those portions of agriculture, animal husbandry, industry, trade and services which supplement the activities of the governmental and cooperative sectors." In addition to these provisions for national independence, social justice, and a mixed and self-sufficient economy, the Constitution also emphasizes such fundamental matters as promoting democracy and national traditions and culture. It must be noted that the 1989 revision of the Constitution does not change any of these major goals.

However, subsequent attempts to formulate a coherent and consistent development strategy on the basis of the preceding principles have run into many ideological obstacles, political conflicts, and practical difficulties.[200] The problem was already evident during the preparation of the ORPs Program and then the first plan. The debates on the meaning of development in the Islamic Republic at the time focused on several key issues. The most suitable geographic unit for development was one. The debate here focused on nation *vs.* provinces. A secondary controversy took up the urban-rural dichotomy. As has already been indicated, the sectoralists were able to impose their "national" perspective. The rural areas were also fortunate to have such a strong supporter as the Reconstruction Crusade. The controversy over the alleged conflict between sectoral and efficiency goals, on the one hand, and geographic and equity goals, on the other, took even a sharper tone in a declining economy where revolutionary fever also ran high for social justice. The outcome remained indeterminate, although those advocating a strategy of "growth first, redistribution later" had taken the lead in practice. As a consequence, "development" became a long-term goal and "growth" was considered an immediate need in the Islamic Republic.

Extensive debates also took place over the pros and cons of the introverted and extroverted strategies of resource use and the degree of openness to the international economy. Full utilization of national resources to achieve self-sufficiency was unanimously upheld. However, consensus could not be reached on the application of outside resources except that they must be modified to suit the national capabilities and needs and that their use should not increase or perpetuate dependency on the world economy. A related debate concerned a proper mix of tradition and modernity. Even more controversial was whether the two apparently contradictory modes of life were at all reconcilable. This debate turned out to be an endless one, leading to competing interpretations of Islam and divisions among the Islamic leaders along "traditional" and "modern" lines. Vastly debated also were the role of the private sector in the economy and a proper limit on its holdings. Article 49 of the Constitution lists several illegitimate means of obtaining wealth and Article 47 states that wealth obtained by legitimate means are honored and that the relevant criteria would be determined by law. This dispute remained unresolved as did the debate over the specific roles of the cooperative and public sectors in the economy. The function of the state in the management of the society was also endlessly contested. Advocates of "the least government is the best government" were not at all insignificant in number or strength. A similar polemic revolved around public participation in the leadership of the country, which meant different things to different people. Some viewed it in terms of democracy and decentralization of the state's functions whereas others wanted to use it to further capitalist development. Last, political *vs.* economic notions of defense and national strength were also debated at some length among the top leaders of the Republic. At the heart of the matter was whether to invest in military industries or the civilian economy. A related issue was whether to export the Revolution by use of force or through development of an Islamic model society. Initially, notions of military strength and the use of force seem to have prevailed in the war environment.[201]

Thus, although consensus was reached on a few issues, for the most part disagreements prevailed. Indeed, the ORPs Program and the first plan were of various orientation. It is not, therefore, surprising that the plan should use specific terminology to define some issues, for example, self-sufficiency and growth targets for economic sectors, but remain silent or vague about other matters including social justice, property relations, and public management. Specifically, on the state's goals, the plan simply restated the Constitution, and it remained silent on matters of land reform, regional development, nationalization of foreign trade, the role of cooperatives, management of the plan, and population control. This last had not been even raised as an issue during preparation of the first plan as it was considered non-Islamic. Thus, the plan reflected a compromise over issues it included. However, most fundamental matters had not been defined within the plan and this prevented its implementation. The plan was rejected in its first presentation in the Parliament in July 1983. A revised plan could not be implemented either, although the Parliament had approved its Framework for Objectives and Long-Term Strategies.[202] The postwar revision of the plan, the Reconstruction Plan, also waits to be implemented (see Chapter 4).

The majority in the Parliament, dominated by the "radicals," argued against the plan, in almost the same terms that the Economic Council had earlier used to criticize the document.[203] They charged that the plan would lead to increased dependency on foreign markets and was antithetical to the goal of national independence and self-sufficiency. They particularly disliked the plan's projection that a high share of the government's foreign exchange earnings would continue to come from the oil sector, as high as 85 percent by the last year of the plan period. The opposition was also adamant about the plan's too ambitious and overly optimistic growth targets for economic sectors and lack of any clear relationship between such targets and the Islamic values (meaning social justice here). Gross domestic production had been projected to sustain a growth rate of 7.1 percent per year over a twenty-year period, 9 percent per year during the first five years (1362–66). The annual growth rates (over the first five years) for agriculture, industry, and construction had been established at 7 percent, 14.1 percent, and 9.8 percent, respectively. These economic growth rates were to be achieved and sustained by the help of the oil sector that was expected to grow at 12.3 percent a year over the same twenty-year period. The oil price was not expected to drop below $29 per barrel under the worst market conditions. This was while the country was at war, the oil installations had already sustained significant damage, and demand for oil in the world market was shrinking at an alarming rate. Other ambitious targets included building 2 million houses, 1,000 hospitals, and 25,000 hospital beds, and train some 7,000 agricultural engineers, 3,000 engineers of technical sciences, and 8,500 medical doctors all within a five-year period (1983–87). The economy was also to attain self-sufficiency in agricultural production by 1991 despite a very high population growth, of some 3.9 percent per year. Compared to the Republic's own performance in the 1979–82 period and that of the Shah's achievements, these targets seemed unrealistic to say the least. The representatives also voiced concern about the lack of a definite relationship between the sectoral plans and the plan's objectives. Additional problems were cited about the incoherent structure of the proposed strategies and the absence of a scheme for implementating the plan. The plan's objective were also criticized as vague and overambitious, particularly with respect to predictions about target growth rates, oil revenues, taxes, and public expenditures.

In retrospect, whereas the technocratic opposition to the plan and the development strategy built into it was genuine, the real stumbling blocks were elsewhere. This became evident in the course of subsequent debates over the political economy. Specifically, the war played a major role in making the state hesitant to go along with a planned economy with a specific direction. However, the primary reason was the ideological differences among the various factions of the middle-class leadership on the nature and extent of the postrevolutionary social change. Broadly speaking, three factions may be distinguished, each comprising several tendencies. For the lack of better terminology, I shall refer to them as *conservative, radical* and *pragmatist-centrist*. I shall also use the terms *faction* and *tendency* interchangeably. It must be noted, however, that most members of these leadership factions come, by and large, from a traditional middle-class background, although their supporters include both the upper and lower classes. This unique character of factional politics within the Islamic leadership is often misunderstood. Specifically, the ideological contests *within* the middle class and its consequent political manifestations are mistaken for *interclass* political conflicts or rivalries. It should not, thus, be a surprise to anyone that frequent predictions concerning inevitable disintegration of the leadership has not yet materialized. This misunderstanding of the nature of factional politics within the Islamic leadership is partly rooted in the fact that different factions subscribe to different types of economic policy and development strategy. But such policy-strategy differences are best understood in terms of different interpretations of the same cross-class and universal Islam. The two extreme interpretations have become known as *American Islam* and *Islam of the bare feet*.[204] Broadly speaking, the latter interpretation calls for change whereas the former is known for its defense of the status quo. Thus, factional politics in the Islamic Republic is rooted in *intra* ideological contests rather than interclass conflicts. Moreover, most Iranologists and Islamicists have tended to reduce factionalism in the Islamic Republic to personal rivalries among certain individuals within the leadership. Although such rivalries are an important source of the ongoing conflict within the leadership, the role of various institutions and the many young idealists within the Islamic movement must not be forgotten.

It is known that a "conservative" faction within the ruling power bloc, supported by wealthy merchants, landlords, and some high-ranking Ayatollahs, oppose planning, state ownership, and public management of the economy. Instead, it advocates a free enterprise system accompanied by some degree of public participation and administrative decentralization. The tendency also runs counter to cooperatives and planned industrialization but favors development of agriculture and expansion of services. This is understandable because farming, small trading, and service activities depend on big merchants and middlemen for marketing their commodities, whereas industrialists could be independent. The conservative faction has opposed the land reform bill, an increase in direct taxes, a limit on the private sector, policies designed to fight profiteering and inflation, the urban land reform laws, the labor law, free schooling, and the bill for nationalization of foreign trade—to name the most important cases. The tendency advocates free trade and openness to international economy; favors trade with Western Europe, Japan, and the Islamic countries; and prefers agricultural exports over oil exports. At the same time, the tendency is culturally impermissive and ideologically strict. It rejects extensive ties with non-Muslim countries and is opposed to introduction of any major reform in Islam's tenets. This particular position reflects the dominant merchant-clergy alliance within the tendency. Finally, conservatives supported a peaceful resolution of the Iran-Iraq war and are against those articles in the Constitution that contradict their perspective on the economy, including Articles 43 and 44. They supported the movement for revision of the Constitution but were unable to achieve most of their aims.[205]

The opposite tendency may be called *radical*. It is supported by most revolutionary organizations, the lower to middle-ranking clergy, and a fair number of the religious intelligentsia. This faction is also supported by the traditional middle and lower classes in the urban centers and rural areas. It advocates public ownership and management of large enterprises, central control and planning of the economy, and nationalization of foreign trade. They are not, however, against free markets or small private holdings. Radicals advocate land, tax, and other socioeconomic reforms, which are normally rejected by the conservatives. The tendency also supports revolutionary foundations and consultative councils, cooperative establishments, and planned industrial development. They remain sympathetic to agriculture (for consumption rather than export) but are opposed to the expansion of services. Members of this camp are also for a self-reliance strategy and against free trade and complete openness to the international economy. They advocate a more confrontational foreign policy vis-à-vis the superpowers and are against the peace with Iraq. Radicals are virulently opposed to establishing any close links with the United States but remain less wary of Europe, including the Soviet Union. They support expanding a relationship with Japan and Third World countries, including Muslim societies. Like their rivals, members of the radical tendency also follow the traditional teachings of Islam *(fegh-e sonnati),* although their interpretation of the *fegh* is significantly different and more modern. Although they are ideologically the most dogmatic of the three factions, this does not make them culturally less permissive in domestic affairs. In particular, radicals equate the conservatives' interpretation with "American Islam," and characterize their own version as "Islam of the oppressed" or "the pure Mohammadian Islam" *(Islam-e nab-e Mohammadi).*[206] In exchange, the conservatives have dismissed the radicals' interpretation as "the Soviet Islam," implying that their version is influenced by socialism. Finally, the radical tendency defends most of the articles in the Constitution, particularly those concerning the economic system. It should be noted, however, that the Constitution was written in the radical environment of 1979, and as such it is more reflective of the radical faction's perspective than those of the other two. Members of the tendency supported the 1989 revision of the Constitution because it did not call for changes in articles concerning the economic system or matters of social justice. But the radicals disliked the elimination of the premiership position and transfer of its functions to the office of the president, although in the past they had called for more centralization of the state's power, and more power for the executive branch in particular.[207]

Between these two extremes is the *centrist-pragmatist* tendency.[208] It gets most of its support from such social groups as the religious intelligentsia, the new middle class, and the technocrats. Their basis of support is, however, much wider and includes a full range of classes and institutions. They maintain that a mixed approach is the most appropriate for the Islamic Republic. Specifically, they favor a controlled market economy guided and regulated by an indicative state planning and supported by limited public ownership and management. The complementary role of the privately organized cooperatives is the most valued. Members of this faction take an equivocal stand toward socioeconomic reforms and, like the other two tendencies, are wary of any major political reform. Public participation and decentralization is upheld but only at the local and lower sectoral levels and where it does not interfere with the responsibilities of the government offices. Pragmatists are the strongest advocates of consolidating parallel organizations by dissolving the grass-roots organizations into the more institutionalized state appa-ratuses. The tendency is, however, distinguished for its defense of oil-led industrialization as the basis for rapid economic growth and modernization. They also advocate a somewhat controlled free trade and cautiously guarded openness to the international economy. Ideological considerations are the last factor that enter into their cal-culations for establishing ties with the outside world. Pragmatists advocate a policy of peaceful coexistence and wish to build a model Islamic society that could be emulated by other nations. In other words, they are opposed to exporting the Islamic Revolution. They are the most flexible of the three factions on modern interpretation of Islam *(fegh-e puya)*. This fact is well reflected in the following statements made by President Hashemi Rafsanjani at a Friday Ser-mon:

> The important point here is that the Islam, which developed some 1400 years ago on the Arabian peninsula—in a settlement where the people were fundamentally nomads—a peninsula where matters of economic importance amounted to a few dates, sheep, camels, minor agricultural products and limited commerce with Syria and Iran and where culture consisted of a few lines of Pre-Islamic poetry—was a legal code specific to that society. And even that code was promulgated slowly over a period of seven or eight years. Now the legal code, which was executed in those days for that particular nation, aspires to become the code for a world in which humanity has plunged the depths of the earth and mined resources thousand of meters below its surface, has competed in space to conquer Mars, has built formidable weapons of defense and offense from particles of atom, and has conquered the sky, the earth and the mountains. In the realm of law, the advances in leg-islation, legal scholars have progressed to the very core of hypoth-eses and theories of the administration of the state. In addition, books, treatises, and universities are devoted to exploring legisla-tive policies; thus, at this very moment millions of people are en-gaged in legal research to better human society. The Islam, which was revealed some 1400 years ago for the limited society of that time, now desires to become the fulcrum of [modern] social admin-istration, and [our] nation wants to use this fulcrum [as a weapon] to wage war on the entire imperialist world, testing its mettle by those means. Unique circumstances have arisen during the course of time. How can Islam cover all these contingencies?[209]

The tendency is also culturally more permissive although it dislikes secularism, as do the other two factions. Finally, the centrist or pragmatist tendency was in the forefront of the movement for the revision of the Constitution. They wanted, and got, a centralized decision-making apparatus under a powerful presidency.

The contests between the factions, the two extreme ones in particular, reached a new height in 1986–87, first as a result of a showdown between the radical deputies of the Second Majlis and the Guardian Council *(showra-ye negahban)*, then at the threshold of the parliamentary elections for the Third Majlis. Factional contests took a new turn in the first half of 1988 over the role of the government and the peace question. In the postwar period the conflict has focused on a reconstruction strategy and political reforms.[210] To begin with, the Guardian Council vetoed many of the bills passed by the Second Majlis leading to a virtual halt in all socioeconomic reforms in 1985–87 period. The impasse between the two legislative bodies led Ayatollah Khomeini to intervene, on a personal plea from the Speaker Rafsanjani, and impose a condition that has become known as the "Two-Third" rule. Accordingly, laws, which passed the Majlis by a two-thirds majority, did not need to be approved by the Guardian Council before implementation. This rule was meant to limit the power of the conservative council in stopping certain reforms from being implemented. The 1987 parliamentary election led to domestic unrest, which grew so critical, that the government had to use troops to bring it under control.[211] A major split also occurred in the Society of the Revolutionary Clerics *(jame'h-e ruhaniyat-e mobarez)*, following which the more radical clerics formed a new Society of the Revolutionary Clergies *(jame'h-e ruhanion-e mobarez)*. The split was endorsed by Ayatollah Khomeini who also helped the radical tendency finance the formation of its new organization.[212] Then followed a series of *fetvas* (religious decrees) from Ayatollah Khomeini on the rule of the Islamic government and the absolute power of the *Vali-ye Faghih* (the highest religious/political authority in an Islamic government).[213] The decrees made the role of the Islamic government among the "primary rulings" of Islam and declared that the *Faghih* is in a position to introduce "secondary rulings" whenever societal conditions necessitated. Accordingly, the Ayatollah ordered appointment of a new Collective for Determination of the Exigencies of the System *(majma'-e tashkhis-e maslahat-e nezam)* to make decision, on behalf of the *Faghih*, about urgent issues facing the Republic. The collective included the Guardian Council, chiefs of the three branches of the state, the prime minister, the respective minister, and experts on the issues being debated. The collective was a great help to the radicals in their struggle against the Guardian Council.[214]

Since the end of the war, however, the centrist-pragmatist tendency has gained considerable influence and is making rapid strides in the direction of consolidating its hold over state power and policies. Many among the conservatives have also joined the pragmatists in their call for more moderation in international and domestic matters. The pragmatists were particularly assisted by the worsening economic conditions and increasing setbacks in the war. The radicals were indeed unfortunate to have been in power during the worst years of the young Republic. The pragmatists were also assisted by a few postwar proclamations by Ayatollah Khomeini in which he, for the first time, openly endorsed factionalism within the state, called for a limited market economy, and advocated a controlled free international trade.[215] He also limited the role of the collective in the law-making process. Under these new circumstances and given the ongoing economic crisis, the radicals found themselves increasingly alienated and powerless. In the meanwhile, the Prime Minister Musavi's offer of resignation in September 1988, like his previous attempts, was turned down by Ayatollah Khomeini.

The situation somewhat changed in the aftermath of the uproar caused by Salman Rushdie's *Satanic Verses*. The episode became an annoying affair for the pragmatists, causing a temporary setback in their drive for more state power. In sharp contrast, the event helped the radicals regain part of their lost influence and disrupt the undergoing normalization process with the West.[216] The dismissal of Ayatollah Montazeri, the would-be successor to Ayatollah Khomeini, also came as a relief for the radicals in the government: the ayatollah had severely criticized them for not keeping up with the Revolution's initial goals and for the country's economic malaise.[217] A few months later, Montazeri was dismissed by Ayatollah Khomeini for his alleged lack of leadership ability. As became known later on, the real reason had to do with the ayatollah's criticism of those responsible for mass execution of prisoners following the cease-fire, harboring a Mohammad Hashemi figure, who had been executed earlier for alleged conspiracy against the Islamic Republic (the man is believed to have made public the Iran-U.S. rapprochement that led to the Iran-Contra fiasco), and defending the rights of the liberal and other opposition groups.[218] The radical faction continued to wield considerable power within the middle-class leadership until the death of Ayatollah Khomeini in 3 June 1989 and the election of Ayatollah Kamanei as his successor. A more severe setback came with the revision of the Constitution and the presidential election in late July 1989. President Hashemi Rafsanjani's cabinet does not include some of the most influential members of the radical tendency.

Although the radicals will continue to wield considerable power in the Majlis, a few key governmental offices, and in certain grassroots organizations, their role in the leadership of the Islamic Republic will continue to diminish unless surprises happen. It must be noted that the centrist tendency has a better chance for consolidating its hold on the Islamic state. Weary of abrupt change in the aftermath of the Revolution and the Iraqi war, and unhappy with the status quo, most Iranians are looking forward to a *gradualist* and *predictable* approach to change in the socioeconomic and political systems of the country. Whereas radicals are unfortunate to have held power during a period of general economic decline, conservatives are having a difficult time defending a more or less *a la Shah* model that failed to benefit the majority. Under these circumstances, the centrist are finding it easier to defend a mixed approach. Equally favorable to the centrist tendency is the ongoing rapprochement between the socialist and capitalist camps and the global restructuring in the direction of a mixed system. Finally, the centrists' interpretation of Islam could be expected to gain wider support within the Islamic movement particularly given that it is also backed by similar interpretations by many influential ideologues of the modern Islamic movement throughout the world including Iran.[219] This particular interpretation, it must be noted, is also closer to the vision of the traditional middle class in the country, including the majority in the state organizations.

Ayatollah Khomeini was a radical and the most ideologically inspired leader of the Islamic Republic. He was a charismatic visionary with immense authority and a cultural model for social change.[220] However, being at the head of an Islamic leadership torn by ideological divisions, the Ayatollah took contradictory positions, defending this or that faction on different occasions. He also played the role of an arbiter of the last resort to bring the conflicting parties together or strike a balance between them.[221] He also remained equivocal and ambiguous about what position he actually favored. The Ayatollah denounced the rich and injustice and gave lip service to radical changes such as land reform. Occasionally, the Ayatollah was also forced into tactical or strategic retreats as in the case of the cease-fire with Iraq. On other occasions, he had to take pragmatic positions as in the case of the Irangate fiasco. Yet, at other times he was the most uncompromising and dramatic, as in the Salman Rushdie affair. In short, Ayatollah Khomeini was an embodiment of the three ideological factions in a most challenging circumstance, and in this lies the source of his difficulties in creating a coherent and consistent leadership. It must be noted, however, that the Ayatollah had encouraged ideological factionalism as a natural and useful phenomenon for Islam and the Revolution.

Factionalism in the Islamic Republic has had positive and negative impacts on the society. Specifically, whereas it has allowed for *intrastate* political democracy (a rather rare phenomenon in Iranian political history), it has led to economic difficulties, for it prevented the state from formulating a coherent development strategy and implementing consistent economic policies. Because factionalism in the Islamic Republic emanates from the cross-class nature of the state's ideology and the extreme heterogeneity of the middle class, it will continue to persist in the foreseeable future unless one of the following three scenarios occurs: (1) one faction will eliminate the others, establishing itself as the hegemonic power; (2) the three factions will come together by increasingly distancing the state from the Islamic ideology; and (3) they will institutionalize their differences in partisan groupings, more probably into a two-party system. The first is improbable as the contestants come from the same class (or some say cast) and ideological backgrounds and, as such, they have common interests rather than antagonistic ones. The second scenario is also doubtful as the Islamic state is bound to embrace the Islamic ideology, which will continue to remain cross-class and thus a source for differing interpretations. This leaves us with the last scenario, which I consider the most plausible given the political thinking of the pragmatists in power.[222] Note that everyone in the leadership realizes that what is needed most is an economic upturn that requires *intrasystem* political stability and *intrasocietal* social security (for everyone, from the existing suppliers and prospective investors to the government officials, workers, and general consuming public). But the formation of partisan groupings, that is, institutionalization of factionalism into a multiparty system, faces tremendous odds. The past experience on this is too limited in the country and the nation's political culture (not just that of any particular group) is too obsolete to allow for pluralism in the immediate future. Yet, certain developments in the postrevolutionary Iran point toward the eventual development of a multiparty political system. The encouraging openness of the ruling pragmatists to the idea and the ongoing debates within and outside the state over the issue are among such positive signs. The obsolete political culture (see Chapter 4) is also coming under attack from many sides and could well be totally abandoned by the aspiring young Iranians. Even more significant is the fact that democracy has gradually become an ideal in the country. These and other changes notwithstanding, the future of factionalism in Iran will continue to remain a largely unpredictable matter.

Eccentric Policies and Pragmatic Solutions

In the absence of planning and a coherent development strategy, the postrevolutionary economy has been managed by means of annual budgets and largely idiosyncratic policies. Here I wish to focus on the state's policies in coping with a declining economy and leave an examination of the annual budgets for the next chapter. These policies have largely reflected the middle-class nature of the state, factional politics within the leadership, and various domestic and international constraining forces crippling the economy. The need for speedy adaptation to mostly unconventional and surprising movements in the economic and extraeconomic spheres explains the eccentric and reactive nature of these policies. In particular, the oil factor, the war, and the factional conflicts were the most influential factors in decisions setting economic policies in the postrevolutionary Iran. The nature and direction of the State policies were equally influenced by market forces, especially in the powerful service sector and the so-called black market. Moreover, such policies, although cloaked in ideological and long-term development objectives included in the Constitution, have been essentially pragmatic, as opposed to ideologically guided, and focused on managing the immediate problems, rather than the long-term direction, of the economy. Only occasionally, and mostly in the initial postrevolutionary years, were state policies directed toward structural change or lasting reform.

By the end of 1978, a sizable portion of the economy and major sectors of the civil society had fallen into the hands of various revolutionary organizations including workers' and employees' councils. The Revolution's focus on the economic problems was well reflected in the Ashoura March of 11 September 1978. The resolution of the march underscored the goals of social justice, end to exploitation, elimination of foreign exploitation, termination of dependency on imperialism, and eradication of oppressive profiteering.[223] These were subsequently included in the 1979 Constitution, and earlier in the postrevolutionary period, attempts focused on practicing the constitutional goals.[224] Thus, much emphasis was placed, in practice and in public debates, on self-reliance, domestic contentment, social reforms, asset redistribution, expansion of the public sector, and structural changes in sectoral-spatial dimensions of the economy. Planning was proclaimed essential in guiding the market forces in a mixed economy as mandated by the Constitution. As we shall see in the next chapter, a significant portion of the country's industries and all its banks and insurance companies were nationalized, a land reform bill was drawn, and proposals were made for implementation of various reform projects.

The changes were initiated by the Provisional Revolutionary Government (PRG), who established the Office of Revolutionary Projects (ORP) to draw the new regime's economic policies. The office soon came up with a program that outlined the structure of property relations in the Islamic Republic and proposed a plan for development of the new society. Following the Constitution, the economy was to be composed of three sectors: (1) Free or People's Sector, (2) People-State Sector, and (3) State Sector. The latter would lead the economy whereas the cooperative sector would function as a balancing force between the public and private sectors. Development was to be achieved in three stages. In the first stage (1979–80), agriculture, cooperatives, and infrastructures were named as top priorities. In the second stage (1981–87), relative self-reliance was to be achieved by reducing industrial dependency. By the end of the last stage (1988–99), the economy was to sustain its growth without dependency on oil and gas exports, which were to have stopped by that time.[225] However, before this program was to take off, it was killed by internal political struggles that led to the hostage drama and the collapse of the PRG.

The next major step began with the formulation of the first plan in 1982.[226] The plan bill was subsequently sent to Majlis for ratification but failed to pass for reasons identified earlier, most important for lack of clarity about the underlying development philosophy, which reflected intraideological contests, and the stages of development in the Islamic Republic. The government revised the plan in 1983 and tried to be more specific about the stages of development but continued to remain silent on the ideologically sensitive matters of property relations and reforms. The revised plan also took into account the "new realities" including the consequence and requirements of the ongoing war with Iraq. It argued that the "destined society" as depicted in the Constitution must be arrived at in stages, the first and the most important of which was determined to be the "Stage of Elimination of Obstacles to Development," referred to as the *preliminary* or *preparatory* stage.[227] According to this new though in planning and development under the Islamic Republic, the preliminary stage had to be implemented before the "regular development planning" could be staged. Additionally, it was argued that during this first stage, socioeconomic development should be based on the following "axes": (1) elimination of organizational and legal obstacles to development; (2) maximum utilization of the existing production capacities; (3) establishment of a coherent system of statistics, information, and planning; and (4) design of institutions and structures suitable to the conditions, values, and demands of the post-revolutionary society.[228] In the face of significant bottlenecks and underutilized capacities, new investment was not considered feasible or even desirable.

As an initial step toward implementing the first stage, the Ministry of Plan and Budget established a "Planning Headquarters" (PH) to undertake certain studies for revising the plan. After several meetings, the PH approved a framework for revision and implementation of the plan on 14 Day 1362 (4 January 1983). It then undertook the following activities: (1) estimated existing productive capacity in service delivery and commodity production for all socioeconomic sectors; (2) estimated financial and material needs for maximum utilization of the existing capacity; (3) identified legal, organizational, managerial, and physical limitations and obstacles for maximum utilization of the existing capacity; (4) reformulated the ongoing development projects to bring them into conformity with the general view of the first stage; (5) initiated the work on the Spatial Strategy Planning *(Amayesh-e Sarzamin);* (6) prepared a Model and Strategy of Development; and (7) undertook the National Census of Population and Housing (in November 1986). The results were published in a series of documents, most of which have been cited in this book.

In the meantime, the Majlis established a Spatial Plan Commission on 21 Aban 1363 (12 November 1984) to look into the proposed revised plan. It took a year for the Parliament and the government to agree, on principle, on what strategies and long-term objectives should guide planning and developing processes in the Islamic Republic.[229] Specifically, agriculture was to serve as an "axis" of development, a rather normative decision since, while important, the sector has only limited interindustry linkages. Moreover, investment in basic industries were to be given priority over the consumer goods industries, rural development was to be favored over a policy of urban expansion, and development efforts were to be focused on short-term objectives, maximum utilization of the existing capacities, and removing obstacles to development.[230] No agreements were reached on the specifics of medium-term courses of actions including the quantitative targets, economic management, the role of private sector, and the extent of openness to outside world.

The revised plan was subsequently shelved indefinitely in favor of annual budgeting. This happened partly because of factional contests within the state over issues surrounding the future economic system, and partly due to the lack of motivation on the part of the government to commit itself to a planned economy under conditions of war and an uncertain oil market. Thus, a more pragmatic approach to economic development was adopted and emphasis was placed on yearly management of the economy and maximum utilization of the exiting capacities, as opposed to initiation of major new investments.[231] The earlier self-reliant policy was also changed somewhat into a policy of diversifying sources of dependency and promoting barter. In the meantime and as attempts to find a more suitable strategy for immediate reconstruction of war damage and prevention of further destructions were frustrated, the government increasingly took a nonideological, quick-fix approach to reconstruction.[232] This process of gradual lapse into a nondevelopmental and pragmatic approach to economy continued and was exacerbated after the sharp decline in oil prices in 1986.

To cope with the critical situation that had developed following the collapse of oil prices, the conservative tendency urged a policy of privatization and less governmental control. The radicals in the government, however, introduced an even more restrictive economic policy under the austerity Plan for New Economic Conditions. The austerity plan covered the last two years of the first plan (1986–87) and remained in effect until the end of 1987. The plan indeed represented a second revision of the original first plan. The plan was predicated on the believe that, under the given circumstances, Iran could not afford a growth strategy based on increased capacity utilization or the introduction of new investment.[233] Rather, it should attempt to maintain the status quo economic condition. As indicated by Masᶜoud Zanjani, then Minister of Plan and Budget, the austerity plan was not a plan in the classic sense of the term; that is, it was not a developmental plan, a plan for economic growth or intersectoral integration. Rather, the austerity plan's main objectives were to prevent further exacerbation of the economic difficulties and make the general budget less dependent on the vacillations in the oil revenue.[234] The plan reduced the general budget and the country's expenditures of foreign exchanges by two-thirds. It also aimed at reallocating the scarce foreign currencies on the basis of a new priority list: the war having top priority followed by the defense-related industries and basic needs (home production and imports). Agriculture, which had the least dependency on oil revenue, was made the axis of the plan and measures were included for coping with inflation. Particular attention had been paid to promotion of nonoil exports as a means of earning the much needed foreign exchange. The government also looked upon the austerity plan as an opportunity for changing the country's consumption and production patterns.

Toward this end, certain "nonnecessary" commodities were eliminated from domestic consumption and exported.

Soon however, "the war of cities" began in early 1988 and led to further decline in the economy. The government was then forced to introduce yet another more restrictive nondevelopmental policy focusing on minimizing the economic decline and the war damage.[235] The new "Survival Policy" (rather than plan) of economic management was predicated upon the assumption that even the status quo was hard to maintain. This was the clearest indication that the economic trends were irreversible under the prevailing conditions of war and that the economy needed to be managed on a day-to-day basis rather than on the basis of any plan, no matter the duration. The Survival Policy was followed right up to the end of the war, when factional debates began to focus on postwar reconstruction. As we shall see in Chapter 4, it is yet too early to make firm predictions on the nature of the emerging postwar development strategy or economic policy. Indications so far, however, suggest that the new pragmatist government plans to return to a "growth first redistribution later" strategy, implemented in stages, along the lines proposed in the 1983 revision of the First Plan, using a combination of oil revenue, foreign assistance, and domestic resources. This policy orientation is reflected both in the plan for the postwar reconstruction and in President Hashemi Rafsanjani's general policy statement published when he was running for president and in his practice thus far.[236]

The new policy is built around selective privatization of the productive public sector, deregulation of certain sections of the economy, limited import liberalization, and controlled financial liberalization. It contrasts with the strategy earlier in the postrevolutionary period which was built around emphasis on the productive role of the public sector, central planning (at least in theory), import substitution, and control of domestic and external finance. The new policy is detailed in Chapter 4, where I shall also indicate the main obstacles that the transition to it faces. For example, the state's attempts so far to reactivate Tehran's stock exchange market and sell public enterprises to local private investors have largely failed and deregulation of the economy and its reintegration into the world market is proceeding extremely slowly. It is also uncertain whether the state can redirect investment away from services toward productive activities, a shift that is critical for the success of the new growth strategy. Nevertheless, it is expected that the government will move further in the direction of a market economy in the 1990s. This will be aided by the kind of stabilization or structural adjustment policies that are prescribed by IMF and the World Bank. However, the extreme "shock therapy" approach may not be adopted as it will be too unpopular with the radicals and the poorer supporters of the state.

3

Economic Trends, Problems, and Policies

In the foregoing chapter, I explained the most important features of some seven categories of forces, which I see as having been among the strongest determinants of the postrevolutionary political economy. In this chapter, which is focused on an examination of the post-revolutionary macroeconomic, sectoral, and territorial trends, problems, and policies, I will show why, how, and to what extent the constraining and facilitating forces have affected the economy and the state's policies and in what particular direction. Both quantitative and qualitative impacts are given, as are structural and superficial trends. Also indicated is the regressive-progressive balance of such impacts and the degree that the general influences have been translated into specific impediments. Finally, the state's policies and efficacy in coping with the problems and the specific impacts of the intervening forces are also detailed and explained.

DOMESTIC PRODUCTION, SECTORAL SHIFTS, AND POLICIES

As shown in Table 3.1 and Figure 3.1, real gross domestic production (GDP), that is, the market value of all goods and services produced in final form by residents of Iran during a year, has been fluctuating since 1976. It registered its sharpest increases in 1976, 1982, and 1983, and its steepest decrease during the 1977–80 and 1984–87 periods. Broadly speaking, the following three periods or cycles may be identified: sharp decline (1977–80), strong growth (1981–83), and sharp decline (1984–87). As indicated in figure 1.1, these periods correspond to significant turning points or events since 1977 when the Revolution began to take root. The impact of the oil factor, the war, and politics is the most noticeable. Moreover, the sharp decline began in 1978, the year preceding the revolutionary overthrow of the Shah, when strikes and workstoppages had become normal events.

Table 3.1 Gross Domestic Production at Factor Prices and Its Sectoral Composition, 1976–87 (billion rials, 1974 constant prices)

Year (a)	GDP Billion Rials	GDP Growth Rate	Non-Oil GDP Billion Rials	Non-Oil GDP Growth Rate	Agriculture Share	Agriculture Growth Rate	Oil Share	Oil Growth Rate	Industries(c) Share	Industries(c) Growth Rate	Services(d) Share	Services(d) Growth Rate	GDP (current prices)(e) Billion Rials
							Sectoral Composition of GDP and Growth Rates (%) (b)						
1976	3658.9	17.8	2274.8	23.2	8.9	7.3	37.8	9.9	16.4	26.6	41.5	26.3	4480.3
1977	3922.3	7.2	2558.9	12.5	8.7	4.5	34.8	-1.5	16.5	7.3	44.7	15.6	5207.8
1978	3266.9	-16.7	2337.1	-8.7	10.8	3.4	28.5	-31.8	17.0	-14.2	49.6	-7.6	5354.4
1979	3070.5	-6.0	2302.9	-1.5	11.6	1.0	25.0	-17.4	16.7	-7.6	50.8	-3.7	6337.8
1980	2568.0	-16.4	2237.5	-2.8	14.1	1.9	12.9	-56.9	20.3	1.6	57.5	-5.5	6758.9
1981	2639.4	2.8	2365.8	5.7	15.3	11.3	10.4	-17.2	20.3	2.7	57.0	1.9	8218.5
1982	3040.3	15.2	2513.5	6.2	14.3	7.9	17.3	92.5	19.4	10.5	50.9	2.8	10621.5
1983	3417.8	12.4	2886.7	14.8	12.6	-1.6	15.5	0.8	20.0	15.6	53.7	18.6	13471.3
1984	3421.3	0.1	2968.8	+2.8	13.1	4.1	13.2	-14.8	20.6	3.2	54.7	2.1	14600.7
1985	3376.0	-1.3	2939.8	-1.0	14.4	8.9	12.9	-3.6	20.4	-2.8	54.0	-1.3	15948.2
1986	2974.9	-11.9	2597.2	-11.7	16.8	2.6	12.7	-13.5	19.2	-16.4	53.0	-11.9	17512.6
1987(f)	2931.0	-1.5	2493.0	-4.0	17.7	4.0	14.9	16.0	18.3	-6.3	50.8	-1.5	21890.8
Annual Average Figures													
1976–78	3616.0	2.8	2390.3	9.0	9.5	5.1	33.7	-7.8	16.6	6.6	45.3	11.4	
1979–83	2947.2	1.6	2461.3	4.5	13.6	4.1	16.2	0.4	19.3	4.6	54.0	2.8	
1979–87	3048.8	-0.7	2589.5	0.3	14.4	4.6	15.0	1.7	19.5	0.06	53.6	0.2	

Year (a)	Billion Rials	Growth Rate	Billion Rials	Growth Rate	Share	Growth Rate	Share	Growth Rate	Share	Growth Rate	Share	Growth Rate	Billion Rials
Percentage Change													
1976–78/ 1979–83	-18.5	-42.9	3	-50	43.2	-19.6	-51.9	105.1	16.3	-30.3	19.2	-75.4	
1976–78/ 1979–87	-15.7	-125.0	8.3	-96.7	51.6	-9.8	-55.5	121.8	17.5	-99.1	18.3	-98.2	

Sources and Notes:
Compiled and calculated on the basis of various tables in *Gozaresh* (1363 and 1365). See also *Salnameh* (1364), p. 782; (1365), pp. 810–811 and (1366), pp. 452–453; and *Taraznameh* (1361, 1362, and 1363). Note that for certain years these sources give slightly different figures.

(a) 1976/1355 (Iranian Shamsi Year); 1979 is the first postrevolutionary year, whereas 1978 is the year of Revolution; war with Iraq began in September 1980.

(b) Sectoral shares total more than 100 percent because imputed service charges (*Karmozd-e ehtesabi*) are deducted from the sectoral value added to arrive at GDP figures. For an explanation of these charges and why they are not included in GDP and cannot be distributed among the sectors, see *Hesabha-ye Meli-ye Iran, 1338–56* (Iranian National Accounts, 1959–77) (Tehran Bank Markazi Iran, 1360), p. 93.

(c) Includes water and power (electricity, gas), construction, manufacturing and mining.

(d) Trade, restaurants and hotels; transportation, communication and storage; banking, insurance and brokerage; housing ownership, and professional and specialized services; social, private, and household services.

(e) GDP in current prices is given for the purpose of comparison with GDP in constant prices. The figures here are not used for calculation of other figures in this or other tables in this book.

(f) Figures are preliminary.

Figure 3.1

Change in GDP and Sectoral Production, 1976–87
(1974 constant prices)

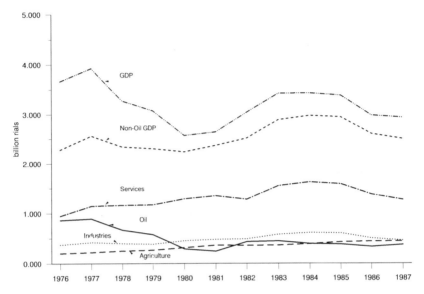

Overall, the indicator has declined drastically from its prerevolutionary level. The average annual GDP for the 1979–87 (postrevolutionary) period indicates a 15.7 percent decline (at fixed 1974 prices) when compared to the corresponding figure for the 1976–78 (prerevolutionary) period. The declining trend began with the 1976–77 recession under the Shah, which had followed a sharp decline in oil revenue in 1975 and the mismanagement of the economy after the oil boom of 1973–74. The trend was exacerbated in 1978 as increased revolutionary movement led to strikes, work stoppages, reduction in oil revenue, the flight of capital, and decline in the rate of capacity utilization. The declining trend reached its highest rates in 1979 and 1980 with the sharp drop in oil revenue, flight of skilled workers, start of conflict over state power and the social question of the Revolution, Iraq's invasion of Iran, and the takeover of the American Embassy in Tehran by the students of the "Imam's Line" *(daneshjouyan-e khatt-e Imam).*

Gross domestic production picked up in 1981 as the Islamic forces gradually consolidated their hold over the state and ended the hostage drama. But the growth trend became significant only after oil revenues increased in 1982 and 1983, following a major price hike in the preceding years and the liberation of the oil-producing zones from the Iraqi occupation forces. A good part of the increased foreign exchange was used to mitigate infrastructural obstacles and import inputs of various types, particularly intermediate inputs, for the mostly dormant industries. The growth trend, however, stopped in 1984, for which a 0.1 percent growth rate is reported. By 1984, oil revenue had begun to decline, the war had come to a stalemate as the Republic's efforts to take over Basra, a city of 1 million in northeast Iraq, was frustrated, and the factional conflicts within the power bloc intensified and crippled most economic policies of the government. All these led to significant capacity underutilization and thus to reduction in actual output. At the same time, potential output also suffered as new investments were negligible.

The "optimistic" government projections in 1984 had indicated a GDP growth rate of 5.4 percent for 1985.[1] But the actual growth rate was −1.3 percent (Table 3.1).[2] The anticipated increase in oil revenue did not materialize; on the contrary, it declined sharply, to $14 billion from about $16.7 billion in the previous year. In the meantime, war expenditures had soared to about $6.3 billion (at 85 rials to a dollar) and most government projects were on virtual hold. Industries were strangled by the lack of inputs and increased bottlenecks leading to significant underutilization of the existing industrial capacities. Even this low rate could not be sustained in 1986 when potential production declined by 11.9 percent from the 1985 level.[3] Spot prices declined to about $10 a barrel in April 1986 from just under $30 in October 1985.[4] This caused the nation's oil revenue to decline from a predicted $15 billion for the year to an actual $5.8 billion. In the meantime, the war expenditures had reached the astronomical figure of about $11 billion. Although the declining trend has slowed since 1987 (for which a −1.5 percent growth rate is reported), because of a slight improvement in oil revenue, the nation's potential GDP growth rate continues to remain sluggish.[5] Overall, GDP registered an average annual growth rate of −0.7 percent over the 1979–87 period (Figure 3.2).

The depth of the crisis is well-illustrated by the following quote from an official publication: "To provide its rapidly growing population with a subsistence life and to eliminate poverty and deprivation within an acceptable framework of income and wealth distribution, Iran needs a sustained GDP growth rate of 5 percent per year for about 20 years"[6] (My translation). Indeed the real growth rate must be much higher than given in the quote if the population is to maintain a subsistence life. A high inflation rate has been eating into the purchasing power of the people and the population has been growing at an average annual rate of 3.9 percent over the 1979–88 period. In 1989, the annual addition to the population was about 2 million, whose maintenance even at a subsistence level requires some $2 billion a year. Moreover, as we shall see, a solid majority (about 65 percent) of the country's population (about 53 million in 1988) still live below the poverty line and some 45.3 percent are under fifteen years of age. Indeed, each year some 600,000 people enter the job market for the first time, and creating this number of jobs requires about 2,000 billion rials a year in new investment. If the growth trend is sustained, the country's population will reach 100 million by the year 2010. The need to create income, jobs, and social services, therefore, would be tremendous.[7]

Noticeable changes have also occurred in the sectoral composition of GDP as exemplified by the significant decline in the share of the oil sector and consequent improvements in those of agriculture, industries, and services (Table 3.1 and Figure 3.2). Specifically, the average annual contribution of oil to GDP over the 1979–87 period (15 percent) dropped by about 56 percent (in 1974 constant prices) when compared to the corresponding figure for the 1976–78 period

Figure 3.2

GDP and Sectoral Growth Rates, 1976–87
(1974 constant prices)

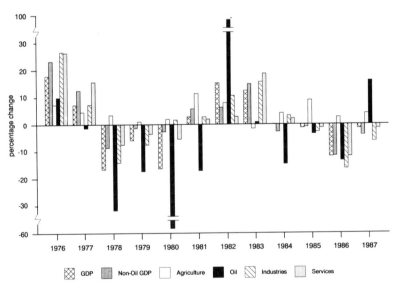

(about 34 percent). Oil production began to decline in 1977, a trend that worsened as a result of strikes by the oil workers in 1978 and the subsequent revolutionary upheavals. The new regime also made it an explicit policy to produce and export oil at the minimum level possible in an attempt to reduce the country's dependency on the capitalist world market.[8] This policy could be pursued because international markets faced shortages of crude oil and spot markets were willing to pay increasingly higher prices. The new government had already abrogated the country's marketing agreements with large international oil companies and was making direct sales to governments and companies.[9]

Soon, however, the war erupted (September 1980) and oil production plunged undesirably, dropping to its all time low of 1.3 mb/d in 1981, the first full war year (see Table 2.3). Suspension of the sale of natural gas to the Soviet Union in February 1980 had already reduced the oil sector's contribution to the economy. Oil production picked up again in 1982 and was sustained at over 2 mb/d through 1985. Thereafter oil production dropped below the 2 mb/d level. As a result, the real value of the sector's production grew at an annual rate of only 1.7 percent over the 1979–83 period (Table 3.1 and Figure 3.2). The aggressive price cutting policy of 1982–83 was particularly effective in increasing oil revenues in these years.[10] The share of oil in GDP, however, continued to drop due to the gradual decline in oil prices, which in 1986 reached their lowest since the price hikes in 1973–74 period (see Figure 2.5).[11] The shrinking demand for oil in the West and Saudi Arabia's malicious policies had combined to produce a significant oil glut in international markets and, in a relatively short time, a situation that came as a surprise to the government in Tehran. Following the hostage crisis, the American government also made it extremely difficult for Iran to carry out business as usual in international oil markets.

The slack caused in GDP by the relative decline in oil was only partially compensated by the continued expansion of services. The sector grew at 2.8 percent per year over the 1979–83 period. In the subsequent years, however, the sector gradually declined, registering only a 0.2 percent annual growth rate over the 1979–87 period. Its share, however, increased from 45 percent in 1976–78 period (average per year) to 54 percent in the 1979–87 period, a 20 percent jump (Table 3.1, Figures 3.1, and 3.2). Although the rate of expansion in the latter period has been slower, the trend is nevertheless considered harmful for the economy. The sector offered the most profitable, quickest return investment opportunity in the postrevolutionary war environment and is a major diversion of the scarce resources from the more productive sectors of the economy.[12] For example, the data from seventy-eight cities for 1985 indicates that out of a total of 8,042 companies registered, 57.9 percent related to services as compared to 4.9 percent for agriculture; the remaining registered as industrial concerns. The share of the sectors in the total investment of 66,650 million rials was 3, 57, and 40 percent, respectively.[13] Within the sector itself, most investments have also been diverted to more unproductive services of trade, restaurants, hotels, and housing rental (Figure 3.3). Most services are controlled by the big bazaaris, including international and domestic merchants, traders and middlemen, who also control the main channels of commodities distribution in the country. They supported the Revolution and continue to be influential in the government and the economy through close political and economic connections with representatives in the Parliament, Council of Guardians, high ranking government officials, and many grand ayatollahs. The bazaaris' opposition to the Nationalization of Foreign Trade Bill is the main stumbling block against its implementation. According to semiofficial *Kayhan* daily, 5,000 bazaaris made 50 billion rials in after-tax profits (about $715 million) in 1986 alone.[14]

Figure 3.3.

Changes in the Service Sector, 1976–86 (1974 constant prices)

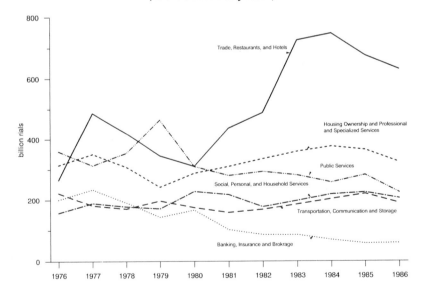

The service subsector most touched by the Revolution was the banking system. In early summer 1979 all banks were nationalized and then in the fall of the same year they were consolidated to form six commercial and three specialized banks. Beginning in 1985, interest-free banking was also introduced. The Law for Usury-Free Banking was enacted back in 1983.[15] In practice, however, banks continued to pay 8 to 9 percent interest (in the name of profit). Functions of the banking system and its relationship with other economic sectors were also to alter significantly. Specifically, banks were to become partners in development projects and their credit policies and priorities changed.[16] For example, agriculture, non-oil exports, backward regions, rural activities, and small-scale industries began to receive more credit at the expense of such previously favored activities as domestic and international commerce, large-scale industrial establishments (units employing ten or more workers), and construction. These changes were to help incorporate banks into productive sectors in the hope of generating significant long-term benefits. (In the short-term, however, they have led to a substantial decline in banking's contribution of services to the GDP [Figure 3.3]) Competition from two financial institutions were the most responsible for the failure of the banking system to contribute to the economy. They are *Sandoughha-ye Gharzulhasaneh* (interest free loan funds) and *Sherkatha-ye Mozarebeh'i* (limited partnership companies).

Emergence of Islamic interest-free loan funds (IFLFs) was the most important development next to nationalization of the banking system. These seemingly Islamic private financial institutions had their origins in similar institutions which had been established long before the Revolution or sprang up during the revolutionary movements in 1978. Various interest groups, mainly from among the bazaaris, drew on parts of these funds to create seemingly charitable organizations. Their formation was also anticipated and encouraged by the Law for Usury-Free Banking. The nationalized banks, however, lost the market to the private sector. Before the Revolution, officially registered IFLFs numbered around 200 but after the Revolution their number increased to 3,000.[17] They have been gradually transferred into giant private economic entities with dealings in all major areas of economic activities but primarily in commerce (including imports and exports), brokerage, and services. These institutions hold some 1,000 billion rials of savings largely from the high-income groups in the country. The Islamic Economic Organization (IEO), the largest of such institutions, was originally organized as the Islamic Bank in 1979 by a group of influential religious leaders and bazaaris. IEO later changed its name to avoid the nationalization law. The organization controls over 50 percent of all IFLFs in the country, is now totally owned by the bazaaris, and was until recently headed by the same family that controls Iran's chamber of commerce (the Khamoushi family).[18] The Echo of Iran and the critics have characterized the organization as "being a state within a state." In 1987, IEO's loanable funds stood at 500 billion rials, roughly equal to 5 percent of the country's total liquidity, of which half was controlled by the parent IEO and the rest by its various subsidiaries.[19]

Since 1986, these institutions have come under increasing attack from the government, which has been holding them responsible for various corruption schemes, illegal activities (including commodities hoarding and black market foreign exchange), defrauding the public, and neutralizing the state monetary and fiscal policies. Both IEO and Nobouvvat Foundation, the second largest of such institutions in the country, were temporarily suspended in 1987 but became active again under new management. The IEO was accused of injecting huge sums into unproductive services thereby undermining the government's attempts to stabilize prices and the money supply and to develop productive sectors. Charges against the Nobouvvat Foundation were even harsher and came from the government and the conservative daily *Resalat* of the Resalat Foundation (20–21 Mehr 1366), which was using the case to demonstrate that public management could not but be ineffective. The organization was accused of failing to pay taxes on its "big deals and hefty profits," "illegally engaging in export of goods," and entering into illicit activities.[20] The organization's chief officers were put on trial and its executive director even received a death sentence, which was subsequently withdrawn by a higher court.

Sherkatha-ye Mozarebeh'i had their emergence as a reaction to the interest-free banking system. These limited partnership companies supposedly are organized in accordance with the Islamic teaching on commerce. In reality, however, and according to *Kayhan* daily, they have been turned into "Mafia-like organizations." They are established by a group or an individual who will then invite the public to invest their cash in the company and receive profits ranging from 24 to 48 percent (compare this with the 8 to 9 percent that banks offer!). The investors have no control over the management or activities of the company and receive no guarantee concerning the principal invested. The high risk is said to be worth the high profit. These companies supposedly are specialized in different lines of business but in reality they get involved in whatever activities they find profitable. Among the most well-known of these companies are Sahar and Elika, Baqali-ye Bozorg-e Dowlatkhahan, Pishgaman, and Mah Afarin (all active primarily in food and nonfood commodity distribution), Afshin (active primarily in production and distribution of food items including lemon juice), and Vigean (active primarily in real estate and construction). Some of these companies control "billions of tumans" (ten rials to a tuman) and vast amount of commodities in their warehouses. The Sahar and Elika Company is reported to have "billions of tumans" in the Melat Bank alone, its executive director is protected by armed guards, and, according to *Kayhan* daily, "nobody knows who has permitted the guards to carry weapons." The same newspaper also reports that the owner of the Baqali-ye Bozorg-e Dowlatkhahan, originally a taxi driver, purchased a 20-million-tuman house for his daughter at 35 million tumans in a deal that took only five minutes.[21]

Clearly, to stay in the business, these companies must make profits at least 10 percent over and above what they pay to the public investors. Given that some of these companies have been extremely successful in accumulating wealth, one may assume that their profit rates are much higher. How then are such huge profits made in a society that already suffers from hyperinflation? According to my personal survey in Tehran and the Iranian newspapers (*Kayhan* and *Ettalaᶜat* in particular), these companies make such hefty profits by engaging primarily in black and intermediary markets and illegitimate activities such as hoarding and repetitive sales and purchase. Most commonly, they concentrate on one commodity at a time, collect all the available supplies of it, hoard, and then offer the commodity to the consumers at exorbitant prices. They are also involved in illegal foreign exchange deals, import-export markets, and various brokerage activities. A few companies are reported to have gone bankrupt or the owner has simply fled the country, taking the people's money with them. For example, one Yousef Khairkhah is reported to have escaped the country taking 2 billion tumans of the people's money with him. His company is not registered anywhere or known to have filed any bankruptcy papers.[22]

In the last months of 1989, *Sherkatha-ye Mozarebehʾi* came under heavy fire from the government and religious decrees *(fetvas)* were secured from the high-ranking religious authorities against them. The campaign was motivated primarily by a number of major concerns. These companies proved the most effective in competing with the banking system in collecting small and large private savings and turning them into a powerful purchasing power in the trade and service markets. The immediate consequences were increased inflation and reduced capital for the productive activities. Inflation further worsened as these companies engaged in hoarding and the black market. Even rationed commodities were not spared, making the government particularly concerned about the fate of the lower-income people. The companies' activities also ran counter to the state's policy of redirecting the wandering immense private liquidity into productive use and for reconstruction. One such policy sought to redirect the private liquidity toward Tehran's newly reactivated stock market where the government of President Rafsanjani is offering to sell shares of the nationalized industries. Finally, a large number of people began complaining about the abuses of some companies that took the people's money then suddenly disappeared. As of December 1989, the uproar against the *Sherkatha-ye Mozarebeh'i* continues; it is not clear, however, what the government plans to do with them. If the fate of the interest-free loan funds are of any indication, these companies will survive the present attack although they may be forced to reduce their scale and accept some regulatory measures.

The slight jump in the industrial share of the GDP reflects the decline in the share of the oil sector rather than a real increase in industrial value added, which has remained sluggish throughout the postrevolutionary years, with the exception of the 1982–83 period (Table 3.1, Figure 3.1). On the average, the industrial sector grew at 4.6 percent a year between 1979 and 1983 and improved its share by 16.3 percent, from 16.6 percent in 1976–78 period (average per year) to 19.3 percent in 1979–83 period. This relatively good performance, however, could not be maintained during the 1984–87 period, when the sector experienced significant contraction as a result of continuing decline in its rates of capacity utilization and capital formation. As a consequence, the sector registered an average annual growth rate of only 0.06 percent over the 1979–87 period, compared to a 6.6 percent rate during the 1976–78 years (Table 3.1, Figure 3.2). The immediate prerevolutionary recession and the revolutionary movement in 1978 had already led to significant decline in the nation's industrial production. In the 1979–80 period, most industries remained closed or functioned at significantly reduced capacity. In some cases, owners had fled the country or declared themselves bankrupt. In other instances, industries suffered from shortage of intermediate and raw material inputs or were caught in the struggle between the workers and the state over the workers' councils among other issues.[23]

The industrial problems led the new government to introduce the Law for the Protection and Expansion of Iranian Industry in midsummer 1979, which provided for the nationalization of industries in three categories: heavy (i.e., basic) industries, industries of fifty-one individuals or families closely associated with the Shah's regime, and industries whose liabilities exceeded their assets.[24] By late 1983, large industrial establishments (defined as industries employing ten workers or more) owned and managed by the public sector accounted for about 14 percent of all such enterprises (986 units out of a total of 6,142 units), mostly in the basic metals (28 percent), chemical (24 percent), paper (23 percent), and wood (24 percent). Moreover, public industries produced 71 percent of value added, were responsible for some 62 percent of industrial investment, and employed 70 percent (about 432,000) of the work force in all such units.[25] It must be noted that most public industries are among the largest in the nation. Indeed, over 62 percent of public industries employ 100 or more workers whereas only 8 percent employ 19 workers or less. The government's dominance of the sector may be better appreciated if we recall that the large industries account for over 85 percent of the nation's industrial value added.[26]

Significant changes were also introduced in the organization of the sector, as the Ministry of Industries was divided into three ministries (Heavy Industries, Mines and Metals, and Industries), and numerous new offices were created and the old ones demolished or reorganized. The Organization of Nationalized Industries *(sazman-e sanaye'-e melli)*, Foundation of the Oppressed *(bonyad-e mostazafan)*, and Foundation of the Martyrs *(bonyad-e shahid)* are the biggest such new organizations. The Industrial Development and Renovation Organization, which existed prior to the Revolution, was almost completely reorganized. These four organizations together control almost all of the nation's nationalized and large industries.

However, what produced the significant growth rates of 10.5 and 15.6 percent for 1982 and 1983 were not these enormous changes but the significant increases in 1982–83 oil revenues and the consequent expansion of production in large manufacturing industries. In sharp contrast to manufacturing, construction and mines declined significantly and electricity, gas, and water remained stagnant (Figure 3.4). The fact that both oil and most large industrial capacities were under the single ownership and management of the state explains the connection. Moreover, large industrial establishments depended on the world capitalist economy for over 57 percent of their raw materials and 63 percent of their spare parts.[27] Their dependency on foreign exchange was therefore quite profound, about $6 to $7 billion a year.[28] Yet, industries oriented to Iranian consumption produce largely for the domestic market and generate hardly any foreign exchange, a resource for which they rely on the

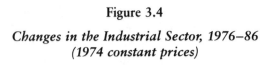

Figure 3.4

*Changes in the Industrial Sector, 1976–86
(1974 constant prices)*

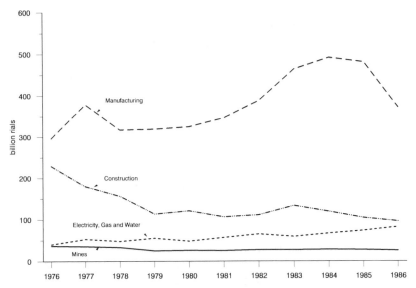

oil sector. Although the war has destroyed many of the industries, its impact on the large establishments may have been positive, given that they have benefited from both the change toward war-related production and the increasing amount of foreign exchange earmarked for the war and defense.[29] Presently (1989), Iran produces a variety of heavy and light ammunition, both defensive and offensive, as a result of which the country's import bill for military equipment has been reduced by some $500 million a year (i.e., about 10 percent) since 1985.[30]

The situation of defense industries in the postrevolutionary period needs some explanation. As may be expected, for security reasons, information on these industries is scanty at best. Although the history of military industry in Iran goes back to the turn of this century, most modern military industries were established in the decade of the 1970s. By the late 1970s, the Royal Armaments Factories in Tehran were manufacturing a wide variety of small arms, including basic infantry rifles and machine guns. Placing emphasis on the air force, the Shah had established Iran Aircraft Industries (IACI) as a joint venture with Northrop in 1970. In 1975, the government bought out Northrop, and signed service contracts with Lockheed and General Electric. By 1977, IACI had a work force of 2,600. A repair facility for U.S.-made missiles also was set up at Shiraz. Iran's sizable automobile assembly industry also had a military component. A joint venture with Bell Helicopter in Esfahan was incomplete by the time of the Revolution in 1978. It was set up (under Iran Helicopter Industries, IHI) not only to train 1,500 pilots and 5,000 mechanics but to also assemble a military transport helicopter. The Shah had also sought, unsuccessfully, to expand Iran's nuclear power generating capacity. In the meantime, the Military Industries Organization (MIO) was set up under the jurisdiction of the War Ministry (Defense Ministry since the Revolution). By the mid-1970s, MIO had become the country's largest importer of machine tools.[31] Also known as Defense Industries Organization, MIO supervised IACI, IHI, and many other military-related industrial establishments.

In the postrevolutionary period, after a short period of inactivity and confusion, military industries continued to extend and expand their production, service, and repair capacities. The impetus came from the war with Iraq, the desire to achieve self-sufficiency, and the international arms embargo. (Helpful also were the fact that the new regime could build upon the existing industries and experience and the willingness of international arms dealers and certain governments to secretly cooperate.) The Islamic Republic's military project was begun by the islamization of the armed forces, the creation of the Revolutionary Guards Corps (RGC), and major administrative changes. The War Ministry was reorganized and renamed the Defense Ministry and the RGC was authorized to establish its own military-industrial operations, most of which competed with those under the Defense Ministry. By 1986, the RGC was reportedly directing some thirty-seven classified R&D and weapon development projects in addition to its cooperative defense efforts with the Ministry of Construction Crusade. Presently (1989), the Islamic Republic's military-related production and service units include, in addition to those under the management of MIO, the IHI, the IACI, and the RGC, some 240 major factories and some 12,000 privately owned workshops. These units are geographically well distributed and employ some 40,000 to 45,000 people, nearly one-third of such employment in Israel, Brazil, or South Africa.[32]

As for production of military machines, the Islamic Republic has concentrated on missiles production as this best serves its military needs and corresponds to its technological capabilities. According to *Jane's Defence Weekly* (23 July 1988), units producing missiles, in-particular surface to surface, number "over a 100," employing "several thousand" employees. The Scud–B, the Oghab (Eagle) I and II, and the indigenously developed IRAN–130 are just a few among many types of missiles produced in the Islamic Republic. The RGC has concentrated mostly on missiles and air power. In addition to creating a significant "missile infrastructure," the Republic has also achieved a level of "adolescence, if not total maturity" in production of light arms, ammunition, mortars, howitzer and artillery barrels, and aircraft parts, produced mostly in the MIO factories.[33] The IHI and IACI continue to provide repair and maintenance expertise and the IACI in particular is now capable of servicing jet fighters (such as the F–5, the F–4, and the F–14), certain transport planes, and aircraft engines. With Iran Helicopter Maintenance and Over-hauling Industries, the organization also services certain types of helicopter engines.

Returning to the discussion on the large manufacturing units and the reason for their relatively better performance, the foreign exchange dependency of these establishments was attractive to the private sector. If the investment itself was not profitable, the oppor-tunity that it provided for access to valuable foreign exchange was very lucrative. In May 1988, for example, the market rate of the U.S. dollar in Iran was over twenty-two times higher than the official rate. Indeed, over the 1979–83 period, the private sector's invest-ment in industries increased 3.3 times as compared with 2.1 times for the public sector.[34] The ratio of private to public investments in housing construction was even higher, 9 to 1, to be specific.[35] It is also common knowledge that many small manufacturing workshops have sprung up and prospered in the postrevolutionary period. In-creased private investment is partly a reflection of the new establish-ment. To avoid government regulations and taxes, around 20,000 such units remained unregistered in 1983 throughout the country, mostly in Tehran.[36] Reportedly, a large number of them, about 15,000, are involved in the production of industrial parts and small consumer items previously imported. The war and the Western trade sanctions against Iran along with certain protectionist policies have particularly benefited these largely informal industries.[37] However, since 1984, the productive informal sector increasingly lost its growth momentum as the economic recession deepened. Thus, it is simply incorrect to assume that under the Islamic Republic only merchants are prospering, although this social group has come to occupy a prominent position among the proprietors in the postrevo-lutionary period, particularly since 1984.[38]

The relatively good performance of manufacturing until 1983 has to be considered in relation to its significant decline in the

1984–87 years (Table 3.1, Figures 3.1 and 3.2). With the decline in foreign exchange earnings beginning in 1984, most nondefense industries were assigned an increasingly smaller share.[39] For example, the annual foreign exchange requirements of the Ministry of Industries, with 7,000 largely medium-size units under its coverage, amount to $5.5 billion. Yet, the ministry received yearly allocations of only 3.8, 2.8, 3.0, and 2.8 billion dollars between 1982 and 1985. Such allocations were much lower for nonmilitary industries, declining from $3.8 billion in 1982 to $0.9 billion in 1986. In sharp contrast, such allocations increased for military-related industries. With the sharp decline in oil prices and introduction of the austerity Plan for New Economic Conditions in 1986, foreign exchange allocated to the nondefense-related large establishments was further curtailed, by as much as 25 percent, leading to a sharp decline of manufacturing industries in that and in the subsequent years. Specifically, the industrial sector declined by 16.4 and 6.3 percent in 1986 and 1987, respectively, which resulted in tremendous contraction of its value added. For example, according to a report by the minister of Plan and Budget, industrial value added fell by 50 percent in 1986 alone.[40]

The industrial sector continues to remain undeveloped and suffers from an unevenly developed structure and dependency on the capitalist world economy. Specifically, the sector accounts for less than 20 percent of value added and is oriented largely toward consumption. In 1981, for example, consumer goods producing industries accounted for 68 percent of the industrial production whereas the share of intermediate and capital goods producing industries were 24 and 8 percent, respectively. By comparison, the corresponding figures for industrialized countries, on average, are 27, 40, and 33 percent.[41] The sector also suffers from various infrastructural, material, managerial, and institutional bottlenecks; shortage of trained and skilled personnel; and an inappropriate technological structure. Although efforts have been made to remove or mitigate such problems, they continue to constrain the attempts to increase the rates of capacity utilization, which remain significantly low. Such rates that were, for example, reported 82 percent for manufacturing and 72 percent for energy production in 1985 (see Table 2.4) have declined to 30 percent in 1988. The role of the private property remains unclear, a definite labor law has not been introduced, and, despite attempts to the contrary, industrial policy remains as eccentric as it was in 1979.[42] In the meantime, the policy of focusing on basic industries has received inadequate support until the end of the war, largely due to the oil-dependent nature of the policy.[43] Beginning with the cease-fire, however, attention again has been shifted to promoting these industries.

Agriculture improved its share of GDP by 51.6 percent, from 9.5 percent in 1976–78 (average per year) to 14.4 percent in 1979–87 (Table 3.1, Figures 3.1 and 3.2). The share figure for 1987 was reported at 17.7 percent.[44] The sector's actual growth rate, however, was a moderate 4 percent a year on the average, slightly higher than the average annual growth rate for the decade preceding the Revolution. This growth rate should be considered against a 3.9 percent population growth rate, among the highest in the world. Agriculture experienced its sharpest postrevolutionary increases in 1981 and 1982 (11.3 and 7.9 percent, respectively) although some of the most fertile lands in provinces of Khuzestan, Kurdestan, Bakhtaran, West Azerbaijan, and Ilam were either occupied by Iraqi forces or were located in war zones. The rapid growth had indeed followed the approval of a new Land Reform Bill by the Revolutionary Council and Ayatollah Khomeini in April 1980, following an intense struggle over the land beginning in the early days of 1979. This struggle may have been responsible for most of the decline in agricultural production during the 1979–80 period.[45] Although opponents of the bill were able to delay its approval by the Parliament until December 1982, the Seven-Person Councils for Land Redistribution continued its work in the rural areas. Before the bill was finally killed by the Council of Guardians in January 1983,[46] the Seven-Person Councils had distributed a total of 185,015 hectares to the poor peasants, of which 150,000 hectares were *movat* (barren land). They also intervened in the cultivation of land left idle by its owners and mediated disputes between landlords and peasants.[47]

The sector's reaction to the Council of Guardians' action was swift and surprisingly negative. Production in 1983 declined to an all time low of −1.6 percent, with agronomy suffering the most (Figure 3.5). Low rainfall was also an important contributing factor. Recall that in 1983 industries and services experienced their highest growth following a noticeable increase in oil revenues in 1982. Agriculture is only loosely connected to the oil sector and has the least dependency among the economic sectors on foreign exchange and international markets. This was why, and despite its low interindustry linkages, the sector's development had received the highest priority, after the war, in the postrevolutionary period particularly following the 1986 sharp decline in oil prices. Although agriculture regained part of its 1983 decline in 1984, for which a 4.1 percent growth rate is reported, it has been unable to replicate the 1981–82 performance except during 1985.

Figure 3.5

Value Added in Agriculture, 1976–85
(1974 constant prices)

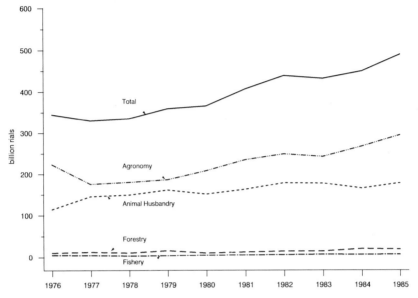

Concerned with the rising demand for food items and increasing rural-to-urban migration, in 1985 the government sent a much revised version of the rejected Land Reform Bill to the Parliament. The bill passed after the "two-third majority vote" rule was introduced but not before substantial changes were made to its major provisions.[48] Accordingly, about 800,000 hectares of the "temporarily cultivated lands" *(arazi-ye kesht-e muvaqat)*, that is, lands seized by the peasants or given to them by the government up to 1980 (1981 in Kurdestan), was sold to the actual cultivators if they had no other means of subsistence and resided in the area. These lands were located mainly in Khuzestan, Kurdestan, Gonbad-e Kavus and Gorgan, and East Azerbaijan. In addition, the new bill gave the government the right to expropriate lands left uncultivated for over a year and sell it to peasants previously working on it. The total number of peasants effected by the bill is estimated at 1 million.[49]

Growth of the sector's 1985 production, by 8.9 percent was, according to Prime Minister Mir Hosain Musavi, in part due to these reforms. However, much of the improvement resulted from the increased rainfall in the southern and western parts of the country and increased cultivation after the expulsion of the Iraqi forces from the occupied lands.[50] The sector has been experiencing a moderate growth since the introduction of the austerity Plan for New Economic Conditions in 1986. The foreign exchange crisis led the government to place the sector high on the priority list, immediately after the war, and before such top priority areas as higher education, health care services, price control, and provision of basic commodities. Nonetheless, agriculture in 1986 grew only at 2.6 percent, not enough to sustain a population growing at about 3.9 percent a year. The 1987 growth figure of 4 percent showed a slight improvement over the year before but not as much as was claimed by the government (Table 3.1). The 1988 growth rate is also projected at 4 percent.[51]

The goal of self-sufficiency in food was also at the root of the Islamic Republic's "agriculture first" policy. The concern and the policy are well indicated by debates in the Parliament and in several policy documents including the original and the revised First Economic, Social, and Cultural Development Plan of the Islamic Republic and the austerity Plan for the New Economic Conditions.[52] Indeed, the government claims to have made agriculture the "axis" of its development policy if only because "the leadership of the religious community wants wheat more than anything else."[53] Assuming that the concern is genuine, one would have expected the performance to have been much better. The import bill for food and nonfood agricultural items is substantial ($4–$5 billion a year, at the minimum); productivity in the sector is extremely low; many rural areas lack most basic socioeconomic and infrastructural services; and agricultural regions suffer from selective migration. The problem seems to lie with the policy.[54] For example, the country still does not have a comprehensive plan or policy for rural development, irrigation systems, soil management, appropriate technology, agricultural infrastructure, investment priorities, training and extension, and credit-price support.[55]

In 1988, one-third of the country's water capacity remained unutilized and, of about 30 to 50 million hectares of arable lands, only 10.1 million were under cultivation (of which only 4.5 million hectares were irrigated).[56] The average size of arable lands per farming household in 1988 was reported at 6.13 hectares. Productivity also remains low, perhaps as low as one-third of what is now considered average in developed nations. Indeed, of the irrigated cultivated land only 87.5 percent is tractor-plowed. As a result, actual agricultural production is only around 12 percent of potential production.[57] The attempted corrective measures have been either limited and eccentric in nature or constrained by enormous domestic and international forces. The work in rural areas by the Ministry of Reconstruction Crusade *(jehad-e sazandegi)* has been beneficial but not sufficiently so to make a significant change in the life of the peasantry or infrastructure of agriculture. The problem with the sector also lies outside it, among others, in the lack of a development strategy and the fact that activities competing with the sector for human and material resources generate substantially more income, resulting in selective migration from rural areas.

In sum, postrevolutionary production is characterized by wide fluctuations, tenacious problems, and largely negative trends. Noticeable changes have also occurred in the sectoral composition of GDP as indicated by decline in the share of oil sector and increase in that of services. As we shall shortly see, these trends also correspond to similar changes in the sectoral employment shifts in the postrevolutionary period. The state's policies have largely failed to cope with the economic decline effectively. However, some of the implemented reformist or pragmatist policies did produce noticeable changes in the structure of the economy. The Republic's expressed and intended goals for the economy were frustrated by a variety of constraining forces. It is clear that some of these factors, including the war and the oil market, were imposed on the middle-class leadership or remained, to a large extend, outside its control. Others, however, were the leadership's own creations, originating from a misguided drive for monopolization of state power or lack of a transparent conception of managing domestic affairs and international relations. As a consequence, much of the Revolution's transforming potentials, including opportunity factors, were wasted. In particular, any sense of national unity disappeared, enthusiasm for cooperation gave way to destructive competition and distrust, and such valuable resources as millions of young volunteers and the newly created grassroots organizations were increasingly drawn into a destructive war. The political narrow-mindedness also led to further alienation of most creative and technocratic forces in secular sectors, leading to a significant and chronic underutilization of the existing capacities.

DOMESTIC EXPENDITURES AND FIXED CAPITAL FORMATION

The crisis of GDP growth and its sectoral distribution in the postrevolutionary period has been closely correlated with largely similar trends in the volume and distribution of domestic gross expenditures (GDE). As indicated in Table 3.2, Figure 3.6, GDE

Table 3.2 Gross Domestic Expenditures, 1976-86 (1974 constant prices)(a)

Year	(1) Gross Domestic Expenditures		(2) Private Consumption Expenditures		(3) Public Consumption Expenditures		(4) Gross Domestic Fixed Capital Formation		(4) as % of (2)+(3)
	Billion Rials	Growth Rate	Percent Share	Growth Rate	Percent Share	Growth Rate	Percent Share	Growth Rate	
1976	3,785.0	18.3	41.4	17.1	22.7	17.3	31.4	35.1	49.0
1977	4,043.3	7.6	45.5	18.3	19.8	-6.4	26.6	-9.0	40.7
1978	3,359.7	-16.9	51.9	-5.1	23.7	-0.2	27.6	-13.6	36.5
1979	3,069.2	-8.6	49.7	-12.6	20.7	-20.1	18.8	-61.2	26.7
1980	2,636.9	-14.1	55.4	-4.3	22.0	-8.8	21.0	-3.8	27.1
1981	2,676.7	1.5	57.8	6.1	22.7	4.6	21.0	1.6	26.1
1982	3,084.1	15.2	53.3	6.1	18.9	-3.8	20.1	9.9	19.7
1983	3,486.1	13.1	51.8	9.9	16.4	-2.0	24.7	39.0	36.2
1984	3,495.0	0.2	52.9	2.4	15.7	-4.2	22.0	-10.5	32.1
1985	3,443.4	-1.5	55.1	4.2	16.7	6.2	18.5	-15.7	25.8
1986	3,150.4	-8.5	55.1	-8.5	15.2	16.3	14.8	-27.1	21.0
Annual Average Figures									
1976–78	3,720.3	3.0	46.3	10.1	22.1	3.6	28.5	4.2	42.1
1979–86	3,130.2	-0.3	53.9	0.4	18.5	1.5	20.1	-8.5	26.8
Percent Change 1976–78/1979–86	-15.9	-110.0	16.4	-96.0	-16.3	-58.3	-29.5	-302.4	-36.3

Sources and Notes:
Calculated on the basis of Table 5 (p. 111), in *Gozaresh* (1363), vol. 1; *Salnameh* (1365), p. 812, and (1366), p. 454; and *Fashnameh* (1365), p. 26 (Table 4–1).

(a) Note that percent shares do not add up to 100 because changes in inventories, net exports of goods and services, and statistical errors are not accounted for in the calculations. For details on these items see the sources cited earlier.

Figure 3.6

Gross Domestic Expenditures, 1976–86
(1974 constant prices)

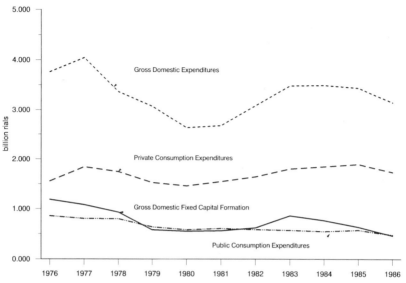

has been fluctuating since 1976, registering its sharpest increases in 1976, 1982, and 1983, and its steepest decrease during the 1978–80 period and then in 1986. All in all, the indicator had declined drastically from its prerevolutionary level. The average annual GDE for the 1979–86 period indicates a 15.9 percent decline (at fixed 1974 prices) when compared to the corresponding figure for the 1976–78 period.

The declining trend began with the prerevolutionary recession starting in 1976 and reached its highest rate in 1978 with the beginning of the revolutionary movement and the subsequent decline in oil production. The start of the war in 1980 led to the indicator's further decline in this year. GDE picked up in 1981 as oil revenue increased and reached its best performance in 1982 and 1983, when it hit its postrevolutionary peak. The growth trend, however, stopped in 1984 with the decline in oil prices and a stalemate on the war front. Consequently, GDE grew only by 0.2 percent in 1984 and declined by 1.5 percent and 8.5 percent in 1985 and 1986, respectively. Overall the indicator registered an annual growth rate of −0.3 percent for the 1979–86 period.

It is doubtful if the average annual growth rate for the period 1986–87 has been any better given the tenacious recession that began in 1984, the sharp decline in oil revenue in 1986, and the subsequent sharp cuts in domestic public expenditures.

Distribution of GDE into its main components has been unfavorable, too, for growth of production and, consequently, economic development. In absolute terms, consumption and investment expenditures have both declined in the postrevolutionary period, reflecting decline in the nation's production and income generating capability. However, the drop in gross domestic fixed capital formation (GDFCF) has been disproportionately higher, leading to a higher share of GDE going to consumption and largely nonproductive savings. In 1985, for example, consumption accounted for almost 71.8 percent of GDE as compared to 18.5 percent for investment; the corresponding figures for 1976 were 64 and 31 percent, respectively (Table 3.2)—per capita GDFCF declined from 293,000 rials in 1977 to about 9,400 rials in 1986 (in constant prices) and the trend continues. Decline in the share of public consumption expenditures (PUCE) in the postrevolutionary years have been more than offset by an increase in the share of private consumption expenditures (PCE).

The share of public ownership in GDFCF also declined by 10.7 percent over the 1979–85 period as compared to the 1971–77 years. The corresponding figures for the private sector indicates a 13.6 percent increase (Table 3.3). Investment in residential construction was the most responsible for the shift.[58] The private sector has also outinvested the public sector in construction as a whole and in machinery in the postrevolutionary period (Table 3.4), but the private sector's investments went mostly to construction (largely residential),

Table 3.3   Gross Domestic Fixed Capital Formation, 1971–77 and 1979 –85 (percent shares, 1974 constant prices)

	1971–77	1979–85	Percent Change
Public	56	50	−10.7
Private	44	50	13.6
Construction	63	64	1.6
Machinery	37	36	−2.7
Agriculture, Manufacturing, and Mining	58	59	1.7
Oil and Gas	11	5	−54.5
Services	31	36	16.1

Sources:
Gozaresh (1363), vol. 1, pp. 46–47; and (1365), vol. 1, p. 18.

Table 3.4   GDFCF in Construction and Machinery (public and private),
1982–86 (billion rials, 1974 constant prices)

	1982	1983	1984	1985	1986	1983	1984	1985	1986
						Growth Rate from Preceding Year			
Construction	402.8	485.5	416.9	364.6	322.7	20.5	−14.3	−12.5	−11.5
Private	186.7	266.5	254.3	236.4	193.4	42.7	−4.6	−7.0	−18.2
Public	216.1	219.0	162.6	128.2	129.3	−1.3	−25.8	−21.2	0.9
Machinery	215.7	374.1	352.8	273.8	142.5	73.4	−5.7	−22.4	−48.5
Private	53.1	197.2	204.7	141.3	52.2	271.4	3.8	−31.0	−63.1
Public	162.6	176.9	148.1	132.5	90.3	8.8	−16.3	−10.5	−31.8

Sources:
Faslnameh (1365), p. 26; and *Salnameh* (1365), p. 816; and (1966), p. 458.

as opposed to machinery, which has also suffered from reduction in the public sector's development budget. The share of machinery in GDFCF declined from about 46 percent in 1975 to about 21 percent in 1986. With the beginning of the recession in 1984, both sectors reduced their investment in construction and machinery. Such cuts were particularly sizable in the private sector (Table 3.4). In the absence of significant public investment the private sector was unwilling to undertake major investment projects (this indeed indicates that public investment has a "crowding in" effect on private investment rather than a "crowding out" effect as assumed by conventional economics). As a consequence, the nation's productive capacities have not increased much in the postrevolutionary period.

Sectoral shares in GDFCF and their changing patterns are given in tables 3.3, and 3.5, and figures 3.7, and 3.8. Agriculture has constantly received the lowest share, ranging from 4.3 percent in 1977 to 6.7 percent in 1986, which is an increasing trend. Oil and gas, on the other hand, have suffered from significant declines in their already low share in GDFCF. From 16.2 percent in 1976, their share dropped to 6.0 percent in 1986. The sector's share in GDFCF declined from 11 percent per year over the 1971–77 period to a 5 percent during the 1979–85 years, indicating a 54.5 percent decline between the two periods. Petroleum regions were located in the war zones and gas production remained dormant until 1989 when a new contract was signed with the Soviet Union. The share of services has always been appreciably large and increasing, except for the first two years of the postrevolutionary period, when sentiments against the sector ran quite high. The sector improved its share from 29.1 percent in 1976 to 31.1. percent in 1985. Its total gain between the two periods of 1971–77 and 1979–85 was some 16.1 percent. Most

Table 3.5   Sectoral GDFCF, 1976–86 (percent of total, 1974 constant prices)

	1976	1977	1978	1979	1980	1981	1982	1983	1984	1985	1986
GDFCF (total)	100.0	100.0	100.0	100.0	100.0	100.0	100.0	100.0	100.0	100.0	100.0
Sectoral Share											
Agriculture	5.0	4.3	4.0	4.9	4.4	6.2	5.6	7.2	7.1	7.2	6.7
Oil and Gas	16.2	8.0	10.0	5.9	4.9	5.4	7.2	4.6	3.8	3.3	6.0
Industries	49.7	54.8	49.4	56.7	59.7	49.9	51.6	48.7	50.5	50.1	56.1
Manufacturing and Mining	28.5	28.3	22.6	19.1	14.7	17.3	18.0	19.0	21.2	14.8	14.1
Water and Electricity	18.7	24.3	19.1	8.8	9.4	12.6	13.9	12.2	9.9	8.4	8.0
Construction	52.8	47.3	58.4	72.1	75.8	70.2	68.1	68.8	69.0	76.8	77.9
Residential	90.3	89.1	91.9	89.5	88.0	90.5	91.0	94.5	93.0	94.8	94.1
Nonresidential	9.7	10.9	8.1	10.5	12.0	9.5	9.0	5.5	6.3	5.2	5.9
Services	29.1	32.9	36.6	32.5	31.0	38.5	35.6	39.5	38.7	39.4	31.1
Transportation	52.3	47.0	60.7	43.6	45.7	52.1	57.2	63.7	64.9	66.1	53.8
Communication	10.6	9.2	10.7	4.7	4.6	5.0	10.3	6.0	6.9	5.8	6.5
Others	37.2	43.9	70.3	51.7	49.7	42.9	32.5	30.4	28.2	28.1	39.7

Sources:
Salnameh (1360), p. 749; (1361), p. 785; (1362), p. 706; (1363), p. 785; (1365), pp. 815, 817; and (1366), p. 457.

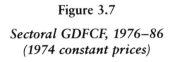

Figure 3.7

Sectoral GDFCF, 1976–86
(1974 constant prices)

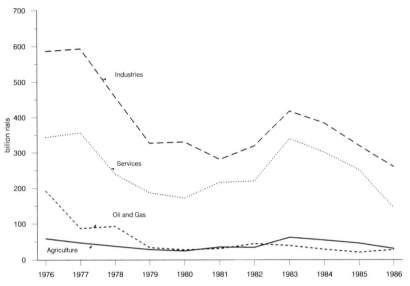

investments in services are concentrated in transportation, which has also enjoyed the most improvement in its share of postrevolutionary GDFCF perhaps because of rural road construction in early postrevolutionary years and later war-related road construction. However, most of the GDFCF belonged to heavy industries, both before and after the Revolution. In the immediate postrevolutionary years, the sector benefited from the proindustry stand of the nation; but with declining oil revenue, the war, and an expanding dominance of the bazaar over the economy, industries began to loose their privileged position to services. In the absence of any significant incentive policy for industrial investment, this trend worsened overtime. Thus, from 49.7 percent in 1976, the sector's share increased to 59.7 percent in 1980 and then dropped to 50.1 percent in 1985. The service sector, on the other hand, improved its share from 29.1 percent in 1976 to 31 percent in 1980 and to 39.4 percent in 1985. Except for residential construction, mostly private housing in the first few years of the Revolution, the rest of the industrial subsectors suffered from a reduction in their GDFCF. The worst hit were water and electricity, followed by mining and non-residential construction. Whereas over the 1979–86 period, credits from specialized banks for manufacturing and mining declined by about 80 percent, those for residential construction increased by about 450 percent. The private sector produces some 95 percent of housing units in the country and residential construction was responsible for about 62 percent of investment in construction. The corresponding figure for 1976 was about 39 percent. This low share of non-residential construction investment is indicative of a low public investment in infrastructures in the postrevolutionary period.

Comparable statistics beyond 1986 are not readily available. Data for 1986 indicate that the government's payments for the fixed investment credits *(hazineha-ye omrani)* declined by 34.2 percent relative to the figure for 1983 (from 1,148.6 to 756 billion rials), while operating expenditures experienced only a 4.4 percent decline over the same period (from 2,523.7 to 2,411.4 billion rials). The amount of investment credits going to "economic affairs" and "social affairs" also declined rather sharply, by 31.4 and 30.6 percent over the 1983–85 years.[59] With the exception of agriculture, the amount of investment credit going to various economic sectors also declined

Figure 3.8

Industrial GDFCF, 1976–86
(1974 constant prices)

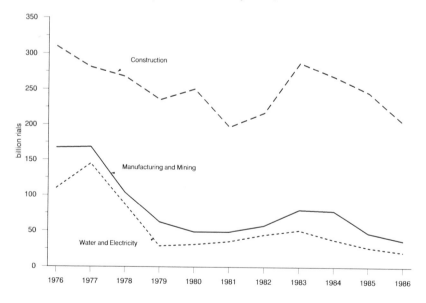

appreciably after 1983. For example, between 1983 and 1984 invest-ment credits going to industries, mines, and non-residential con-struction, housing, and urban development declined by 33.6, 18.9, and 29.7 percent, respectively, while agriculture and natural re-sources and water resources experienced the modest credit growth rates of 4 and 1.7 percent.[60]

The post-1984 economic crisis led to an even larger absolute de-cline in the amount of GDFCF (public and private) going to various economic sectors. Public investment credits to industries and mines, for example, were 43.9 and 45.9 percent less in 1985 compared to the 1983 figures.[61] Indeed, the austerity Plan for New Economic Conditions introduced in 1986 allowed for significant new invest-ments only under exceptional circumstances and where they would help increase utilization of the existing capacity. A similar idea had already been incorporated in the revised first plan that was never implemented.[62] However, trends in sectoral shares in investment credits seem largely to have remained unchanged: services have con-tinued improving their shares at the expense of industries, while ag-riculture has been barely able to maintain its share.

Decline in postrevolutionary GDFCF was due to a number of domestic and international factors which combined to produce what is called a "saving-investment gap." The declining oil revenue was quite damaging, as most investment depended on foreign currency to pay for capital goods imports. Even more devastating was the war, which, as we have explained, destroyed a significant portion of the existing capital stocks, reduced production and became a burden on the general budget and an obstacle to the use of the existing capac-ities. Private capital flight also contributed to a reduced domestic savings. The newly created revolutionary institutions and the in-creased public responsibility toward the poor after the Revolution helped increase public spending and the country's propensity to con-sume. Equally devastating was the lower profit rates and longer turnover times in the productive sectors as compared to services which benefited from disproportionately high mercantile margins. Consequently, the increased savings of a tiny minority, as a result of increased income concentration, did not go to productive investment as stipulated in conventional economic literature. Indeed, not only did inequality not lead to efficiency as some economists in the gov-ernment had expected, but it also led instead to a vicious circle of increased inefficiency and inequity. Specifically, the productive sec-tors were increasingly drained of their scarce savings as these were transferred abroad or put into the more lucrative investments in trade and business services. The unsettled political environment and lack of any degree of effective public control also encouraged this trend. The appreciable decline in real wages and business taxes did not help reverse the trend. The government's policies seemed also to have exacerbated the trends toward less funds for GDFCF. In particular, by making the war a top priority and shifting an increasing amount of resources from development to current expenditures, the government discouraged new investment in both the public and the private sectors. The trends in distribution of GDFCF among various economic sectors has been another factor in an increased share of less productive investments in the postrevolutionary period, a distortion for which the government's priority policy and lack of discipline was partly responsible.

A major consequence of the declining GDFCF has been a rather significant drop in the nation's economic productivity which may not be remedied in the medium-term given the huge labor surplus and the need for generation of millions of jobs. For example, the ratio of investments to added production was 21 to 1 (3170.5 to 150.9 billion rials) over the 1979–82 period as compared to 2.9 (4123.3 to 1416.0 billion rials) during the 1973–77 years.[63] Although the situation was somewhat rectified in the following years, it still remains unacceptable. According to a recent report, "about 317,0500 million rials were invested domestically in the period between 21 March 1979 to 21 March 1988, but the production increment was only in the amount of 150,900 million rials."[64] This gives an extremely low incremental capital-output ratio (0.048) and underscores the need for effective economic planning to increase utilization rate. The postrevolutionary GDFCF also had little effect in changing the highly imbalanced dualistic structure of the country's production technology that continues to suffer from the lack of a clear policy, particularly concerning issues of transfer, adaptation, and development. Clearly, the situation calls for increased public intervention and investment, particularly in R&D, infrastructures and industries. However, the success of such intervention and investment policy would depend on how efficiently it is implemented. This is why effective investment planning has become indispensable to the country. To redirect investment toward industries, the government must also introduce incentives for the private sector and implement it with vigor and rigid discipline. Such a policy should incorporate specific measures for increasing the share of industrial profit in the surplus pie. Also needed are strong tax efforts and reduction in current public expenditures to boost public savings and reduce the public sector's borrowing requirements (PSBR).

THE GENERAL BUDGETS AND BUDGET DEFICIT

In the absence of national planning, annual budgets have functioned as the primary public tools for management, as well as transformation of the postrevolutionary economy. The chaotic revolutionary situation, expansion of the public sector as a result of economic nationalization, the war with Iraq, and dependency on the precarious oil markets have all increased the importance of budgeting in the Islamic Republic. Thus, the absolute size of the postrevolutionary general budget, in current prices, has constantly increased, particularly in the years following the outbreak of the war. In constant prices and relative to the size of the country's GDP, however, the general budget indicates significant decline. Specifically, the amount of the general budget (i.e., public expenditures in current prices) decreased from about 43.2 percent of GDP (at current prices) in 1977 to about 32.5 percent of the indicator in 1979, then to 22.4 percent of GDP in 1985. Moreover, the 1986 per capita budget for current and development expenditures in constant prices was almost equal to the figures for 1971.[65] In other words, the role of the government in economic management, measured in constant prices, has indeed declined given the added responsibilities of the public sector in the postrevolutionary period. Note, however, that the general budget is only part of the total national budget, which also consists of the state-owned companies' budgets. In the postrevolutionary years, this latter budget has also been expanding in absolute and nominal terms; it is now larger than the general budget. Yet, through the instrumentality of the general budget the state sets its priorities and controls the direction of the socioeconomic system.

A careful reading of the ten annual budgets implemented under the Islamic Republic will indicate significant changes in priorities of the state; such changes have been largely in the direction of more unproductive expenditures and provision of basic needs items.[66] Initially, the state favored a budget less dependent on oil and more on taxes. The public incomes were to be spent largely on such activities as agriculture, rural development, producers goods industries, electricity, and transportation. The least developed provinces, the working people, and small-scale productive operations were to receive more assistance from the state. These and similar policies were to be implemented to help realize the goals of economic self-reliance, restructuring of the consumption patterns, and social justice. But before much could be achieved in these areas, struggles over political and social question of the Revolution began, the war erupted, and oil revenues declined. These led to fiscal and monetary constraints, increased bottlenecks, and forced the state to change its priorities and policies in favor of more allocation for the war and basic needs largely at the expense of development funds.[67]

Agriculture and basic needs items continued to receive support but major changes were gradually introduced in other high priority areas, particularly beginning in 1984. The 1986 sharp decline in oil revenues set the stage for even more dramatic changes under the disguise of the austerity Plan for the New Economic Conditions. The idea of economic growth was shelved for the time being and attention focused on system maintenance, maximum savings in foreign exchanges and their transfer to the defense sector, and tapping new sources of foreign exchange earnings. The war budget was further enlarged, imports were reduced except for military supplies and basic needs, incentives were announced to expand the nonoil exports, many large-scale industries were reoriented toward defense production, and initiation of new projects was not allowed except where nationally indispensable; for example, for generation of new jobs. Instead, emphasis was placed on the completion of the incomplete projects and full utilization of the existing capacities by means of bottleneck-removing investments. Agriculture, higher education, and research and development in defense also received added attention, and disciplinary measures were introduced to fight inflation and corruption.[68]

Thus, it is not at all surprising that the growth of the general budget should be led by a corresponding significant increase in current or operating public expenditures including those of the war. In 1977, for example, current expenditures accounted for about 63 percent of the total public expenditures, the remaining 37 percent going to development funds. With the intensification of the revolutionary movements in 1978, the Shah tried to purchase loyalty from the public sector employees by increasing wages, a decision that resulted in a major shift in the structure of the general budget. Thus, current expenditures rose to 70 percent, while development expenditures dropped to 30 percent of the total budget. With the exception of the 1982–83 period, the trend toward increasing current expenditures has continued in the postrevolutionary years and was exacerbated with the beginning of the war in 1980 (table 3.6). Indeed, "the war expenditures rose from 18 percent of the general budget in 1359 [1980] . . . to 32 percent in 1365 [1986] and 34 percent in this year's [1987] budget bill," reported the minister of Plan and Budget. "These figures," he asserted, "are only a portion of the actual war expenditures as other resources of executive bodies [were] also deployed for requirements of the fronts, not stated in any official fig-

Table 3.6 General Budgets: Major Components, 1976–88 (billion rials, current prices)(a)

| | Actual Figures | | | | | | | | | | | Approved Figures | Estimated Figures |
	1976	1977	1978	1979	1980	1981	1982	1983	1984	1985	1986	1987	1988
Public Incomes (br)	1743.9	2126.7	1699.3	1791.8	1348.7	1702.9	2391.7	2600.2	2645.2	2692.0	1782.0	2626.0	2727.0
Taxes (%)	19.7	20.9	27.4	20.6	25.2	32.5	25.7	30.6	34.3	38.4	57.5	43.4	42.7
Oil and Gas (%)	76.2	74.8	59.6	68.1	65.9	55.1	65.4	61.0	48.5	44.2	23.4	32.6	30.9
Others (%)(b)	4.1	4.3	13.0	11.3	8.9	12.4	8.9	8.4	17.2	17.4	19.1	24.0	26.4
Public Expenditures (br)	1913.7	2492.2	2207.8	2061.0	2251.8	2707.1	3167.4	3672.3	3377.8	3351.0	3167.0	3971.0	3979.0
Current (%)	69.1	62.8	70.2	74.6	74.8	75.1	71.1	68.7	73.9	77.9	76.9	82.3	79.3
War (%)(c)	0.0	0.0	0.0	0.0	0.0	18.7	17.7	21.8	17.8	20.1	18.9	21.4	17.4
Development (%)	30.9	37.2	29.8	25.4	25.2	24.9	28.9	31.3	26.1	22.1	23.1	17.7	20.7
War (%)(d)	0.0	0.0	0.0	0.0	0.0	0.0	7.7	7.9	6.8	6.7	3.6	13.9	N/A
Budget Deficit (br)	169.8	365.5	508.5	269.2	903.1	1004.2	775.7	1072.1	732.6	659.0	1385.0	1345.0	1252.0
Domestic Loans (%)	0.0	92.0	49.0	99.0	76.0	78.0	73.0	65.0	51.0	84.0	93.0	96.0	91.0
Foreign Loans (%)	15.0	8.0	1.0	1.0	0.0	0.0	0.0	0.0	0.0	0.0	0.0	0.0	0.0
Others (%)(e)	85.0	—	50.0	0.0	24.0	22.0	27.0	35.0	49.0	16.0	7.0	4.0	9.0

Sources and Notes:
Compiled and calculated on the basis of *Gozaresh* (1363), vol. 1, pp. 118–119, vol. 2, Chapter 4, pp. 1–19; *Salnameh* (1363), p. 762; *Taraznameh*, various issues (1355–63); *Tabavvulat*, pp. 606–607; *Economic Bulletin* 6, no. 20 (26 March 1987), p. 4, no. 35 (15 September 1987), p. 8, no 11 (17 March 1987); no 19 (19 May 1987); *Kayhan-e Hava'i* (19 Esfand 1366), p. 24; and *Salnameh* (1365), p. 785.

(a) Note that discrepancies exist among figures reported by the various sources listed in the table. I have used figures more frequently cited or reported in the most recent publications. In all cases, government sources were preferred over nonofficial statistics.

(b) Includes income from government's monopolies and public ownership; incomes from public services and sales of goods; insurance premiums, receipts from assistance, and transfer and miscellaneous incomes; and profit and interest on investments abroad.

(c) Operating expenditures of the war as percent of total operating (current) expenditures. Note that the figures do not reflect total expenditures of the war.

(d) Reconstruction expenditures as percent of total development expenditures. Note that the figures do not reflect total reconstruction expenditures.

(e) Includes forwarding from previous years.

ures or statistics."[69] The war expenditures continued to rise and in 1987, according to Prime Minister Musavi, they accounted for 41 percent of the general budget and 52 percent of the government's operating expenditures. He further indicated that certain development expenditures were also spent in war-related projects and that "hundreds" of war- and defense-related research projects were financed in the universities.[70]

The war was initially funded out of operating expenditures, but as the costs of its continuation increased, a growing amount had to be paid out of development funds. This shift became particularly indispensable as, along with the war and domestic political struggles, the newly created revolutionary institutions, including several foundations, military and paramilitary organizations, courts, and committees, expanded and became an added burden on the operating budget. "Whereas they received 20,000 million rials in 1359 [1980], some 230,000 million rials [were] appropriated for revolutionary institutions in the 1366 [1987] budget bill," reported the minister of Plan and Budget at the open session of the Parliament investigating the 1988 budget bill.[71] In the meantime, the government had to subsidize costs of basic needs items, particularly food, to mitigate the impact of rising prices on the declining real income of the poor. In 1986, expenditures on food subsidies accounted for about 5 percent of the budget and were 10 percent higher than the figure for the preceding year. As a consequence of all these and other changes, by the end of 1987, the share of current expenditures rose to 82 percent of the general budget, while that of development expenditures declined to 18 percent, an extremely unhealthy budgetary allocation.[72]

Along with the increase in public expenditures, state income also increased (with the exception of 1986) in the postrevolutionary period. It increased by about 50 percent between 1979 and 1985 (Table 3.6). It rose (in current prices) from 54 percent of GDP (at 1974 fixed prices) in 1977 to over 77 percent of the indicator in 1984. Only part of this increase can be attributed to a decline in the GDP. Much of the growth came from increases in taxes. The share of oil revenues in public incomes declined in the postrevolutionary period. Indeed, between 1976 and 1985, tax incomes increased by 95 percent whereas oil incomes declined by 42 percent. Tax incomes, which accounted for about 19 percent of total government income (average per year) over the 1974–78 period, jumped to 54 percent in 1986 and was expected to increase to 65 percent in 1987 and 1988.[73] Incomes from nonoil, nontax sources increased, from 4 percent of total public income in 1976 to 19 percent of the indicator in 1986 (Table 3.6). The tax structure also moved in the direction of more indirect taxation (Table 3.7). In 1976, for example, of all taxes 55 percent came from direct taxes and 45 percent from indirect taxes. In 1984, the reverse was the case.[74] In the succeeding years, however, the share of indirect taxes declined somewhat (Table 3.7). Indirect taxes hurt poorer consumers the most, many of whom faced declining real incomes. Of the direct taxes, taxes on private companies, occupations, and wealth remained largely underpaid, whereas taxes on wages increased appreciably, from 55 percent of income taxes in 1976 to 69 percent of that indicator in 1984 (Table 3.8).[75] Since the sharp drop in oil income in 1986, the government made successful attempts to collect more direct taxes. During the first nine months of 1986, for example, taxes on occupations and real estate grew by 88.4 and 36.5 percent, respectively, whereas indirect taxes dropped by 3 percent. The prime minister cited these changes as "indications of progress toward justice in taxation,"[76] The improvement in the tax structure was even more significant in 1987. For example, the ratio of taxes on occupations to taxes on wages and salaries increased to 91.4 percent in the first eight months of 1987 from about 56 percent in the previous years; the trend was expected to continue

Table 3.7   Structure of Taxes, 1976–87 (billion rials, current prices)

Year	TT(br)(a)	Direct Taxes As % of TT	Direct Taxes Growth Rate	Indirect Taxes As % of TT	Indirect Taxes Growth Rate	Direct Taxes as % of Indirect Taxes	TT as % of current price GDP
1976	342.9	54.8	23.6	45.2	30.4	121.2	7.5
1977	443.6	51.9	22.6	48.1	37.5	107.9	7.7
1978	465.9	57.8	17.0	42.4	−7.9	137.0	8.7
1979	368.3	61.9	−15.4	38.1	−28.6	162.5	5.8
1980	340.4	38.0	−43.4	62.0	50.6	61.3	5.0
1981	554.1	58.1	149.1	41.9	9.9	138.7	6.7
1982	613.9	48.1	−8.3	51.9	37.2	92.7	5.8
1983	796.5	41.7	12.4	58.3	45.9	71.5	5.9
1984	908.2	44.6	21.9	55.4	8.4	80.5	6.2
1985	1033.7	51.0	12.5	49.0	−11.6	104.1	6.9
1986	1024.5	56.6	11.0	43.4	11.4	130.4	6.5
1987(c)	984.5	56.1	−0.9	43.9	1.2	127.6	—

Sources and Notes:
Gozaresh (1363), vol. 2, ch. 5, p. 8 and (1365), ch. 6, p. 3; and *Taraznameh* (1363), p. 158; and *Salnameh* (1365), p. 809.

(a) TT: Total Taxes

(b) Approved figures.

Table 3.8 Structure of Direct and Indirect Taxes, 1976–87 (billion rials, current prices)

	1976	1977	1978	1979	1980	1981	1982	1983	1984	1985	1986	1987(a)
Direct Taxes	187.8	230.3	269.5	228.1	129.2	321.9	295.5	333.0	406.0	531.5	579.8	552.0
Companies Tax	128.9	160.2	200.1	143.0	46.0	227.6	173.9	208.7	258.3	358.7	373.5	303.6
Income Tax	47.9	57.5	58.4	72.3	65.9	78.3	96.8	90.8	106.4	136.9	136.5	199.6
Wages	26.2	39.7	44.3	60.0	51.6	55.7	65.1	59.0	73.2	87.0	93.2	70.0
Occupations	14.2	11.2	8.7	7.9	9.0	16.9	21.5	22.1	24.6	36.4	54.8	100.0
Others	7.5	6.6	5.4	4.4	5.3	5.7	10.2	9.7	8.6	13.5	15.5	29.6
Wealth Tax	11.0	12.6	11.0	12.8	17.3	16.0	24.8	33.5	41.3	35.9	42.8	48.8
Indirect Taxes	155.1	213.3	196.4	140.2	211.2	232.2	318.4	464.6	494.0	504.2	444.7	432.5
Imports Tax	122.6	169.2	143.7	100.9	161.3	169.7	217.5	346.3	345.7	273.9	224.7	204.8
Sales and Consumption Taxes	32.5	44.1	52.7	39.3	49.9	62.5	100.9	118.3	148.3	230.3	220.0	227.7

Sources and Notes:
Tahavvulat, pp. 608–609; *Gozaresh* (1365), vol. 2, Chapter 6, p. 9; and *Qanoun-e Budgeh-e Sal-e 1367 Kol-e Keshvar* [The 1988 Budget Law of Iran] (Tehran: Parliament, 18 Esfand 1366).

(a) Approved figures.

in 1988.[77] Nevertheless, the existing trends depicted in figure 3.9 are not encouraging. For example, the personal income tax has been transformed into a levey mainly on workers and civil servants, the majority of whom face dire economic conditions.

Despite the growth trend, public incomes are insufficient to meet the rising expenditures, and the state's attempts to further increase its income have not met with much success.[78] There are a number of reasons for the development of this "fiscal gap". The declining oil revenues have been the primary contributing factor. The decline has resulted from a combination of influences including the government's initial policy of reducing reliance on oil, the war and the consequent decline in oil production and exports, the sharp drops in spot prices in 1986, and the decline in the value of the U.S. dollar in recent years. The state's inability to collect taxes owed by the private sector, services in particular, is another major reason for the relative decline of state revenues. Indeed, according to an inside account, between September 1980 and the end of 1986, about 7,000 billion rials in taxes have remained uncollected from the superrich (those with 3 million plus rials monthly incomes) in the nonpublic services sector.[79]

Figure 3.9

Structure of Public Tax Income, 1976–87
current prices)

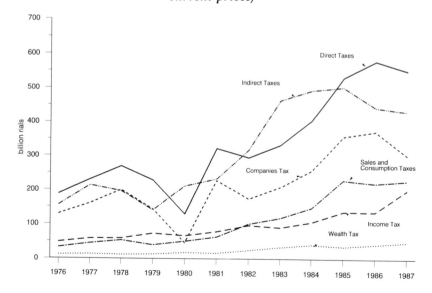

In 1980, the state collected taxes amounting to 8.7 percent of the gross national income. The corresponding figure for 1986 was only 5 percent.[80] "The unpaid taxes from the astronomical profits made under war conditions," in the prime minister's words, are only part of the problem with tax collection.[81] Tax revenues remained constrained because of the drop in oil revenues, which resulted in reduced imports, capacity utilization and production and, thus, reduced taxes on imports and value added. Additionally, the tax administration in Iran kept 5 to 6 million files in a country with 10 million households of which around 60 to 70 percent are estimated to live below the poverty line. It is clear that such a tax system is totally inefficient and unequal. To increase the system's efficiency and equity, perhaps no more than 500,000 files should be kept and the rest destroyed altogether.[82] This would allow better targeting of the superrich for tax collection and would relieve the burden of the middle- and lower-class taxpayers. The tax administration is also in need of radical legal reforms to become more progressive and mitigate the present excessive favoritism and corruption.

The gap between growing public expenditure and constrained income was further exacerbated by the surprisingly constant underestimation of expenditures and overestimation of incomes by the government budget makers. To take an extreme example, in 1986 only 50 percent of the income forecasted was realized. The situation was even worse concerning the foreign exchange earnings for the year: forecasted at $15 billion, the actual figure turned out to be only $5.8 billion. On the other hand, the year's foreign exchange needs for defense, estimated at $2.3 billion, turned out to be "much higher," reported the prime minister.[83] This only proved that oil income was not a policy variable in domestic economic calculations and that the budget's foreign exchanges requirements may not be predicated upon the sale of oil. Aside from the dependency of public income on international oil markets, the forecasting problem was also rooted in factional politics and unexpected movements in the domestic economy. Deeply concerned and engaged with the war, the government planners seemed to have also lost touch with the trends in the capitalist world economy, particularly the sweeping restructuring processes that were (and are) underway in oil supply and demand. Equally unproductive was the reactive behavior of the government vis-à-vis changes in international oil markets.

The chronic imbalance between incomes and expenditures resulted in a tenacious and rising budget deficit (Figure 3.10). This phenomenon was not peculiar to the postrevolutionary period. Indeed, from 1976 to 1978, the budget deficit rose continuously,

Figure 3.10

Main Components of the General Budgets, 1976–88
(current prices)

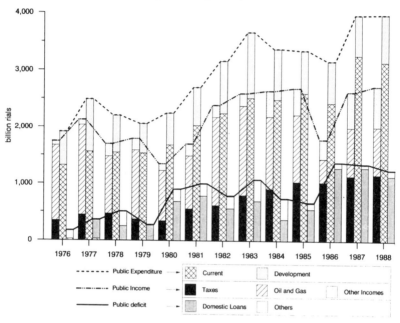

reaching 509 billion rials in the latter year (Table 3.6). In the first year of the Revolution, 1979, the government was able to reduce the deficit by almost 47 percent. With the start of the war and the gradual enlargement of the newly created revolutionary institutions, the budget deficit grew again, reaching 1,004 billion rials in 1981. From this date to 1985, the budget deficit remained high but under control. Beginning in 1986, however, the situation increasingly worsened and became cause for serious concern within the leadership. The estimated deficit figure for the 1988 budget was 1,252 billion rials, but the opposition in the Parliament charged that the figure was an underestimation and that the real figure would be in the area of 2,000 billion rials.[84] This was equivalent to about 73 percent of the 1988 general budget and 2.4 times larger than the estimated oil income for the year.

Yet, the most serious problem concerning the budget deficit was not its huge size but its financing by loans from domestic banks and the resulting increases in the domestic public debt/GNP and the PSBR/GNP ratios, money supply, and liquidity (Table 3.6). The public debt to the banking system increased from 333.3 billion rials in

1979 to 981.3 billion rials in 1983.[85] By the end of 1988, such loans had exceeded 3,000 billion rials. Much of the burden was shifted to the Central Bank that became a virtual appendage to the government with little or no autonomy in managing the country's money markets. The bank's share in payments to the state increased from 28 percent in 1979 to 71.5 percent in 1983 to over 85 percent in the most recent years. As a consequence, the money supply and liquidity rose from 2,203 and 4,508 billion rials in 1979 to 4,558 and 7,967 billion rials in 1984 and then to 5,811 and 10,723 billion in 1986.[86] In 1986, liquidity grew by 15 percent and the government blamed the interest-free Islamic financial institutions (i.e., the IFLFs) for the increase.[87] The inflationary pressure of these increases on the economy was enormous particularly given that the bank credits were used to finance current expenditures. Although such spending increases aggregate demand, it hardly stimulates aggregate supply. The resulting demand-pull inflation became a constant feature of the postrevolutionary economy.

Finally, there are the misconceptions concerning the size and structure of the general budget. According to a senior economic expert at the Ministry of Plan and Budget, "wrong budgetary conceptions have become fixed in our minds and are now part of our cultural conceptions."[88] Complaints about the increasing size of the general budget and budget deficit are very common in parliamentary debates; current expenditures are considered a drain on the economy whereas development funds are defined in very positive terms, and public income is given primacy over public expenditure. Yet, in constant prices, the 1986 budget was hardly larger than the one for 1976; thus, the country may not benefit from a balanced budget, for development funds could end up in wasteful projects and the income sources (oil and taxes) have always proven to be the least reliable. What is needed is a complete change of attitude toward the general budget, so that it could be reevaluated in the light of new conceptions. For example, expansion of the general budget in real terms may indeed be the solution to the decreasing inability of the state to manage the unplanned economy where an enormous amount of problems remain outside the influence of the market forces; where current expenditures, if targeted and economized, could prove more beneficial than money spent on poorly conceived development investments. It may also be more beneficial to exclude the unreliable oil income from the list of policy variables and rely only peripherally on income taxes. Instead, the general budget may stand on a firmer base if it is largely founded on a sound choice of targeted expenditures, both operating and developmental.

INFLATION AND ANTIINFLATIONARY MEASURES

The upward movement of prices that began in the prerevolutionary years continued into the postrevolutionary period. The rate of demand-pull inflation stood at 25.1 percent in 1977. With the beginning of the war in 1980 and the subsequent decline in production and oil revenue, prices jumped by over 23 percent. The subsequent economic sanctions imposed by the United States following the hostage episode further exacerbated the cost-push inflation as it made imported industrial inputs and consumer commodities scarce and more costly. In the absence of any significant price control measures, the increased oil revenue in 1982 and 1983 did not lead to a much lower inflation in the war economy. In 1984, however, the growth trends in prices declined sharply and reached a minimum (slightly over 4 percent) in 1985 following a number of stringent antiinflationary measures including administrative pricing. Expansion of production and increase in imports due to increased oil revenue in the 1982–83 period were among other major antiinflationary influences. Since 1986, however, prices continued to rise at a rapid rate as the economy and imports continued to decline with the reduction in oil revenue while population grew rapidly (Table 3.9, Figure 3.11).

Thus, the wholesale general price index increased from 119.5 in 1976 to 501.7 in 1986 (1974 = 100). Although the annual growth rate of the index declined from 30.5 percent in 1980 to 5.5 percent in 1985, it increased again to 23.5 percent in 1986.[89] The rising trend seems to have been exacerbated in 1987, when "prices showed a sudden jump upward," rising by "two or three times compared with last year" for such items as fruits, household goods, health, and education.[90] The figure reported for the first quarter of the year is 32.9 percent. The situation got even worse following the missile attacks on Tehran in late 1987 and early 1988.[91] Generally speaking, of the major categories of goods and services included in the construction of the wholesale general price index, food items experienced the highest price hikes, followed by industrial raw materials and textiles and clothing (Table 3.10, Figure 3.12).[92] As people with a per capita income of less than a 100,000 rials a year spent between 40 to 45 percent of their income on food, inflation was the most devastating to these poorer sections of the society.

The cease-fire in August 1988 initially led to a significant drop in the price of foreign currency in Tehran's black market, as a consequence of which prices of most major consumer durable goods declined substantially, by 50 percent in some cases. The event

Table 3.9   Wholesale and Retail Price Indices, 1976–87 (1974 = 100)

Year	Wholesale General Index (Iran)(a)	Percent Annual Change	Retail General Index (Urban)(b)	Percent Annual Change
1976	119.5	13.5	128.1	16.6
1977	136.9	14.6	160.2	25.1
1978	149.9	9.5	176.2	10.0
1979	179.6	19.8	196.3	11.4
1980	234.3	30.5	242.5	23.5
1981	279.7	19.4	297.9	22.8
1982	318.1	13.7	355.2	19.2
1983	358.0	12.5	418.1	17.7
1984	385.2	7.6	462.1	10.5
1985	406.2	5.5	480.9	4.1
1986	501.7	23.5	580.9	20.8
1987(c)	666.8	32.9	769.7	32.5

Sources and Notes:
Gozaresh (1363), vol. 2, Chapter 7, pp. 7–11; and (1365), vol. 1, pp. 73–74, vol. 2, Chapter 11, p. 5–8; and *Iran Dar Aʾineh-e Amar*, no. 5 (1364), pp. 203–205.

(a) Goods only.
(b) Consumer commodities and services in urban areas.
(c) First quarter of the year.

Figure 3.11

Wholesale and Retail Price Indices, 1976–87
(1974 = 100)

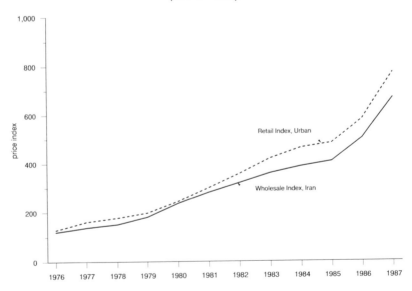

Table 3.10   Average Yearly Wholesale Price Index in Iran, 1976–87 (1974 = 100)

Year	General Index(a)	Goods Produced & Consumed in the Country	Imported Goods	Exported Goods	Food Items	Industrial Raw Materials	Textiles & Clothing	Transportation, Machinery, & Vehicles
1976	119.5	123.0	110.7	125.2	120.1	123.6	123.4	125.9
1977	136.9	142.2	124.1	140.5	139.1	126.5	138.7	140.6
1978	149.9	155.4	137.1	145.8	158.8	156.8	144.5	153.3
1979	179.6	188.4	157.7	178.6	203.2	183.7	177.2	169.9
1980	234.3	251.4	191.8	233.9	272.3	257.7	248.1	201.7
1981	279.7	307.1	211.9	278.1	333.8	318.3	312.5	220.4
1982	318.1	351.6	234.6	324.3	381.8	361.9	381.1	246.1
1983	358.0	400.0	254.5	354.1	461.0	392.7	399.8	253.3
1984	385.2	432.9	265.3	401.5	511.3	463.8	410.2	253.7
1985	406.2	456.0	281.5	420.4	529.7	534.2	408.1	261.8
1986	501.7	558.5	358.7	517.9	699.1	627.1	457.8	313.1
1987 (b)	666.8	677.5	463.8	975.0	821.9	766.5	571.9	424.5

Sources and Notes:
Gozaresh (1363), vol. 2, Chapter 7, p. 10; (1365), vol. 2, Chapter 11, p. 5; and *Salnameh* (1365), p. 747.

(a) Goods only.
(b) First quarter of the year.

Figure 3.12

Average Yearly Wholesale Price Index,
Iran, 1976–87 (1974 = 100)

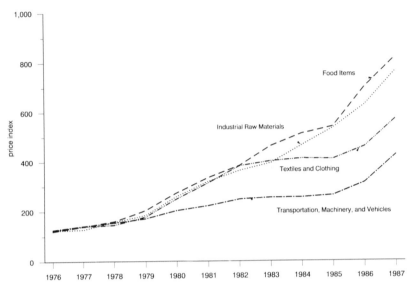

generated optimism among the people who were expecting a rapid postwar economic turnaround. It was also hoped that the foreign exchange saved in the postwar period would be used to import more consumer goods. However, the declining trend was soon arrested and then reversed in the following months, when it became clear that the economic reconstruction would be a very slow process and that the saved dollars would be spent energizing the oil industries and rebuilding the army. Additional influence came from the government policy of relaxing control over the foreign trade sector that caused the rial to fall sharply again relative to foreign currencies.

Increases in retail prices were even more alarming, particularly for consumer goods and services. In urban areas, the retail general price index increased to 480.9 in 1985 from 128.1 in 1976 (1974 = 100). The annual growth rates of the index were double digit for the 1979–84 period. A major decline occurred in 1985; however, the rate ever since has been rising rapidly, reaching 32.5 percent in the early 1987 (Table 3.9). Of the major items whose price indices have gone into the construction of the general retail price index, transportation and communications have led others followed by foods, drinks, tobacco, clothing, household furniture, and housing and heating (Table 3.11, Figure 3.13). Health services prices rose moderately until 1985 when they began their present steep rise.[93] In the absence of price indices for rural areas, the general index of expenditures may be used to detect price movements there. As reported in a government source, the index increased from 217.6 in 1979 to 479.7 in 1983 (1974 = 100). The comparable figures for urban areas were 225.1 and 474.5.[94]

It is clear that the rural areas have suffered equally, if not more, from upward movements in prices.[95] Note that statistics on prices reported here are for the official market (i.e., the market directly under the supervision of the government). For a more realistic picture to emerge, the unofficial market (including free and black market) prices should also be taken into consideration. To give one extreme example of the gap between the two markets, the unofficial price of a pair of tires in 1987 was 11.6 times the official price, at 65,000 and 5,600 respectively.[96]

The causes of the inflation are manifold and vary from sector to sector. The domestic and international factors have both been responsible, but most blame goes to the domestic sources. These include various agencies in the public sector and the private market. However, the private sector, the profiteering merchants in particular, have been the most responsible for the sometime exorbitant prices. Two institutions should be particularly noted for their role in inflation; namely, *Sandouqha-ye Gharzolhasaneh* and *Sherkatha-ye Mozarebeh'i*. Other causes of the postrevolutionary inflation include the war with Iraq and struggles among various political factions in the country; increase in the nation's money supply and liquidity; decline in production, oil revenue, and foreign exchange; rise in factor costs; increase in the population, particularly the urban population; postrevolutionary cultural constraints on imports; and expansion of welfare for the poor and thus effective demand.[97] Mistaken government policies or lack of well-designed measures and corruption on the part of agencies responsible for distributing rationed and subsidized goods also have contributed to inflation, for they have fueled the expansion of the so-called black markets. Other influences on the inflation have included structural bottlenecks, external influences such as trade embargo and exchange rate fluctuations, and the uneven income distribution in the country. The drive for higher profits, even in the public sector, and a high demand for foreign exchange in the country have been no less significant.

The war, however, should be considered a root cause of postrevolutionary inflation. At the same time that the war reduced production, it increased demand on various scarce commodities and

Table 3.11   Average Price Index for Consumer Goods and Services, Urban Iran, 1976–87 (1974 = 100)

Year	General Index	Foods, Drinks, & Tobacco	Clothing	Housing & Heating	Health Services	Transportation & Communications	Household Furnitures & Services
1976	128.1	118.6	121.1	159.2	122.4	123.0	128.3
1977	160.2	142.2	146.7	217.0	147.0	162.2	146.5
1978	176.2	168.8	163.6	216.7	170.0	176.6	156.7
1979	196.3	206.5	187.2	205.5	186.5	193.4	175.3
1980	242.5	272.5	232.1	220.4	193.2	249.1	229.7
1981	297.9	342.2	282.1	241.9	198.9	328.7	321.1
1982	355.2	404.4	351.8	271.3	205.6	422.7	409.0
1983	418.1	463.7	424.5	324.0	225.2	508.6	466.3
1984	462.1	504.5	496.4	364.7	247.6	594.8	488.2
1985	480.9	532.2	501.5	379.1	266.9	627.3	480.7
1986	580.9	679.4	544.1	431.7	288.0	739.7	594.1
1987(a)	769.7	818.6	647.6	466.1	293.1	902.4	839.4

Sources and Notes:
Gozaresh (1363), vol. 2, Chapter 7, p. 8; (1365), vol. 2, Chapter 11, p. 7; and *Salnameh* (1365), p. 749.

(a) First quarter of the year.

Figure 3.13

Price Index, Consumer Goods and Services,
Urban Iran, 1976–87 (1974 = 100)

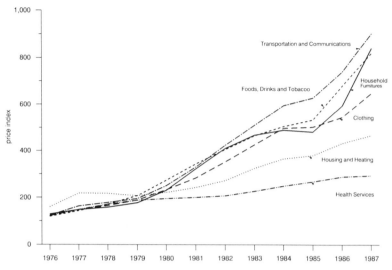

encouraged black markets. Although consumption declined more than production and the state made conscious attempts to dampen the population's propensity to consume, demand remained high relative to supply. The resulting cost-push–demand-pull inflation was exacerbated by the increasing factor costs, rapidly growing population, and rising expectations in the revolutionary environment.[98] The war also reduced the country's oil production and consequently had a negative effect on its foreign exchange earnings. This in turn, as we have seen, led to increased deficit and liquidity, resulting in higher prices.[99] It also negatively affected nonoil exports, exacerbating the nation's foreign exchange crisis. The war further contributed to the expansion of the profiteering services sector, precipitated a multiintermediary distribution system, and propagated hoarding, which engendered black markets for most commodities.[100]

The postrevolutionary black market in consumer commodities and foreign currencies contributed significantly to inflation. This market was in turn developed because of profiteering, corruption, and mismanagement of the numerous distribution channels that came into existence in the postrevolutionary period. The drive for profiteering led the mostly corrupt big private distribution agencies, with the help of certain public offices, to amass goods in their huge warehouses and create a black market. As was noted earlier in this chapter, *Sandouqha-ye Gharzolhasaneh* and *Sherkatha-ye Mozarebeh'i* were attacked on several occasions by the government for engaging in such illegitimate activities. In 1986 it was reported that "enough medicine for 17 years of national consumption had been uncovered in secret warehouses."[101] The black market, so created, was then used to push prices to exorbitant rates. The Echo of Iran quotes "experts" as saying that "a major portion of the inflation is due to the domestic free market and distribution network."[102] A research pamphlet published by the Ministry of Commerce also indicated that the "profit making of circulation capital," centered in the bazaar was among "the most important factor in inflation."[103] The deputy minister of Labor and Social Welfare was quoted as saying: "Expansion of the services sector, limits in domestic production, and bottlenecks in imports have paved the way for involvement of a number of people in the distribution of the commodities. So, if any of them is to make some profit, prices of commodities and services have to go up."[104]

However, to better understand the interplay of the black market, the profiteering in the bazaar, corruption, and inflation, one must consider the particular web of distribution in the country. The postrevolutionary period is characterized by a vast and complex system of goods distribution.[105] The channel has two main lanes, one public and the other private. The private distribution system is created of a hierarchy that has in its zenith the big merchants in control of domestic trade and imports. Between them and the consumers at the bottom are various layers of intermediaries, each hoping to profit greatly. Not all such intermediaries are legitimate agents either. Some are professional smugglers and thieves with the help of whom the big merchants control the black market in given commodities. The sector also has substantial control over the official market and through such control encourages corruption in the public distribution system. For example, whereas cooperatives distribute less than 5 percent of the commodities, the private sector, according to Tehran's governor general, "is even distributing rationed commodities."[106] It must also be noted that the executive boards of a good many cooperatives have been penetrated by intermediaries and merchants, who also happen to have their hands into corruption within the rationed markets.

The public channel is also crowded by many intermediaries some of whom are corrupt. A majority of them are controlled by the Headquarters for Economic Mobilization (HEM) and the Ministry of Commerce. They distribute commodities through a vast number of cooperatives and private agencies headed by big merchants in the bazaar. A fundamental flaw in the public distribution system concerns a lack of coherent policy or the existence of policies that indirectly encourage black market. This is despite the fact that a vast array of institutions are supervising price movements in the economy. They include the Economic Council, the Organization Supporting Consumers and Producers (OSCP), the Council Determining and Fixing Prices (inside OSCP), the Pricing Commission (in provincial commerce offices), and the county supervising commissions. Rationing, which is most needed in a society where production has declined and income distribution is extremely uneven, in the absence of government control, has become a tool for corruption and expansion of the black market. Indeed, a sizable portion of such commodities are sold openly in the black market. Only HEM has been guided by some degree of planning and has attempted to control its various distribution channels. But even goods under this organization have found their way into the black market. The price control and the rationing system in the absence of the state's control over a large part of the economy (which remains in the hands of the private sector) has further led to transfer of resources from production of rationed and price-controlled basic necessities toward production and trade in luxury items and commodities that offer a larger margin of profit. This transfer has in turn exacerbated the situation in the rationed market, expanding the black market for such goods and leading to numerous largely illegitimate intermediary channels.

Deficit financing and the growth of private liquidity resulting from the war, declining production, and thus the tax-revenue basis of the government, among other influences, have been equally powerful forces in the tenacity of postrevolutionary inflation. Public debt between 1979 and 1983 experienced an almost threefold increase, and by 1988 the amount of such debt exceeded 3,000 billion rials or 20 percent of the country's 1984 GDP at current prices. Coupled with the expansionary credit policies of the banking system and the so-called interest-free institutions, increased public borrowing has led to the expansion of the money supply and private liquidity. These have increased by 107 and 78 percent between 1979 and 1984 and have grown at 18 and 19 percent in 1986.[107] In the absence of a radical redistributive policy and because of income concentration in the hands of a few, who pay the least taxes, increased money supply and private liquidity has led to a considerable growth in the purchasing power of both the public sector and the wealthier segments of the private sector and thus has contributed to the high inflation rates particularly for less essential and luxury imported commodities.

Note that the relationship between production, liquidity, and inflation is also influenced by the country's dependency on foreign exchange.[108] For example, the nation's industries depend on foreign markets for no less than 65 percent of their inputs. The country's ability to earn foreign exchange, in turn, depends almost entirely on its oil production and price. Thus, changes in oil revenue is directly responsible for inflation, for this determines the level of industrial production and foreign exchange that the government sells to the Central Bank for rials. The smaller the amount of foreign currency, the lower is the level of production (and imported goods) and smaller is the amount of rials transferred to the government from the Central Bank. While the lower production and imports produce a supply pressure, the rial shortage increases the general budget deficit and the government's borrowing from the banking system. The resulting liquidity increase feeds directly into inflation, which, in turn, negatively affects production, for it causes transfer of resources to the more profitable trade sector, and depresses the foreign trade balance of the economy. A vicious circle thus operates so that inflation becomes a major cause of its own existence. Faced with monetary and fiscal crisis, the state put considerable pressure on the public sector production units to achieve self-sufficiency. This in turn has forced the managers of state-run enterprises to increase their products' prices considerably. The private sector has constantly emulated such moves. In 1987, for example, "factories run by the government organizations raised the prices of their commodities . . . by 30 to 50 percent, which was followed by a similar price rise by companies not affiliated with the government."[109]

Whereas much of the price inflation, particularly the wholesale index, resulted from increases in the prices of domestically produced goods (Table 3.10, Figure 3.14), the impact of international trade and the world monetary system on domestic prices was considerable.[110] The exchange rate for the nonoil export-earned foreign currency was five to six times higher than the official rate and imports paid for this currency tended to be extremely overpriced.[111] The imported inflation was particularly high at the retail levels and during times of Western economic sanctions, for example, following the hostage crisis in 1980 and when the country's balance of payments deficits increased. Its influence on prices was the highest in 1982 and 1983 when oil revenue and consequently imports in-

Figure 3.14

Average Yearly Wholesale Price Index, 1976–87 (1974 = 100)

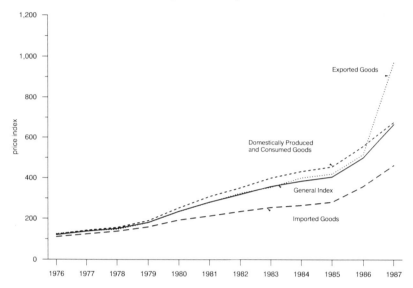

creased to their postrevolutionary peak. Since 1984, however, when oil revenue and imports were declining, imported inflation was also less significant.

Various consequences have followed from the tenacious post-revolutionary inflation. Those in the distribution networks have frequently passed on the cost of inflation to consumers by such methods as overpricing, underweighing, and quality reduction.[112] Inflation has also reduced the purchasing power of the poorer sections of the society and those on fixed incomes including public employees. In sharp contrast, it has led to increased income for owners of fixed assets and for those in trade and distribution networks. These groups benefited from the flexible pricing pattern in the service sector and from a relatively high mercantile and rental margins. Commenting on the causes of overpricing, in the summer of 1987, the deputy minister of Labor and Social Welfare noted that "some sectors of trade have earned higher profits [after the Revolution] than the prerevolution[ary] period. The rise in the incomes of such groups are merely due to [the] overpricing of commodities [which] in turn is due to the free [market] activities of [the] nongovernment distribution network."[113] On the other hand, according to one estimate, "earners of fixed wages have lost two-thirds of their income in the form of [an] inflation tax" since the Revolution,[114] and "the fall in purchasing power of the average low-income families has led them to sell their durable holdings such as carpets and jewelry as a means of meeting their most fundamental requirements."[115]

The depressing effect of inflation on the purchasing power of the public employees was also noticeable. In 1981, for example, some 78.6 percent of the government employees earned less than the average consumption expenditures of an urban family. By 1984, the figure had increased to 97.2 percent.[116] In addition to its impact on purchasing power and income distribution, inflation was also a powerful force neutralizing efforts to expand domestic production, to promote nonoil exports, and to reduce dependency on oil and international markets. Higher profitability of services led to a concentration of investment in that sector. Inflation also drained the government of its high-quality personnel, who either moved to the private sector or took a second job. Most of these people were absorbed in service occupations that had little need for expertise. The result was that the value of education of a sizable portion of the nation's graduates and experts was lost. Inflation cheapened the rial, making imports expensive, while nonoil exports did not benefit. The devalued rial led to speculation in foreign currency, gold, and real estate. To preserve the value of their rials, the superrich converted them into these assets, sent part of the first two out of Iran, and used the rest for speculation at home.

Since 1982, the government has become increasingly sensitive to inflation, as indicated by the expanding administrative and economic measures taken against it. The government has attempted to rationalize its budget primarily by cutting "unnecessary" expenses, increasing tax revenues, and lessening reliance on the credits from the banks for financing budget deficits. To lower its deficit and pay for the war, the government even reduced its development budget to a very significant degree. However, these measures became less effective in 1984 when the economy entered the present recession.[117] The state was nevertheless able to bring the credit policies of the banking system under its close supervision, and it successfully encouraged the private sector to channel a large part of its huge cash holdings into the nationalized banks.[118] In 1980, following the outbreak of the war, the government had already introduced price control and rationing of necessities. In an attempt to control demand increase, the state also fixed wages and salaries for an indefinite period of time. Beginning in 1983, such policies became stricter and new ones were introduced. Soon all imports came under the government's control, and goods were priced and distributed on the basis of a complex formula that supposedly accounted for the needs of various provinces and economic sectors. The government fixed the exchange rate between rials and foreign currencies in an attempt to control imported inflation. This policy was reinforced with zeal and complemented a new foreign exchange assignment system introduced following the 1986 oil price crash. However, at the time when the value of rial was continuously depreciating, such a policy simply did not work.

In addition to fighting inflation, the government had hoped to use rationing, among other price-fixing measures, to control imports, modify the distribution system, and procure the minimum essential requirements of the poorer social groups. Although helpful in these respects, the policy led to a dual market economy where a rationed market competed with free and black markets.[119] Whereas the former was characterized by long lines, relatively lower prices, and shortages of commodities, the latter offered plenty of various supplies, at sky-rocket prices, obtainable just by placing a telephone call.[120] In the absence of effective public control, the rationing system led to corruption and expansion of the black market where most rationed items could be readily found at exorbitant prices. Other side effects of the rationing system included increased corruption in the public sector,[121] changes in consumption patterns, and disruption in production as a result of investment shifts to production of nonrationed items. To ease the impact of inflation on lower-income groups and those who had seen their purchasing power largely eroded and to encourage domestic production of farm products, early in the postrevolutionary period, the government also initiated an extensive subsidy program covering the most essential goods. With the worsening economic conditions and budget deficits since 1984 and growing conservative criticism to the program, subsidies were reduced for most items. Nevertheless, items such as fertilizer, sugar, vegetable oil, wheat, and milk continued to be subsidized heavily.[122]

The most recent attempts at fighting inflation include stiff legislation against overpricing and hoarding, which followed Ayatollah Khomeini's *fetva* (religious decree) in late 1987, giving the government power and legitimacy to control and supervise various channels of distribution.[123] Depending on the extent and frequency of the offenses, an offender can face penalties ranging from cash fines to cancellation of work permit. Some have even called for execution of these "economic terrorists."[124] Since 1988, provincial governors have been charged with supervision of the fight against overpricers.

The critics, however, claim that the policy unjustly punishes only the minor offenders. After "working in the public prosecutor's office [PPO] for a number of years" said an employee of the PPO in charge of fighting overpricing, "I have never seen a [major] hoarder or overcharger charged for such offenses here, whereas only small retailers and peddlers are charged and sentenced as soon as they make minor offenses."[125] The government has also tried to control liquidity by paying its employees' New Year bonuses in the form of commodities coupons, an initiative that the working people seem to have welcomed: "It has been some time since the children had sugar with their tea," remarked a worker. "However, with the commodities coupons we may meet some of our family's requirements," he continued.[126]

Despite these and other measures, inflation continued to remain a major political-economic problem in the Islamic Republic. Although more radical measures had to be introduced, the big bazaaris and their conservative allies in the various state apparatuses would not allow implementation of the conventional policies. Given that the private sector distributes "even the rationed commodities," remarked Tehran's governor general, it "will keep its position even though it is subject to the rule and regulations instructed to trade unites."[127] Indeed, the effectiveness of the antiovercharging plan came into question only three weeks after its introduction, as commodities covered by the plan became scarce and began to show up on the black market at higher prices. Moreover, despite stiff penalties for transactions in coupons, "they are being freely transacted on the streets of Tehran."[128] As noted by the director general of the Administrative and Employment Affairs Organization: "Instead of making the individuals the main targets of such campaigns, the economic system should be changed so that no persons may find opportunity to abuse their positions."[129] This requires, above all, comprehensive planning and public management of the major economic operations. Only then could the private sector be brought under control and cooperatives become effective distribution networks. Clearly, ending the war was the first right step; but reaching a comprehensive peace settlement with Iraq, developing a suitable reconstruction strategy, taxing the rich, and changing priorities in the general budget remain among important other steps the state should take toward stabilizing the economy. The postwar policy to relax control on trade was a step in the wrong direction and will lead to higher prices given that the supply will not change to any dramatic degree in the near future, even if more imports enter the country. The foreign exchange constraint will continue to remain a major obstacle.

Unemployment and Sectoral Employment Shifts

Chronic unemployment has been another major characteristic of the Iranian economy since the late 1970s. The problem has worsened in the postrevolutionary period because the labor force has grown rapidly while employment opportunities have declined.[130] The country's population has increased at an annual rate of about 3.9 percent over the 1979–87 period as compared to 2.7 percent in the 1970s.

The 1986 population was reported at about 49.7 million, of which about 33.8 million were ten-years-old or more. The corresponding figures for 1976 were 33.7 and 23 million respectively. The size of the active and employed population also steadily increased, from 9.8 and 8.8 million in 1976 to 12.8 and 11.0 million in 1986 respectively (Table 3.12).[131] However, the rate of activity and employment declined consistently leading to higher rates of unemployment particularly since the Revolution. Thus, the unemployment rate jumped from an already high 10 percent in 1976 to 18.7 percent in 1984 and 14.1 percent in 1986 (Table 3.12, Figure 3.15).[132] Unofficial statistics put the unemployment rate for 1986 at about 28.6. (See note to Table 3.12.) A sizable underemployed population—around 20 percent of the active population—must be added to these figures to arrive at the actual number of the nonproductive and less-productive population. Thus, of about 12.3 million

Table 3.12   Structure of Employment, 1976–86 (million persons)

	1976	1979	1980	1981	1982	1983	1984	1985	1986(a)
Total Population(b)	33.7	37.8	39.3	40.8	42.4	44.1	45.8	47.6	49.7
10 years and over	23.0	24.9	26.1	27.3	27.6	28.4	29.3	30.6	33.8
Active	9.8	10.4	10.9	11.0	11.6	12.0	12.3	12.6	12.8
Employed	8.8	9.2	9.5	9.4	9.4	9.8	10.0	9.9	11.0
Unemployed	1.0	1.2	1.4	1.6	2.2	2.2	2.3	2.7	1.8
Rate of Active (%)	42.6	41.8	41.8	41.8	42.2	42.1	41.9	41.2	38.9
Rate of Unemployed (%)	10.0	11.5	12.8	14.0	19.0	18.3	18.7	20.4	14.1

Sources and Notes:
Gozaresh (1363), vol 1, p. 113; and (1365), vol. 1, p. 80; vol. 2, Chapter 14, pp. 1–6; *Salnameh* (1360 and 1366), p. 65; and *Taraznameh* (1359), p. 201.

(a) Unofficial sources report a much higher unemployment rate for 1986. See, e.g., *Political Bulletin* 6, no. 10 (10 March 1987), p. 8, where the number of unemployed is reported at 3.8 million with an unemployment rate of about 28.6 percent.

(b) Population of 1979–85 years are calculated using the average annual growth rate of 3.91 percent for the 1976–86 period.

Figure 3.15

Structure of Employment, 1976–86

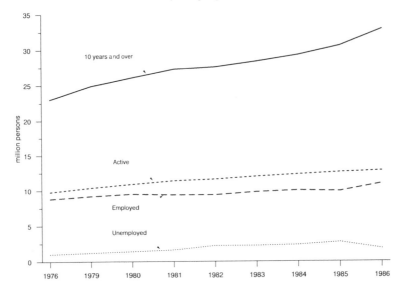

of the employable population in 1984, only 61 percent or 7.5 million (i.e., about 16.5 percent of the country's total population) were actually engaged in productive activities. In other words, each working person had to support 6.1 nonworking persons.[133] Indeed, during the 1976–86 decade, on the average, some 302,000 (population of ten-years-old and over) entered the job market each year, while only some 224,000 jobs were created (including 74 percent for new entrants and 56 percent for all job seekers during the decade).[134]

Generally speaking, over 70 percent of the unemployed are under thirty years of age and about 64 percent are concentrated in urban places where some 89 percent of the new job entrants live (i.e., some 2.7 million out of a total of 3.03 million for the entire 1976–86 period). Unemployment is also unevenly distributed across provinces. Thus, less-developed provinces and provinces in the war zones show larger rates of unemployment than the rest. Factors responsible for these trends have included a high natural increase and an extensive and increasing rural-to-urban migration particularly in the first few years during the postrevolutionary period. Such migration might have been responsible for as much as 20 percent of the new job entrants in urban areas. Over 40 percent of urban unemployed have been employed in the past and the remaining 60 percent are new entrants into the job market. Of the urban unemployed, 28 percent are illiterate and 30 percent hold high school diplomas. However, on the national level, the majority of unemployed are simple agricultural and construction workers. Moreover, of the total employed population only 40 percent are literate with only 4.7 percent having education above a high school diploma, of whom some 90 percent work in urban centers.[135] Compared to 1976, however, there has been some improvement in the educational level of the employed population. For example, the proportion of the employed population with a higher education has increased from 3 percent in 1976 to 4.7 percent in 1986. Similarly, of the employed population in 1976, only 41 percent were literate, whereas the corresponding figure for 1986 was 60 percent. However, the quality of education has declined in the postrevolutionary period. Finally, there are fewer women working in the postrevolutionary period, and their employment growth rate has significantly declined.[136]

The public sector has been responsible for most of the new jobs created after the Revolution, for some four-fifth of the new jobs (about 1.9 million out of 2.24 million over the 1976–86 period), of whom about 77.8 percent were service related and 67 percent worked in urban places.[137] As a result, the public sector's employment increased from about 1.7 million in 1976 to about 3 million in 1986, increasing its share in total employment from 19 percent in 1976 to slightly over 31 percent in 1986. Moreover, the number of government employees in urban areas increased by 80 percent in 1986 compared to 1976, while its employees in rural areas increased by 3.9 times over the same period. The share of the public sector in sectoral employment changed from 1.3, 9.1, and 48.7 percent for agriculture, industries, and services in 1976 to 1.3, 19.8, and 56.8 for the sectors in 1986. The large increase in public industrial employment was due to the nationalization of some of the largest industrial units following the Revolution. Large industries (units employing 10 workers or more) were responsible for 50 percent of industrial employment, of whom 70 percent were in large publicly owned enterprises producing some 71 percent of the large industries' value added. Indeed, no less than 50 percent of all industrial value added in the nation were produced in government-owned enterprises, making it an economic giant with tremendous influence on the economy. It must be noted that the share of public services' value added in total gross domestic production declined by some 35 percent over the 1976–86 period despite a doubling of the sector's employment. This points toward the very low productivity of public employees, whose average per capita income of 96,000 rials a year was comparable to earnings of employees in such low-paid sectors as agriculture and construction. Note also that most employees of these latter sectors were illiterate or had a low-level of education whereas those in the government sector were among the most educated Iranians. Indeed, 82 percent of the country's 497,000 graduates of higher education, 85 percent of the nation's 1.1 million scientific, technical, and specialist cadres, and 52 percent of some 45,000 top managers and administrative personnel work for the government.[138]

The role of the private sector in the postrevolutionary job creation was negligible at best. The sector's total employment of some 7.13 million people in 1976 increased only slightly to 7.6 million in 1986. Almost all of the newly created jobs were service related. Indeed, the private sector's employment share in nonservice activities declined by 284 jobs despite increased employment capacity in the agricultural sector largely because of the infrastructural improvement undertaken by the state since the Revolution. More important, a sizable portion of the private sector's employment in recent years was self-employment rather than wage-paying jobs. As a consequence, the share of the sector's wages and salary earners dropped from about 35 percent of the country's total employed population in 1976 to about 17 percent in 1986. In absolute terms, the decline amounted to about 1.2 million lost jobs. Part of the decline was rooted in the postrevolutionary economic nationalization, rapid population growth, uncertainty concerning ownership limits, and eccentric public policies. For the most part, however, the sector was responsible, for it focused on nonproductive and quick-return activities and followed a very nonpatriotic line of operation within a war environment (e.g., black market, hoarding, withholding cash from the banking system, transfer of wealth outside the country, and foreign currency deals).[139]

Sectoral employment shifts in the postrevolutionary period were moderate and largely in favor of agriculture. As indicated in Table 3.13, the share of agriculture increased, to 33 percent in 1984 from 28.2 percent in 1976. Although the sector's share declined to 29.2 percent by 1986, it still accounted for the largest portion of jobs created after the Revolution. In absolute terms, about 3 million people were working in the sector in 1976. The figure grew to over 3.2 million in 1986, or 20,000 a year. This performance simply indicates that agriculture cannot be relied upon as a major source of employment. The wages and salary earners in the sector, however, declined over the same period, from 662,000 in 1976 to only 332,000 in 1986. The sector also experienced a significant drop in its unpaid family workers, from 587,000 in 1976 to about 390,000 in 1986. The declines reflected a drop in the number of landless peasants in

Table 3.13 Sectoral Structure of Employment, 1976–86 (1,000 persons)

	1976		1982		1983		1984		1986	
	Number	Share(%)	Number	Share(%)	Number	Share(%)	Number	Share(%)	Number	Share(%)
Agriculture	2,292	28.2	3,160	33.6	3,243	33.2	3,294	33.0	3,276	29.2
Industries and Mines (a)	3,013	37.2	2,928	31.2	3,081	31.6	3,115	31.3	2,859	25.5
Services (b)	2,795	34.6	3,668	35.2	3,432	35.2	3,559	35.7	5,075	45.3
Total (b)	8,100	100.0	9,756	100.0	9,397	100.0	9,968	100.0	11,210	100.0

Sources and Notes:
Gozaresh (1363), vol. 2, Chapter 10, p. 9; and (1365), vol. 2, Chapter 14, p. 6. See also Salnameh (1366), p. 70.

(a) Includes manufacturing and mining; electricity, water, and gas; and construction.

(b) Figures for 1986 include 376 unclassified jobs.

the postrevolutionary period. The result was obtained due to a few limited land reform programs, expansion of arable lands, and increased rural-to-urban migration. In sharp contrast, the postrevolutionary agriculture experienced a real growth in the number of landed peasants and agricultural entrepreneurs in rural Iran, their total increasing from about 1.6 million in 1976 to about 2.2 million in 1986. It was perhaps due to these positive changes that the sector's per capita labor productivity also improved by some 4 percent a year (in 1974 fixed prices) over the 1976–86 period (from 109,000 rials in 1976 to 161,000 rials in 1986).[140]

The share of employment in industries and mines dropped from 37.2 percent in 1976 to 31.3 percent in 1984 (Table 3.13). Thus, the number of people employed in the sector in 1986 was about 1.5 million, that was 212,000 less than the figure for 1976. The loser, however, was rural Iran. Thus, although the rural areas lost some 295,000 industrial jobs (from 783,000 in 1976 to 488,000 in 1986), the industrial employment situation in urban areas improved only slightly, from 889,000 to 971,000 in the same period. Considering that over the 1976–86 period, urban population has increased by a rate of 5.4 percent a year, the grim employment situation in urban Iran becomes even more evident. As most rural industries were small and labor intensive, their decline was translated into a decline in the production and employment of small industries in the postrevolutionary period. For example, in 1976, small industries were responsible for about 75 percent of the country's industrial production. The figure declined to less than 60 percent in 1986. (In terms of number of units, however, there are more small industries in 1989 than anytime in the past.) In terms of productivity, too, the industrial sector showed no significant improvement in the postrevolutionary period. Thus, in 1974 fixed prices, average productivity per capita of the employed population in the sector increased from 177,000 rials in 1976 to 255,000 in 1986. Among industries, the share of employment in construction declined the most (down to 10.6 percent of the total industry and mine employment in 1984 from 13.5 percent in 1976) followed by the share of manufacturing. Between 1976 and 1986, only 18,000 new jobs were created in construction, which, in 1974 fixed prices, lost some 57 percent of its per capita productivity.[141] Employment in water and electricity has slightly increased.

The sectoral composition of employment also changed in favor of the least productive activities and low-paying jobs with depressing effects on production and per capita income. Thus, of 224,000 new jobs created each year on average over the 1976–86 period, some 94 percent were service related. Indeed, the service sector has significantly increased its share in total sectoral employment, from 34.6 percent in 1976 to 45.3 percent in 1986. Within the service sector, trade and restaurant industries generated most jobs, followed by transportation and communication. Employment in the low-paying informal sector and illicit activities also increased in the postrevolutionary period, for the productive and formal sectors could not absorb the increasing number of new entrants into the job market. Employment in the least productive activities seems to have expanded at a faster rate since the beginning of the current economic recession in 1984. For example, the share of services was reported at 45.3 percent in 1986 as opposed to only 25.5 percent for industries and mines and 29.2 percent for agriculture (Table 3.13). After a 60 percent drop in the foreign exchange earnings from oil in 1986, the government closed down or drastically reduced the production of factories considered foreign currency intensive and producing nonessential goods; it further reduced the number of the better-paying jobs.[142]

This structural change in favor of the public sector, services and low-paying jobs led to a significant decline in the rate of productivity and in per capita income particularly in the nonservice sectors of the economy. Thus, per capita productivity (in 1974 fixed prices) of the population (employed and unemployed) declined from 112,000 rials in 1977 to 62,000 rials in 1986. The corresponding figures for the employed population (ten-years-old and over) were 436,000 and 278,000 rials, respectively. During the same period, however, per capita productivity in most private service activities increased appreciably, from 397,000 rials in 1976 to 720,000 rials in 1986 in the case of commerce, restaurants, and hotels.[143] However, the service sector as a whole absorbed most of the new low-paying jobs concentrated in trade and transportation, and in such government institutions as revolutionary foundations, education, and culture. As most such low-paying service jobs are concentrated in the public sector, the postrevolutionary wage gap between the private and public sectors increased tremendously, with those in the private sector making almost 5.8 times more in per capita income than those in the public sector.[144] The public sector also suffers from what may be called an employment inflation, making the private sector the only hope for the generation of any major new employment in the economy.

Many structural and cyclical factors contributed to increased unemployment rates and the relative reduction in productive employment. The dependent economy did not inherit from the previous regime a balanced sectoral employment structure; it experienced a double digit unemployment in its final years. However, the war exacerbated the imbalanced structure and unemployment by destroying many productive units, eliminating thousands of jobs, creating a significant number of refugees, and encouraging investment in the highly profitable services and retail trade. The shift in the structure of the general budget in favor of more operating expenditures reinforced the negative consequences of the war as investment for the formation of fixed capital decreased. Decline in capacity utilization and production in the face of increased demand and profiteering by the bazaar forced the government to introduce antiinflationary measures that also increased unemployment and diverted investment to services. Added to these was a fast growing young population (over 45 percent below age fifteen) that viewed the Revolution as a means to improve its lot.

So long as the structure of the economy remains unchanged, the postwar reconstruction remains dormant, population control policies are lacking, the development budget remains low, and inflation is unacceptably high, little can be done to remedy unemployment and the structural imbalance in employment. Among other factors that must be considered for improvement of the job market are a more appropriate technology, increased investment in job-generating activities, industries in particular, introduction of fiscal and monetary policies that will attract private savings to productive investment, and skillful management of the human and material resources. Other options include placement and training services, recruitment subsidies for employers, and legislation of unemployment benefits. The state's focus, however, must be on "employment principle" rather than on "benefit principle." Whereas the private employers have every incentive to maintain a high level of unemployment (the so-called reserve army) (e.g., to keep wages down and increase control over the work force), the government must pay serious attention to the problems, particularly unemployment, as they have caused extensive damage to the political economy and sociopsychological makeup of the country. The increasing incidence of family breakdown and crime, the growing political passivity of the population, the decreasing production and per capita income of the majority, and the worsening income distribution are only a few among such critical consequences.

PER CAPITA INCOME AND INCOME DISTRIBUTION

Decline in GDP in the face of a rapidly growing population has led to a drastic reduction in the average living standard of Iranians in the postrevolutionary period. Per capita GDP has declined by 47 percent (in 1974 prices) between 1979 and 1987, at an average rate of 5.2 percent per year (Table 3.14, Figure 3.16). Again, as in the case of GDP, per capita GDP registered its sharpest declines over the

Table 3.14   Per Capita GDP, 1976–88 (1,000 rials, 1974 constant prices)

Year	Amount	Change From Previous Year
1976	108.6	14.6
1977	113.0	4.1
1978	91.3	−19.2
1979	83.3	−8.8
1980	67.5	−19.0
1981	67.3	−0.3
1982	75.2	11.7
1983	82.0	9.0
1984	77.4	−5.6
1985	68.0	−12.1
1986	58.0	−14.7
1987	54.0	−6.9
1988 (a) "about"	50.0	−7.4
Change: 1979–87	−46.7	
Annual Average	−5.2	
Change: 1976–88	−54.6	
Annual Average	−4.2	

Sources and Notes:
Figures for 1976–83 are taken from *Gozaresh* (1363), vol. 1, p. 106; the figure for 1984 is calculated using GDP figure given in *Faslnameh* (1365) and the figure for the year's population. Figures from 1985–88 are quoted by Gholam Hossein Naadi, Parliamentary representative, and are taken from *Kayhan-e Hava'i* (19 Esfand 1366), p. 24. See also *Gozaresh* (1365), vol. 1, p. 68 where slightly different figures are reported.

(a) Estimate.

1978–80 period, the most turbulent revolutionary years. It fell by 19 percentage points immediately following the war in 1980. In sharp contrast, the indicator experienced rapid growth during the 1982–83 period, for which an average growth figure of about 10 percent has been reported. This reflects increased oil revenue in the period, by 92.5 percent in 1982 alone. Per capita GDP has consistently declined since 1984 when the current economic crisis began following the decline in GDP, oil revenue, and capacity utilization, and the intensification of the war, unemployment, and inflation. (In 1987, it was reported at 54,000 rials [in 1974 prices], which is 50 percent less than the figure for 1976 [Figure 3.16].) It must be noted that part of the decline in per capita is related to the rapid growth of the postrevolutionary population.

Given the high inflation, unemployment, underemployment, and dependency ratio (5.7 in 1984),[145] the decline in per capita GDP has deprived many of a decent living standard. The poorer sections of the society are, however, the main losers. Ironically, these groups were among the main beneficiaries of the reform measures that were

Figure 3.16

Changes in Per Capita GDP, 1976–88
(1974 constant prices)

introduced in the first two years of the postrevolutionary period including a series of wage increases, land redistribution programs, and
expropriation-nationalization projects.[146] The middle-class wage
earners have also lost most of their purchasing power despite the
leadership's continued struggles to build a middle-class society after
its image. Consequently, the postrevolutionary Iran has increasingly
become polarized into a two-class society of the rich and the poor.
Quoting a "recent census" to Parliament, Parliament representative
Gholam Hosain Naadi reported: "Of the total population, around
12 million are very deprived, 22 million are badly vulnerable and
11.7 [million] are semivulnerable and 1.3 million are affluent people. It is clear that if the potential rate of inflation remains in place,
around 72 percent of the population, to say the least, would be
badly damaged and harmed or face very serious problems in their
daily living."[147] He then gave the following breakdown of the 72
percent he cited:

1. In the very deprived group: the unemployed family;

2. In the badly vulnerable group: 50 percent of the farm workers, 90 percent of the construction workers, 90 percent of

government employees and 90 percent of the industry and mines workers;

3. In the semivulnerable group: the remaining 50 percent of the farm workers, the remaining 10 percent of the industry and mines sector and the administrative system and 90 percent of the population covered by the services sector.[148]

Naadi's observation that the incidence of absolute poverty is increasing among Iranians is also supported by a variety of other sources and information. In an article in *Kayhan* daily, Ezzatollah Sahabi, the chief of the Plan and Budget Organization under the 1979 provisional government, has written that absolute poverty has increased by 43 percent over the 1979–85 period and the situation is further deteriorating.[149] The same newspaper in a recent article reported that "the real purchasing power of salaried people had fallen by 60 percent since the revolution."[150] Other sources indicate that "the fall in the purchasing power of the average low income families has led them to sell their durable goods such as carpets and jewelry as a means of meeting their most fundamental requirements."[151] Official statistics indicate a progressive decline in real wages and compensation in large-scale industrial establishments since the start of the war in 1980 (Table 3.15, Figure 3.17).

Prior to this date, real wages in the sector had risen considerably. Specifically, on the average, the index of wages and compensa-

Table 3.15   Index of Wages and Compensation in Large-Scale Industrial Establishments and General Index of Retail Prices for Main Goods and Services in Urban Iran, 1977–85 (1974 = 100)

	Index of Wages and Compensation		Index of Retail Prices	
Year	Index	% Change from Previous Year	Index	% Change from Previous Year
1977	251.4		160.2	25.1
1978	325.7	29.6	176.2	10.0
1979	527.2	61.9	196.3	11.4
1980	625.0	18.6	242.5	23.5
1981	680.2	8.8	297.9	22.8
1982	760.7	11.8	355.2	19.2
1983	880.5	15.7	418.1	17.7
1984	897.2	1.9	462.1	10.5
1985	985.7	9.7	480.9	4.1

Sources and Notes:
Gozaresh (1363), vol. 2, Chapter 13, p. 28; *Salnameh* (1386), p. 726; *Majaleh* (1364), p. 112.

Figure 3.17

Indices of Wages and Retail Prices, 1977–85
(1974 = 100)

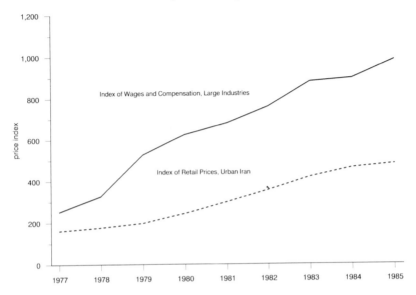

tion rose by 36.7 percent a year between 1978–80 and by 11.1 percent a year over the 1980–85 period as compared to 15.0 percent and 16.3 percent increase for the index of retail prices, respectively.[152] The gap between the two indicators narrowed during the 1982–83 growth period; it widened again thereafter. In 1987, wages of a "simple worker" was 760 rials a day and those of a "regular worker" 1,800 rials, as compared to 9,000 rials for a tin of cooking oil.[153] Even more disturbing was the report that some 5 million Iranians earn no more than 60 rials a day.[154] The declining trend in real income was further exacerbated in 1988.[155]

The per capita daily consumption expenditures of the bottom 10 percent of the population was only 60 rials in 1983, whereas the figure for the next 10 percent was no more than 135 rials. This bottom 20 percent represented 8.4 million (10 million in 1984–85) who must have been living in destitution given their extremely low expenditures and the extremely high prices.[156] According to an economic expert of the Ministry of Plan and Budget, about 60 to 70 percent of the population lives below the poverty line.[157] Statistics also indicate a growing imbalance between the urban and rural families in terms of income and consumption expenditures. The income imbalance has been traditionally more pronounced than the imbalance in consumption expenditures between the two population groups. Again such imbalances declined in the first two or three years following the Revolution, but began to rise thereafter as indicated in Table 3.16. In 1985, for example, the ratio between the yearly consumption expenditures of an urban family and its incomes was 124 : 100, up from 98 : 100 for 1977. The comparable figures for a rural family were 128 : 100 and 125 : 100. It is clear that the ratios increased significantly, particularly for the urban families who have been more affected by the war, the high rate of population growth, and the postrevolutionary economic dislocations including unemployment, inflation and low productivity rate.

The decline in postrevolutionary income and purchasing power was not equally distributed among the various segments of the society. This was partly due to the extreme socioeconomic inequalities that characterized the previous regime and partly due to certain developments in the postrevolutionary period, including the war, the profiteering private services sector, inflation, unemployment, underemployment, and improper or lack of proper government policies. In 1972, for example, 13 million or 67 percent of the population, including 8.8 million urban dwellers, "lived below the poverty line" and the situation worsened over the 1972–76 period.[158] Moreover, the coefficient of inequality in distribution of consumption expenditures increased from 0.45 during the 1966–71 period to 0.51 during the 1972–79 period.[159] The share of the bottom 40 percent of the income group in consumption expenditures declined from 14 percent in 1968 to 12 percent in 1979. In sharp contrast, the share of the top 20 percent of the income group increased from 53 to 58 percent for the same years.[160] The ratio of urban to rural per capita consumption expenditures also increased in the prerevolutionary years, from 1.6 in 1959 to 2.7 in 1977.[161] Although no reliable measure exists for the coefficient of income inequality in Iran, it is generally agreed that the coefficient is much larger than the one for consumption expenditures, varying between 0.60 and 0.70 over the 1959–77 period and that the trend in the postrevolutionary period has been increasing.[162] Even more unequal is wealth distribution, for which reliable data is almost totally lacking.

Consumption inequality trends were narrowed in the early postrevolutionary years until 1982. Thus, the coefficient of inequality in consumption expenditures declined to 0.43 in 1982, and slightly increased to 0.44 in 1983.[163] The food rationing system, subsidies, and price controls on basic commodities were among policies that helped reduce the gap. Improvement also occurred in the ratios of

Table 3.16 Yearly Incomes and Expenditures (food and nonfood), Urban and Rural Households, 1976–87 (1,000 current rials)

	1976	1977	1978	1979	1980	1982	1983	1984	1985	1986	1987
Urban (a)											
(1) Expenditures (b)	—	438.2	—	528.2	545.5	883.5	1113.1	1240.5	1280.5	1314.6	1488.8
(2) Incomes	—	448.7	—	514.4	608.8	709.6	918.4	1034.2	1037.1	1126.6	1149.3
(1) as percent of (2)	—	97.7	—	102.7	89.6	124.5	121.2	119.9	123.5	116.7	129.5
Rural (c)											
(1) Expenditures (b)	152.1	207.2	234.9	288.4	—	505.4	611.7	670.7	677.6	761.6	908.4
(2) Incomes	120.9	166.3	192.2	227.3	—	391.8	471.9	524.6	531.1	568.6	723.2
(1) as percent of (2)	125.8	124.6	122.2	126.9	—	129.0	129.6	127.8	127.6	133.9	125.1
Ratio of Urban to Rural Expenditures (d)	—	2.1	—	1.8	—	1.7	1.8	1.8	1.9	1.73	1.64
Ratio of Urban to Rural Incomes (d)	—	2.7	—	2.3	—	1.8	1.9	2.0	2.0	1.98	1.59

Sources and Notes:
Iran Dar A'ineh-e Amar, no. 5 (1364), pp. 208–209, 212; *Salnameh* (1362), pp. 667, 669, 670, 672; (1360), pp. 710, 716–117, 722; (1361), p. 757; (1365), pp. 767, 772, 773, 778; and (1366), pp. 426–428. See also *Natayej-e Tafsili, Rusta* and *Natayej-e Tafsili, Shahr* (1976–88 issues).

(a) Statistics have not been collected for urban household budget in 1976, 1978, and 1981.

(b) Statistics have not been collected for rural household budget in 1980 and 1981.

(c) The original sources give monthly figures except for 1986 and 1987.

(d) Calculated by the author.

urban to rural expenditures and income, which declined from 2.1 and 2.7 in 1977 to 1.7 and 1.8 in 1982 (Table 3.16). However, socioeconomic inequalities remain high and have increased since 1984, a trend that began in 1980 with the beginning of the war and was exacerbated as the war dragged on, oil revenue decreased, and the state's nondefense expenditures were substantially curtailed. It was reported that in 1987, the bottom 10 percent of the population received no more than 1.3 percent of the national income, whereas the top 10 percent received 33.0 percent.[164] According to another report in 1988, some 50 percent of the national income was paid to the top 10 percent of income group, 38 percent was earned by the middle 40 percent, and the remaining 12 percent belonged to the bottom 40 percent of the population.[165] Moreover, some 60,000 families earned monthly incomes of about 3 million rials,[166] as compared to about 30,000 rials for an average working family.

Among those who became richer after the Revolution, since 1980 in particular, merchants and traders in control of the country's distribution channels were the most notable. According to *Kayhan* daily, their profits amounted to over 90 billion rials in 1983, and in 1986 some 5,000 bazaaris made 50 billion rials in after-tax profits.[167] According to a report by the daily *Resalat,* the number of "billionaires" (in tumans; each tuman equals 10 rials) increased from about 100 families in the prerevolutionary years to over 900 families in the postrevolutionary period.[168] In sharp contrast, the groups who have suffered the greatest decline in their incomes include the urban poor, the farm laborers, the workers in construction and industries, and government employees.[169] For example, "some 99 percent of government employees received wages less than the average expenditures of an urban family in 1364 [1985]," and the average working family could not afford "rice for a few days" or "sugar with their tea."[170] Incidentally, these were the same group of people whose income substantially increased in the prewar postrevolutionary period.

The gap between the rich and the poor may also be detected by looking at the relationship between savings and consumption in gross domestic expenditures. In 1982, about 31 percent of GDE, that is, 4,138 billion rials, was saved. This is an astronomical figure indeed. The question then is, who saved the money? By looking at the sectoral employment and value added, and the unemployment rate in 1983, it becomes clear that most of the savings have been concentrated in nonpublic services such as commercial affairs, intermediation, and brokerage business. Given that the majority of the people working in these services are not owners of the means of production and are low-paid, the savings must have been concentrated in the hands of a small number of owners, about 100,000 families in the country.[17]

As acknowledged by a government source:

> The aforementioned model of income and expenditure distribution remains one of the principal obstacles to economic development of the society within the framework set by the Constitution. On the one hand, this model limits the possibility of effective participation by a major section of the country's population in economic development, and on the other hand, by provision of possibilities for undesitable expansion of services, it will intensify the present structural problems of the country's production.[172] (My translation).

To remedy the situation, the government introduced a number of important policy measures. The new state's redistribution policies included asset and income redistribution. Both nationalization and expropriation strategies were used. As was noted, a significant portion of the large industries and all banks and insurance companies were confiscated or nationalized. As a result, the income and wealth gap between the "haves" and "have nots" narrowed temporarily in the country, and in the industrial sector in particular. Revolutionary foundations, including the Construction Crusade and the Foundation for the Oppressed, also helped expand supportive and welfare services in the rural areas and among the urban poor. The less developed provinces received a larger socioeconomic development funds on per capita basis.[173] Subsidies were paid for the basic commodities and many antiinflationary measures were pursued. Taxes on the rich were, in recent years, increased. A temporary labor law was introduced, and laws for unemployment benefits, social security, and minimum wages were enacted. Attempts were made to balance wages in the private and the public sectors and to increase wages of the working people. Finally, the government tried to limit the share of capital in value added.

Although not all these policy measures have been fully implemented or successfully applied, the government has at times introduced policies that have tended to exacerbate socioeconomic inequalities. For example, following the sharp decline in oil revenues in 1986 and the introduction of the austerity Plan for New Economic Conditions, "the government reduced the work shifts and hours and imposed certain other austerity measures in the factories such as cutting cheap food served to workers, reducing overtime, etc."[174] Moreover, many reforms, which are needed to achieve social justice, remain to be introduced. These include radical land reform,

increases in direct taxes (on the wealthy and occupations in particular), control of the private sector, expansion of public schools,
effective means to fight inflation and overpricing, nationalization
of urban land, introduction of a definite labor law, nationalization
of foreign trade, and reorganization of regional administration. The
struggle over these and other reforms intensified following Ayattolah
Khomeini's *fetvas* in early 1988,[175] and again after the cease-fire,
when they surfaced in the context of debate on a suitable reconstruction strategy. However, as we shall see in Chapter 4, the current
trend is in the direction of neglecting social justice in favor of rapid
economic growth.

PROVINCIAL DEVELOPMENT AND POLICIES

Interprovincial disparity has long been a characteristic of the
Iranian society and its rectification has become a prominent issue in
the postrevolutionary period. This section will provide an overview
of interprovincial disparity before the Revolution and will examine
the various forces affecting provincial development since the Revolution. Whereas the emphasis is on the state's policies, the impact of
the war and the popular movements is also evaluated. Although interprovincial disparity has somewhat narrowed in the postrevolutionary period, the gap between the rich and the poor provinces
continue to remain wide and unacceptable from the perspective of
what I have elsewhere called *territorial social justice*, which was
among the aims of the Revolution.[176]

Provincial Disparity in Postrevolutionary Iran

A study by Amirahmadi and Atash using 1976 data, indicated
that the gap was particularly wide between the more developed
provinces (MDPs) of Markazi (including Tehran), Khuzestan, Esfahan, Yazd, Fars, and Semnan on the one hand, and the less developed provinces (LDPs) of Kurdestan, Chahar Mahall and Bakhtiari,
Lorestan, Ilam, Hormozgan, Zanjan, Sistan and Baluchestan, West
Azerbaijan, and Boyer Ahmadi and Kohkiluyeh on the other. Indicators for the remaining intermediate provinces (IPs) were closer to the
national averages for most of the thirteen socioeconomic variables
that the study examined.[177] Similar results were also obtained in a
subsequent study by Amirahmadi, a summary of which is given in
Table 3.17.[178] For example, the gap between the MDPs and the
LDPs was 2.4 times for degree of urbanization, 2.6 and 3.9 times for
number of physicians and hospital beds per 100,000 population, respectively, about 3 times for percent of houses with electricity,

Table 3.17 General Characteristics of the Three Categories of Iranian Provinces, 1976

Characteristics	Iran	More Developed Provinces	Intermediate Provinces	Less Developed Provinces
1. Population (% of nation)	100.0	41.5	41.4	17.1
2. Area (% of nation)	100.0	31.7	42.8	25.5
3. Density (per sq km)	20.5	26.8	19.7	13.6
4. Percent of urban population	47.1	66.9	35.1	27.8
5. Average total food and nonfood consumption expenditures of an urban family in 30 days, US$(1980)	650.0	602.0	652.0	728.0
6. Average total food and nonfood consumption expenditures of a rural family in 30 days, US$(1980)	343.0	411.0	343.0	265.0
7. Primary employment as percent of total employment	35.1	27.9	36.5	46.5
8. Secondary employment as percent of total employment	33.1	37.8	31.1	27.8
9. Value added per worker employed in large industrial establishments (1,000 rials)	740.0	620.0	513.8	361.0
10. Percentage of population that is literate (6 years and over)	47.5	54.7	41.8	32.3
11. Number of physicians per 100,000 population	39.8	45.4	22.9	17.8
12. Number of hospital beds per 100,000 population	160.1	185.1	101.2	47.5
13. Percentage of dwelling units with electricity	51.7	64.1	36.6	22.9
14. Number of public sector employees per 1,000 population	49.6	54.2	35.1	28.3
15. Development budget (share)	100.0	31.4	39.6	29.0

Sources and Notes:
Constructed on the basis of data compiled from the various issues of *Salnameh* and other publications by the Plan and Budget Organization including *Natayej-e Tafsili, Rusta* and *Natayej-e Tafsili, Shahr.*

For the list and location of provinces on the Iranian map see Figure 2.1.

2 times for public employees per 1,000 population, 1.7 times for literacy rate, and 1.5 times for productivity in large industrial establishments. Interregional disparity became even more pronounced when the least and the most developed provinces were compared. To take two extreme cases, in 1976, for example, Markazi was 80 percent urbanized as compared to 13 percent for Boyer Ahmadi and Kuhkiluyeh and the ratio for per capita gross regional product (including oil) between the poorest, Sistan and Baluchestan, and the richest, Markazi, provinces was on the order of 1 to 10 (U.S. $313 and $3,132 respectively). (The extreme nature of interprovincial disparity has been also documented in a few other studies.)[179]

Alternative explanations have proposed different factors to underlie interprovincial disparity. International consulting firms have generally emphasized uneven distribution of resources among the provinces.[180] A few independent researchers, on the other hand, focused on the ethnic and cultural differences among provinces, national oppression via unequal interprovincial exchange (by means of, for example, a policy that sets the terms of trade between agriculture and industry in favor of the later), or legal, policy-related discrimination.[181] The impact of foreign investment and multinational corporations have been only scantly considered.[182] Most writers, however, seem to point toward structural causes including political centralism, dominance of sectoral planning for national economic growth and inappropriate policy measures or lack of any such measures.[183] The postrevolutionary government seems to operate also on the basis of an understanding similar to structural explanations. However, in the absence of any officially published statement on the issue, this proposition may be supported by the government's provincial development policies.

Impact of the War and Popular Movements on
Provincial Development

As was noted in Chapter 2, the collapse of Phalavi state's centralized machinery in the face of the popular revolution led to dual sovereignty over the state's power. This in turn encouraged an intensive struggle over the social question of the Revolution including movements for land reform and regional autonomy. Although difficult to determine, the impact of these spontaneous, popular factors on provincial development and interprovincial disparity must have been significant. Such impact was particularly strong concerning central-local government relations. To begin with, they weakened the central government's control over provincial politics and resource management, leading to de facto territorial and functional decentralization, increased local initiatives, and popular participation. They also sharpened the public focus on and consciousness about the regional issues, thus creating pressure for introduction of popular legal measures and policies. Further, the movements radicalized the regional people, increased their territorial consciousness, taught them the value of organized and united action, and led to propagation of the idea that grass-roots organizations were indispensable for an introduction to democratic measures. There were also more tangible results. The autonomy movement in Kurdestan, for example, forced the central government to somewhat improve conditions there. The state also wanted to improve its image with the Kurdish people as part of a campaign against the regional opposition. Similarly, the movement in Turkoman Sahra led to significant changes in land redistribution in favor of the landless peasants.[184]

Another factor affecting the provincial development in the post-revolutionary period was the war with Iraq. As noted earlier, the war inflicted extensive damage on the country's settlements. Specifically, a total of 51 cities and some 4,000 villages were reported destroyed or damaged in varying degrees. Recent data also indicate slower population growth in the war zones compared to the rest of the country. For example, Khuzestan grew at an average annual rate of only 1.77 percent over the 1976–86 period, less than 50 percent of the national average. In sharp contrast, the comparable figures for Tehran province (excluding the city of Tehran) and Bushehr, a province adjoining Khuzestan, were 8.7 and 5.5 percent, respectively.[185] The war also had a major impact on population redistribution, for it caused death, destruction, and migration. Some 2.5 million fled the war areas to settle in large cities and refugee camps in other parts of the country, particularly in cities located in the center and in areas adjoining the war zones. Karaj, Qom, Shiraz, Arak, and Zanjan were examples. A good many also fled the country into exile. An equally large number migrated from the village areas and smaller towns to refugee camps and the provincial capitals within the war zones, where people were better protected. Examples include cities of Ahvaz, Urumia, and Bakhtaran that continued to grow at over 5 percent per year over the 1976–86 period. In sharp contrast, smaller towns in the war zones had a significantly lower growth rate. Dezful in Khuzestan, for example, grew only at 0.2 percent over the 1976–84 period.[186]

Although the war destroyed a good portion of the socioeconomic activities in the war zones, it led to concentration of significant war-supporting activities and expenditures in the neighboring provinces.[187] Increased war-related imports also promoted development in the southern coastal provinces with port facilities. The improved development position of Kurdestan and Ilam in the war zones may be explained by the same factors that were responsible for the improved relative development of other LDPs, namely, policies of the government in support of the LDPs. Yet, the impact of the war must have been equally powerful, for it destroyed Iranian industries and consequently led to the relative decline of the MDPs. The war also triggered a development program implemented in the strategic Persian Gulf islands. Finally, the war led to drastic changes in investment priorities of the government, both in terms of location and types of production. Most defense industries and strategic establishments moved to more secure areas in the central and eastern parts of the country, and many existing capacities were altered in the direction of military production.

Administrative Changes and Provincial Policies

State policies for provincial development included legal, planning, and administrative changes and specific measures to redistribute social services, and investment and relief funds in favor of certain less developed provinces. Constitutional and planning changes were discussed in Chapter 2. In what follows, I shall focus on administrative changes and specific provincial policies in the postrevolutionary period. Gross deficiencies characterized provincial and planning administrations in prerevolutionary Iran. The Shah's government was of a unitary and centralized nature (as opposed to federalism) and the society was organized socioeconomically along sectoral (vertical) administrations, and politically into provincial (horizontal) administrations. The country's twenty-three provinces were headed by governors, in most cases a nonnative politician. The invariably male governor represented the central government and was in theory responsible for the supervision and coordination of all provincial affairs. In practice, however, the governor's office largely was unable to carry out its functions. Heads of provincial sectoral offices were responsible only to their ministers in Tehran and the sectoral ministers were independent of the interior minister to whom the governor reported. Consequently, territorial and sectoral integration and coordination were weak. These relations were equally weak among the socioeconomic sectors, many of which were headed by largely self-serving nonnative technocrats. Moreover, this organization made provinces subordinate to the nation and to the socioeconomic sectors on matters of development. As a consequence, vertical hierarchies from the Shah to local offices dominated horizontal relationships between various territorial units. Under this arrangement, only at the very top of the state hierarchy did the two bureaucracies meet; there was almost no coordination at the local levels.[188]

Although the postrevolutionary state is based on a republican model (as opposed to the monarchy under the ancien régime), its organizational structure has changed only very little. The system remains unitary and centralized and based on a dominant vertical-sectoral organization of the society. Only in a few areas have noticeable changes been introduced. These include measures to remedy gross deficiencies that have characterized provincial and planning administrations. The number of provinces have increased to twenty-four (by the addition of Tehran Province); existing sectoral offices have largely been reorganized (particularly those concerned with agriculture, industries, and infrastructure); a few suprasectoral offices have been created with primarily spatial concern (such as *Jihad-e Sazandegi* or Construction Crusade and a number of *bouniads* or foundations); and the old leaders have been replaced by new ones, some of whom are appointed from among the local people. The power of the governor seems to have somewhat increased as has the interplay among various sectoral offices and between them and the governor office. Under the new administrative arrangement, heads of sectoral, as well as suprasectoral, offices report to both their respective ministers and the governor.

By strengthening the position of provincial governors, the Islamic Republic has reduced the gap between the horizontal and vertical administrations. Provincial governors are also involved in provincial development planning. The governor exercises increased power through a powerful Provincial Planning Committee (PPC).[189] The PPC has also increased the interplay between various economic sectors at the provincial level. The governor heads the planning committee and the director of the Provincial Planning Office is its secretary. The committee frequently brings together heads of sectoral and suprasectoral offices and district governors, under the supervision of the governor, to discuss matters of policies and priorities sent down from Tehran. Distribution of provincial budgets, proposals for the next year's budget, and examination of the reports and views received from the representatives of the province in the Parliament are also taken up in the committee's meetings. Additionally, the planning committee receives detailed reports from the implementing agencies concerning the quality and quantity of their operations and is charged with coordination of their activities. The governor is responsible to report the committee's work plan and minutes of its meetings to the representatives of the province in the Parliament and receive their comments and reactions for presentation to the committee. A new Law of Islamic Councils demarcates functional divisions of labor between the central and local governments in all matters of strategy determination to implementation, supervision, and evaluation.[190] For example, the PPC not only can propose national projects, but it also is allowed to plan and implement provincial projects, given that it would not require resources beyond local capabilities. On the other hand, whereas the national budget remains centralized, local governments may collect and retain certain taxes. These changes notwithstanding, participatory decision making and management, and administrative decentralization remain in the Islamic Constitution.

A number of changes were also made in the planning administration. An early attempt came in December 1983 (Azar 1362) when the government created ten planning regions by juxtaposing two to three contiguous provinces with a similar culture or level of development into one region. The larger or the more influential provincial capital was then made the regional center from which a regional planner would oversee the planning affairs of the whole region. (A similar regionalization scheme had also been attempted in 1972 under the Shah.) Just as this early experience, the new scheme was soon abolished largely because of the opposition from sectoral ministers, and also because of interprovincial cultural and political conflicts and the inability of the regional centers, as well as the central administration in Tehran, to provide effective leadership and technical services. Termination of the regionalization scheme was followed by a new design for regional administration on the basis of a complete reorganization of the Plan and Budget Organization (PBO). Under the Shah, PBO was part of the prime minister's office and had a staff or advisory role within the hierarchy. It was administered by a managing director, who was assisted by two powerful deputies of planning, and budgeting supervision. Almost a year after the Revolution, PBO was made into a ministry with an interdisciplinary portfolio and moved from the prime minister's office. The new administration eliminated the earlier two deputies but horizontally expanded the organization to incorporate nine new deputies (Figure 3.18), each with planning and budgeting supervision offices. Among the newly created deputies was Deputy for Regional Affairs (DRA), among the largest in the organization. Figure 3.19 indicates the various planning administrations under the DRA including twenty-four Provincial Plan and Budget Organizations (PPBO), with over 200 staff members, and the Office of Regional Planning (ORP), which is located in PBO in Tehran and charged with the *Amayesh-e Sarzamin*.

Figure 3.18

Administrative Chart of the Ministry of Plan and Budget since 1983

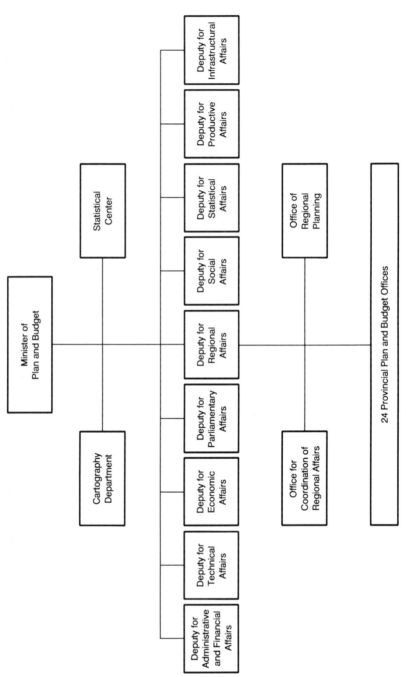

Source: Drawn by the author on the basis of interviews 1986.

Figure 3.19
Administration of Regional Planning since 1983

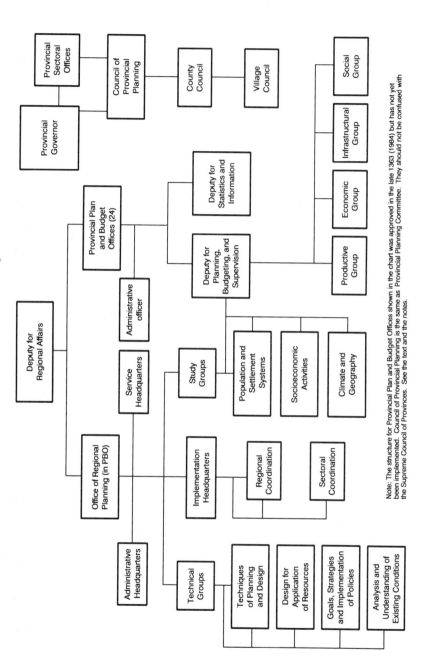

Note: The structure for Provincial Plan and Budget Offices shown in the chart was approved in the late 1363 (1984) but has not yet been implemented. Council of Provincial Planning is the same as Provincial Planning Committee. They should not be confused with the Supreme Council of Provinces. See the text and the notes.

These reorganizations could not be fully implemented or sustained. In 1989, following constitutional changes and in an attempt to recentralize the system, the Ministry of Plan and Budget was again made into an organization and moved to the president's office. Moreover, while the ORP is a reality, with a tight structure and an active agenda, the PPBOs largely existed on paper except for a small core of regional planners and an administrator in a few large provinces. And there remained other problems. For example, boundaries of certain provinces must be redelineated to correct for extreme disparities in size, revenue basis, and resources among provinces. Spatial and sectoral councils must be fully operationalized before a centrally controlled decentralized regional government and a participatory planning system can emerge. Provincial governors must be delegated considerably more power than they presently wield. They should also be given a more articulate body of regional and technical staff than they presently have. The link between horizontal and vertical bureaucracies must be expanded by creation of certain *meso* organizations such as an interministerial coordinating body. Finally, the state should gradually move away from rigid centralism and sectoralism toward what I have elsewhere called "an associative system of regional governments in which common interests and purposes are the primary integrating forces, and where regionalism is subordinate to nationalism but not to sectoralism."[191] Considerable factors militate against such a development under the Islamic Republic. These include the unitary system of the government, the sectoral-vertical organization of the Republic's institutions, the predominance of the sectoral interests over regionalism, and the lack of a well-defined and unified perspective about a more productive and integrative relationship between the central administration and the regional governments.

The impact of the legal, planning, and administrative changes on the provincial development in postrevolutionary Iran cannot be easily determined. Most such changes remain to be implemented and others put in practice have not been subjected to any impact analysis. Scarcity of information is not the only problem with such an assessment. Even more troubling is the impossibility of separating the impact of these changes from other state measures, incidental factors (such as the war), and popular movements. Certain safe generalizations, nevertheless, can be made. For example, most regionalists in the country continue to receive legitimacy for their radical demands from the Constitution; the new spatial planning system (*amayesh-e sarzamin*) has generated significant interest in provincial development and produced a considerable amount of information about various aspects of the provinces; and finally, administrative changes have helped to increase the power of provincial governments and the efficiency of resources use at local levels. Although such impacts have not led to any significant short-term changes, their long-term consequences for regional development could be tremendous.

We now come to the state provincial policy. Broadly speaking, the Islamic Republic lacks a coherent system of policies for provincial development. It has implemented a number of isolated policies. These include both explicit spatial policies, aimed at improving certain conditions in given regions, generally the LDPs, and implicit policies, that is, nonspatial policies with significant repercussions for regional development. After the Revolution, particularly following the war, the government began directing part of the private and public investment toward the LDPs. In 1976, for example, of all Agreements in Principle and Permits issued by the Ministry of Industries, only 0.42 percent went to the LDPs. The figure increased to 1.5 percent in 1981 and then to 8.7 percent in the first six months of 1986.[192] The policy of making agriculture an "axis" of development was equally helpful to the LDPs. Price support programs, cheap and easy credit arrangements, services provision, and low-level technical assistance were among the major components of the policy.

Most economic and social service sectors have also transferred part of their operations to the LDPs. This is particularly true of the newly established Ministry of Reconstruction Crusade (RC), which has carried out extensive socioeconomic and infrastructural works in the rural areas particularly electrification, road construction, and provision of certain social services including health and housing. The war zones have also benefited from activities of the Foundation for the Affairs of the War-Inflicted Population, the Foundation for the Oppressed, and the Headquarters for the Reconstruction and Renovation of the War-Damaged Areas.

A number of policies focusing on tribal areas, rural settlements, and small urban centers also tend to benefit the LDPs. Most helpless residents of rural and tribal areas over sixty-years-of-age receive welfare payments under the "Shahid Raja'i Program" from the Imam Relief Committee. Each month, the relief committee pays up to 3,000 rials to such individuals in the forms of cash or essential capital or consumer goods. Since 1987, the monthly allowance has increased to 5,000 rials for eligible individuals heading a family of more than one person (Article 11 of the budget laws since 1983). Of the funds allocated each year to municipalities under Article 19 of the budget laws, 80 percent must be distributed to cities other than provincial centers.[193] Article 6 of the budget laws also targets the most backward spots in the country. The Plan and Budget Organization has identified forty-one such areas.[194] In addition to normal allocation from their respective provincial budgets, these areas receive special funds directly from the central administration in Tehran. In 1988, for example, 16 billion rials were allocated to be spent on fixed investments in "essential" and "specified" development projects in designated depressed areas. At least 70 percent of the funds must be expended in development projects in rural and tribal areas.[195]

Among the most important regional policies of the Islamic Republic designed to benefit the LDPs are Articles 3 and 16, Note 66, of the budget laws since 1985. In instituting Article 16, the state also follows other aims, namely, to receive financial help for its projects from the wealthy and encourage public participation in smaller projects with local significance. Each year, the central government allocates a specified sum of funds (for example, 10 billion rial in 1986 and 15 billion rial in 1988) to be allocated to provinces relative to their shares in the nation's general budget. Each province may spend the fund on new small projects or completing projects that were initiated by the private sector. The law prohibits initiation of projects requiring more than 50 billion rials of expenditures. In rural and tribal areas, at least 30 percent of the investment for such projects must be committed by the private sector. The figure is 50 percent in urban places. The credit from the private participants could include cash, labor, or materials. Implementation of the law is collectively supervised by the governor, the Provincial Planning Committee, and the respective executive agency.[196]

"To allow participation of private entrepreneurs in development of their respective regions," Article 16 also allows the Council of Provincial Planning to retain up to 50 percent of the monthly occupational taxes it collects, as well as any sum that it collects in provincial capitals (with the exception of Tehran) over and above the sum collected in the same month in 1985. Such taxes must be placed under the Provincial Planning Committee and exclusively invested in provincial development projects of the following types: public education and health, urban development, physical training, water projects, and rural roads. "In these sectors, projects favored by the taxpayers must receive priority," the law stipulates. The council identifies various projects, for each of which a trustee and a bank account is established. Taxpayers are free to choose among the projects announced by the council and deposit their taxes to the corresponding accounts. Moreover, the taxpayer may request that his or her taxes be invested outside the region of residence excluding cities of Tehran, Mashad, Esfahan, Tabriz, and Shiraz, which are among the largest provincial centers.[197] This policy benefits the generally tax-losing LDPs, but is of little help to the poor as the provincial wealthy, including the landlords and the capitalists, choose projects directly benefiting their own investments and activities.

Article 3, on the other hand, allows the government to use the banking system to support private local initiatives with little or no start-up capital and to assist reactivation or expansion of the existing operations. Such initiatives and operations must be technically and financially sound and feasible, economically needed, and organized into cooperatives. Originally, the law did not apply to individual applicants, however, that has been changed in most recent budget laws, which only require a 50 percent minimum expenditure of the funds in the cooperative sector. The stated purpose of government in advancing this article is to generate jobs and increase production in agriculture and industries, particularly those organized into cooperatives and located in rural areas. The Central Bank is obliged to provide the needed credits for the eligible projects from the internal sources of the Provincial Banks (provincial branches of the Exports Bank) and, when needed, from resources of other banks.[198]

Most funds under this article have gone to agriculture, rural industries, and the LDPs. For example, of the 60 billion rials allocated for the purpose in 1988, 30 billion have been given to agriculture and rural industries, 8 billion to construction materials, 5 billion to industries, 5 billion to mines, 5 billion to the Foundation for the War Migrants, and the rest has been divided among many social services and cultural activities. Of the amount allocated to agriculture and rural industries, Sistan and Baluchestan, an LDP, has received 3 billion rials as compares to 0.03 billion for Tehran and 1 billion for East Azerbaijan. The LDPs of West Azerbaijan and Kurdestan have been allocated 0.915 and 0.7 billion rials respectively.[199] Despite these higher shares going to the LDPs, critics remain unhappy with implementation of Article 3. For example, Movahedi Sajedi, a Parliament representative, has charged that the Article 3 has not benefited the poor, created the expected number of jobs, or increased production, and that the beneficiaries have been people with connections and friends within the bureaucracy. He demands a more just and correct distribution of such funds.[200]

The government also encourages provincial export production by providing the producers and exporters with various production, financial, and marketing services. This export-promotion regional policy is complemented with another policy that allows inhabitants of the deprived regions of the border provinces in the south to engage in import and export activities given that such transactions do not create foreign exchange commitments and do not exceed a 100,000 rials ceiling. The law is lucrative, for black market exchange rates between rials and foreign currencies are sometimes fifteen times higher than the official exchange rates. The original law in 1986 required that the inhabitants be members of certain cooperatives. (This condition was relaxed in the subsequent year by the Council of Guardians.) This change had led to corruption, for nonmember individuals are poor and illiterate; they are hardly able to benefit from the law. They usually sell their rights to merchants and middlemen who reap the benefits.[201]

Another policy mandates that a predetermined number of entrants to the country's universities each year must include applicants from the LDPs. These students, most of whom receive scholarship from the government, must, in turn, undertake to work in their native province for a specified period after graduation. The LDPs also receive an additional budget for education. Under Article 8 of the 1988 budget, for example, 3 billion rials were allocated for the purpose and distributed among provinces on the basis of relative educational deprivation. Half of the funds were allocated for the creation of model schools and the other half paid for upgrading the quality of education where it had noticeably dropped. The article also allocated 20 billion rials for free nutrition programs in the LDPs.[202]

In the absence of a migration policy, the government has adapted a number of measures to influence movement of the population, particularly the state employees, away from the MDPs toward the LDPs. Working in the deprived areas for at least a limited period, usually a year, has become obligatory for most government employees and certain professions including medicine, dentistry, and higher education. The prerevolutionary policy of differential wage rates for the government employees serving in different regions continues to be in force. In a few LDPs, the wage rates are three times as high as in Tehran for comparable jobs. This should be a powerful incentive where inflation runs high in large cities and overtime pay is restricted on most regular jobs. (The war had, however, reduced the effect of such population redistribution policies to a significant degree.)

Finally, the government has made a conscious effort to change its budget allocation priorities from one based on regional comparative advantage to one based on need for immediate relief. Thus, the shares of the LDPs in the development budget have increased relative to the figures for the MDPs, and in comparison with the LDPs' shares in the years preceding the Revolution. For example, as indicated in Table 3.18, over the 1982–86 period, the LDPs have received, on the average, about 33 percent of the nation's regional development budget, whereas the figure for the MDPs is below 30 percent, although the latter's population is more than twice as large as the former's. The corresponding budget figures for the LDPs and the MDPs over the 1973–77 prerevolutionary period are 28.4 and 32 (Table 3.19). The intermediate provinces (IPs), on the other hand, have experienced only a slight improvement in their budget shares. However, the war made it increasingly difficult for the government to continue its pro-LDPs policy as indicated by the decline in their budget shares since 1984 (Table 3.18).

Although extensive, the state's regional policies remained inadequate. They were hardly coordinated or put into a broader development perspective. Incentives were not directed to well-targeted objectives and most projects were funded for no apparent reason or any meaningful eligibility criteria such as desirability, feasibility, replicability, and affordability on a national scale. Equally absent was an impact analysis from an efficiency or equity perspective. Locational requirements remained also largely unspecified and the policies were not given proper legal protection to reinforce their implementation. They also lacked adequate managing organizations. Supporting policies were equally absent and many major provincial problems were not covered by any of the explicit policies. Specifically, incentives wer not extended to include project- or locale-specific grants; control instruments (concerning migration or activity location) were not instituted; and territorial development agencies were not established. Finally, most policies took a "place prosperity" approach, ignoring the social dimensions of territorial issues.[203]

Despite the shortcomings, the extensive policy measures adopted must have made certain contributions to various aspects of provincial development in the country. However, in the absence of data and the presence of other impacts, it is impossible to be specific about the extent or quality of the policies' effects. The only significant evidence, a recent study by Amirahmadi and Atash, indicates a moderation in the disparity gap among the LDPs and the MDPs, a trend that seems to have lasted until 1984.[204] The study used coefficient of variations and standardized scores to examine changes in regional disparity for seven socioeconomic variables between 1976 (before the Revolution) and 1984, the last postrevolutionary year for which statistics were available. The variables examined included percentage of urban population, consumption expenditures of urban and rural families, value added per worker in large industrial estab-

Table 3.18   Provincial Distribution on Development Budgets (fixed investments), 1982–86 (percent share)

Provinces	a 1982	b 1983	c 1984	d 1985	e 1986
More Developed	30.9	30.8	29.2	28.2	28.8
Markazi	5.5	7.0	6.7	6.6	6.9
Esfahan	5.4	5.4	5.4	4.7	4.8
Yazd	2.7	2.6	2.4	2.1	2.2
Khuzestan	8.6	7.1	6.6	6.7	6.6
Fars	6.5	6.2	5.8	5.7	5.9
Semnan	2.2	2.5	2.4	2.4	2.4
Intermediate	35.2	35.2	38.0	40.1	39.9
Bakhtaran	3.7	4.1	4.1	3.8	3.9
Khorasan	6.1	7.4	7.2	8.2	7.9
E. Azerbaijan	6.6	5.5	6.9	8.0	7.9
Gilan	3.4	3.2	3.9	4.1	3.7
Hamadan	1.7	1.9	3.4	2.9	2.6
Kerman	6.2	5.0	4.9	4.6	4.9
Mazandaran	4.0	5.1	4.4	5.3	5.8
Bushehr	3.3	3.0	3.1	3.2	3.2
Less Developed	33.9	34.0	32.8	31.7	31.3
Chahar Mahall and Bakhtiari	4.2	3.9	3.0	2.9	2.9
Hormozgan	4.1	3.4	3.7	4.1	3.6
Kurdestan	2.9	3.8	3.6	3.3	3.7
Ilam	2.9	2.7	3.0	2.6	2.9
W. Azerbaijan	4.8	5.5	4.6	4.5	4.7
Lorestan	3.0	3.7	3.7	3.5	3.7
Boyer Ahmadi and Kohkiluyeh	3.7	3.3	3.2	2.9	2.8
Sistan and Baluchestan	5.3	4.6	4.4	4.7	3.9
Zanjan	3.0	3.1	3.6	3.2	3.1
Iran (percentage)	100	100	100	100	100
Iran* (million rial, current prices)	150,609	195,627	194,309	186,077	160,406

Sources and Notes:
1982 data from *Salnameh-e Amari* (1362) (1983), p. 694; 1983–85 data from *Salnameh-e Amari* (1363) (1984), p. 769; and *Iran Dar Aʾine-he Amar*, no. 5 (1364), p. 220.

a. Provincial distribution of the following budgeted development funds were not available and are not included in the year's statistics: (1) *Jihad-e Sazandegi* [Construction Crusade]: 7,200 million rials; and (2) Special Funds: 11,870 million rials.

b. Provincial distribution of the following budgeted development funds were not available and are not included in the year's statistics: (1) *Jihad-e Sazandegi* [Construction Crusade]: 89,279 million rials; and (2) Special Funds: 6,534 million rials.

c. Provincial distribution of the Special Funds, 9,010 million rials, were not available for the year and are not included.

d. Provincial distribution of the Special Funds, 2,500 million rials, and war expenditures were not available for the year and are not included. Figures are approved, not actual.

e. The amount of 9,136 million rials development credits on the basis of special permission are not included because their distribution among various affairs were not available. Figures are estimates.

* Please note that the absolute figures of this row are not comparable to the corresponding figures in Table 3.19.

Table 3.19   Provincial Development Budgets 1973–77 (percent share)

Provinces	1973	1974	1975	1976	1977
More Developed	41.1	29.1	28.9	31.4	29.6
Markazi	18.2	7.9	7.5	8.0	7.2
Esfahan	6.0	4.8	5.3	5.5	5.6
Yazd	1.7	2.7	2.5	2.1	3.1
Khuzestan	7.3	6.6	5.5	10.2	5.3
Fars	6.3	4.9	5.6	4.1	5.5
Semnan	1.6	2.3	2.5	1.5	2.9
Intermediate	38.3	38.5	41.4	39.0	40.5
Bakhtaran	3.9	4.0	4.0	3.9	5.0
Khorasan	7.5	7.2	8.4	7.6	6.3
E. Azerbaijan	6.8	4.6	7.5	8.7	8.3
Gilan	5.3	4.5	4.3	5.0	5.5
Hamadan	3.7	3.5	3.7	2.2	3.4
Kerman	2.9	5.6	4.9	4.4	4.0
Mazandaran	6.8	5.3	5.4	4.5	4.9
Bushehr	1.4	3.7	3.3	2.7	3.1
Less Developed	20.6	32.4	29.7	29.6	29.9
Chahar Mahall and Bakhtiari	1.4	2.5	2.4	5.2	2.4
Hormozgan	2.5	5.2	3.9	4.2	5.6
Kurdestan	2.5	4.2	3.8	3.0	3.7
Ilam	1.3	2.6	2.8	2.1	2.6
W. Azerbaijan	4.9	4.4	4.1	3.0	2.0
Lorestan	2.8	3.0	3.6	3.1	3.8
Boyer Ahmadi and Kohkiluyeh	1.3	3.0	2.3	2.2	3.1
Sistan and Baluchestan	2.3	5.1	4.0	4.8	4.1
Zanjan	1.6	2.4	2.8	2.0	2.7
Iran (percentage)	100.0	100.0	100.0	100.0	100.0
Iran* (million rial, current prices)	6,539.5	18,618.6	24,740.0	22,866.0	22,329.3

Source and Notes:
Sair-e Barnamehrizi-ye Mantaqeh'i Dar Iran [Evolution of Regional Planning in Iran] (Tehran: Plan and Budget Organization, 2536, 1977).

1973–77: Includes funds for Special Regional Projects and additional funds allocated to provinces after revision of the fifth plan following the fourfold increase in oil revenue in 1973 (the Law of Article One). 1976–77: Also includes money allocated to provinces under Development Funds for Regional Projects (fixed investments).

* Please note that the absolute figures in this row are not comparable to the corresponding figures in Table 3.18.

lishments, number of post offices per 10,000 sq km, number of hospital beds per 100,000 population, and number of physicians per 100,000 population. Of these, provincial dispartiy increased only for the last variable, whereas it declined in all other cases. Indeed, shortly after the Revolution, medical schools were closed for about three years and the existing physicians either fled the country or were sent to war zones and hospitals in large cities, particularly Tehran. The study also found that, during the 1976–84 period, most of the IPs and the LDPs improved their relative position within the provincial hierarchy, while four of the six MDPs suffered relative decline. However, and as Amirahmadi and Atash concluded, "except for a few cases, the relative position of the provinces did not change in any significant way and thus their place in the provincial hierarchy remained largely unaffected by the socioeconomic development processes."[205] It is not clear if this spatial change made any significant impact on the conditions of the poor in the LDPs.

Regional issues continue to remain a major source of tension between the local people and the central government. The Kurdish struggle is a case in point. They need greater attention from the state. The existing measures must be institutionalized and better managed. Restructuring territorial socioeconomic systems, sectoral administrations, and sector-space interactions are of paramount importance. New policies must also include a regionally balanced distribution of power, decision making, and development resources. Respect for cultural diversity and autonomy must also be preserved. Greater improvements are needed in the state's implementation capacities. However, it is not yet certain if the emerging reconstruction strategy will favor a more balanced provincial development. Given that the pragmatists in power need and are focusing on rapid economic growth to raise the generally declined living standard in the country, disparity could be expected to widen again.

FOREIGN TRADE AND THE BALANCE OF PAYMENTS

An export-promotion strategy was introduced in Iran in the 1970s as the growing joint-venture consumer industries began supplying the neighboring Persian Gulf states with products. However, the incredible power of the oil sector to earn windfall foreign exchange made it impossible for the state to develop any significant appetite for nonoil exports. Moreover, as the industries producing such exports depended on the foreign exchange earnings from oil, their further development was hampered by the gradual decline in the oil revenues. The dominance of oil also made foreign trade less relevant as a stabilizing tool, particularly for controlling prices and employment. On the contrary, the sector had been the primary enemy of economic stability and development. Specifically, earnings from oil increased demand for imports and drained the economy of a significant portion of its savings. Between 1953 and 1983, some $205 billion were paid for imports, about $92 billion during the 1978–83 period alone.[206]

With the decline in oil revenue and the GDP in the postrevolutionary period, the imbalance in the country's foreign trade exacerbated. The war and the lack of coherent and coordinated plan for the transformation of the economic structure, the allocation of foreign exchange, and the reorientation and control of foreign trade were among the major contributing factors.[207] Other causes included the externally oriented consumption pattern, expansion of the credit system due to an increasing budget deficit, a low-level of tax collection from the rich, and the largely overvalued exchange rates between rial and foreign currencies—the U.S. dollar in particular. The Constitution included foreign trade among the activities of the "public sector" and the Law of Nationalization of Foreign Trade was enacted by the Parliament in March 1980. However, opposition from the big merchants, who draw immense amount of profit from international trade, and their conservative allies in the government had prevented the state from implementing the law fully. Consequently, state control of foreign trade remained inadequate despite the decline in the share of the private sector in current payments for import of goods, from 69 percent in 1980 to 34 percent in 1985 (Table 3.20).[208]

Between 1977 and 1979, the value of imports dropped by 34 percent as the GDP and the oil revenues gradually declined to their lowest levels. (Table 3.21 gives the trends in volume and structure of imports.) Cancellation of certain military purchases and the general apathy for "foreign" goods at a time when struggle for national sovereignty was underway helped bring about the declining trends. With gradual improvements in the economic conditions after 1980 and the increased needs of the war front, imports picked up again and reached their postrevolutionary peak in 1983, when the oil revenue and the GDP were also at their postrevolutionary peaks and the war had moved onto Iraqi territory. In just four years, between 1979 and 1983, the indicator increased by 131 percent. Since 1984, imports have been declining: from about $18.3 billion in 1983 to $8.5 billion in 1986. Although the 1987 and 1988 figures were projected to be still lower, imports relative to domestic production remained significantly high. The steep decline in imports after 1984 was induced by the decline in oil revenue, which reached its lowest level in 1986.

The most discouraging aspect of the imports, however, is its structure. Specifically, most Iranian import items are for consumption. In 1984, to take a year when imports of capital goods were at their postrevolutionary peak, capital goods accounted for only about 26 percent of the imported commodities, whereas the year's figures

Table 3.20 Current Payments for Import of Goods, Total Value, and Percent Shares of Public and Private Sectors, 1976–85 (million U.S. dollars)(a)

	1976	1977	1978	1979	1980	1981	1982	1983	1984	1985
Total Value (b)	16,060.0	16,553.1	13,551.4	11,545.1	15,743.4	15,344.2	13,408.6	22,316.4	16,912.3	11,751.0
Public Sector (%)	51	54	45	35	31	42	58	58	66	66
Private Sector (%)	49	46	55	65	69	58	42	42	34	34

Sources and Notes:
Salnameh (1363); and (1365), p. 740; *Tehrani*, vol. 2, p. 393; *Taraznameh* (1363); and *Majaleh* (1364), p. 62.

(a) For exchange rates between rial and dollar see note 10 in Chapter 1.

(b) Note that the figures do not include payments for services.

Table 3.21   Industrial and Consumer Imports and Their Composition, 1976–86 (million rials, current prices)(a)

Year	Total Value (million rials)	Annual Growth Rates (%)	Intermediate Goods (%)	Capital Goods (%)	Consumer Goods (%)
1976	901,761	—	52.6	29.8	17.6
1977	1,034,211	14.7	54.1	37.5	18.4
1978	732,293	−29.2	52.7	28.1	19.2
1979	684,491	−6.5	54.7	18.9	26.4
1980	776,841	13.5	57.2	16.1	26.7
1981	1,081,951	39.3	60.9	15.9	23.2
1982	1,002,326	−7.4	57.9	19.5	22.6
1983	1,582,717	57.9	59.9	24.0	16.1
1984	1,322,673	−16.4	57.8	26.1	16.1
1985	1,058,345	−20.0	66.7	20.2	13.1
1986(b)	720,691	−31.9	55.6	22.5	17.4

Sources and Notes:
Gozaresh (1363), vol. 2, Chapter 8, Tables 1, 2, and 4; *Salnameh* (1365), pp. 715, 732; and *Faslnameh* (1365), pp. 204–205. Figures for 1985 and 1986 are from *Economic Bulletin* 6, no. 35 (15 September 1987), p. 18.

(a) For exchange rate between rial and dollar, see note 10 in chapter 1.

(b) Percentage figures for 1986 do not add up to 100. For the year some 4.5 percent of imports are reported under the category "Others."

for intermediate and consumer goods were about 58 and 16 percent, respectively. Note that most imports in the intermediate category are used in the consumer goods industries. The postrevolutionary import structure has also suffered from a reduction in the share of capital goods, from a prerevolutionary peak of 37.5 percent in 1977 to as low as 16 percent in 1980 and 1981. This sharp decline has reflected the war shock and the low-level of capital formation in the period. It was not until 1983 that imports of capital goods began to increase to above 20 percent of the total imports bill (Figure 3.20).

Since 1979, the state has attempted to reduce the level of consumer goods gradually and increase that of the capital and intermediate goods, particularly the parts going to defense-related production. This policy began to work only after the 1982 oil price hike and following the introduction of a more stringent exchange control policy in 1984, when oil income began to decline and imports had to be brought under tighter control. The sharp decline in oil prices in 1986 forced the state to introduce the most extensive foreign exchange assignment system ever instituted in the country. A Committee for the Assignment of Foreign Exchange was formed to implement the policy.

Accordingly, expenditures of foreign exchange were to decline by one-third, but the burden was to be borne by certain specified sec-

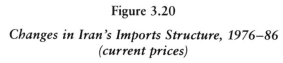

Figure 3.20

*Changes in Iran's Imports Structure, 1976–86
(current prices)*

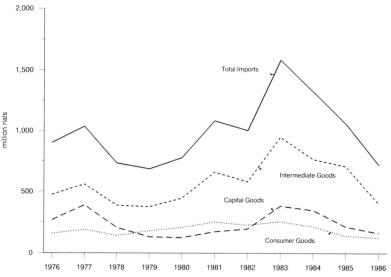

tors and activities. The war was given the highest priority and its share in the official-rate foreign exchange appreciably increased. Consumer goods were classified into "essential" and "secondary"; the former received a high priority for official-rate foreign exchange whereas the latter was to be largely imported at free market-rate foreign change. Industries were also classified into various categories: those producing "essential" or "strategic" goods were given high priority and received the official-rate foreign exchange; those that produced "less essential" goods would only receive a portion of their foreign currency needs at the official rate; and industries that did not fall in either of these categories were to secure their foreign exchange needs on the free market or from the government at similar rates. Certain national industrial projects and "job-generating" industries were also treated favorably and given the right to official-rate foreign currencies. Agriculture, with the lowest foreign currency dependency among the economic sectors, was also given access to the official-rate foreign exchange as were activities producing nonoil exports.[209]

The dollar value of oil exports, which had declined to its lowest level immediately following the war in 1980, increased thereafter and reached its all time postrevolutionary high of about U.S. $20.5

billion in 1983. (Table 3.22 gives trends in volume and structure of exports.) However, the impact of declining prices could not be offset by increased export volume, and this led to a reversal in the trend in oil export earnings beginning in 1984. Oil income dropped to its lowest point in 1986, to $5.8 billion, following the sharp fall in spot prices earlier that year. The 1987 figure was reported by then Prime Minister Musavi at $11 billion, which is close to the figure given in Table 3.22 ($10.7 billion).[210] The decline in the value of the U.S. dollar in recent years became another annoying factor in the oil-dependent Iranian budget.

The importance of oil for the Iranian economy was explained earlier and may be underscored here again. For example, the sector earned over 95 percent of the country's foreign currency and, in 1983 and 1984, was responsible for about 74 percent of the public income, which were either directly drawn from oil or indirectly through taxes on goods paid for by the oil revenues. The decline in oil exports could be potentially beneficial to an economy that had suffered heavily from dependency on a single export commodity. In the absence of a planned production shift, however, no measurable

Table 3.22   Oil and Nonoil Exports, 1976–88 (million U.S. dollars, current prices)(a)

Years	Nonoil Exports	Oil Exports	Nonoil as % of Oil Exports
1976	540	20,488	2.6
1977	625	20,735	3.0
1978	543	17,867	3.0
1979	812	19,315	4.2
1980	645	11,607	5.6
1981	340	12,456	2.7
1982	284	20,050	1.4
1983	357	20,457	1.7
1984	361	16,663	2.2
1985	357	13,968	2.6
1986	764	5,800	13.2
1987 (b)	1050	10,718	9.8
1988 (b)	—	7,900	—

Sources and Notes:
Economic Bulletin 6, no. 18 (12 May 1987), p. 4; and no. 17 (5 May 1987), p. 11; *Gozaresh* (1363), vol. 2, Chapter 8, p. 17; *Taraznameh* (1356, 1357, and 1358); *Salnameh* (1365), p. 740; *Gozaresh* (1365), vol. 1, p. 61; vol. 2, Chapter 12, p. 1; *Majaleh* (1364), p. 62; *Tahavvulat*, p. 632; *Tarh-e Moghadamati*; and *Iran Focus* 1, no. 2, p. 19.

(a) For exchange rates between rial and dollar see note 10 in chapter 1.

(b) Figures are estimates.

benefit has as yet been gained. On the contrary, the economy suffered tremendously from the declining oil exports.

The nonoil exports also fluctuated in the postrevolutionary period and, on the whole, made little progress. They made a jump in the first year of the Revolution (1979) and declined each year thereafter until 1983 when they began to increase, but made their second jump only in 1986, followed by another major increase in 1987, when they reached their postrevolutionary peak of about $1,050 million (Table 3.22).[211] Estimates for 1988 showed a slight decline relative to 1987 performance.[212] The huge decline in oil revenues in 1986, along with increasing international isolation, had left the government with almost no other option but to devise means to increase nonoil exports. Particularly effective was the government's preferential exchange rates for nonoil exports. An array of other promotional incentives were also offered to producers of nonoil export commodities.[213] Nonetheless, the nonoil export earnings remained[213] insignificant compared to earnings from oil exports. With the exception of the 1986–88 period, over 95 percent of foreign exchange was earned through the oil exports in the postrevolutionary period as in the years immediately preceding the Revolution.

Equally undesirable is the structure of nonoil exports (Table 3.23, Figure 3.21).[214] In 1976, for example, industrial goods accounted for 28 percent of nonoil exports, whereas the shares of agricultural and traditional goods and mineral ores were 70 percent and 2 percent, respectively. Even this uneven structure could not be maintained in the years following the Revolution. The share of industrial goods has steadily dropped, reaching 8.7 percent of the total nonoil exports in 1985, as compared to 82.8 percent for agricultural and traditional goods. The trend seems to have accelerated in the subsequent years; comparison of data for the first four months of 1985 and 1986 indicates a 78 percent drop in industrial exports as opposed to a 100 percent increase in agricultural and traditional exports.[215] Thus, the 1986 figures for the share of industrial goods, agricultural and traditional goods, and mineral ores were 2.2, 94.8, and 3 percent, respectively (Table 3.23). The corresponding figures for 1987 are reported at 8, 85, and 5 percent.[216] Iranian exports are thus becoming increasingly concentrated in primary products, and this is resulting in a deterioration in the country's terms of trade. In the first nine months of 1985, for example, nonoil exports increased by 99 percent in volume but only by 26 percent in foreign exchange value. The state also helped to reduce the nonoil exports prices, and this led some countries, United States included, to accuse the Islamic Republic of "dumping." "When I was in Dubai," reported a reader

Table 3.23 Composition of Nonoil Exports, 1976–86 (current prices and percentages)

Main Nonoil Export Categories	1976	1977	1978	1979	1980	1981	1982	1983	1984	1985	1986
Total (million dollars)(a)	539.9	625.2	542.8	811.8	645.2	339.5	283.7	356.6	361.1	357.0	764.2
Industrial Goods (%)	28.3	21.1	30.0	8.2	3.7	3.9	7.5	7.3	7.6	8.7	2.2
Agricultural and Traditional Goods (%)	69.8	68.9	68.0	89.3	93.3	94.6	90.0	89.2	81.7	82.8	94.8
Mineral Ores (%)	1.9	10.0	2.0	2.5	3.0	1.5	2.5	3.5	10.7	8.5	3.0

Sources and Notes:
Tabavvulat, p. 632; *Gozaresh* (1365), vol. 2, Chapter 2, p. 15; and *Majaleh* (1364), p. 65.

(a) For exchange rates between rial and dollar see note 10 in chapter 1. Note that exports reported under categories "Other" is included here in Agricultural and Traditional Goods category. A part of such exports for 1985 and 1986 (probably around 2 percent) actually belong to Industrial Goods category. See *Gozaresh* (1365), vol. 2, Chapter 12, p. 15.

Figure 3.21

Changes in Nonoil Exports, 1976–86
(current prices)

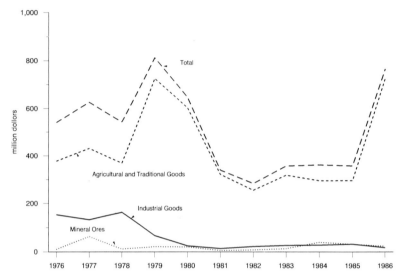

of *Kayhan* daily, "I saw a 320 rial washing powder of ours being sold at 220 rials. . . . It is not right to have a shortage of detergent for our own requirements at home while the government exports them abroad."[217] Earlier, between 1979 and 1984, however, Iranian exports were experiencing a disproportionate rise in price, making them too expensive to compete in the international markets.[218]

Concentration on a few trading partners has long been a major source of dependency and vulnerability for Iran. Although a certain degree of diversification occurred in the postrevolutionary period, the country's trade still remained largely dominated by the developed capitalist markets (Table 3.24). Imports from these economies declined from 85 percent in 1976 to 63 percent in 1982, reflecting the impact of the United States's trade sanctions and the freezing of Iranian assets following the seizure of the American Embassy in Tehran in 4 November 1979.[219] Imports rose again (in 1983) when oil revenues grew large in 1982–83 and restrictions on Western trade with Iran were lifted after the resolution of the hostage crisis on 20 January 1981.[220] After 1984, however, imports from the Western countries declined along with the drop in oil prices (Table 3.24). They were reported at 67 percent of the country's imports in 1986.[221] In contrast, nonoil exports to developed capitalist markets

Table 3.24 Distribution of Foreign Trade by Type of Economy, 1976–86 (percentages based on current price figures)(a)

	Developed Capitalist Countries(b)			Socialist Countries(c)			OPEC Member Countries(d)			Others		
Years	Imports	Nonoil Exports	Imports as % of Nonoil Exports	Imports	Nonoil Exports	Imports as % of Nonoil Exports	Imports	Nonoil Exports	Imports as % of Nonoil Exports	Imports	Nonoil Exports	Imports as % of Nonoil Exports
1976	85.1	46.1	184.6	2.9	25.9	11.2	1.1	19.9	5.5	10.4	8.1	128.4
1977	85.4	41.7	204.8	5.4	39.1	13.8	1.1	14.3	7.7	8.1	14.9	54.4
1978	86.8	34.3	253.1	5.1	22.8	22.4	0.1	15.5	0.6	7.3	27.5	26.5
1979	81.9	71.5	114.5	6.2	12.3	50.4	2.9	8.5	34.1	9.0	7.7	116.9
1980	67.8	75.5	89.8	13.7	15.4	89.0	5.2	5.6	92.9	13.3	3.5	380.0
1981	69.9	63.6	109.9	8.4	17.3	48.6	4.6	11.8	39.0	17.1	7.3	234.2
1982	62.6	54.4	115.1	12.7	24.2	52.5	2.1	15.6	13.5	12.6	3.8	331.6
1983	68.1	46.6	146.1	7.3	18.5	39.5	3.5	18.2	19.2	21.1	16.7	126.3
1984	70.7	46.8	151.1	6.5	29.5	22.0	2.9	12.2	23.8	19.9	11.5	166.1
1985	65.8	52.8	124.6	9.7	17.7	54.8	3.5	16.1	21.7	21.0	13.4	156.7
1986	66.7	56.8	117.4	5.8	7.3	79.5	6.4	19.2	33.3	21.1	16.7	126.3

Sources and Notes:
Compiled and calculated on the basis of *Gozaresh* (1363), vol 2, Chapter 8, pp. 12–14; *Salnameh* (1365), p. 717; and (1366), p. 396.

(a) Percent figures may not add up to 100 due to rounding.

(b) The United States, Canada, Western Europe, Australia, Japan, and Turkey.

(c) The USSR and Eastern Europe.

(d) Saudi Arabia, Iraq, Kuwait, The United Arab Emirates, Qatar, Venezuela, Indonesia, Libya, Algeria, Gabon, Equador, and Nigeria.

increased in the postrevolutionary period, from 46 percent in 1976 to around 53 percent in 1985. After 1980, when 75 percent of the nonoil exports were sold to Western countries, the trend declined.[222] On balance, however, the imports of Iran from these economies—as the percent of its nonoil exports to them—increased by about 33 percent between 1976 and 1985, indicating a much narrower gap than that which existed prior to the Revolution.

Trade with the then socialist bloc had also been erratic. Imports from the bloc increased steadily, from about 3 percent in 1976 to about 13.7 percent in 1980, but declined thereafter, to 5.8 percent in 1986, although the expected figure was a 10 percent increase in that year.[223] Nonoil exports to the bloc dropped by about 50 percent between 1976 and 1979, from 26 to 12.3 percent. They increased in 1984, to 29.5 percent, but dropped again to 7.3 percent in 1986 (Table 3.24). Overall, the imports of Iran from the bloc—as the percent of its nonoil exports to the bloc—decreased by 390 percent between 1976 and 1985. The largely negligible imports from the OPEC member countries increased to a peak of 5.2 percent in 1980. (Since then the trend has been fluctuating but largely on the downward side.) In sharp contrast, Iran's nonoil exports to these countries dropped steadily to 5.6 percent in 1980, from 20 percent in 1976, but increased again to 18.2 percent in 1983 and 19.2 percent in 1986. In 1984, the figure dropped to 12.2 percent, registering its sharpest one year decline in the postrevolutionary period. Finally, imports from the remaining Third World countries were equally erratic, increasing to 17 percent in 1981, from 10.4 percent in 1976, and then declining to 12.6 percent in 1982, increasing again to 21 percent in 1986. Iran's nonoil exports to these countries, however, declined sharply from a high of about 28 percent in 1978 to a low of 3 percent in 1982 increasing again to 16.7 percent in 1986.

Among the fifteen major trading partners of the Islamic Republic in 1983, none was located in the then socialist bloc (Table 3.25). The list included Japan, eight Western European countries, and six developing nations among which Turkey, South Korea, and Pakistan were particularly infamous for their repressive regimes and close ties with the United States. It has been speculated that much of the trade with these countries, as well as with the Unites Arab Emirates, originated from the United States. The fact that trade with these nations increased sharply in 1980 makes the speculation all the more credible. Recall that the United States imposed trade sanctions on Iran in that year following the hostage crisis. Iran's postrevolutionary trade relations remained more or less steady with the Federal Republic of

Table 3.25 Distribution of Iran's Imports by Fifteen Major Trading Partners in 1983 for the 1976–85 Period (percentage figures are based on current prices, U.S. dollars)(a)

Major Trading Partners	1976	1977	1978	1979	1980	1981	1982	1983	1984	1985	1986
1. Federal Republic of Germany	17.8	19.4	20.6	18.0	15.1	16.7	16.3	19.0	19.1	15.8	18.3
2. Japan	17.4	15.7	16.9	13.8	9.8	12.0	10.6	16.7	14.2	13.4	13.6
3. United Kingdom	6.8	6.9	8.1	6.9	7.3	6.3	6.0	6.0	8.4	5.7	6.8
4. Turkey	NL	NL	NL	NL	1.0	2.2	6.5	4.7	3.6	7.5	6.3
5. Italy	5.8	5.6	5.7	5.6	5.5	5.3	4.6	4.6	4.4	4.6	6.5
6. South Korea	1.3	0.9	0.7	1.6	3.9	4.5	3.4	2.8	3.0	2.4	2.5
7. Sweden	1.1	1.4	1.4	0.9	2.2	1.9	1.8	2.7	3.2	1.6	1.5
8. Brazil	0.5	NL	0.6	0.7	NL	0.6	1.9	2.3	3.3	2.0	2.6
9. Argentina	NL	NL	NL	NL	NL	0.5	1.3	2.3	2.6	4.0	2.7
10. Belgium	2.4	2.4	2.5	2.6	2.5	2.4	2.9	2.3	3.9	2.9	3.6
11. Holland	3.5	3.3	2.1	3.1	3.1	3.3	2.6	2.2	2.5	2.4	3.1
12. Spain	1.0	1.0	1.7	1.1	2.2	3.0	3.0	2.1	2.1	1.8	1.4
13. Switzerland	3.8	3.1	2.7	2.8	4.1	3.9	2.5	2.0	1.8	8.1	2.5
14. Pakistan	NL	NL	NL	NL	NL	NL	0.9	1.9	1.3	0.6	1.0
15. United Arab Emirates	NL	NL	NL	NL	4.3	3.0	1.1	1.9	2.1	2.9	5.7

Sources and Notes:
Compiled and calculated on the basis of *Taraznameh* (various years: 1355–63); *Salnameh* (1365), pp. 720–723; and (1366), p. 398.

NL = Not Listed as a major partner for the year.

(a) For exchange rates between rial and dollar see note 10 in chapter 1.

Germany, Japan, the United Kingdom, Italy (among the five largest partners in 1985), and most smaller Western European countries. In sharp contrast, such relations experienced volatile shifts and fluctuations vis-à-vis the United States, France, the USSR, Rumania, and most developing nations. The United States was the main loser in postrevolutionary Iranian trade. From the third largest exporter of goods and services to Iran in 1977, after the Federal Republic of Germany and Japan, its trade with Iran dropped so low that it never again appeared even among the fifteen major trading partners.[224]

Iran has had a negative and deteriorating trade balance with most of its trading partners, particularly with the major ones and those who buy the country's oil. For example, the Federal Republic of Germany and Japan, the top two trading partners of Iran for some time now, had positive trade balances with Iran, respectively, of $22 billion and $18.5 billion between 1950 and 1983.[225] The FRG's imports from Iran as a percent of its exports to Iran dropped from 13 percent in 1971 to 2.9 percent in 1977 and then to 2.1 percent in 1983. The corresponding figures for Japan were 7.6, 0.05, and 0.03 percent.[226] (The declining trends have continued and are expected to worsen in the postwar period, when Iran will rely on these two countries for most of its reconstruction needs.) (See chapter 4.) As a consequence, Iran's balance of payments, even when oil was included, were negative for most years since the 1960s, particularly in the postrevolutionary period. (Table 3.26, Figure 3.22). With the economic recession in 1984, the size of the balance of payments deficit almost doubled relative to the year before, but the trend was reversed in 1985 when the balance of payments developed a sizable surplus. However, in 1986, when the sharp decline in oil prices could not be compensated for by a proportional reduction in imports, the balance of payments became negative. Note that between 1979 and 1984, over $4,243 million left the country in the form of capital, whereas the trade balance, that is, net current account, earned about $2,504 million, generating a deficit of around $1,739 million in the period. Capital flight became a major drain on the postrevolutionary economy, and the government control of exchange rates could not counteract a growing black market for foreign currency in Tehran.

Finally, the introduction of the austerity Plan for the New Economic Conditions ushered in a period of significant decline in the government's foreign currency payments and an increase in nonoil exports. The expansion of domestic defense production and productive capacities of major import-substitution industries, including steel, glass, cement, petrochemicals, machinery, and motor vehicles,

Table 3.26　　The Balance of Payments, 1976–85 (million dollars)(a)

Year	(1) Net of Current Account	(2) Net of Capital Account	(3) Balance of Payments(b)
1976	4157.0	−1766.0	2288.0
1977	1094.1	1505.2	2014.5
1978	−501.0	316.5	−579.0
1979	6109.7	−110.2	5651.0
1980	−4599.4	−306.6	−4051.0
1981	−2736.9	−288.5	−2361.1
1982	6551.8	−5184.5	1304.6
1983	−2116.5	2066.3	−584.5
1984	−702.8	−421.3	−1195.2
1985	1578.4	−161.1	707.9

Sources and Notes:
Gozaresh (1363), vol. 2, Chapter 8, p. 17; *Faslnameh*, p. 203; and *Taraznameh* (1356–63); *Majaleh* (1364), p. 62.

(a) For exchange rates between rial and dollar see note 10 in chapter 1.

(b) Note that (3) is bigger or smaller than the arithmetic sum of (1) and (2) by "discrepancies, currency rate adjustments and unregistered transactions." This category has at times been very high; reported figures for 1983 and 1985 were −534.3 and −709.4 million dollars, respectively. See *Majaleh* (1364), p. 62.

Figure 3.22

Changes in Balance of Payments, 1976–85

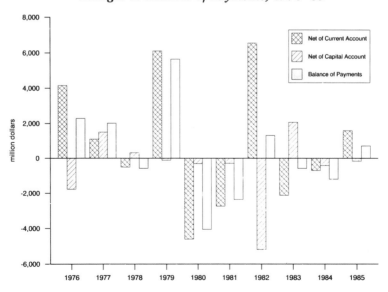

was particularly critical in saving foreign currency and reducing the country's "foreign exchange gap." Iran was reported to have saved $1.3 billion in military imports in 1986 by relying on domestic production. Such savings amounted to $3 billion in 1987.[227] Consequently and despite the decline in oil revenue, the nation's balance of trade improved in 1987 and could experience an even lower deficit in 1988. Additionally, although Iran's reserves in foreign banks have experienced wild fluctuations in the postrevolutionary period, the Islamic government has managed to retain its credit worthiness. In 1988, Iran increased its shares in the World Bank by $236 million and the country's reserves (including gold) in foreign banks was reported at about $6 billion for the first three months of the year.[228]

It is also to the credit of the Islamic Republic that, despite all economic hardships, it has maintained a very low debt/output ratio; it has paid off some $700 million of the Shah's foreign debts of about $4.7 billion and has not incurred any major long term borrowing from the international lending markets.[229] In addition to a $4 billion debt left from the Shah's period, the Republic might have accumulated around $2 to $3 billion in short-term debts to its suppliers by 1987 (about $800 million according to the Prime Minister Musavi).[230] (However, the Republic's short-term debt in 1989 was put at $10–$12 billion by President Rafsanjani. See note 2, Chapter 5.) Instead, the Republic can mobilize some $7 billion in assets frozen by the United States and another $2 billion from money loaned by the Shah to foreign governments. For the present (1990) however, a high import bill and the postwar reconstruction needs, in the face of low oil revenues, are putting increasing pressure on the government to borrow money from abroad.[231] The pressure had already become significant in 1988. Conversion of "much of the country's trade to bartering" does not seem to have helped contain the pressure and the country was "beginning to default on payments to suppliers" in mid-1988.[232] The public sector borrowing requirement (PSBR) will continue to increase as foreign interest payments and government spending grow faster than the local revenues and net transfers to the government from abroad. Further pressure for foreign borrowing may be generated as politically motivated capital flight continues. In the presence of exchange control, underpricing of exports and overpricing of imports have become the main means of capital flight. Direct underground channels are also widely used to smuggle out foreign currencies purchased in the black market.

4

The Postwar Reconstruction

The cease-fire between Iran and Iraq initially raised considerable hope among the two peoples for a lasting peace and a speedy postwar reconstruction. The war had encouraged the most degrading immorality and shattered the economies beyond easy or immediate repair. The desire for peace and reconstruction also arose out of the need for genuine national reconciliation and international cooperation. Whether these intertwined goals can or will be realized in any reasonable time frame or at an acceptable level is not yet certain: the two sides continue refusing to trust each other, Iraq is making unwarranted claims, including total sovereignty over the Shatt-al-Arab waterway, and the world community seems to have lost much of its initial interest in the peace between the two nations. In the foreseeable future, therefore, a volatile situation of no-peace no-war may prevail between the two countries, encouraging continued transfer of the scarce resources into military sectors, perpetuating national discord, and increasing international tensions.[1] Yet, there is no alternative to peace and reconstruction or to national reconciliation and international cooperation. Immediate realization of these objectives is the most needed in the postrevolutionary Iran where national dissension and economic destruction are the most critical.

In what follows, I shall focus on the conceptual and practical aspects of the postwar reconstruction in Iran. More specifically, I outline the most important elements of a postwar reconstruction strategy and apply it to the experience of the Islamic Republic. The issues discussed include (1) meaning and stages of the postwar reconstruction, (2) differing positions on the goals and priorities, (3) the role of the public and private sectors, and (4) the type of policies needed to be implemented. Special attention is paid to the debates and problems associated with mobilizing domestic and foreign resources and removing bottlenecks particularly in the areas of financial, institutional, and infrastructural resources. As most such obstacles are detailed in Chapter 2, I shall focus on two critical obstacles, which I believe are central to the success or failure of the postwar reconstruction: the foreign exchange shortage and the Iranian obsolete political culture. I shall conclude with a few observations about the future for peace between Iran and Iraq and the global indifference toward it. Although the most general elements of a reconstruction strategy has emerged out of the extensive debates among the various political factions within the state, implementation of most initiatives by the pragmatists in charge of the executive branch awaits the resolution of disputes over specifics and mobilization of resources. In the meantime, certain urgent and revenue-generating projects are being implemented, while the economy continues to suffer from the problems discussed in Chapter 3.

DEBATE ON A RECONSTRUCTION STRATEGY

A major aspect of the postwar reconstruction concerns establishing a suitable strategy, an issue on which most postwar societies engage in lengthy and arduous debates, thus wasting much time and energy so critically needed for reconstruction. By "strategy" I refer here to that body of knowledge that helps determine the most important tasks that must be implemented at each stage of reconstruction, the type and amount of resources needed, and the location of reconstruction projects. A strategy, therefore, involves defining goals and objectives, setting priorities and targets, making plans or facilitating market mechanisms, and formulating policies for implementation. Thus, it is not surprising that the debate over a reconstruction strategy usually has centered around these issues. The long debate over strategy is perhaps inevitable given that it varies across ideologies, social groups, over time, and in different cultural contexts. It is also an issue that directly depends on the nature of the war itself and the extent of the damage inflicted on the society. Although each nation should find its own strategy for the postwar reconstruction, a framework could be developed to guide such debates toward conclusive results using the past postwar experiences and the experience with disaster planning.[2] (I shall use the word *disaster* here to also refer to war in general, the Iran-Iraq war in particular.)

A suitable reconstruction strategy is one that is flexible for adaptation to specific sectors and governmental levels and modifiable at various stages. It must also be borne in mind that different socioeconomic sectors demand differing strategies for rebuilding. Beyond these general principles, a well-structured postwar reconstruction strategy should incorporate unmistakably clear, broad, and long-term national and international *goals*. National defense, independence, development, self-reliance, democracy, and social justice are among the most important of such goals, which are usually included in national constitutions. In general, however, postwar governments become primarily concerned with economic normalization, growth, and efficiency, and tend to favor international integration over an isolationist approach. It is important that the reconstruction goals be decomposable into their economic, political, ideological, social, sectoral, territorial, and cultural constructs, and that they be reflective of global trends and restructuring as well as international and national constraints and opportunities. To implement such goals, however, they must be decomposed into workable, feasible, and specific *objectives* at social, sectoral, and territorial levels, covering all spheres of the society's political economy. In setting objectives, the government should be realistically modest and not utopian, accounting for resources, needs, perceptions, expectations, potentialities, and constraints. Moreover, as no society can afford to accomplish everything at once, it is forced into selecting an appropriate sequence for the tasks that must be implemented. Moreover, not all damaged items are equally difficult or easy to reconstruct or have equal input problems. Therefore, a hierarchy of objectives must be established with the most important ones at the top of the list for earlier implementation. Generally speaking, *priorities* may be set based on immediate needs, long-term goals, or resources availability. As the immediate postwar is a period of economic decline and financial austerity, concern with identification of growth sectors and revenue-generating activities dominate considerations for setting priorities.

Clearly, setting the goals, objectives, and priorities right is very important, but even more portentous is the facility to *implement* them. A broad-based *planning* system seems indispensable for the postwar reconstruction particularly at the replacement and developmental stages. (See later.) Otherwise, the risk of chaos, duplication, and wasteful use of scarce and valuable resources would be high. A totally planned approach to reconstruction is neither possible nor desirable, for it encourages bureaucratic red tape and inflexibility no matter how decentralized it might be. Even the Soviet Union did not rely solely on planning for its postwar reconstruction. Their reconstruction was largely planned for large-scale, strategically important projects while *market mechanisms* were allowed to operate at the local level and in small-scale activities.[3] Further, for private initiatives to thrive, market mechanisms have proven the most effective. It is unfortunate that *market* is always associated with *private* cause and considered *capitalistic*, whereas it could contribute equally to a public cause and be part of a broader social policy. A good example is West Germany's "social free market" experience in the postwar period.[4] The Gorbachev's *perestroika* also recognizes this new conception of market mechanisms.[5] Yet, there are activities that are best organized and developed by *cooperatives*. They may be found in production in rural settlements or in consumer services in urban areas. It is therefore more appropriate to adopt a *mixed approach* for implementation of reconstruction programs. It must be noted, however, that there cannot be a fixed formula for such a mix, for the amount of the ingredients in the mix vary from case to case and time to time.

Equally indeterminate and case-specific is the extent to which the *public* and *private* sectors should participate in ownership and management of the economic society. Although both sectors have a role to play in the postwar reconstruction, the share should be determined in terms of their burden and absorption capacities (real and potential). These are hard to determine in the case of the private sector, but they may be calculated for the public sector using a combination of indicators. For example, public sector's burden may be estimated by the size of the general budget deficit relative to GNP and in comparison to similar measures for other successful nations. Organizational capacity, ratio of public investment to its ownership, and the sector's effectiveness should all be considered when its role in reconstruction is debated. As is generally understood and acknowledged, the private sector is only peripherally concerned with provision of basic needs, public goods, strategic investments, and social welfare-related services. These activities are either not profitable or too risky, for they involve huge investments and a continued reinvestment commitment. The line between public and private sectors is also sector specific. In agriculture and housing, for example, the line should be drawn near the public sector (thus, leaving more for private sector). In considering a division of labor between the public and private sectors, two opposite forces of conservativism and reformism must also be balanced. These forces tend to be particularly active in the postwar societies.

Implementation also needs to be guided by well-defined *policies* concerning economic, social, political, ideological, cultural, infrastructural, territorial, educational, technical, and legal changes. *Economic policies* should become active in both fiscal and monetary matters. Wars generate budget deficits next to huge private liquidity, inflation, unemployment, and poverty among other problems. Considerable need, therefore, exists for policies to be directed toward generating more public revenue, redirecting the wandering cash toward productive use, creating jobs, and undertaking redistributive reforms. Past experiences indicate that a progressive tax policy is particularly helpful. The post-WW II French government, for example, imposed a national reconstruction tax to redirect part of the windfall profit that some businesses and individuals had made during and because of the war to finance the reconstruction. The government should also design an incentive package for the private sector to invest in productive activities. This could include tax relief, soft loans, loan guarantees, and subsidized business services among other assistance. At the same time, however, the state must prevent the wandering savings from going into nonproductive uses by specific disincentives such as higher taxes and cumbersome licensing requirements. Export promotion can be a useful policy for generating foreign exchange but this should be undertaken in close correlation with an import-substitution strategy based on domestic resources in order to save foreign exchange. Consideration for financing must also include beneficial alternatives that might exist beyond the national borders. Buyback, and usance are, generally speaking, the least damaging to national independence. Direct foreign investments, loans, and other alternatives might also be sought if they can be secured with no strings attached.

Social policies should include considerations for the provision of basic needs in such areas as health, education, housing, and recreation. Additional services must be provided to those who have suffered in the war, particularly the disabled. These include new building code regulations and modification of the existing structures to accommodate such a population. Policies that make the refugee population and other war inflicted groups accustomed to a victim mentality, which leads to their increased dependency on the state, must be avoided. Rather, they should be provided with start-up capital, technical assistance, and social support to begin a new life. Such incentives are particularly critical for those who wish to return to their war-shattered residences. Assistance should be given to them for housing provision and job creation. The critical point to remember is that the state's policies should lead to increased affordability or self-reliance of the war-inflicted families rather than their dependency. Clearly, the state must be ready to provide housing for those who otherwise will become homeless.

Education is the most critical policy area for postwar reconstruction. This is particularly true in the case of the Third World where professional and technical education remains low. In addition to training policy makers, planners, managers, local leaders, public work officials, credit administrators, producers, and builders, reconstruction education should also facilitate the transition of a large segment of the population from fighters to producers, thereby making their future employment easier. Whereas schooling (e.g., crash course programs) is important, on-the-job training must receive top priority. To be effective, such education should be extended to all territorial levels, economic sectors, professions, and social groups.

Carefully thought out *cultural policies* are equally needed in reconstruction to help preserve the cultural symbols and continuity. This is particularly critical in the case of rebuilding national monuments and historic quarters in old towns. Recycling old architectural components such as doors, windows, precious metals, and reusable timber can not only help preserve culture but also minimize the use of scarce resources. Historical preservation needs development of appropriate techniques and community participation, women in particular. Reconstruction of Warsaw after the WWII provides a unique example and invaluable lesson.

Generally speaking, after housing, wars leave their most devastating impact on infrastructures. This is why well-designed *infrastructural policies* are usually considered the most needed for a more successful reconstruction. Yet, infrastructural projects are costly and must be given high priority and undertaken in stages. Even then, as past experiences indicate, a bottleneck-removing policy should be followed. It must be also noted that specific economic sectors and regions have their own (what may be called) lifeline infrastructures, without reconstruction of which they may not be successfully reconstructed. Cities and rural areas suffer indiscriminate damage during the war and their reconstruction is a major policy problem in the postwar. Habitats are better rebuilt with the direct participation of the inhabitants, and the government must take a more active role in reconstructing the inhabited centers. Scales of operation, kinds of activities, and ways of life are among many issues that differentiate problems of rebuilding rural areas and urban centers. Decisions must be made concerning the location of the new facilities and the nature of property changes that might occur. Even more important is recreating new links between the towns and rural centers in a war-damaged region.

It is therefore critical that an appropriate human *settlement policy* be followed. An integrated regional approach seems particularly useful. This requires creating a hierarchy of cities and rural areas linked together not only by transportation and communication networks but also, and more important, by functional interdependencies. Function-specific cities must be carefully designed and this demands restructuring the prewar urban structures. Intermediate cities should be selected as market centers serving smaller towns and rural areas and mediating interactions between them and regional capitals. An integrated rural policy should focus on regrouping smaller dispersed villages into larger settlements with social service areas and marketing centers. Small-scale industries should be adapted to rural conditions and linked to industries located at higher levels of the territorial hierarchy. The successful implementation of this rural development policy requires that agriculture be given a high enough priority in the country's sectoral development strategy. The integrated human settlement policy must also be accompanied with a policy for repopulating the war-damaged areas and this, as we argued, required an appropriate incentive policy. However, care must be exercised in offering such incentives, for they tend to depopulate surrounding backward areas, just as reconstruction activities tend to do. Even more critical is the security consideration in planning settlement system in the war-damaged areas. A helpful approach is to create what might be called satellite buffer settlements around more strategic and larger urban centers.

For these policies to become reinforceable, they must be provided with proper *legal frameworks* in terms of new laws and proper enabling legislation. Specific laws are also needed for a variety of actions including changes in the old urban zoning and expropriation of substandard properties or properties that stand in the way of planned urban restructuring. Finally, reconstruction must account for some very critical *political issues*. These include managing the postwar military and paramilitary forces and factionalism within the state. Reconstruction of intrastate relationships is not an easy job particularly in societies that suffer from an obsolete political culture. Even more difficult is reconstructing the state-society relationship, particularly those between the state and its opponents. Whereas democratization and public participation are the only means for creating political legitimacy, most postwar states are too fragile and unstable to allow for their implementation in the short-term. Therefore, it is not surprising that most postwar societies are characterized with political discord and national conflicts.

A suitable reconstruction strategy has also been the subject of lengthy and arduous debate in the Islamic Republic and issues involved are more or less the same as those just outlined. Specifically, ever since the cease-fire in August 1988, the three political factions have offered three different views of what the postwar reconstruction should mean within the Iranian context.[6] After wasting much time and energy, the debate should be settled over the most general elements of a definition but it continues over the specifics. Generally speaking, all parties to the debate seem to take the constitutional goals as also applicable to the postwar reconstruction. Consequently, the debate has been the least concerned with the broader long-term national goals. In sharp contrast, specific objectives, priorities, policies, and the role of government and the market have been the subject of whetted debates, for resources are minuscule compared to the amount needed; and the course *chosen* will shape the nature of the emergent system in the country. Specifically, the debate has centered around how to reconstruct the society along the goals that correspond to those in the Constitution. It focused on the following four basic issues: (1) rebuilding the military (both the institution itself and equipment), (2) energizing the national economy, (3) promoting economic ,ell-being of the population (especially the families of those killed in the war), and (4) reconstructing war-damaged areas. Social justice, which had been the subject of continued concern after the Revolution, has been deliberately eliminated from the list of top priority items for the time being.[7]

Of the four top priority areas, the first two, rebuilding and energizing, were considered more important then the last two, promoting and reconstructing, but the policy makers could not agree on whether defense or economic growth should be placed at the top of the priority list. One group, largely radicals, argued for a higher defense spending; they maintained that military strength was still the most effective tool in foreign policy and that Iraq could not be trusted to stand by its declared peaceful aims. Another group, a combination of conservatives and pragmatists, on the other hand, insisted on giving highest priority to economic growth, arguing that economic strength was the most powerful weapon in international diplomacy today. They gave the example of Japan, which has dominated the world without firing a bullet! At the end, however, the debate seemed to have settled at a point between the two extremes, but one closer to the second position. Economic growth was also considered more important because the state needs to generate, in a reasonable time frame, some 4 to 5 million jobs and control the everrising prices. However, at the same time that the state is revitalizing productive capacities, it must rebuild the military, if the Islamic Republic is to match Iraq's strong army. The need for resources for the reconstruction is thus enormous and domestic resources may not be sufficient for the purpose. Among the main problems, as we shall see later on, are the foreign exchange constraints and various socioeconomic, political, institutional and infrastructural bottlenecks.

The main question then becomes whether Iran will reconstruct the society through an open-door strategy, with the participation of the domestic private sector and foreign investments or follow a strategy of self-reliance with extensive state involvement. Or should there be a mixture of the two approaches.[8] So far the Islamic Republic has used very little foreign assistance and has basically relied upon domestic resources. But the open-door advocates, mostly the conservatives with bazaar links, argue that the policy of self-reliance would not work for reconstruction because the country must move quickly and the needs are so great. They insist that the people have sacrificed and do not want to wait much longer to see their lives improve. They, therefore, advocate a rapid growth policy to which they sometimes refer to as a *goshayesh* (relief) policy. The government, they argue, should take steps to import consumer goods and encourage the private sector to do the same; this requires trade liberalization policies. Investment in quick-return projects directed toward the immediate welfare of the population should also receive priority over long-term projects.

Conservatives also argue that the private sector should be offered fiscal and monetary incentives to take risks and introduce initiatives. They are against price control, rationed markets, and subsidies, but favor wage control, devaluation of the rial to the level of black market rate, the closing of loss-making state firms, and sales of nationalized industries to the private sector. A rapid growth policy may also require the use of foreign resources and expertise, in which case they should be employed. The open-door advocates oppose any extensive state intervention in the economy and the reconstruction beyond acting as an indicative planner and regulator of the last resort. They also maintain that unless the economic pie is made bigger by a strategy of rapid growth, there would be little to share with those under the poverty line, currently about 65 percent of the population. Ayatollah Ali Khamenei, the new leader of the Islamic Republic, who succeeded Ayatollah Khomeini upon his death on 3 June 1989, is known to favor a somewhat similar line before he became the leader, although he has also been open to certain aspects of the opposing view and is better defined as a pragmatist. According to him, economic growth assists the poorer sections by boosting employment opportunities and wages, while it, at the same time, increases production and thus reduces inflation.[9] The most controversial members of this faction are, however, organized around the *Rasalat* newspaper under the editorship of Ayatollah Azari Qumi.

Others, mostly the radicals, argue that the pace can be slower and that the country must invest in the industries it needs to produce the materials needed for reconstruction—like the cement, construction, steel, and machine tools industries, and in social services to help the neediest. Under this option, Iran can also rebuild the sectors that use mostly domestic resources; they do not need much foreign exchange like agriculture and small-scale industries. They say that the people, who have lived in extreme hardship for ten years, will not mind waiting a little longer to see their life improve. Moreover, instead of encouraging the private sector, the government should expand and further develop the cooperatives in production and distribution spheres. The government should also continue to encourage a policy of self-reliance with a measure of protection for domestic production and resist the temptation of the quick-fix solution that the open-door policy promises. Otherwise, they maintain, the country will soon become indebted to foreign governments and companies, and multinational corporations in particular. The result, as indicated by Egypt's post-Nasser *Enfitah* (open-door) policy, will increase foreign dependency and income inequality along with the creation of a minority consumer market and a relative reduction in the level of industrialization.

Radicals also favor price control, defend subsidies and rationing of basic necessities, and are opposed to privatization of public industries. They also argue against devaluation of the rial for nationalistic and economic reasons. They maintain that devaluation will increase prices of imports while it will have no major impact on the country's nonoil exports, which have always been negligible. The consequences will increase trade deficits and inflation from which the poorer sections will suffer the most. Devaluation, they argue, will also increase the cost of production as industries import most of their inputs, and this will hurt the already depressed productive units. As a good number of such units are owned by the government, the state's budget deficit will become even larger, causing inflation to worsen and production to decline further. The most controversial figure of this faction is Hojjatoleslam Ali Akabar Mohteshami a Majlis representative from Tehran (formerly minister of Interior). Mir Housain Musavi (formerly prime minister and currently an advisor to President Rafsanjani and a member of the Collective for Determination of the Exigencies of the System) is known to favor the radical alternative, although at times he has shown significant flexibility in accepting largely moderate or pragmatic policies.[10]

Which course seems likely? It is still up in the air, but policy makers and planners are probably heading for a mixture in which the private sector will play a major role with the state maintaining a strong economic and controlling position.[11] Advocated by such pragmatist-centrist leader as President Ali Akbar Hashemi Rafsanjani, the strategy would also incorporate a mixed market and planning framework to guide the coexisting public, private, and cooperative sectors.[12] But the sector most favored is the privately organized cooperatives that bring, in Rafsanjani's words, "a large number of people together as a private sector" and activate a balanced economic growth. Opposed to this middle course to development is "Western capitalism," which is both "unjust and exploitative," and the "Eastern communism," which "kills private initiatives" and "instigates antagonism between the state and the populace."[13] In the mixed approach, the public sector is most likely to dominate industries and mines, banking systems, exports, some social services, and all infrastructures, while the other two sectors will expand in housing, agriculture, small-scale productive activities, imports, and most services relating to consumption and distribution. Pragmatists favor a selective price and wage control policy, want to do away with most subsidies and rationing except where indispensable, and are for a multiple exchange rate system. Advocates of this strategy also favor a certain degree of political openness and have a positive attitude toward the educated Iranians living outside the country (exiles and self-exiles).[14]

The mixed approach is predicated on a nonconfrontational foreign policy based on economic and military strength and one that seeks to export the Islamic Revolution by means of an emulative model rather than by the use of force. It was indeed this new thinking in foreign policy, along with economic hardship, that was responsible for ending the war. The policy is also supposed to lean the Islamic Republic toward more openness to the East and West and reliance on foreign assistance.[15] Normalization of relations with the Soviet Union in summer 1989 was a step in the realization of this new policy. The $15 billion accord with the USSR was among the largest Iran had ever signed with that country in a single deal. It included a vast area of cooperation ranging from production of natural gas, to construction of dams and railroads, to cooperation in commercial and military areas.[16] Relations with the West and the Republic's "enemies" in the Middle East are also expected to normalize in the near future. Steps have already been taken to reverse the negative effects of the Rushdie affair. The pragmatist government even used the June 1990 earthquake disaster in Iran as an opportunity to improve its international relations; aid were accepted from *all* nations, except Israel and South Africa. Relations with France and Germany have been normalized to a large extent and these countries are involved in major economic projects in the country. For example, a French financial group was reported in November 1989 to have concluded a $3.6 billion contract with the Islamic Republic involving some 15 percent of Iran's oil exports.[17] Negotiations are perhaps also underway to normalize relations with Great

Britain and the United States. The United States released some $567 million of the frozen Iranian assets in fall 1989, and another $400,000 in spring 1990 reportedly hoping that this will give an incentive to the Iranian leadership to open a dialogue for normalizing relations with the U.S.[18] Although the Islamic radicals remain fiercely opposed to any rapprochement between the two countries, the most pragmatic leaders are expected to overcome such resistance and establish some sort of a more formal relationship with the United States in the not so distant future. Thus, in the coming years, foreign policy will have more to do with economic policy in the Islamic Republic than has been the case.

Despite their differences, all parties to the debate hitherto are in agreement over a number of fundamental issues concerning the nature of the Islamic system they wish to construct and over the less ideological policy matters. In particular, they all agree that domestic resources should be used to their maximum capacity, foreign dependency should be avoided, public participation (meaning various things to different factions) should be encouraged, and the war-damaged areas and peoples should receive added attention. They also agree that highest investment priority should be given to the following critical areas: (1) promoting defense industries and related establishments; (2) repairing and expanding infrastructures (such as science and technology research, power plants, roads, and port facilities); (3) rebuilding oil industries (including oil wells, refineries, and petrochemicals), and oil export facilities including pipelines and wharves; (4) developing agriculture and its supporting infrastructures, including dams, canals, and other irrigation networks; (5) rebuilding and expanding construction industries including cement and glass factories; (6) reconstructing damaged basic industries including steel and machine tools complexes; (7) redeveloping certain war-damaged localities and cities; and (8) attending to the immediate needs of the war-inflicted families. They also agree that economic reconstruction should be undertaken in stages and that oil revenue would have to be relied upon in the beginning.[19]

Ayatollah Khomeini was largely equivocal toward the three approaches, taking ideological and pragmatist positions in different circumstances. The Rushdie affair indicated an ideological position as did a number of decrees the Ayatollah issued in 1987 concerning the need for the government intervention in the economy and other matters. In sharp contrast, although he continued to distrust the West and the East, particularly the United States and the Soviet Union, he approved policies that were put forward by the pragmatists and went counter to some of the declared aims or policies of the

Islamic Republic. For example, he accepted the cease-fire and sanctioned the postwar policy of gradually normalizing relations with France, Britain, and Canada to name the most important cases. Ayatollah Khomeini also took a centrist stand in economic matters. In a fall 1988 communique, he issued a response to a letter from the chiefs of the three branches of the state and the prime minister who requested his views on priorities for the postwar reconstruction.[20] The communique listed the priorities as follows: (1) provision of all kinds of socioeconomic and cultural privileges for the martyrs' families and those who helped the war efforts; (2) improvement of the country's defense capability and development of military industries; (3) self-reliance in agriculture and expansion of scientific and research centers; (4) planning for the welfare of the general public; (5) liberalization of international trade in certain consumer commodities; and (6) participation of the people, that is, the private sector, in the reconstruction. However, he made it clear in the communique that he continued to consider the U.S. and the USSR as enemies of Islam and of the Islamic Republic.

Subsequently, the Council of Policy Making for Reconstruction made the Ayatollah's recommendations the basis for the reconstruction priorities and policies for rebuilding the war-damaged areas. Seyyed Ali Khamenei, then president, in a letter to Mir Hosain Musavi, then prime minister, outlined the Directive on the Comprehensive National Reconstruction Plan (hereafter referred to as *Directive*) in the following terms and asked that they be made the basis for planning and implementation (partial text):

> *On policies*: **1.** Participation of local people and helpful popular forces in each area in reconstruction works by specifying the subject and the manner of their participation in such activities (reconstruction of residential and commercial units shall be undertaken to the extent possible by the owners of such units in accordance with a program guided and supported by the Government); **2.** Linking the damaged areas to other areas which can help in the reconstruction works in order to invite and attract popular aid and support from other regions for the damaged villages and towns; **3.** Observing the cultural, traditional and psychological characteristics of the people in each area in reconstruction works and provision of services; **4.** Creation of cooperative societies and other types of companies by giving priority to the war combatants and volunteers (*Basiege* or Mobilization forces); **5.** Construction of residential units [on a] minimum [of] useful areas making the necessary provisions for future expansion; **6.** Reviewing the possibility of integrating rural areas (villages) and agricultural lands, improving irrigation resources and canals and preparing lands for housing

development by protecting ownership rights of natural persons and legal entities in order to facilitate supply of services, optimum use of water and land for reconstruction of villages and agricultural lands and economization of national expenditures; **7.** Provision of the necessary materials for reconstruction of the war-stricken areas by coordination of various sectors; **8.** Provision of the necessary safety arrangements and facilities in densely populated areas, especially in the border towns and villages, against any likely enemy assaults or invasions; **9.** Taking the necessary safety precautions and observing the criteria on inoperative defenses in the reconstruction of industries, strategic areas and vital installations; and **10.** Keeping and preserving some of the areas destroyed in the war to show the extent of the generosity, self-sacrifice and resistance put up by the martyr-fostering people of Iran.

On priorities: **1.** Oil and energy (reconstruction, renovation and commissioning of refineries and petrochemical complexes and power generating stations); **2.** Agriculture; **3.** Reconstruction and commissioning of the factories producing construction materials; **4.** Housing (priority is given to residential units requiring certain repairs and remedial works, especially for those belonging to families having occupations); **5.** Priority is given to reconstruction and commissioning of factories and industries having the following three characteristics: highest rate of employment and production, anti-inflationary nature, and low foreign exchange requirement; **6.** Reconstruction of villages.

On foreign exchange requirements: will be procured by obtaining the necessary legal permits in the following ways: **1.** Barter trade accounts (with due attention to the amount in the accounts belonging to the Islamic Republic of Iran); **2.** Special account; **3.** Usance, with minimum two-year term; **4.** Advance sale of products of each unit's surplus to the domestic requirements (like oil products by the Abadan Refinery); **5.** Utilization of foreign resources within the criteria and regulations prescribed by the Economics and Finance Ministry and of the Central Bank of the Islamic Republic of Iran in the case of special production projects approved by the legal authorities concerned.

On stabilization and decentralization policies: **1.** Decentralization and expansion of authorities vested in provinces and smaller geographical divisions of the country in relation to the superior units or authorities as well as the related organizations and committees within the framework of the country's general policies and plans and the applicable regulations; **2.** Popularization of the municipality organizations and expansion of the scope of their services in various fields by restoring the activities of town councils, reducing the burden of government organizations and assigning some of their duties to popular organs; **3.** Decentralization of Tehran and other large cities: **a.** By transferring and preventing the creation of new organizations and industries which are not necessary in these cities and appointing a competent authority for the determination, supervision and implementation of this matter, b. Development of new industrial and nonindustrial townships and centers for the purpose of the gradual transfer of nonessential industries and organizations from the Tehran urban areas to other suitable areas, c. Adoption of certain policies and resolutions such as the provision of government services and the extension of certain duties and tax exemptions for directing the population, skilled personnel, experts and capital towards deprived and sparsely populated areas. d. Recommendations to the government and the Majlis (Islamic Consultative Assembly) on consideration of the possibility of transferring the state administrative headquarters from Tehran to other suitable locations.

Energy and oil sector: 1. Planning and investment for the energy requirements of the country's socioeconomic development; 2. Compilation of a comprehensive national energy plan with due attention to the following policies: relying on the energy produced by natural gas and economizing in consumption of middle distillates; 3. Maximum use and substitution of natural gas for other fuels and electricity by expanding gas distribution networks, changing the fuel systems of public transport vehicles to natural gas, substituting gas-burning equipment for electric equipment and supplying gas requirements of petrochemical units; 4. Completion and commissioning of the refinery projects under construction, maintenance, mobilization, and improved exploitation of the existing oil and gas installations, construction and expansion of refineries and expansion of oil and gas industries for export of surplus petroleum products; 5. Improving installations, maintenance and operation of the existing power generating stations, completing the power generating stations under construction and creating new capacity; 6. Preventing energy losses by insulating living environments and selecting suitable population growth areas in order to make better use of fuel and energy in all sectors; 7. Studying and carrying out research on the use of new sources of energy and reviewing and deciding on the use of atomic and other types of energy; and 8. Development of new hydroelectric power generating stations on the Karoun River and the Siah-Bisheh power generating station in order to prevent water waste and to generate low-cost electricity.

Expansion of oil and gas resources: 1. Increasing oil and gas production capacities and facilities by observing the socioeconomic criteria with due attention to the present known oil and gas resources throughout the country; 2. Export of natural gas, petrochemical products, and other petroleum derivatives for the purpose of substituting for crude oil exports; 3. Protecting oil and gas resources throughout the country and increasing oil and gas recovery; **4.** Making every effort towards attainment of self-sufficiency in the oil industry; **5.** Giving priority to exploitation of the common oil and gas fields shared with neighboring countries; **6.** Investment in exploration, exploitation and production of oil and gas from revenues derived from such investment(s); **7.** Diversification of export terminals; **8.** Giving special priority to the petrochemical sector and petrochemistry, the creation, expansion and completion of petrochemical industries and allocation of a portion of revenue to research work and studies in the above-mentioned fields; and **9.** Providing suitable bases for participation of the private sector in the downstream petrochemical industries, affiliated gas industries, and distribution of petroleum products. (Original translation by Pars Associates, Attorneys-at-Law, Tehran, published in *Middle East Executive Report* 12, no 9. The reprint here is shorter and rearranged.)

As can be noted, the Directive remained silent on the defense sector and a development strategy, but listed reconstruction priorities and policies for damaged areas and economic sectors, and indicated sources for financing the required foreign exchange. In particular, the oil and agricultural sectors and reconstruction of industries producing construction materials appeared at the top of the priority list. Attention was also given to housing, rural areas, and the welfare of the war-inflicted population. On specific policies, the Directive emphasized promoting local participation and cooperative societies, linking the damaged areas to areas willing to patronize their reconstruction and observing the sociocultural and psychological traits of the war-inflicted people. Other policies included encouraging administrative and economic decentralization, increasing the defensive capacities of the border areas, and preserving sections of damaged structures as historical records. As for securing the needed foreign exchange, the Directive recommended barter trade accounts, special account, usance with a minimum two-year term, advance sale of products of each unit's surplus (in excess of the domestic requirements), and utilization of foreign resources including loans and credits. The Directive also pointed out that repayment of such loans or credits must begin concurrent with exploitation of the relevant projects and sales of their final products.

The Directive became the basis for a revision of the original First Plan (1361–65) and its subsequent revised versions—which was prepared by the government of Prime Minister Musavi following the cease-fire with Iraq on 20 August 1988 (hereafter referred to as the *Musavi Plan*).[21] (See Chapter 2.) Like its predecessor, this plan was also predicated upon a stage of development thinking. In particular, economic reconstruction will go through three stages. In the first stage, the economy will be restored to its normal functioning by directing resources and efforts toward the maximum use of existing productive capacity, infrastructures, and human resources. In the second stage, oil revenues will be used to achieve economic growth and a higher per capita income. In the final stage, the growth process will be consolidated and made independent of oil exports.

The plan gives nine broad goals and provides specific policies to achieve them. The first three goals concern rebuilding the country's defense capability, reconstructing the damaged productive capacity and infrastructure, and expanding scientific and technical education. Next comes economic growth that should lead to increased productive employment and per capita income, and reduced inflation and economic dependency by emphasizing production of strategic agricultural goods. The remaining goals concern promotion of social justice, provision of basic needs, administrative and judicial reforms, and spatial reorganization of population and activities on the basis of regional comparative advantage.

Policies for economic growth make up the core of the plan. Higher priority is given to incomplete projects and production of capital and intermediate goods. Income from oil and mineral exports will be primarily invested in productive investments, technology transfer, and the development of science and technology. A center for the development of industrial technology will be established along with a supporting credit institute for technology development. Imports for production of rationed, sensitive, and necessary goods as well as for the production of industrial machinery will receive foreign exchange at official rates. Imports for production of all other necessary goods along with imports of industrial machinery will be allocated for foreign exchange at preferred rate (*arz-e tarjihi*). The remaining imports would have to involve no transfer of the state's foreign exchange.

The agricultural sector, rural areas, and deprived regions will continue to receive special treatments. Nonoil exports will be promoted by establishing free trade zones in coastal areas and by other measures. Material incentives will be offered to the private sector to redirect its huge liquidity toward productive investment, including purchase of public enterprises and participation in mineral exploitation. Public ownership of industries will be limited to basic industries (vehicles and transport [*khudrou*], petrochemical, and metal industries) and large scale industries (with over 2,000 employees, over 2 billion rials in fixed capital investment, or over 50 percent of domestic production market share for basic and sensitive goods).

Foreign trade will continue to remain under government control. Nontechnical public jobs will be reduced by 20 percent but technical jobs will increase from the existing 60 percent to 70 percent. Select members of the defense forces will be utilized in civilian jobs. And a large part of the state's functions will be transferred to the private and cooperative sectors.

The plan's quantitative targets are ambitious and optimistic. Gross domestic production (GDP) and fixed investments are estimated to grow at 8 percent and 10.8 percent a year on the average and in 1988 fixed prices, respectively. Some 25,552.9 billion rials is expected to be invested during the five years and the industrial value added is projected to grow at an average annual rate of 14.2 percent (in 1988 fixed prices). Public income is projected to increase from 2,098.7 billion rials in 1988 to 5,622.3 billion rials in 1993, indicating a 21.8 percent annual growth rate. Income tax, oil revenues, and other incomes are expected to increase by 25.3 percent, 13.7 percent, and 21.4 percent a year on average. The share of income tax in public revenue and GDP will increase from 49.1 percent and 4.3 percent in 1988 to 56.6 percent and 8.8 percent in 1993, respectively.

The ratio of income tax to current expenditures is expected to increase from 28.8 percent in 1988 to 73.6 percent in 1993. Over the same years, budget deficits will decrease from about 2,146 billion rials to only 245.7 billion rials, reducing its share in the total budget from 51 percent to 4.2 percent. The share of development expenditures in total public expenditures will increase from 19.4 percent in 1988 to 26.4 percent in 1993. Total oil and nonoil exports over the entire plan period will amount to $89,690 million, of which 85.66 percent will come from the oil exports ($76,833 million oil and $12,857 million nonoil, respectively). Oil exports is expected to reach $18,118 million in 1993, whereas nonoil exports are projected to increase from $1,675 million in 1989 to $3,634 million in the last year of the plan.

The plan is intended to reduce population growth rate from the current 3.9 percent to 3.1 percent in 1993. Based on the assumption that some 394,000 jobs will be created each year (almost twice the current number), unemployment is projected to drop to 14 percent by 1993. Inflation is also expected to drop from 28.5 percent (for consumer goods and services) in 1988 to 8.9 percent in 1993. This will partly result from a significant projected drop in private liquidity. Projections for the social sector also paint a rosy picture. Some 2.5 million houses will be built during the plan period; literacy rate will increase from 78.8 percent in 1988 to 97.2 percent in 1993; and the number of college and university students will increase by 61.4

percent. Accessibility to primary health care will increase from 70 percent to 95 percent, and the number of doctors for each 1,000 population will more than double (from 0.18 to 0.37). Finally, the population covered by health insurance will increase by 64 percent (from 17.41 million to 28.17 million).

The Musavi Plan was extensively discussed in the Majlis but before it could be made into law, the government was changed. The new pragmatist cabinet of President Hashemi Rafsanjani decided that it needed a bolder, flexible, more open, and largely market-oriented plan. Thus, a new revision of the Musavi Plan (hereafter referred to as the *Hashemi Plan*) was undertaken and sent to the Majlis in August 1989. The Hashemi Plan makes significant changes in a number of policies, quantitative targets, and areas of emphasis. In particular, it intends to move the economy toward a mixed and semiopen economy with a more powerful private component. The major changes, as indicated by President Hashemi Rafsanjani in a press interview on 8 September 1989, concern a more extensive sale of nationalized industries to the private sector and freedom for the public and private agencies to enter into contracts with foreign sources.[22] Yet, the plan accepts the general framework of goals, priorities, and policies of its predecessor.

Just like the Musavi Plan, the Hashemi Plan is predicated on a theory of growth in stages, but, unlike its predecessor, it puts more emphasis on economic growth by increasing industrial production. Thus, the proposed total fixed capital investment is increased to 12,478.6 billion rials, from 11,869 billion rials in the Musavi Plan. Expansion of industrial production is hoped to reduce unemployment and inflation and increase per capita income. In the Hashemi Plan, foreign exchange budget (expenditures) has increased from about $96–97 billion to an approved $111,652 million. Another $7.5 billion (approved figure) may be also created in liabilities by the Central Bank to be repaid in installments of no more than $2 billion a year. The foreign exchange is to be secured by oil exports (some 72 percent), nonoil exports (about 16.5 percent), and foreign credits (about 11 percent), among other negligible miscellaneous sources (such as tourism and return on Iran's trifling foreign investments).

The plan gives more autonomy to ministries and public agencies to manage their affairs. It also makes it easier for certain economic units to directly enter into contracts with foreign sources and use their credits. Such credits, however, must be used only for expanding the economy's productive capacity. The corresponding projects would also have to regenerate their own foreign exchange requirements or else produce some $2,500 worth of value added. The plan further imposes a ceiling on the amount of foreign exchange liability such contracts can involve, for example, $3.2 billion in the oil sector, $3 billion for various dams, and $2.2 billion for petrochemical industries. Partnership with foreign sources will assist in easing the foreign exchange constraint and help in the transfer of technology.

The plan allows for a more extensive privatization of the public industries, and this is expected to reduce the budget deficit and inflation and redirect the wandering liquidity toward productive activities, away from trade and brokering. Reactivation of Tehran's Stock Exchange in the last months of 1989 was intended to facilitate implementation of this policy. Incentives are also anticipated in the plan to involve the private sector in productive activities. The Hashemi Plan focuses on basic industries and large-scale units (as were defined in the Musavi Plan) and pays special attention to oil, gas, petrochemicals, cement, mines, plastics, and paper products. The plan also proposes to build some 208,000 houses more than the figure proposed by its predecessor. Other high-priority areas are the military, transportation, communications, and agriculture. Their budgets have increased, in comparison to the Musavi Plan, by $1.5 billion, $2 billion, $1 billion, and $1.5 billion, respectively.

Tourism has also entered the new plan as a high-priority sector and a new source of foreign exchange. This novelty should be considered as indicating a major policy shift. As part of the new tourism program, the government has declared Kish Island, in the Persian Gulf, a "Free Island" where goods and services may enter or exit the country with substantially reduced bureaucratic red tape, taxes, and duties. The island's economy will include tourist attractions and facilities, extensive commercial activities, and a number of export-promotion industries, intended for the markets in the Persian Gulf states. The private sector is hoped to respond to various incentives that the state is making available. The government will also invest but such investments are expected to be concentrated in providing infrastructures and services. This policy of the President Hashemi Rafsanjani is hoped to help ease shortages of consumer goods and foreign currency, reduce inflation, and assist in the development of the larger Persian Gulf area. It is also seen as part of a security plan for the Persian Gulf as well as a plan to encourage a gradual economic link between the Persian Gulf states and Iran.[23]

The Hashemi Plan was sent to the Majlis in August 1989 and has been the subject of extensive debate ever since. The plan was approved in its first reading, but its final ratification, although achieved, was not smooth. Already the radical opposition was charging the government with focusing too much on economic growth and, thus, undermining the more important concerns about socio-cultural changes. They were also demanding more attention to agriculture and its supporting infrastructure, including rural areas and irrigation. Additionally, the critics maintained that the plan's liberal openness to international trade, investment, and borrowing will exacerbate Iran's dependency, make it a debtor nation, worsen domestic socioeconomic inequalities, and increase the influence of Western culture. The plan has also been criticized for its unconditional support of the private sector. Defending the plan's intention to borrow from other countries, President Hashemi Rafsanjani rejected the proposal that his government will make Iran a debtor nation. He revealed that the country was already in debt to the amount of $10–12 billion, mostly in short-term credit.[24] He also defended his policy of promoting the private sector by suggesting that such a policy had been in place before his term began and that it also had the approval of the country's top leaders.

By taking a flexible position, President Rafsanjani has been able to sell most of the market-oriented ideas in the plan to the hardliners; he continues his dialogue with them on other contested issues including social reforms and a more self-reliant development path. The plan was ratified with minor modification and put in practice in 21 March 1990, in the beginning of the Iranian year 1369. Its adequate implementation, however, will continue to face domestic and international obstacles of major magnitude. Such obstacles could include factional politics; foreign exchange bottlenecks; shortage of a skilled labor force, particularly competent managers, administrative, and organizational hurdles; infrastructural constraints and incidental factors such as the June 1990 earthquake disaster. Political stability, economic security, and a more flexible foreign policy are particularly critical for the plan's implementation. The government is cognizant of these and other obstacles and the plan offers policies to deal with most of them. Nevertheless, the obstacles may not easily go away because of their enormity, structural character, and long-term nature. Assuming that the plan will be implemented, the outcome will still fall short of realizing the "destined society" as propagated in the Constitution and other official ideological documents. As noted in the plan, it will, at best, implement the first stage of a three-stage development process, the stage of maximum utilization of the existing capacity, largely by means of an obstacle-removing strategy.

Thus, the pragmatist government plans to return the economy to its normal functioning by a combination of oil revenue, foreign assistance, domestic resources, and the private sector. It will build a mixed economy in which the role of the private sector will expand while that of the government will be confined to basic and strategic sectors and activities. This means that planning will continue to be considered a major tool for economic management. However, it faces insurmountable difficulties for becoming anything but an ad hoc and partial activity, devoid of comprehensiveness and novelty. Yet, implementation will remain the real difficulty with planning in the Islamic Republic of Iran.

The pragmatic approach is most likely to be implemented in the Islamic Republic, largely because the state power in large part has fallen into the hands of the pragmatists since the July 1989 presidential election. In the meantime, the July constitutional revisions have increased the pragmatist president's power by eliminating the rival office of prime minister and by creating a more centralized decision-making system.[25] However, for a successful postwar reconstruction, the pragmatists also need to create necessary conditions for a more efficient interplay of the following three sets of factors: (1) domestic resources including national reconciliation and a more coherent development strategy, (2) an efficient management system to coordinate and optimize the use of national and international resources, and, (3) international assistance in the form of capital, technology, and export markets. This is indeed why President Hashemi Rafsanjani and his largely pragmatist-technocratic cabinet members have indicated their commitment to conclude a comprehensive peace with Iraq, reshape Iran's foreign policy, and put almost all of their energy and resources into reviving the economy by an obstacle-removing stage of growth strategy. (The state continues to remain ignorant of the importance of a national reconciliation for postwar reconstruction). The policy permanence, however, would depend on a number of factors, including the president's ability to contain or control factional politics, advances in the peace process with Iraq (for which the pragmatists are held responsible), improvement in the economic conditions, and incidental occurrences.

The pragmatic policy of the mixed approach remains the most vulnerable to unexpected developments that normally occur in or in relation to the Islamic Republic. The latest example of such an event was Nicolae Ceausescu's trip to Tehran just before he was put to death; his government was toppled in Rumania. Ostensibly, he had gone to Iran on an invitation from the pragmatists, a cause that gave sufficient pretext to some radical member of the Majlis to question the wisdom of the pragmatists' foreign policy. But the most significant event occurred in relation to the Salman Rushdie's *Satanic Verses*, which caused a major uproar in Iran and the world (vastly reported in the *New York Times*, February 1989). No doubt Ayatollah Khomeini's distrust of the West deepened in the aftermath of the affair. To most members of the Islamic leadership in Tehran, the event was set up purposefully by the West to inflict damage on Islam. The insensitive manner with which the British government and their Western allies handled the event before the Islamic Republic issued the death threat to Salman Rushdie only exacerbated such misgivings. Incidents such as these particularly weaken the pragmatists whose "liberal" policies were attacked by the radicals and Ayatollah Khomeini in a speech he gave after relations with Western Europe deteriorated over the episode. This event, indeed, indicated the immense difficulty that the pragmatists face in implementing a more moderate foreign policy so critical for the postwar reconstruction.

Aside from being vulnerable to unexpected developments, the mixed approach also faces problems in formulating a more coherent development strategy, creating a more efficient system of management, and securing international assistance. As dimensions of the first two problems have been explained elsewhere in this book, I shall concentrate on the last one. The Islamic Republic may not be able to repeat the experience of, for example, South Korea in attracting Western and Japanese assistance in rebuilding its economy. To acquire such resources, the Islamic Republic must abandon its present international policy, accept total reintegration into the capitalist world market, and abide with world market roles and regulations. Pragmatists in power may wish to take such a gigantic policy shift but they will have a hard time selling it to their radical opposition in the Majlis and in the society in the near future. Even some of their own constituents would voice concern over a total return to the Shah's foreign policy. The present global changes are generating new opportunities for the mixed approach, but they may not be of much help in the short run. Indeed, the changes in Eastern Europe could make the Third World a less desirable place for the Western and Japanese capitalists. Eastern Europe offers an extensive market and a more secure environment. The labor there is also cheap and well-disciplined, though less, now that the iron control is lifted. Most international aid will also go to Eastern Europe, for the capitalist world is anxious to develop a free market economy before the present euphoria for such a system is put off by the likely worsening of the peoples' lives under the new arrangements. Iran's ability to compete with Eastern Europe (and with the more established Third World governments friendly to the West) over international resources is further constrained by the unfavorable domestic and regional conditions including cultural changes and the no-peace no-war stalemate with Iraq. Moreover, given the U.S. and USSR rapprochement, Iran may in the future lose its geopolitical and strategic importance and thus attractiveness to the West. Although politically healthy, such a development can be economically harmful as the economy continues to depend on the West and Japan for much of its oil markets and industrial inputs, including technology. All these suggest that Iran rather should look toward developing nations, within and outside the Islamic world, for trade, technology transfer, and capital investment.

The mixed approach also has the potential of generating certain important problems. For example, it can perpetuate the ongoing ideological debates within the state. Specifically, given its eclectic combination of elements from the open-door and self-reliance strategies, proponents on both sides would continue to struggle for a bigger ideological representation in the mix, leading to much waste of time and energy so badly needed for reconstruction. The mixed approach could also lead to a worsening of the economic situation. In particular, the relaxation of international trade could lead to a diversion of the existing huge private investable savings (some 12,000 to 15,000 billion rials) to profitable import-export services and away from productive sectors. Although employment may not rise significantly, income concentration and inflation would certainly worsen. Demand for foreign exchange would also rise as would the trade deficit, leading to further decline in the value of the rial. The inevitable consequences would be an even higher inflation and a further worsening in the purchasing power of the majority. Indeed, some of these predicted problems are already realities in Iran under President Hashemi Rafsanjani.[26]

The situation on the price side, for example, got so out of hand that the government had to intervene in the black market for the foreign exchange by indirectly depreciating the rial substantially. The move produced significant short-term results in terms of bringing down the prices of goods, services, and foreign currency. For example, the exchange rate between rial and the dollar declined from around 1,400 rials to one dollar to about 950 rials to one dollar in just less than two weeks. This experience indicated that the mixed approach might avoid these pitfalls if the state would not only put a stricter control on the black markets and the cancerous expansion of international trade and domestic services but also make significant changes in its foreign exchange policy. However, in March 1990, the government had to suspend this policy of indirectly depreciating rials due to insufficient currency for foreign exchange. The government could also impose higher taxes on investment in these activities and make them subject to cumbersome licensing. A recent bill imposing value-added taxes on luxury consumption goods and services was a step in the right direction.[27] Another similarly wise policy was legislation of a National Cooperation Tax for Reconstruction (NCTR) to help finance infrastructural projects and fixed capital formation. The tax was also hoped to reduce private liquidity and considered a step toward redistribution of wealth. According to this law, legal entities (afrad-e haghighi) with a wealth of over a 100 million rials will pay a onetime NCTR at the rates determined by the law (up to 45 percent for immobile wealth).[28] The state could also devise effective incentive policies to guide the wandering savings in the direction of productive investment.

At territorial level, some important decisions vis-à-vis reconstructing the war-damaged urban areas and economic activities are being established.[29] The Directive, as was noted earlier, outlines the major considerations in planning and reconstructing the damaged cities, towns, and villages. First, before plans can be developed, authorities want to know how many people will return. So, population projections are developed. Second, they study what should be the various cities' functions, rather than presupposing that they will assume their previous roles. Third, they have decided to take a regional view of development; that is, in planning the reconstruction, cities will be seen as integral parts of their provinces and the provinces will be seen in relation to each other. According to this strategy, the National Spatial Strategy Planning (NSSP) (amayesh-e sarzamin), reconstruction of rural settlements and agriculture would precede that of the cities.[30] It is hoped that the strategy will prevent the unwanted migration of rural people to the cities as they are rebuilt. Moreover, the strategy is consistent with the government's policy of making agriculture an axis or pivot of development and helping rural settlements in the first stage of economic growth and reconstruction.

Next, cities would rebuild on their old sites but not necessarily as they were. In the past, there were no parks, but lots of markets, narrow streets, and mixed land uses—with housing and trades all together. Now, the plan is to create modern cities, with industrial and commercial sites separate from residential areas. This means that significant changes are going to take place in landholding patterns within these cities. Attempts will certainly be made to enforce Islamic building codes and architecture. The new spatial structure of the cities is also expected to affect patterns of social and economic interactions between the residents and property relations. Old neighbors, for example, could find themselves spatially separated. The new land-use pattern will undoubtedly increase demand for modern communication networks and affect the transport system, as people will no longer be able to walk to work.

This particular urban reconstruction strategy conforms nicely to the government's priority of economic normalization and growth. The plan is to reconstruct the productive sectors first, responding to the infrastructure, housing, and service bottlenecks as they develop. Clearly, this is a different strategy than the one followed in the pre-cease-fire period, when the government put some 44 percent of its reconstruction budget into housing.[31] The new strategy will also make the displaced population return gradually, in stages and as planned, according to the government's ability to rebuild. Otherwise, there will be no housing or jobs for those who wish to return to their cities, except of course for those who will build their own housing with little or no reliance on the government.

THE NATURE OF THE RECONSTRUCTION PROCESS

Conceptualizing the postwar reconstruction also requires identifying the most critical aspects or attributes of the reconstruction process. To begin with, reconstruction is an orderly and predictable process. For example, damaged cities and industries are usually rebuilt on the same sites, the predisaster trends in population and urban growth continue during the reconstruction period, and dominant economic sectors and social groups continue to dominate. The tendency for the prewar trends to continue is reinforced by two powerful forces: (1) the uncertainty attached to changes in policies, and (2) the biases of the existing institutions in restoring the prewar order. It is also easier and faster to restore the old than to create the new. Moreover, under normal conditions, the enormous resources poured into the reconstruction process largely benefit the richer section of the population and therefore make the position of the disaster victims more unequal. This occurs for several reasons including "a desire on the part of the business community to take advantage of the disaster to improve its own position."[32] Indeed one person's catastrophe becomes another person's marketing boom during reconstruction following a disaster. All this attests to the need for a planned reconstruction in the direction of restructuring existing trends and relationships with a view to maintaining continuity so that conservative forces are not antagonized. It must be recognized that it is impossible to completely maintain the status quo, for it is impossible to implement a tabula rasa.

Beyond these general features and just as in the case of formulating a suitable strategy, there is no consensus on what should or should not characterize a more acceptable process as it will differ from case to case. Notwithstanding the specificity problems, it is possible to identify, on the basis of the existing literature and past experiences with disaster planning and postwar reconstruction, a few critically important properties of postwar reconstruction. I outline them here as a set of propositions along with the experience of the Islamic Republic.

Politics and Reconstruction

Reconstruction tends to become *politicized,* and politics postpone reconstruction. The war increases the expectations for the postwar period but, at the same time, the postwar period is a time of shortage that tends to increase societal tensions and pressures for implementation of immediate corrective measures. Two factors tend to exacerbate this tension: (1) the economic crisis that usually follows the cease-fire and (2) factional struggles over political power in a postwar period largely in flux. The economic crisis encourages disagreements over a reconstruction strategy, which is pulled toward a planned or market approach, and reduces political will for reconstruction of war-damaged areas, while it tends to encourage regeneration of the national economy. Political factionalism, on the other hand, tends to prolong the disagreements and prevent practical initiatives to be implemented. Thus, it is not surprising that, whereas in recent years the need for reconstruction has increased throughout the world, the political will for reconstruction has diminished. Most governments tend to regenerate their national economies at the expense of reconstructing war damage.

As we have just seen, postwar reconstruction has been the most politicized in the Islamic Republic and one-year-and-a-half since the cease-fire, only a few major reconstruction projects have been implemented largely focusing on oil and infrastructure related projects. Housing reconstruction had been a high priority area before the cease-fire. Some 74,456 houses had been reconstructed by the end of the war—out of 114,860 houses that were damaged from 50 to 100 percent. Industries, agriculture, and damaged settlements were also being reconstructed but the pace had been very slow. In the meantime, the government continued to revise its First Plan, which had already been revised a few times. The latest version of the revised plan was sent to the Parliament by President Hashemi Rafsanjani in the last days of 1989. It was approved and went into operation in March 1990.

Public Participation and Reconstruction

Reconstruction should be considered a "therapy for the wounded society," and thus it demands not only *public participation* but also attention to the social psychology of those affected. This means, among other considerations, that reconstruction, as a process of therapeutic readjustment, should bring in the affected population as partners and engage them in rebuilding their communities; the caring professional societies and humanitarian organizations have a critical role to play in this therapeutic activity. The Iranian administrative system is, however, very centralized, though less so since the Revolution.

Prior to the cease-fire, particularly during the earlier years of the war, public participation in reconstruction was significant.[34] This was partly because many such activities involved rebuilding housing and certain public places. Additional enthusiasm came from the people themselves who believed their revolution was being destroyed by its enemies. In the meantime, the concept of controlled decentralization had gained significant ground among the early revolutionaries. For example, and as we noted in Chapter 2, the original First Plan was made by the participation of some 6,000 individuals throughout the country and it incorporated top-down and bottom-up approaches to administration and the implementation of economic development. Also favored was the notion that reconstruction should bring the people into the process through committees, grass-roots organizations and, above all, private undertakings.[35] The emphasis on the "people" was, and continues to be for some, a ploy to legitimize increasing privatization of the economy; for others, however, it means real participation.[36]

Over time, however, public participation in reconstruction has diminished as the initial enthusiasm has faded away and the government has moved, particularly since the cease-fire, in the direction of a more substantive program of reconstruction and recentralization. The focus is now on major revenue-generating projects and basic infrastructure and industries, all of which demand central control as well as expertise and skill not possessed by the majority. An example of the attempts to recentralize the government is the bill that demoted the Ministry of Plan and Budget from an independent ministerial body to a staff organization within the Office of the President (as under the Shah), changing its function from a line to an advisory authority over other ministries. The summer-1989 changes in the Constitution were also aimed at creating a more centralized policy-making body.[37] Moreover, it is expected that the sectoral forces in the society will oppose and perhaps effectively neutralize the ongoing attempts by the provincial forces to institutionalize a more participatory territorial system of management and decision making. In the meantime, the talk about incorporating people in the reconstruction process continues and, as we have seen, the Directive gives particular attention to the issue.

Safety Codes and Reconstruction

Reconstruction tends to be an emotionally charged process during which pressure for quick response is high. *Safety considerations* therefore are usually relaxed for speedy satisfaction of needs and emergencies. Yet, reconstruction is characterized by many hazards and risks. For example, patched-up buildings, temporary shelters, or structures with apparently minor damage could collapse on residents, general users, reconstruction workers, or emergency crews, with devastating moral and material consequences. Strict and specifically designed legal *safety codes* are needed, covering individuals, groups, and family units. This must be accompanied with social insurance covering the victims. Also needed are well-trained and responsible inspectors in various fields.

In the absence of information, it is hard to speculate about the Islamic Republic's safety concerns. Reconstruction, just like the war, has been the most emotionally charged issue in the country, and religion has been used for the most part to mobilize the masses in both cases. Therefore, the risk of hazard must have been high. Yet, I know of only a few laws and regulations specifically designed for safety purposes. Although property damage has been paid for in full or in part, depending on the type and extent of damage, social insurance remains largely underdeveloped. The absence of enough trained inspectors must have also helped increase the number of potentially fatal accidents.

National Security, Defense, Integrity, and Reconstruction

Reconstruction must be most attentive to *national security, defense, and integrity.* Achieving these requires domestic political stability, which in turn depends on democratic means and the role of law. Reconstruction must begin by denouncing the war, any war, as all wars are inhumane. The risk of another war could best be reduced by *incorporating* the cause of the war into the reconstruction itself. A good defense policy is also based on a prudent diplomacy based on the understanding that the utility of offensive force is diminishing while economic development has become a real force within the international balance of power. Changing people's attitudes toward the old enemy and war in general is particularly important. Education is a valued tool for this purpose. Reconstructionists should think of themselves as *peace activists* (both as peacemakers and peace-keepers). Although they cannot prevent war from happening, they can lessen the chance of war. Reconstructionists should also be defenders of law and order and of civil defense planning. Care must be taken particularly to strengthen the defensive capacity of the border areas. This requires an immediate but well-planned repopulation of the war-damaged areas. Empty land is an invitation for invasion. Dispersion of economic activities and their relocation to safer places, expanding both military and civil defense structures, institutions, and forces, and increasing national integration of the border people are equally helpful. National integration demands a territorial balance in the standard of living and development, regional specialization, and establishment of a well-articulated system of regional government. Among other measures to increase national defense include building air-raid shelters and redesigning public and residential constructions to accommodate security concerns.

Theoretically, a high concern for national security is incorporated into the Directive. In practice, however, the Republic's experience with all these requirements of national defense has so far been modest at best. Democracy and the role of law remains to be broadened to include the opposition and a comprehensive peace with Iraq remains out of sight largely due to Iraq's unacceptable claims. The state has, however, changed its international policy toward more accommodation of old antagonists and emphasis on the role of economic tools and negotiation rather than politico-military force. In the meantime, the defense budget has been increased even after the war, by $1.5 billion a year during the 1989–93 five-year plan period. However, little has as yet been accomplished in expanding the defensive capability of the war zones. The reconstruction of the war-damaged areas is expected to be complete in two years, a rather ambitious and unrealistic proposition.[38] During the war some industries were relocated to safer areas in the north and east of the country, but industrial dispersion has not been a major concern of the government. Most industries are being reconstructed in their original (prewar) locations. These include the highly damaged Abadan oil refinery, the world largest, Navard industrial complexes in Ahvaz, and the huge petrochemical complex in Bandar Khomeini (formerly Bandar-e Shahpour).[39] Finally, national integration of border regions remain a national long-term goal.

War Damage and Reconstruction

War damage and reconstruction needs must be carefully determined and assessed. Generally speaking, they are vast, diverse, and complex, necessitating an *interdisciplinary* approach to postwar reconstruction. War damage, for example, differs in extent, type, importance, ownership, age, priority for or difficulty of replacement, and financial value. Different types of war damage may affect human, material, institutional, financial, cultural, and historical resources. They may have been damaged beyond repair or may be repairable. Moreover, different types of damage are repairable or replaceable at different costs and with different degrees of difficulty. War damage also differs in terms of age, structure, and importance to nation, locality, family, and individual. Finally, ownership is a critical matter. The damaged item could be publicly or privately owned, it could belong to a wealthy or a poor family. The ownership consideration is important because wars usually create confusion about ownership, while reconstruction tends to restructure the old property arrangements in damaged areas. Damage determination requires adaptation of suitable methods. A careful record of all variations of damaged items should also be kept, preferably by an independent agency with specialized branches. The condition of independence may be guaranteed by institutionalizing different representations within the organization. Record keeping is important because it can help the state compensate the war victims (particularly the poor) as soon as possible; determine the available resources and the needs; set objectives and priorities; and finally, determine the stage to which a particular reconstruction task belongs.

In the case of Iran, as we have seen, the war inflicted a variety of complex and extensive damage on the society involving human, economic, physical, political, and psychocultural aspects. Iran's lack of experience with war in recent history particularly has contributed to the vastness of the war damage. As was explained in Chapter 2, these damages are identified and computed using an acceptable methodology, and are well classified both for compensating the victims and in reconstructing the society. The Islamic government also acknowledges the comprehensive and extensive nature of the war damage in official reports. Most governmental proclamations underscore the need for a more comprehensive and flexible reconstruction strategy. In practice, however, and as we have seen, the state has narrowed its options to rebuilding the economy as its top priority.

Resources for Reconstruction

Resources for reconstruction must be *identified* and *mobilized* without wasting time. Reconstruction needs resources and resources need to be identified before they can be utilized. Finding resources in an exhausted economy is not an easy task. Existing and potential resources must be distinguished and the latter must be further identified in terms of their immediate and long-term exploitability. Resources must also be classified by type (e.g., human, physical-material, serviceable, credit, or financial), quality (e.g., interinstitutional cooperation and coordination, skilled work force, training institutes, dynamic and modern sectors), amount (e.g., abundant, scarce, or sufficient), distribution (e.g., concentrated in certain areas or in the hands of a few families), cost (cheap, expensive, or competitive), function (e.g., local leadership), ease of use (e.g., accessibility, availability, and convertability), and impact (e.g., dependency or self-sufficiency). Finally, indigenous resources must be distinguished from external resources; these latter must be carefully identified in terms of the foregoing characteristics: national origin, and the conditions attached to their purchase, transfer, or adaptation. These conditions particularly apply to transfers of technology. Resource identification should also account for territorial distribution and interdependency. This is best done by means of a careful analysis of regional resources, settlement systems, spatial links, and functional gaps. Suitable methods should be devised for proper identification of all these resources and interdependencies.

The identified resources must be mobilized before they can be utilized, for mobilization aims at widening accessibility to resources. Resources mobilization is a largely government-led and -organized action but private groups are equally indispensable. For the government or the private sector to act, it must have resources, skills, confidence, and authority. Different types of resources are mobilized differently and by different agencies. People are more effectively mobilized by propaganda, nationalism, patriotism, and democratic practices. Popular organizations, self-help projects, incorporation of women into the reconstruction process, and patronage (e.g., cities not affected by the war will rebuild damaged cities) have been equally important. Coordinative, cooperative, and collective work and training are particularly effective in mobilizing resources. A combination of these methods have been used in almost all cases of reconstruction. For example, the main slogans in the Soviet Union were "aids to the liberated areas" and "producing for the reconstruction."[40] Another important aspect of resource mobilization relates to the role of the military and paramilitary in reconstruction.

The transition of these forces *from fighters to reconstructors* should be carefully planned. Financial resources may also be mobilized by means of public and private initiatives. Methods used have included "War Loan Drive," selling war bonds, and self-financing by the people. Finally, material resources may be mobilized by expanding mineral exploration and exploitation, extensive use of local materials and simplified techniques, particularly in construction, and energizing small factories, workshops, farms, and services. Creating communication channels and transportation networks are particularly important.

The Islamic Republic has done an extensive statistical survey of the existing resources in the country and the results are available in numerous volumes published by various ministries and government agencies notably the Plan and Budget's Statistical Center and the Central Bank. The ten-year national census and the census of agriculture are among the significant steps the government has taken in the direction of identifying domestic resources. Sources cited in this book should provide a useful guide to the government publications on various aspects of the society since the Revolution. For mobilization of the country's resources the Islamic Republic has used religion as a powerful force and organized "Week of War" and "Day of Struggle for Economic Development," among other similar initiatives. It has also used popular organizations, self-help methods, and patronage. For example, Tehranis have been involved in reconstructing Khorramshahr while *Astan-e Qods* rebuilt the city of Hovaizeh.[41] The Republic has also used people's savings by channeling parts of them into, for example, Account Number 100 of the Imam and Account Number 222 of Shaheed Raja'i, among other similar accounts. Gifts and other financial assistance have also been collected by a variety of organizations including *Emdad-e Imam* (Imam's Assistance Organization). In the early wartime period, financial assistance from the people amounted to some 40 percent of the total budget of the *Setad-e Markazi*; in 1988 some 20 billion rials were allocated for the reconstruction from the Account Number 222 as reported by Hamid Mirzadeh, director of the Central Headquarters for Reconstruction.[42]

Timing Reconstruction

Reconstruction needs to be *timed accurately.* The first most important step following a disaster such as a missile attack or bombardment is to analyze the area's *vulnerability* to determine the causes and consequences of the disaster and various possible vulnerable conditions. This should lead to better control over the subsequent actions to deal with the disaster. Important among factors to reduce vulnerability are also self-help and the need for propagation of a human ecology of cultural survival. The *best* time to *reconstruct* is after the war, when people are returning or have returned (so that they can participate in the process). Clearly, not all kinds of damage could be left for after the war. These include basic need emergencies, housing, and strategic infrastructures that must be rebuilt as quickly as possible. The best time to plan, on the other hand, is during the war, so that the nation is ready for a rapid reconstruction when the war ends. *Speed* is essential to capture the political will and the public's enthusiasm, which are the most critical for allocation of the ever decreasing resources to reconstruction.

The Islamic Republic became involved in emergency and restoration reconstruction almost immediately after the war had begun in September 1980. Emphasis was put on rebuilding housing, infrastructures, and other basic needs and strategic items. At least four international and national conference were also organized along with a research center, studying various aspects of reconstruction in the country.[43] Despite these attempts, the Republic was unable to formulate a reconstruction strategy during the war. Thus, when the cease-fire at last came, the nation was not ready to go in action in hopes of rebuilding the society. The consequent loss of opportunity for a speedy reconstruction of the economy was further worsened by a prolonged factional debate that followed the cease-fire, delaying formulation of a reconstruction strategy and implementation of many important reconstruction activities.

Stages of Reconstruction

Reconstruction should be *scheduled in stages,* each carefully defined, planned for, and implemented in proper sequence. Elsewhere I have identified the following four stages: (1) emergency, (2) restoration (or recovery), (3) replacement, and (4) developmental reconstruction.[44] Clearly, overlap should and will inevitably occur among these stages as they are not always or totally separated in time or mutually exclusive. The duration of each stage will vary according to a variety of factors, including scale of the disaster, existence of a strong political will for reconstruction, and the degree of the society's preparedness for coping with the given disaster including a strategy and a predisaster plan. Other factors include availability of resources and the government's ability to mobilize them, quality of the leadership, the speed at which decisions are made and implemented, existence of popular and humanitarian organizations, and international cooperation.

The emergency stage immediately follows a disaster and aims at coping with the situation and helping victims survive. It normally includes such activities as search, rescue, mass feeding, clearance of debris, paramedical help, and provision for shelter and other basic needs of the victims. The restoration or recovery stage aims at returning the community to a bearable life. Thus, repairable damaged structures are patched up and made usable again. Considerable overlap exists between this stage and the emergency stage. It is clear that restoration takes much longer and requires more resources than the previous stage. Whereas self-help is important in both stages, restoration reconstruction also requires certain levels of comprehensive planning. Most investments and expenditures during these stages are of a temporary nature. Thus, although double investment (i.e., temporary investment to be followed by a permanent investment on the same project) is unavoidable, care must be taken to reduce its costs. The first two stages are also considered critical from a political and social point of view. They boost the people's morale, prevent migration from the place of residence, maintain the social peace, and postpone (unfortunately) emergence of antiwar movements.

The replacement stage, on the other hand, is concerned with returning the community to its predisaster situation. Thus, rebuilding structures and capital stocks that have been destroyed beyond repair or whose repair requires a national commitment in terms of resources is undertaken at this stage. Other activities include returning refugees to their original places of residence, and helping them start a normal life. Job creation therefore is an essential first step. This stage must be guided by long-term state planning because complex decisions are needed before certain old structures are rebuilt. For example, should the structure be reconstructed at all and, if so, where and at what technological level and capacity? Land-use patterns might also have to be changed, necessitating modifications in property ownership and relationships. A strong tendency exists at this stage to construct prefabricated housing, a policy that leads to double investment and thus waste. The replacement stage should be followed by a fourth stage, focusing on developing the society beyond the predisaster level. This developmental reconstruction is no easy task, as it involves recovering the war's opportunity costs and going beyond such recovery. Wars do not just destroy part of what exists; they also prevent the society from making new investments, utilizing its production capacity and resources, and developing its skills and technical capability. Therefore, developmental reconstruction should not be concerned with damaged items but deficits that would remain after rebuilding all destroyed structures. Reconstruction at this stage enters the field of development and becomes concerned with socioeconomic transformation in the direction of broad national goals. Long-term comprehensive planning and strategic thinking become urgent as does government financing and international assistance. For example, decisions must be made regarding what is usable and useful from the past: some of the old structures must be preserved while others should be scraped or restructured.

The Islamic Republic's reconstruction activities during the war remained limited to the first three stages: emergency, restoration or recovery, and replacement. Developmental reconstruction was not, rightly, included among the responsibilities of the Central Headquarters for Renovation and Reconstruction of the War-Damaged Areas (*setad-e bazsazi va nousazi-ye manateq-e jang zadeh*), the country's main organization for reconstruction during the war. Rather, as its director explained in a press interview, the duties of the headquarters were limited to emergency assistance, provision of basic needs, and restoration of repairable damaged structures (i.e., structures with less than 50 percent damage). Except for housing and certain infrastructures, the headquarters or its supporting branches (*setadha-ye mo'in*) did not even undertake replacement. According to Hamid Mirzadeh, a recent director of the headquarters, during the war, reconstruction was limited to the first two stages, together referred to as *bazsazi-ye maqta'i* (the temporary reconstruction); replacement reconstruction, called *bazsazi-ye addisazi* (normalizing reconstruction), was generally ignored; and developmental reconstruction, referred to as *bazsazi-ye bozorg* (the great reconstruction), was left altogether to the postwar period. He admits that there was opposition to the reconstruction during the war, but dismisses such reaction on the ground that the *bazsazi-ye maqta'i* was needed for social and political reasons. Among such reasons, he cites boosting the people's morale, preventing depopulation of the war zones, maintaining the social peace and basic needs, and postponing development of antiwar movements.[45] As most of what the headquarters was assigned to do became inapplicable in the postwar period, its duties were changed and new responsibilities were assigned, including replacement and developmental reconstruction.

A more serious attempt has been made since the cease-fire to expand the scope of replacement reconstruction. Thus, various damaged industrial, infrastructural, and settlement structures are being rebuilt with emphasis on the oil installations, energy sector, producer goods industries, and basic infrastructure. Developmental reconstruction, however, remains largely neglected, awaiting implementation of a well-detailed reconstruction strategy that was approved by the Majlis in the early days of 1990. A new high policy-making body, called *Showra-ye Siasatgozari Bara-ye Bazsazi* (the Council on Policy Making for Reconstruction) was set up immediately after the cease-fire to determine the basic ingredients of the strategy. As we have seen, the Council produced a Directive and details were worked out later on by Musavi's government and revised by Hashemi Rafsanjani's government.

Proper Management of Reconstruction

Reconstruction must be managed *properly and efficiently.* But no one best way to manage reconstruction activities exists. The existing experiences do, however, point toward a number of principles that should be followed. To begin with, reconstruction is a civilian job and popular grass-roots associations are indispensable for the task. Such organizations may be formed by the citizens or the government. In either case, it is important that they be given adequate resources and authority to act and remain independent and in control of their resources. Examples of such organization in the Islamic Republic are various, for example, *setads* (headquarters), *nehads* (institutions), *bonyads* (foundations), *showras* (councils), *grouha-ye kar* (work groups), *basiege* (mobilization forces), and *comiteha* (committees). These organizations have been not only active in supporting the war but also in the wartime emergency and recovery activities. However, their contributions to the postwar reconstruction have been negligible to say the least. Although indispensable, popular organizations are not sufficient for the complex managerial and technical tasks that replacement and developmental reconstruction demands. Appropriate public offices must be established to assist and complement them.

The choice among various disaster management systems must be made with due regard to the existing governmental organizations and bureaucracy. Three such models are available: (1) establishment of a specialized new ministry for reconstruction, (2) creation of reconstruction offices within the existing ministries, and (3) formation of a headquarters within the prime minister's or the president's office. The last model is the closest to what was adopted by the Islamic Republic during the war, but various ministries also had their own reconstruction offices. In addition, a few freestanding offices were established to carry emergency and recovery aspects of the reconstruction. The main organization in the country concerned with reconstruction during the war was the *Setad-e Markazi-ye Bazsazi Va Nousazi-ye Manateq-e Jangzadeh* (Central Headquarters for Reconstruction and Renovation of the War-Damaged Areas). Among the members of the headquarters were fifteen ministers and director of the Central Bank, with the minister of Interior as president. Other important members included ministers of *Jihad-e Sazandegi* (Reconstruction Crusade), Housing and Urban Development, Plan and Budget, Agriculture, Commerce, and Industries. The organization oversaw the work of many subdivisions including the *Setadha-ye Mo'in* (supporting headquarters at provincial and major city levels) and *Setadha-ye Shahrestan* (county headquarters). It was, in turn, supervised by the *Showra-ye 'Ali-ye Bazsazi Va Nousazi* (Supreme Council for Reconstruction and Renovation) headed by the prime minister. The other three members of the council included a representative of Ayatollah Khomeini, minister of Interior, and minister of Plan and Budget with the last acting as the headquarters' secretary. Members of the provincial headquarters included the governor, representatives of the ministries of *Jihad-e Sazandegi* and Commerce, and the *Imam Jom'eh* (Friday Imam).

Among the freestanding organizations dealing with aspects of the wartime reconstruction, the following ones were notable: *Bonyad-e Maskan (Housing Foundation), Bonyad-e Omour-e Mehajerin-e Jangi* (Foundation for the Affairs of the War Immigrants), *Bonyad-e Mostazafan* (Foundation for the Oppressed), *Sepah-e Pasdaran* (Revolutionary Guard Corps), *Astan-e Qods* (Organization in Charge of the Properties of the Eight Imam), *Owqaf* (the Religious Endowment Institution), and *Helal-e Ahmar* (the Islamic Red Cross). War reconstruction also needed specialized agencies concerned with certain sectoral and territorial tasks such as the Donbas Mine Restoration Administration in the Soviet Union. Although similar sectoral administrations have not been organized in the Islamic Republic, a few specialized territorial administrations are in operation in the country including the Khorramshahr's *Setad-e Mo'in.*

Since the cease-fire, a number of changes have been made in the management aspects of the postwar reconstruction. The most important of these changes include the following: the *Setad-e Markazi* (Central Headquarters) has been given new and expanded responsibilities for replacement and developmental reconstruction, while organizations devoted to the *Bazsazi-ye Maqta'i* (emergency reconstruction) have been dismantled or deactivated to a large degree; the *Showra-ye Ali* (High Council) has been replaced with the *Showra-ye Siasatgozari* (Policy-Making Council), which also has more authority; responsibilities for administration of the reconstruction activities are now vested with the president (Office of the Prime Minister has been eliminated); and sectoral ministries have expanded their reconstruction offices and have been given direct control over implementation of relevant reconstruction projects. The role of the popular institutions in reconstruction has also declined to a significant degree, as more formal governmental bodies have taken up the various reconstruction tasks. Women's roles continue to remain negligible at best. In the wartime period, the lack of coordination between various popular and governmental institutions had created tremendous waste and difficulty. In the postwar system of management, the same problem remains, but the real difficulty now concerns the lack of coordination among various governmental organizations. In particular, intermediate coordinating bodies are lacking and there has been no attempt on the part of the government to classify its functions as decentralizable or nondecentralizable. This is needed for a better division of labor among the various popular, informal, and formal organizations.

Documentation and Evaluation of Reconstruction

Reconstruction should be carefully *documented and evaluated*; the results should be published periodically in various forms and places. This is needed for better management of reconstruction and for the transfer of the experience to the general public (to encourage participation), academic communities (for theoretical development), and practitioners in other countries and in the future. An information bank must be established along with well-defined evaluative criteria. Whereas governments should be involved in documentation and evaluation of reconstruction activities, these goals are best and most accurately achieved by independent agencies outside the governments' spheres of direct influence. Such agencies should have access to key data and policies and be operative at all governmental levels.

In the Islamic Republic, both documentation and evaluation remains a monopoly of the government. No independent agency has been involved in documenting and evaluating reconstruction activities with the exception of consulting firms and universities. A data bank has not been created either but the government has compiled impressive amounts of information on war-damage and, as we have seen, the statistics are fairly detailed. However, for security reasons, the information is disseminated only to a limited number of organizations and individuals, largely within the government. Little is also achieved in terms of designing suitable criteria for evaluation of reconstruction projects.

OBSTACLES TO RECONSTRUCTION

Most radical postrevolutionary societies, we have argued, experience civil or international wars, which in most cases are imposed upon them to prevent social change. We have seen that Iran was no exception. The postwar reconstruction should thus be considered part of a larger struggle to reverse this situation and initiate the building of a new society. As such, it can expect to be hindered by the same, if not more formidable, constraints that hinder social transformation in other postrevolutionary societies. The Ayatollah Khomeini's dictum that "reconstruction should be viewed as another defensive war" reflects this struggle.[46] Indeed, as we shall shortly see, Iran has faced no fewer constraints in rebuilding the society than most postrevolutionary states, despite the Islamic Republic's mostly conciliatory policies and pragmatic approaches. However, just like revolutions, the postwar reconstruction also creates opportunities for political, institutional, structural, and managerial changes and improvements. In the case of Iran, such opportunities are particularly encouraged by the country's vast natural resources, most of which remains untapped. The postwar reconstruction, therefore, presents itself as a process whereby constraints are mitigated or brought under control, while the scope, depth, and types of opportunities or enabling forces are widened. Constraints on the postwar reconstruction are unique to given societies and change as reconstruction enters new phases. As in revolutions, such constraints have their origins in a variety of causes: some generating from the prewar conditions in the country; others created by or because of the war. They also differ in terms of territorial origin: some arising from domestic factors; others imposed by the external forces. I have already detailed the various types of obstacles that the Iranian Revolution had to face. Here I wish to focus on some of the most pressing constraints that the reconstruction is facing. General speaking, these are the same constraints that crippled the economy in the first place. I will discuss them under financing options, obsolete political culture, and major bottlenecks.

Financing Options

Developing the economy leads to the issue of industrial inputs such as raw materials, intermediate goods, machinery, and technology, a significant portion of which must be imported. Iranian industries are dependent on international markets for about 65 percent of their inputs, very little of which could be generated locally regardless of how emphatic the government would be in using indigenous resources. The needed inputs for reviving the industries at the pre-revolutionary level (which is still less than full capacity utilization) will cost some $6.5 billion a year in foreign exchange. The military must also be rebuilt and the annual cost of imported spare parts and equipment will amount to about $3 billion, since only a small amount is produced domestically. Another $1.5 billion is to be added to the annual defense budget during the five-year plan beginning in 1989. Food imports, which were always high, account for another $4.5 billion or so a year. An open-door policy could increase this figure by as much as 50 percent. If another $1 billion is added for yearly costs of scholarships, embassies, missions, and similar items, the total foreign exchange need will add up to $15 to $17 billion a year. Yet, this figure does not include foreign exchange needed for foreign interest payments (which remains low), reconstruction of the war's direct damage, and development of the economy beyond the prerevolutionary level (which will require significant import of capital goods). In 1983, the economy absorbed some $20 billion (mainly paid for imports of industrial inputs and consumer goods). Indeed, the new five-year plan anticipates a larger foreign exchange budget, some $112 billion over the 1989–93 period, or about $22.4 billion a year. The government expects to earn $1.9 billion a year from nonoil exports, which have hardly ever exceeded $1 billion a year. The remaining $20.4 billion would have to come from oil exports and foreign assistance of various forms.

Yet, oil earnings, which account for over 90 percent of Iran's foreign exchange, may not exceed $15 billion a year for the next few years, even if OPEC were able to maintain its recently established production ceiling of 22.5 million barrels a day, at $21 per barrel. The government's budgeted oil revenue of some $15 billion a year could indeed prove an overestimation as it has in the past on a consistent basis if no price-rising crisis occurs in the oil market! Iran's production quota is established at about 3.2 million barrels a day, but less than 3 mb/d is produced, of which around 0.8 million is for domestic consumption and the rest could be exported. Most experts believe that Iran may not increase its production beyond 3.0 million barrels a day without a major investment to inject gas into existing wells. Note also that only a portion of oil-earned foreign exchange, some 50 to 60 percent at most, is actually received by the government and the rest is partly consumed by international inflation and partly goes to pay for costs of production, distribution, transportation, marketing, insurance, parts and repairs, new investments including exploration, and so forth. Thus, of the $15 billion estimated annual oil revenue, only around $7.5 to $9.0 billion is actually available for economic growth and the reconstruction. About $1 billion could also be earned from nonoil exports and another 0.5 billion a year could be expected from loans to foreign countries or other unexpected sources (e.g., the United States released $567 million of the Iranian frozen assets in November 1989 and $400,000 in May 1990).

Although the Islamic Republic will rely on (the unreliable) oil revenue to rebuild the economy, the government would also have to generate some $6.5 to $8.5 billion a year in foreign exchange from other sources (including nonoil exports) to cover its "foreign exchange gap." It seems certain that the leadership will not invite direct foreign investment, at least not in the foreseeable future. Rather, they will attempt to use foreign revenues in buyback or usance schemes.[47] For example, if foreign parties are asked to build or rennovate a plant, or provide raw materials, the idea would be to pay them back by asking them to take delivery of the product or export it to other countries. This financing strategy is also hoped to promote the country's nonoil exports. Alternatively, foreign companies may be asked to consider their investments as medium-term loans to the government. They then will be paid when the project is completed or production begins. The radical faction rejects the buy-back idea because this "trap" will allow the "foreigners to make policies for our basic industries"; in addition, "they will become the real investors while we will be reduced to a broker between them and the Third World where the products will be sold."[48] Responses of foreign firms to the buy-back or usance ideas have not been enthusiastic either.

A proposal presented by Iran's minister of Economics and Finance to the visiting West German's minister of Foreign Affairs in Tehran in fall 1988 could become a model for the involvement of foreign firms in Iranian reconstruction projects. The proposal calls for the establishment of a consortium comprising several of West Germany's major banks, oil companies, and industrial concerns. Iran would borrow money from the banks within the consortium, spend the money on projects contracted to industrial concerns within the consortium, and repay the loans by selling oil to the oil companies within the consortium.[49] Firms from the Federal Republic of Germany, Italy, and Japan will be preferred over their counterparts in other countries, and it would be acceptable if they were to form a single multinational consortium. In this way, the Islamic Republic hoped to get more multinational firms involved in the country's reconstruction without relying too heavily on any single one of them. During the past several years, a number of foreign firms, largely from Western Europe, have kept a more or less active presence in Iran. A short list includes Krupp, Daimler Benze, BASF, Siemens, Deutsche Babcock, Zahnradfabrik, and Lahmeyer International of West Germany; Nissan, Mitsubishi, Mitsui, Kanematsk Gosho, and Itonam & Company of Japan, Saipa, Renault-Peugeot, and Société Générale of France; Agusta, Agip, and Fochi-Sicom of Italy; Rauma Repola of Finland; Talbot of England; Asea Brown Boveri (ABB) of Sweden/Switzerland; SKF of Sweden; and Ciba-Geigy of Switzerland.

Iran also seems to prefer loans from international agencies such as International Bank for Reconstruction and Development (the World Bank) and International Monetary Funds (IMF) rather than from commercial banks and governments which might be asked for help if other sources were to prove insufficient. Indeed the government has approached both IMF and IBRD in the post-cease fire period for loan and technical assistance and the responses from the agencies seems to have been positive and guarded. The Constitution prohibits the government from taking foreign loans except those approved by the Parliament. Nevertheless, this option is being discussed within the state. Reportedly, Ayatollah Khomeini was angered over a confidential letter to him from some influential leaders of the Republic, requesting his permission for foreign loans. However, in a February 1989 press conference (reported in *The New York Times*), Gholamreza Aghazadeh, minister of Oil and Minerals, disclosed that, "The present government has made a number of policies on taking loans. The major policy is that we will be able to get loans for important infrastructural projects." The *Times* reporter also paraphrased the minister as saying that "Iran would strictly limit its borrowing to revenue-producing projects and that such borrowing would not exceed $3 billion over the next five years" and that the decision follows "long debates within the leadership that have been finally settled in favor of a more pragmatic approach backing a vigorous reconstruction of the Iranian economy.[50] Aghazadeh was referring to the oil sector as the five-year plan for 1989–93 period allows the government to use foreign savings, in various forms, of up to $27 billion.

Wealthy Iranians living outside the country are also considered a possible source of foreign exchange and potential investors. This channel, however, will be tightly controlled and may be opened only as a last resort. Other possibilities include increasing solidarity within OPEC for a rise in oil prices—a consideration that led Iran to accept a proposal in November 1988 establishing parity in production between itself and Iraq, a rather major concession. Iran has also changed its Persian Gulf diplomacy in the direction of establishing pragmatic and neighborly relations with the Persian Gulf states, including Iraq, Saudi Arabia and Kuwait.[51] In July 1990, Iran and Iraq cooperated on a proposal that raised OPEC oil price to $21. The new Persian Gulf diplomacy is intended to generate interest on the part of the governments, financial institutions, and investors in the region, helping the Islamic Republic build its economy. The postwar trade liberalization policy concerning prospective importers in the Persian Gulf areas is also directed at encouraging the transfer of foreign exchange to the country. The main theme of the International Conference on the Persian Gulf (Tehran, 20–22 November 1989) was also solidarity among the Persian Gulf states. The Gulf Cooperation Council (GCC) has proposed establishing an international fund (similar to one suggested in the Resolution 598) to help the reconstruction in both Iran and Iraq.[52] The GCC is, however, making the proposal conditional on a comprehensive peace settlement in which it has shown little interest so far.

Promoting nonoil exports is another source for foreign exchange. This alternative, however, remains largely limited, for Iran's nonoil exports have hardly ever exceeded $1 billion in recent history. As was noted earlier, the new five-year plan estimates foreign exchange earnings from nonoil exports at $1.9 billion a year. Although not a difficult target to meet, it will take a significant amount of time, initial investment, and export-promotion incentive programs for this to happen. Note also that export production requires an increase in capacity utilization, which in turn depends on availability of foreign exchange to pay for imported inputs. Mineral resources, which are rich and diverse, have not been fully exploited because of excessive emphasis on the production and export of crude oil. However, the limitation posed by the oil market has made officials think again. In the postwar period, changes have been made in the Mines Act to make it easy for the domestic and foreign private firms to enter into joint ventures with the government for exploration and exports.[53] This potential source of foreign exchange, however, will not bear fruit in the immediate future unless some of what is needed at home is exported. The government target to earn $1.5 billion in 1990 from mineral exports seems highly optimistic. Natural gas is, however, plentiful (Iran's reserves are second to those of the USSR) and ready for exploitation. The government has settled its disputes with the Soviet Union (the country's only customer) over pricing and other technical details and export of natural gas to the Soviet Union resumed in early 1990. The package deal with the Soviet Union also included a $15 billion trade and economic development pact.[54] It must be noted, however, that the deal will not produce foreign exchange for Iran; rather it will result in increased

Soviet technical assistance and technology transfer, as well as certain industrial inputs, to the country. During his 1989 trip to Iran, this author observed many Soviet trucks on the road between Tehran and Rasht, a city on the Caspian Sea.

The government also has its eyes on a number of other sources. The country hopes to make limited use of its assets frozen by the United States government which includes a disputed $10.9 billion in military equipment purchased by the Shah but never delivered to Iran. Money lent to foreign countries by the late Shah amounts to some $7 billion. Against this sum, however, is about $10–12 billion in short- and long-term debt incurred by the previous regime and by the Islamic Republic in recent years. Moreover, some of the debtors, including France, have been unwilling to repay their debts in hard currency. Instead, they have been negotiating deals under which Iran would be paid in commodities of various types. One such deal has reportedly been concluded with France, which will participate in construction of Tehran's underground railway and sell eight airbuses and food items to Iran.[55] The United Nations's assistance and the money made on the limited foreign investments are negligible at best, but savings from the reduced insurance and transport costs for oil exports following the cease-fire are significant. There is also the International Monetary Funds' Special Drawing Rights, which is negligible, and the possibility of a loan from the World Bank in which the Islamic Republic has already increased its share. The Bank's experts have visited Iran twice since the cease-fire and are preparing a package for the country.

Finally, the Islamic Republic is at last learning the real value of its Persian Gulf neighbors. Pragmatists in power now consider the states in this area significant in several ways. First, they are indispensable for solidarity within the OPEC and thus for securing a higher oil prices. Nothing can benefit the Islamic Republic more, as oil export is responsible for over 90 percent of its foreign exchange earnings. Second, the Persian Gulf states offer a good prospect for the Iranian nonoil exports. They have a relatively large and unsaturated market: some 15 million people live in the littoral states (excluding Iraq) with per capita incomes higher than those in the industrialized West. These countries lack mineral resources and are cash exporters of agricultural and light consumer products, in production of which Iran has comparative advantage in the region. Third, proximity and traditional-cultural ties between Iran's southern ports and the sheikhdoms of the Persian Gulf are additional assets. Dubai and Sharja in particularly are very important to Iran as these ports handle a significant portion of exports from international business to the region. In 1987, for example, the nonoil exports through Dubai to the region amounted to $10 billion and the Emirate's reexport to Iran in the same year reached an estimated $365 million. Four, considerable surpluses exist in the current account balances of the sheikhdoms of Persian Gulf, notably Kuwait and the United Arab Emirates. For the 1970–87 period, the two nation's surpluses amounted to $110 billion and $70 billion, respectively. Some $150 billion of the region's private money is also invested abroad. Even a small portion of this wealth, if redirected to Iran, could make a significant contribution to the country's postwar reconstruction. Last, the Islamic Republic hopes to use the Persian Gulf states as mediators between itself and Iraq. A peace settlement will then save Iran billions in defense budgets.[56]

The unity theme of the International Conference on the Persian Gulf (Tehran, November 1989) was predicated upon this analysis of the significance of the Persian Gulf states for the postwar reconstruction of Iran. As was indicated to me by an official of the Foreign Ministry at the conference: "We wish to use reconstruction as a unifying factor in the region and one that would strengthen the economic ties among the Persian Gulf states." The intention is good and sound but tremendous historical and structural constraints tend to work against the Islamic Republic's Persian Gulf policy. Clearly, a precondition to reconstruction is a conclusive, comprehensive peace with Iraq and normalization of relations with Saudi Arabia. The Islamic Republic must also work hard to gain the trust of the Persian Gulf states and capitalists. Prospects for any of these preconditions to be met in the immediate future are negligible at best. Moreover, a policy of unity without reference to the existing contradictions will be viewed as out of line with reality and a sign of weakness. No country will take such a policy from its neighbor with due seriousness.

Major Bottlenecks

Besides a shortage of foreign exchange (the "foreign exchange gap"), there are other major obstacles to reconstruction. We have detailed these in Chapter 2 and partly in Chapter 3. Here I shall focus on those bottlenecks that are having an immediate effect on reconstruction. We have already mentioned the "fiscal gap" and the shortage of skilled human resources. It pays to reiterate and underscore them again. The fiscal gap is well indicated by the imbalance between public expenditures and incomes, resulting in a significantly high public sector's borrowing requirement (PSBR). The number one factor causing the huge budget deficit is the inability of the government to collect taxes particularly from businesses and the rich. Capacity underutilization is another factor that depresses the state revenues. The shortage of skilled, ingenious, experienced, and efficient managers is no less serious. Right from the very beginning of the Revolution, high-level, as well as low-level, management positions have been assigned to loyal ideological supporters irrespective of their ability to carry out the task and the responsibilities. The basis for such appointments have also been personal or family related rather than any predetermined rules or criteria. No wonder that most such assignments have proven disastrous for the economy. There is also the shortage of college and university graduates and technicians. For example, in 1986 there were only 300 graduates in the applied fields per 100,000 population as compared to 5,500 for Japan. The figure for technicians was even more disappointing, 600 per 100,000 population as compared to 25,000 in Japan. The training of technicians is underway, but it is not anywhere close to what is needed.[57] Even more disturbing is the fact that a good number among those available remain unemployed. In 1983, for example, some 37,000 with college or university education were jobless, of whom some 23,000 were previously employed.[58]

The great need for people, who can build complex institutions such as basic industries and infrastructures, will be filled by foreign expertise. The Islamic Republic has already signed contracts with various firms from Japan, West Germany, Italy, France, Turkey, China, the Soviet Union, Eastern European countries, South and North Korea, and Brazil, to create such institutions. There are already a good number of foreign experts working in Iran on different industrial projects such as petrochemicals, steel mills, pipelines, and electric plants.[59] The government is also giving financial support to hundreds of students in universities around the world including many who are on scholarships in the United States. However, the number of financial aid recipients remain much smaller than those under the Shah's regime. Pleas have also been issued for the return of Iranian experts living outside the country. Yet, the most surprising measure taken by the government to remedy the situation involves a contract that was signed with West Germany in fall 1989 (temporarily suspended in the aftermath of the Rushdie affair). According to the contract, West German universities would train Iranian specialists in construction techniques and urban planning to prepare them for designing and implementing more complex reconstruction projects.[60] Similar contracts were numerous under the Shah. Skilled managers and administrators are also in short supply, but the government will not turn to foreign expertise in this area. It may, however, attempt to get help from educated Iranians currently living in the United States and Europe.[61] Again, timing becomes important. If reconstruction goes more slowly, skills could be developed internally (as happened in the oil industry) so they would not have to rely so much on outside help. This is one reason why some defend the more gradual process.

Another significant obstacle to reconstruction is the lack of appropriate institutions or the existence of too many organizations with similar functions and inappropriate practices.[63] The latter include the regular army *vs.* the Revolutionary Guards, the police *vs.* Revolutionary Committees, the Ministry of Agriculture *vs.* Ministry of Reconstruction Crusade, Ministry of Housing and Urban Development *vs.* Housing Foundation of the Islamic Revolution and Housing Organization, interest-free loan institutions *vs.* the banking system, management of the universities *vs.* the Council for Cultural Revolution and other grass-roots organizations, and, most significant, the Foundation for the Eighth Imam (*Astan-e Qods-e Razavi*) *vs.* the government. The postwar addition to this list is the Council of Policy Making for Reconstruction, which is duplicating the government function in drawing a plan for reconstruction of the nation's economy. Specifically, the council and the Ministry of Plan and Budget were both busy drawing their own plans, while still other ministries were going ahead with their own projects and programs.[63] Before reconstruction can be launched, the problem of parallel organizations must be resolved, perhaps by eliminating some and integrating others. So far, attempts in this direction have failed. Examples include bills that are aimed at integrating (1) the regular army and the Revolutionary Guards Corps, and (2) the Ministries of Agriculture and Reconstruction Crusade. None of the bills passed the Parliament; there was a tremendous outcry against them from different quarters in the state.[64] Perhaps the way to tackle this problem is not to address them individually but as part of a complete reorganization of the state structure in the direction of a more controlled decentralism. Such a proposal should be particularly acceptable to the pragmatists, who have come to dominate state power following the 1989 presidential election.

There are other problems of even a more critical nature. The state must decide if there should be limits to private ownership and wealth accumulation. If so, then the specifics of such limits should be clearly spelled out. Otherwise, the wandering private cash holdings will not contribute to reconstruction of productive sectors. Rather, part would remain idle while the rest would continue to be invested in services and leave the country. The state must also decide whether international trade should be nationalized, and, if not, then what should be its specific role in a more liberalized trade policy. As of May 1990, the joint opposition of the bazaaris (that is the big merchants) and the conservatives in the government has prevented any major reforms in private ownership laws and international trade policy. Although there are some indications from the postwar push toward legitimizing limited accumulation of wealth and establishment of a largely private international trade with significant state control, the issues are by no means near a resolution.

Finally, the state also must make quick decisions about such important and pending issues as land and tax reforms, income distribution, women's rights, labor law, political democracy including freedom for political parties and the press, and reorganization of the country's provincial administration. These and other problems of social security remain among the most formidable problems facing the Islamic Republic. Some of these reform issues have been taken up on several occasions since the Revolution and progress has been made in such areas as limited land redistribution, institution of a less regressive tax system, and provision of subsidies for basic needs.[65] In the postwar period, and after a massive execution of political prisoners, the state has taken initial steps toward allowing freedom of activities for political parties within certain constraints.[66] The harsh treatment of "bad-veiled" (*bad hejab*) women has been relaxed as have restraints in a number of other sociocultural areas such as music and television shows. However, more needs to be done before the most pressing demand of the general public for social security (*amniyat-e ejtemaʿi*) is granted to their satisfaction.[67] It is clear that people who do not feel secure cannot contribute to development of their community. In other words, the postwar reconstruction must begin with the resolution of the social security problem of the nation before it can become successful in rebuilding the economy. The fact that these issues are being debated in the postwar period within the state is by itself the most encouraging development. However, it may take time for any noticeable progress and nothing significant may be expected before the Rafsanjani government (in place since July 1989) is firmly in control of the state policies and apparatuses.

The Iranian Obsolete Political Culture

Finally, complicating the obstacles to the postwar reconstruction is what I have termed the Iranian *obsolete political culture*.[68] It is characterized by ideological dogmatism, political extremism, chauvinistic heroism, vulnerability to personality cults, subservience to and fear of authority, cynicism, distrust, disunity, and individualism.

This political culture also demonstrates profound mania for obsolete ideas and exaggerations, encourages self-righteousness, despises self-criticism and critical thinking, advocates political revenge as an acceptable social norm, depends on political spoils and corruption, and knows no limit in leveling accusations against nonconformers. A comrade yesterday becomes a traitor today as a traitor could become a comrade tomorrow! Accusation by association is another characteristic of this political culture. Thus, even being seen with the political opposition could make you a traitor in the eyes of the other side! It is also a culture based on a "divide and rule" concept of politics; it works on the assumption that every political individual is dishonest unless otherwise proven to be true. Further, Iranian politics is assumed to be a puppet show in which the real players, always behind the scenes and invisible, are imperialist plotters, certain religious minorities, or a few sold-out politicians. The paranoia associated with this conspiratorial view of politics is largely cross-class and cross-ideological. It is, however, widespread among Iranian political elites and intelligentsia who continue to use it as a weapon against political enemies or for manipulation of the followers.

The political society, generally speaking, is considered divided into three categories: (1) militants (*nezamikar, mokhalef*), (2) compromisers (*siasikar, sazeshkar*), and (3) the herd (*bitaraf, khonsa*). As this last category is not considered important, friends and enemies are confined to the first two categories. Thus, anyone who is not on your side automatically becomes your enemy and vice versa! Worse yet, in judging political activists a double standard is used; for example, a person of similar traits and beliefs becomes revolutionary when a friend, a reactionary when on the opposite side. In the same vain, conservatives see radicals as destructive and radicals do not want to cooperate with even reformists. This political culture does not allow individuals to decide about their locations in the political spectrum of the society. Rather, it encourages terror tactics to force individuals to change political affiliation. The Iranian obsolete political culture is also distinguished by, among other properties, the lack of a political balance, intolerance for the opposite view, obsession with the use of force, and rejection of political flexibility and compromise. In short, it is a political culture based on "guerrilla tactics" and political puritanism.

Yet, the most destructive property of the obsolete Iranian political culture is its preoccupation—rather obsession—with the concept of "overthrowing" the political rival as an aim in itself rather than a means to a better alternative. The opposition is always there to overthrow those in power. What happens next is irrelevant to such a primitive strategy, which is indeed based on no constructive alternative to begin with. The political opposition cannot see that, aside from the politics of overthrowing and conformity, there is a range of other alternatives. Working within the system is also considered a treacherous act at best. The Iranian obsolete political culture has no respect for political process; rather it is obsessed with results. Process is a burden you undertake for success or victory rather than for its educational value. The longer such a process, the higher is the price of its burden. Defeat is a sign of being wrong, victory proves you are right. The political culture also has no respect for the long term and thus for evolution in politics. Things become relevant only if they apply to the short term and produce immediate political gains. The Iranian political culture also takes appearance for essence and resists learning from other nations.

Clearly, some such attributes are also observable among peoples of other nations, and not all Iranians harbor such a mentality. Indeed, the obsolete political culture is carried largely by the political leaders and political groups, most of whom happen to be among the country's intelligentsia. In fact, the personality cult is largely cultivated from the above, mostly by the charismatic or authoritarian leaders themselves, then imposed on the masses by means of effective propaganda by the intelligentsia and the close associates of the leader. I also wish to point out that this political culture is in sharp contrast with the nation's rich *socioliterary* traditions and not representative of the national identity. Indeed, Iranians have been praised by "foreigners" for being compassionate, benevolent and gracious, brave and rebellious, selfless and magnanimous, and creative, cooperative and dependable.[69] Their contribution to literature, art, and civilization has also been the most significant and recognized. The fact, nevertheless, remains that the Iranian nation today suffers heavily from a centuries-old and deleterious *political* culture, and denying its existence for the sake of preserving national pride will only exacerbate its destructive impact.

The roots of this obsolete political culture must be sought in a variety of historical and structural causes. The Iranian political culture today is only slightly different from the political culture that dominated say during the Qajar or even the Safavid period. This is so because the political leaders in control of the state power, the kings in particular, violently suppressed any meaningful attempts to develop a new political culture. The kings did not even trust their own households, and the Iranian history is full of stories about kings killing or blinding their sons, brothers, or other probable rivals. In addition to living under such cynical and cruel kings, Iranians have also been subjected to frequent civil wars and invasions by nomadic tribes. Imperial domination has been instrumental in reproducing this political culture, particularly the paranoia associated with the conspiratorial view of politics in Iran. Religious institutions have been influential as well in perpetuating the Iranian obsolete political culture, as most of them did not allow the emergence or development of significant dissident views; they remain largely inimical to and skeptical of secular movements in the country. Class domination resulting in mass political alienation has been another important factor in perpetuating this political culture. The twentieth century influences have included Stalinism, fascism, and liberalism. Although this last has never been given a real chance, the others have helped perpetuate the existing political culture.

The deleterious consequences of the obsolete political culture are many. This political culture has prevented most Iranians from developing a sense of *national interest,* which is different from nationalism and national pride. Rather, it has constantly promoted narrow individualistic, class, or group interests. It is, therefore, no surprise that Iranians, generally speaking, lack *a* well-defined national agenda for the future, one based on the consensus of the majority. Another major consequence of the obsolete political culture is what I like to call the *leadership syndrome.* Political leaders on all sides, for example, continue to remain aloof of the ongoing global political-economic restructuring and its impact on the diminishing utility of offensive force and repression.[70] Incarcerated by their outdated values and views, these leaders are also unwilling to acknowledge the increasing utility of negotiation as a medium for settling differences. Rejection of force and acceptance of negotiation would imply political flexibility and compromise, which are considered dirty words in the context of the obsolete political culture of Iran. Democracy and national unity are also misunderstood and are made impossible propositions in the country: whereas many Iranians are crying for such values, only a few are actually ready to tolerate and respect their political opponents and join them in participation and shared responsibility.

"Identity crisis" is another major consequence of this political culture. This is a multidimensional issue encompassing sociopolitical, economic, cultural, and ideological problems. In particular, it is symbolized by national discord, destructive politics, and the lack of what I have termed in Chapter 2, *amniyat-e ejtemaʿi* (social security). Other consequences of the obsolete political culture are no less destructive, and the nation cannot afford to remain indifferent to this antiquated culture. It must be changed; however, this requires a candid encounter with the past and a new political thinking, that is, an *Iranian perestroika* aimed at structural changes in the nation's political behavior. And this must begin at the level of individual and family, the real basis upon which such behaviors are cultivated.

The new political culture must emphasize, among other things, national interest, reconciliation and unity, democracy and social justice, and economic reconstruction under the given domestic and international conditions. This may be a gigantic task but by no means an impossible one. Developing an optimistic view of the future is the most important first step. This may have already begun. I know many young Iranian intellectuals who are looking into the future with great enthusiasm and are determined to reject the obsolete political culture in favor of a more dynamic and humane one. The new political culture must also develop into an ideal before it can be realized. This may not be a project too far into the future given the many positive political changes that have already taken place. These include the balance of power that has developed between the various factions in the state, the pressure that continues to come from the grass-roots organizations, and the increased political awareness of the postrevolutionary population, villagers and urbanites alike. Some changes have also occurred in many centuries-old aspects or institutions of the Iranian political system, including a reduced fear of authority and a change of power relationship between the ruled and the ruler. A positive trend of political deideologization is also discernible.

But, just as with any passing paradigms, the Iranian obsolete political culture will continue to have its own guards among all political groups and in the short term. However, although the loyalists will not give up easily, the critics and dissidents will continue to grow in numbers and strength. There is no real alternative to accepting the fact that the key to success in the changing world of ours is to generate new and more vibrant thoughts and accept the right of others to live in peace and prosperity. Iranians also have a rich socioliterary culture that should be utilized in the restructuring of the obsolete political culture. Unfortunately, the socioliterary culture remains isolated from the political culture. The first step is then to break this wall. Iranians may also learn from the recent experiences of the political reformers in South Korea, Brazil, Chile, the Philippines, and Nicaragua, to name only a few nations that have been trying to create a new political culture and practice democracy after years of repressive control by military regimes and dictators. Recent changes in Eastern Europe and the Soviet Union should provide equally valuable lessons for Iranians to consider and adopt to their own specific situation. Perhaps time has come for Iranian studies to go out of its present narrow-mindedness and nationalistic shell to reach out for new thinking and comparative understandings. Research and analysis toward this end should *not* be based on any apriori assumptions; rather they should aim at disecting the reality as it really is. We need to avoid being one-sidedly normative; instead, we should develop a more positivistic approach, one that emphasizes responsibility in learning and action, and encourages a critical reevaluation of our beliefs, assumptions, and historical "facts."

THE PEACE PROCESS AND RECONSTRUCTION

We have shown that the damage done by the war is truly enormous and that reconstruction faces monumental obstacles of domestic and international origin. Clearly, there also are many options, potentials, and facilitating forces. On the balance, however, the forces of constraint, I believe, are too robust to be coped with by any single political group, within the state or outside it. In other words, the postwar reconstruction is a task no single force in Iran can undertake alone with any noticeable success in the foreseeable future. This is particularly true if the reconstruction is to move beyond the narrow confines of economics to include other spheres of the society. What is needed is a true national union in which a solid majority of Iranians would participate. The primary purpose should be creation of domestic peace, democracy, social security and public participation—all of which are among critical preconditions for a successful reconstruction. These are obviously major political issues and simply may not be achieved in the short run. The political cleavage between the Islamic Republic and its opposition is simply too wide, as are the divisions among various political factions within each camps. Perhaps significant compromises must be made by all sides or else the costs to the nation could be truly relapsing and regrettable.

A lasting reconstruction also needs a lasting peace that faces great difficulty mostly because of Iraq's unacceptable territorial claims, particularly total sovereignty over the Shatt-Al-Arab waterway.[71] A situation of no-peace no-war will not only slow the reconstruction, it will also lead to inefficient use of the scarce resources, which will be detrimental to the Islamic Republic's principal goal of immediate and rapid economic growth. In particular, it will force the government to continue pouring a significant portion of its scarce foreign exchange and skilled labor force into the defense sector. Such a policy has become even more defensible in the wake of increased Iraqi military purchases following the cease-fire.[72] The ensuing arms race will in turn endanger the fragile cease-fire in place. In a speech given while he was still speaker of the Parliament and the deputy commander-in-chief of the army, ʿAli Akbar Hashemi Rafsanjani indicated that the Islamic Republic would not tolerate the no-peace no-war situation for a long time.[73] Although the war may not be easily revived in the face of tremendous domestic and international constraints, such warnings must be taken as indicating uneasiness with the unsettled situation. In the postwar period, both countries have been rapidly building up their military machines and human forces particularly at the fronts, where the two armies were sometimes less than 20 meters apart.

Yet the world community, which at one point was devoting considerable energy and determination to end the war, has in recent months developed a growing apathy toward the conflict. The United Nations has been, for all practical purposes, left alone by the West, East, and nonaligned countries, many of whom are racing for a larger share in the countries' reconstruction projects. Even more alarming is the declining interest of such regional authorities as the Organization of Islamic Conference, the Arab League, and the Gulf Cooperation Council. The last two organizations have even encouraged the unresolved situation by supporting Iraq's territorial claims, a rather dangerous signal to a restless Sadam Hosain. Saudi Arabia's position has been particularly unproductive in the peace process. The Saudis seem to take the cease-fire for granted as they do not consider Iran to be capable of a renewed war. What they forget is that Iran has tremendous potential to build up a strong offensive system and that those in the leadership, who still believe in the use of force to punish Sadam Hosain, are not insignificant in number or political power. The world community must again change its focus from reconstruction to peace between the two nations, if only for the sake of world peace and their own interests in the reconstruction.

In the meantime, the Iranian government should continue to work in the direction of a comprehensive peace with Iraq. In Chapter 2, I outlined the remaining options for Iran now that the peace process is gaining a new momentum. On 4 June, 1990, the two foreign ministers held their first "direct talks" in the presence of the UN Secretary General and within the framework of the Resolution 598. The talks are hoped to result in a summit meeting between the two presidents. Iran and Iraq also cooperated during the OPEC meeting on 27 July to raise oil prices and stop Kuwait and the United Arab Emirates from producing beyond their OPEC quotas. Iran also accepted Iraq's assistance for the tragic earthquake that devasted northern Iran on 21 June. These opportunities must be further harnessed in the direction of a comprehensive peace.

Conclusions: Empirical and Theoretical

Using a modified world-system perspective, this book has offered an analysis of economic transformations under the Islamic Republic, including trends, problems, and politics at macro, sectoral, and territorial levels. It has shown a significant gap between the original vision of the new Republic and its actual performance. The gap is attributed to a set of constraining factors originating from domestic and international sources. The book also offers a framework for postwar reconstruction along with obstacles that continue to cripple the Iranian reconstruction efforts. In what follows, I shall first sum up the empirical findings of the book and then offer a few generalizations about middle-class revolutions in the Third World including Iran.

EMPIRICAL FINDINGS

The economic performance of the Islamic Republic, judged in quantitative terms, is characterized by wide fluctuations, tenacious problems, and largely negative trends in production, sectoral shifts, investment, consumption, government budget, international trade, prices, employment, per capita income, income distribution, and regional development. The expected radical, social transformations in the areas of development, sovereignty, and justice, promised at the outset of the Revolution, have not been achieved either. The poor performance becomes particularly pronounced when comparisons are made with the immediate prerevolutionary years. Although the economy experienced certain improvements in the immediate posttrevolutionary period, only in 1982 and 1983 did the production grow at an acceptable rate, leading to reversal in most economic trends. The economic recession that began in 1984 continues to worsen even though the war has ended. The June 1990 earthquake will further strain the economy's performance in the medium-term.

The latest official estimates give the following figures for the country's socioeconomic conditions.[1] Population, estimated at 56 million in 1989, continues to grow at the excessively high rate of 3.9 percent despite government efforts (since 1987) to encourage family planning and birth control in spite of Islamic teaching (the Islamic government is importing condoms and contraceptives). Gross domestic production in real terms for 1988 is estimated at about 2,961 billion rials (at constant 1974 prices), that is, almost as much as it was sixteen years ago, and real gross per capita income in 1989 was about 50,000 rials, that is, almost equal to what it was some twenty-one years ago (and almost half of what it was ten years ago). More than a year after the cease-fire (in late 1989), most industries (except for the oil sector) were still working at about 20 to 30 percent of their theoretical capacity, and there is a ten-year backlog of investment in most industries, private and public alike. In 1989, only 15 percent of GDP was being allocated to fixed capital formation, down from 27.6 percent in 1978.

Incidents of absolute poverty has increased among as many as 65 to 70 percent of the population; they would have faced difficulty in sustaining their subsistence were it not for the state's food subsidies, the extended family structure, and the traditional system of social support in the country. As indicated by a 1986 census of consumption, at least 17 million Iranians, that is, 34 percent of the population, will be considered poor even if the poverty line is drawn on the basis of the rationed foods that will cost only 140 rials per day. At the same time, well over 1,000 families have become billionaires (in Iranian tuman) since the Revolution. There were only 100 families of that type in prerevolutionary Iran. Another 70,000 families earn over 3 million rials a month in a country where real per capita gross earning is about 50,000 rials. A significant, though undetermined, number of Iranians are undernourished. Indeed, the Iranians' consumption expenditures show a significant drop, down from about 50,000 rials in 1979 to about 30,000 rials in 1989 (at constant 1974 prices). Abject poverty has led to disproportionate increases in personal debt, sale of household items and other family property including real estate in recent years, and noticeable increases in petty theft or dependency on other illegitimate sources of earnings including drug dealings.

The state per capita budget has dropped by 30 percent in real terms over the 1979–89 period, down from about 40,000 rials in 1979 to about 12,000 rials in 1989 (at constant 1974 prices). This reflects the decline in the state's welfare and development expenditures as well as in its revenues both because of a drop in oil earnings and tax revenues. For example, collected taxes in 1988 have amounted to about 1,000 billion rials (in current prices), that is, only 4.4 percent of the year's estimated GDP of some 23,000 billion rials (in current prices). Indirect taxes make up for the largest part of the collected taxes and this hurts mostly the poor. Direct taxes are collected mostly from production units, which pay easy-to-collect taxes, whereas the wealthy and the most profitable services and trade activities are highly undertaxed. Growing budget deficits have also been a major source of concern for the Islamic state. In 1988, for example, budget deficits amounted to 2,146 billion rials, roughly equal to 51 percent of the total budget. A major consequence has been hyperinflation.

Inflation was running at about 20 to 60 percent rate at the end of 1989 for most necessary consumer items (most under price control) with black market rates for some commodities approaching 500 to 2,000 percent. In the meantime, merchants have intensified hoarding and profiteering and are reluctant to either lower prices or put their windfall capital into productive use. The Iranian rial has lost much of its value in the postrevolutionary period and this has led to increased capital flight. The free (rather black) market exchange rate between the U.S. dollar and rial has been some fifteen times higher than the official rate in the fall of 1989. Problems with foreign exchange led the state to design a multiple-tier system that includes, in addition to the official and free market rates, a "competitive rate" (arz-e reghabati), a "preferred rate" (arz-e tarjihi), and a "service rate" (arz-e khadamati). The official rate of 72 rials per dollar assists maintaining prices of basic food items to an affordable level. It is also used to encourage production of "sensitive and necessary" rationed commodities and industrial machinery. The preferred rate (the rate is case specific, ranging from 400 to 700 rials per dollar) is used to help in increasing production of necessary goods and imports of industrial machinery. The service rate is given to certain travelers abroad, patients, and students at about 850 rials to one dollar. It was hoped that the competitive rate, which was lowered to about 800 rials per dollar at the end of 1989, on the other hand, would bring down the free market rate, and reduce the trade balance by discouraging imports (although it is given to a wide variety of importers!) Encouraging nonoil exports (because it cheapens Iranian exports) and eliminating the general budget deficit by transferring part of the wandering private liquidity (estimated at 1.3 trillion rials) to the state sector was also anticipated. Reduced private liquidity and general budget deficit could, in turn, help reduce inflation. However, the wealthy Iranians took advantage of cheaper dollars and transferred significant amounts of wealth outside the country. Inthe meantime, this policy led to a reduction in the state's reserves by at least $3 billion. The government suspended the competitive rate in March 1990, calling it a failure. Nonetheless, the policies' short-term effect on the free market rate was substantial. In less than a few weeks, the rate had dropped to below a 1,000 rials from about 1,400. The real problem with the policy was that it required more foreign exchange than the government could afford to place on the market.

During the first ten years of the Revolution, some 3.1 million people were added to the country's work force (310,000 a year on the average), but only 1.9 million jobs were created over the same period (190,000 a year on the average). Therefore, the net addition to the unemployed population amounted to 1.2 million (120,000 a year on the average). Indeed, open unemployment rate for civilian population was estimated at about 15 percent in 1989 (i.e., some 2 million people). But if military personnel, population with disguised unemployment (women in particular), and underemployed people (e.g., part-time workers and street vendors) were also added, the unemployment figure would go up to as many as 6 million or some 41 percent of the work force (active population in 1989 was estimated at 14.5 million). In other words, only 8.5 million Iranians, out of a population of 56 million, were fully employed, which means every working Iranian was supporting seven people (six not working).

Equally disturbing were statistics on the social conditions of the population. Housing was taking away some two-thirds of the wage earners' income in 1989, and yet some 20 million Iranians with a household size of about four to five members were estimated to live in no more that two rooms. Schools were running at two, in some places, three or four shifts in 1989 to cope with the influx of pupils. More than 45 percent of Iran's 56 million population in 1989 were below fifteen years of age. The health care system was equally underdeveloped. Acute shortages existed for physicians, dentists, physical therapists, nurses, and hospital beds among other health related resources. For example, in 1988, for every 3,200 Iranians there was only 1 physician, and the ratio of dentists was 1 for every 7,200 people. Recreational services was also in short supply, limiting personal activities needed for the development of the population's human capacities. Addiction to opium and heroin, particularly among the youth and unemployed has reached national crisis proportions. Despite stiff policies, the government has failed to stop drug trafficking, which has become among the most lucrative businesses in the country. Corruption is another national problem crippling Iran today by becoming widespread among individuals and families, within businesses and the government, and among members of the ruling groups and of various revolutionary and so-called charitable foundations.

The postwar reconstruction remains in its initial steps although the war ended some time ago. A Reconstruction Plan, after several revisions, has been approved by the Parliament in the beginning of 1990. The plan is formulated along a mixed approach, which emphasizes rapid economic growth, private sector, foreign borrowing, and economic participation. It also advocates an economy more open to international trade, and seeks to privatize most nationalized industries of a less strategic nature. In short, the market mechanism is to be expanded at the expense of the public management. Although the plan gives a clear mandate to the government of President Rafsanjani for action, its execution faces stiff opposition from the radicals. Although they may not be able to stop the plan's implementation, they can create problems to slow down its process. Other obstacles to the implementation of the plan includes a significant foreign exchange shortage, various infrastructural and institutional bottlenecks, managerial inadequacies, a shortage of skilled workers, and the country's obsolete political culture. The no-peace no-war stalemate will not help the situation either. The plan, for example, calls for continued expansion of the defense sector and allocates about one-third of the foreign exchange budget for the purpose. Uncertainty with the peace process has also slowed the reconstruction of the war-damaged areas near the borders with Iraq.

However, although very poor, the Islamic Republic's economic performance would not be considered the worst when compared to the declining economies of most Third World countries in the 1980s. It is also remarkable that an economy so damaged by the war could manage to remain solvent and sustain itself without significant outside assistance and major external long-term debt. In 1989, for example, the government's new long-term foreign debt was reported at $500 million with an additional short-term debt of some $10–12 billion (mostly imports credit).[2] The recognition for this partly goes to the Iranian people, who (except for a rich minority) have patiently tolerated extreme economic hardship in the post-revolutionary period, particularly since 1986. Moreover, the numbers mask significant qualitative changes in the structure of the economy, growth of domestic productive capacity in small-scale and defense-related industries, transformations in rural areas, and changes in the state's objectives, priorities, and policies. Extensive nationalization; creation of a leading state sector in a mixed economy; reorganization of the banking system and concentration on agriculture, rural development, and deprived regions; and higher education particularly in areas of health services and technical research may be also mentioned. Improvements in the conditions of many rural areas are particularly noticeable. A list of such changes includes construction of extensive networks of rural roads, increased urban functions in rural areas, improved literacy rate and health services, and significant electrification and provision of piped water. Other changes include a slight reduction of general budget's dependency on oil as a result of a gradual shift toward more reliance on taxes, increased barter trades, and protection of certain domestic industries from international competition. Additionally, the mix of ideological and pragmatic debates, along with attempts to cope with a dependent war economy, have led to accumulation of considerable knowledge about development needs, obstacles, and available resources for the postwar reconstruction. The country also seems to have become somewhat aware and confident of its capability for a more autonomous development path. Although the positive impact of these changes may not be considerable in the short run, their long-term benefits could be significant if such trends continue and are channeled in the right direction.

Significant opportunities or enabling forces had been generated by or because of the Revolution including enormous potential, energy, enthusiasm, creative ideas, national unity, and international support. However, before such forces could be mobilized for social change, equally powerful domestic and international constraints began to develop. Added to the burden of the Shah's economic legacy (including uneven and dependent development of the consumption-oriented economy) were the Revolution-fueled raised expectations and the unrealistic promises of the new regime. Increasing pressure from imperial powers and domestic political economy were even more damaging. Struggles over state power, a new foreign policy, the land question, regional autonomy, housing for the poor, and the workers' councils further intensified the interlocking nature of the economy, politics, and ideology in the postrevolutionary society. However, the most damaging to the economy was the war with Iraq, dependency on oil and international markets, and Western trade sanction. Equally damaging to the economy was the infighting within the middle-class ruling groups whose social incoherence and lack of a middle-class ideology proper became a source of systemic indirection and conflicting policy pronouncement.

The government's failure to get the legislative branch to pass certain major reform packages and laws, formulate a generally acceptable development strategy, and plan the economy led to further economic chaos and decline. In the meantime, the powerful profiteering bazaaris and their allies in the various state apparatuses effectively killed most government economic policies, particularly those relating to investment, trade, and inflation. The postrevolutionary economy also suffered from significant underutilization of the existing capacities largely as a result of enormous material, infrastructural, personnel, managerial, organizational, and institutional bottlenecks. Additional negative impact came from inexperienced and nonspecialized managers, who were put in charge of economic units for strictly ideological considerations. Finally, the extreme deficiency of the state apparatuses, channels through which most economic activities and decisions must pass, prevented the state from implementing any major policy initiatives. In particular, because of conjunctural difficulties, lack of long-term predictions, the war, poverty of experience, and reflective decisions, among other factors, the state administration suffered from an extended bureaucracy and lacked a proper centralization of decision making and implementation tasks. All these have in turn led to contradictory policies and practices, a rise in the use of personal influence, widespread nepotism, corruption, and the dissatisfaction of the people.[3]

The state's eccentric economic policies have largely reflected economic and extraeconomic forces and the need for speedy adaptation to mostly nonconventional and unpredictable movements in the domestic and international spheres. Such policies, although cloaked in the ideological and long-term development objectives of the Constitution, have been essentially pragmatic and focused on managing immediate problems of the economy. Earlier in the postrevolutionary period, attempts focused on realizing the constitutional goals of economic sovereignty, social justice, and a mixed economy largely by means of planning. A national plan was devised in 1982 but subsequently rejected by the Parliament. The plan was revised in 1983 according to the theory of stages of growth, starting with the elimination of obstacles, maximum utilization of the existing capacities, and institution building. Only then, it was argued, could regular development planning be staged. Subsequently, however, the revised plan was shelved indefinitely in favor of annual budgeting. Various factions could not agree on a definite development strategy, and the government was reluctant to commit itself to a planned economy under the conditions of war and an uncertain oil market.

In the meantime, the government abandoned the earlier policy of self-reliance in favor of a policy of diversifying the sources of dependency, barter trade, and the maximum use of existing capacities.

As damage due to the war continued to grow, the government further lapsed into a pragmatic (i.e., nonideological) quick-fix (i.e., nondevelopmental) approach to economic management. Introduction of the 1986 austerity plan, following the sharp drop in oil prices, signaled another major turning point in policy reversals in the Islamic Republic. The plan was predicated upon the belief that maintaining the economic status quo was the most that the government could hope for. Even that became impossible following the war of cities in 1988, when the Survival Policy was launched. The new policy continued for a while after the cease-fire and was subsequently replaced by a strategy of stages of growth, similar to that incorporated in the 1983 revised First Plan. This new strategy, formulated within a reconstruction plan, resulted from yet another revision of the original First Plan after the cease-fire. However, the new plan was revised again after Prime Minister Musavi left office. President Hashemi Rafsanjani insisted that his technocratic cabinet wanted a more pragmatic and flexible plan for the postwar reconstruction.

As I have argued elsewhere, the middle-class leadership had a lot of ideas but no ideology of its own.[4] This meant that the postrevolutionary leadership coming from this class had inherited problems in formulating or implementing a coherent development model or plan. In particular, the middle-class leadership was handicapped by the tension between the cross-class and universal ideology (i.e., Islam) that it brought to the government and the narrow interests (or vision) of the class it represented. In the meantime, the class's utopia or vision of the future society (as indicated in the Constitution and many policy and planning documents) could not be realized because of enormous domestic and international constraints and as such vision stood in sharp contrast with what the leadership could actually achieve in the real world of the 1980s.[5] It took sometime, however, before the class or its leaders realized this fact. Consequently, after an initial period of ideological struggle and political radicalism, the leaders submitted to the tension between the middle-class vision, its cross-class ideology, and the mandates of the real world. An eclectic, pragmatic approach then emerged that defined the religion in modern terms (*feqh-e puya*) and that juxtaposed various pieces from different strategies to arrive at a workable mixed model. The emergent model was initially reformist but, as pragmatism dominated the mentality of the agencies making policy decisions, ideology lost its potency and the revolution began slipping toward moderation and a more conventional approach in the form of accepting otherwise unacceptable solutions or conditions.

Finally, Iran remains a country divided at the threshold of the postwar reconstruction and faces a national crisis that could have far-reaching implications for its future. The crisis has economic, political, social, cultural, and international dimensions and could lead to a significant decline in the nation's standing within the global community. Various aspects of the socioeconomic and political dimensions are explained throughout this book. The international dimension refers largely to the Islamic Republic's fractured image particularly in the West. The cultural dimension of the Iranian national crisis also needs emphasis. Most significant is the crisis of identity arising from the incomplete cultural transformation under the previous regimes. Specifically, the cultural dualism reflected the failure of the Pahlavi dynasty (1926–79) to create a synthesis between modernity and tradition. As a consequence, the "modernized" members of the national community did not identify with the Islamic ideology, the leadership of the Revolution, or the changes that were taking place. This created a crisis of legitimacy for the traditionalist state, which was amplified by the rejection of the government's decisions and policies by a growing segment of the modernized populace. The result was the crisis of participation by the technocrats and secular intellectuals in societal affairs, a problem that was exacerbated by a long tradition of political centralism and top-down management. However, the roots of the country's badly fractured politics must be sought in its obsolete political culture.

In sum, while the Islamic Republic faces a multiple of domestic and international problems, attempts by the new leadership to adopt reasonable policies continue to be undermined by formidable constraining factors. Significantly, nine years after the hostage drama and more than one and a half years after the cease-fire with Iraq, relationships with the West, and the United States in particular, remain unfriendly; a comprehensive peace with Iraq is nowhere in sight; a plan for economic recovery and reconstruction is yet to be put into practice; and the critically needed national reconciliation is not on anyone's agenda. Clearly, these issues are interrelated as, for example, economic recovery and postwar reconstruction are conditioned by the Republic's reintegration into the new world system, which is possible only if the state would project a better image of itself. But this is in turn conditioned by a successful national reconciliation, a seemingly unattainable objective at this time. Thus, if I am correct about the interrelatedness of the aforementioned problems, then nothing short of a new approach, an Iranian *perestroika* if you will, could improve the status quo in the foreseeable future.

THEORETICAL CONCLUSIONS

Some of the important theoretical implications of this book may be summed up in terms of the following propositions. I contend that lessons from a significant number of other Third World postrevolutionary societies support these propositions. They include Egypt, Algeria, Tanzania, Iraq, Syria, Peru, Burma, Ethiopia, Afghanistan, Mozambique, Angola, Nicaragua, and Somalia to name only a few.[6]

Causes of These Revolutions

The most important lesson to draw on the *causes* of these revolutions is that they do not result from any particular single factor; rather they are caused by complex external and internal factors, covering a multiplicity of social, economic, political, ideological, and cultural dimensions. Aside from this complexity, the causes of these revolutions are varied and unique to each nation. A limited generalization is plausible, however. In particular, these revolutions are made against external domination and dissatisfaction with the internal status quo as reflected by such recurring demands as national independence, territorial integration, political democracy, social justice, economic development, and cultural reconstruction.

How These Revolutions Are Made

How these revolutions are *made* also seems to vary across nations and over time. Nevertheless, the following three modes are identifiable: armed uprising, military coups, and mass demonstrations. They have been used in isolation as the main revolutionary tactics and also in combination for more effective results. What mode is chosen depends largely on the type of the revolutionary leadership, causes of the revolution, and specific revolutionary demands. For example, army officers have preferred coups, while young radicals have used armed uprisings and more established or moderate leaders have preferred collective tactics as in the case of Iran.

Nature of These Revolutions

On the *nature* of these revolutions, three issues seem relevant: *who makes* these revolutions, *who leads* these revolutions, and *what ideology* is adopted. The makers of these revolutions are, generally speaking, urban residents who receive only limited assistance from the rural settlers. All social classes, with the exception of a tiny minority of very rich, participate in the movement. The middle class, however, plays the most important, active, and effective role. This class also assumes the leadership through its intelligentsia, who happen to be the most politically oriented in the Third World. The *middle-class* nature of these revolutions is thus their most defining character. Because the middle-class leadership has no ideology of its own and due to the cross-class composition of these revolutions, the postrevolutionary state assumes a variety of cross-class ideologies. Nationalism, religion, and populism (e.g., African and Arab socialism) are among such ideologies. Experience indicates that the more complex the class character of a revolution, the higher is the change for the middle-class leadership to adopt a cross-class ideology. The state ideology, in turn, becomes a dominant factor in the postrevolutionary social change.

Transforming Potential

On the *transforming potential of the middle-class revolutions,* broadly speaking, there are three views of revolutions as vehicles of social change. The *fatalist* position maintains that revolutions do not go beyond their political state and are only means for redistributing power to another ruling group. In sharp contrast, the *volunterist* position maintains that revolutions are the most effective means for social transformations. The *moderate* view, however, takes a middle position: revolutions are relevant to social change but their impact is variable and thus case specific and determined largely by a complex of economic and extraeconomic forces. These include the social basis of the leadership and its ideology and a set of opportunity and constraining factors that operate at both domestic and international levels. The nature and mix of the determinants also change over time and vis-à-vis different social phenomena. Constraining factors are particularly strong in the case of the middle-class revolutions in the Third World, significantly limiting their ability to transform the postrevolutionary society. Moreover, although some of these determinants exist in all postrevolutionary societies, others are specific to given contexts or conditions. Equally variable is the impact of these determinants on different revolutions and different aspects or sectors of a given postrevolutionary society.[7]

Utopia and Actual

The *moderate* view explains that a big gap exists between the *utopia,* which revolutions generate, and their *actual* achievements. In particular, revolutionary governments confront similar problems to those experienced by most governments, and they are forced to make policy choices and compromises that result in less than perfect achievements of the original goals. Initially, postrevolutionary governments plan for radical social changes, but over the course of time such plans are gradually withdrawn in favor of more realistic projects. In the meantime, the revolutionary leadership gradually moves away from strictly ideological considerations toward pragmatism and moderation. The speed at which this metamorphosis occurs depends largely on the nature of the revolution and on the power of the opportunity and constraining factors. The balance of power between these same factors also determines the degree of the gap that develops between the vision and the actual.

Opportunity or Enabling Factors

Opportunity or *enabling factors* act in the direction of facilitating social change in the postrevolutionary societies. Revolutions initially generate massive energy and enthusiasm for change, innovative thoughts and actions, voluntary and cooperative spirit, and a powerful sense of constructive optimism about the future. They also sharpen the sense of responsibility and accountability for national resources, both actual and potential. Further, revolutions produce a variety of popular and grass-roots organizations dedicated to hard work and revolutionary change. They also receive support from outside their borders, from progressive and friendly forces throughout the world. The ongoing global restructuring of the world political economy should be considered a new factor of opportunity for postrevolutionary societies. This is particularly true in the case of the middle-class revolutions in the Third World, which received only moderate and noncommittal support from the presently less coherent and inactive socialist camp. Note that perceived opportunities are as powerful as real opportunities for social change.

Constraining Factors

Before revolutions can utilize the opportunity forces, they must face *constraining forces* of varying origins and strength, affecting the revolution in the opposite direction. Although such forces are largely time and place specific, a few generalizations may be warranted:

1. The inherited socioeconomic system is usually crisis-ridden (in both efficiency and equity terms) and presents tremendous difficulty for the transformation of the old system. The postrevolutionary crisis is also due to the fact that the old is rejected before the new can be born. In this interregnum, a wide variety of chaotic approaches are experienced.

2. Struggles over state power in the immediate postrevolutionary period prevent the state from achieving political stability, thus delaying economic growth and social change. Such struggles take place within the middle-class leadership and between them, and the upper- and lower-class political representatives. The political discord in the postrevolutionary period is the prime cause of national crisis in these societies.

3. While the general public develops unrealistic expectations, young revolutionaries raise utopian demands and expect the state to meet them at an impossible speed. The inevitable result is destructive contests between the leadership and the utopian revolutionaries.

4. Struggles of the core imperial powers and the old domestic dominant groups` (usually in coordination) against the revolution are extremely damaging to the already damaged postrevolutionary political economy. Postrevolutionary societies continue to depend on these forces for most of their finances (including foreign exchange), industrial inputs, food items, and technology. Such struggles adopt a variety of overt and covert tactics, including wars, coups, and economic embargoes. They are designed to force the leadership into conformity and moderation—(for preserving the status quo at the domestic and international levels)—or else for overthrowing the revolution. The core nations' level of pressure and success depends on the geopolitical importance of the postrevolutionary society and its degree of integration into the capitalist world economy.

5. A close correlation seems to exist between war (civil or international) and revolution, and wars are, generally speaking, imposed on postrevolutionary societies. War against the revolution is used to paralyze the economy and thus to delegitimize the radical leadership in the hopes of forcing it into moderation or else preparing for the eventual overthrow.

6. Revolutions encounter tremendous bottlenecks including shortage of skilled human power and material resources; lack of appropriate infrastructures, institutions and organizations; and absence of a constructive political culture. On top of these, revolutions also generate their own bottlenecks in terms of parallel organizations, chaotic administrative roles and structures, and multiple power and decision-making centers.

Dislocation between Interest and Ideology

The *dislocation* between the leadership's narrow middle-class *interests* and its cross-class *ideology* presents another major constraint for the postrevolutionary transformation. In particular, it leads to factional conflicts within the leadership, a problem that is further exacerbated by the extreme internal heterogeneity of the middle class. The resulting systemic indirection is reflected in the leadership's inability to formulate a definite and coherent development strategy or planning tactic and in the state's eccentric policy pronouncements and practices that are implemented in response to daily pressures and immediate problems. Such policies are also reflective of the tension between the public sector and the free market operations and forces.

National Crisis

Most if not all postrevolutionary societies experience what I like to call a *national crisis* that is distinguished by the lack of a well-defined *national interest*, political division, economic decline, social dislocation, and cultural-ideological confusion. The crisis varies (in terms of type and extent) across nations, but its defining characteristics remain deeply political. Whereas many factors contribute to the emergence and perpetuation of the national crisis, its roots should be sought in cultural dualism and largely obsolete political cultures in most countries of the Third World. The crisis usually deepens over time as domestic and international constraints increase in number and strength. Given the multiplicity of the causal factors, a more complex system of remedial measures may be needed to uproot the crisis. However, the most significant steps in most cases involve developing a strong sense of national interest, scrapping the obsolete political culture, and generating a cultural dynamism amenable to national interest and reconciliation, democracy and social justice, and the rule of law in all aspects of societal affairs.

Prospects

The political and policy implications of my conclusions concerning the limits or consequences of Third World middle-class revolutions remain indeterminate to the candid reader. This book could be read as arguing that middle-class revolutions are doomed to fail and are thus a waste of time; or alternatively, these revolutions contribute little whereas they generate crises of various types and are thus essentially harmful. On the contrary. Although they face tremendous odds and are unable to realize their initial goals, these revolutions do initiate structural and historical changes in otherwise rigid societies. Moreover, these revolutions occur, and will continue to occur, regardless of their probable outcomes, because they demand national independence, democracy, social justice, and cultural revival, all of which are most legitimate and will continue to remain so for the foreseeable future. The motivation for revolution is also drawn from the tension that will continue to remain between socialism and capitalism (despite changes in Eastern Europe) and among various domestic interest groups. Additional aspirations are derived from progressive movements around the world and from such powerful ideological forces as nationalism, populism, and religion.

Although middle-class revolutions have had limited potential for social change within the existing world system, their transforming potential may increase as a result of the ongoing global restructuring of the world political economy. In particular, (1) the current convergence between socialism and capitalism means that the mixed approach, idealized by the middle-class leadership, will receive more acceptance at home and abroad; (2) mitigation of the East-West contradiction will also reduce the burden of wars on the Third World, including postrevolutionary societies. A positive result will be reduction in defense budget in favor of development and basic needs; (3) decreasing power of the two superpowers along with the emergence of a multipolar interdependent world system means that the postrevolutionary societies' choice for alternative sources of support will increase; (4) while the external constraints for social change may decrease, domestic constraints would have to become the main focus of policy makers; and (5) only leadership sufficiently attentive to causes of democracy, social justice, economic growth, and development of a new political culture may succeed in the emerging world community.

To achieve these requirements of a more democratic society, the thoughtful leadership should concentrate on national reconciliation as the absolute first precondition. Such leadership should be aware of the facts that dictatorship cannot be sustained for long, that uneven development is counterproductive, and that democracy and balanced development require democratization of all aspects of social life. Experience also indicates that nationalization of petty ownership and overly centralized planning are counterproductive and that all revolutions ignorant of these facts have paid dearly. The success-inspiring leadership should also take note of the fact that a well-controlled open-door policy in international exchange is hardly inimical to national independence if it is based on the best interest of the nation. Such a policy should be preferable to both free trade and autarky. Self-reliance does not mean outright rejection of outside help; rather, it means a policy that can be sustained if such outside assistance were to be terminated. Last, an ingenious leadership would recognize beyond any shadow of any doubt that development of a strong sense of *national interest* is the key to national integration and development. Realization of these preconditions notwithstanding, the middle-class revolutions may hope to generate only a modest social change in the Third World. To produce a more significant result, they must wait for a remote time when a new middle-class paradigm of social change emerges.

Notes

CHAPTER 1. INTRODUCTION: THE LIMITED TRANSFORMING POTENTIAL OF THE MIDDLE-CLASS REVOLUTION

1. On characteristics of the world system see Immanuel Waller-stein, *The Modern World-System* (New York: Academic Press, 1976), pp. 229–239; and Immanuel Wallerstein, "Patterns and Pro-spective of Capitalist World-Economy," in *Contemporary Marxism,* no. 9 (Fall 1984): 59–70.

2. For an interesting and formidable theoretical analysis of in-ternationalization of the oil industry see Cyrus Bina, *The Economics of the Oil Crisis* (New York: St. Martin's Press, 1985); and Cyrus Bina, "Internationalization of the Oil Industry: Simple Oil Shocks or Structural Crisis?" *Review* 11, no. 3 (Summer 1988): 329–370.

3. Hooshang Amirahmadi, "From Feudalism to Capitalist Manufacturing and the Origins of Dependency and Underdevelop-ment in Iran, 1796–1921" (Ph.D. diss., Cornell University, Ithaca, NY, 1982).

4. Hooshang Amirahmadi, "Middle-Class Revolutions in the Third World," in Hooshang Amirahmadi and Manoucher Parvin (eds.), *Post-Revolutionary Iran* (Boulder, CO.: Westview Press, 1988), pp. 225–244. On differing explanations given for the causes of the Iranian Revolution, see also Said Amir Arjomand, *The Turban for the Crown: The Islamic Revolution in Iran* (New York: Oxford University Press, 1988), pp. 189–210; Ervand Abrahamian, *Iran be-tween Two Revolutions* (Princeton, NJ: Princeton University Press, 1982), pp. 530–537; Dilip Hiro, *Iran under the Ayatollahs* (Lon-don: Routledge & Kegan Paul, 1985); Shaul Bakhash, *The Reign of the Ayatollahs: Iran and the Islamic Revolution* (New York: Basic Books, 1984); Nikki Keddie, *Roots of Revolution* (New Haven, CT: Yale University Press, 1981); Mohsen Milani, *The Making of Iran's Islamic Revolution: From Monarchy to Islamic Republic* (Boulder, CO.: Westview Press, 1988); Farhad Kazemi, *Poverty and Revolu-*

tion in Iran (New York: Pergamon Press, 1982); Hosain Razavi and Firouz Vakil, *The Political Environment of Economic Planning in Iran 1971–1983* (Boulder, CO: Westview Press, 1984); Eric Hooglund, *Land and Revolution in Iran, 1960–1980* (Austin: University of Texas Press, 1982); Robert Graham, *Iran: The Illusion of Power* (New York: St. Martin's Press, 1979); James Bill and W. M. Rogers (eds.), *Musaddiq, Iranian Nationalism and Oil* (Austin: University of Texas Press, 1988); Robert E. Looney, *Economic Origins of the Iranian Revolution* (New York: Pergamon Press, 1982); Jerrold D. Green, *Revolution in Iran: The Politics of Countermobilization* (New York: Praeger, 1982); and Gholam Afkhami, *The Iranian Revolution: Thanatos on a National Scale* (Washington, DC: Middle East Institute, 1985).

5. Arjomand, *The Turban for the Crown*, pp. 189–210; and Asaf Hussain, *Islamic Iran* (New York: St. Martin's Press, 1985).

6. Abrahamian, *Iran between Two Revolutions*, pp. 530–537. On the politics and world-view of the Iranian religious leaders, Ayatollah Khomeini in particular, see Farhang Rajaee, *Islamic Values and World View: Khomeini on Man, the State and International Politics* (Lanham, MD: University Press of America, 1983); Michael M. J. Fischer, *Iran: From Religious Dispute to Revolution* (Cambridge, MA: Harvard University Press, 1980); and Shahrough Akhavi, *Religion and Politics in Contemporary Iran: Clergy-State Relations in the Pahlavi Period* (Albany: State University of New York Press, 1980).

7. On economic development during the reign of Mohammad Reza Shah (1941–78), see Homa Katouzian, *Political Economy of Modern Iran, 1926–1979* (New York: New York University Press, 1981); M. M. H. Malek, *The Political Economy of Iran under the Shah* (London: Croom Helms, 1986); Jane W. Jacqz, (ed.), *Iran: Past, Present, and Future* (New York: Aspen Institute for Humanistic Studies, 1975); George Lenczowski, *Iran under the Pahlavis* (Stanford, CA: Hoover Institution Press, 1978); Graham, *Iran*; Fred Halliday, *Iran: Dictatorship and Development* (New York: Penguin Books, 1979): Bill and Rogers, *Musaddiq*; Bizhan Jazani, *Capitalism and Revolution in Iran* (London: Zed Press, 1980); Hooshang Amirahmadi, "Regional Planning in Iran: A Survey of Problems and Policies," *Journal of Developing Areas* 20, no. 4 (July 1986): 501–529; Hooshang Amirahmadi, "A Theory of Ethnic Collective Movements and Its Application to Iran," *Ethnic and Racial Studies* 10, no. 4 (October 1987): 363–391; Hooshang Amirahmadi and Farhad

Atash, "Dynamics of Provincial Development and Disparity in Iran, 1956–1984," *Third World Planning Review* 9, no. 2 (May 1987): 155–185; Hooshang Amirahmadi and Ali Kiafar, "Tehran; Growth and Contradictions," *Journal of Planning Education and Research* 6, no. 3 (Spring 1987): 167–177; Kazemi, *Poverty and Revolution;* Ahmad Ashraf, "Peasants, Land and Revolution," *Ketab-e Agah* (Tehran: Agah Publishers, 1982); Razavi and Vakil, *Political Environment of Economic Planning;* Hooglund, *Land and Revolution;* Afsaneh Najmabadi, *Land Reform and Social Change in Iran* (Salt Lake City: University of Utah Press, 1987); Looney, *Economic Origins;* and Kamran Mofid, *Development Planning in Iran: From Monarchy to Islamic Republic* (Cambridgeshire, England: Menas Press, 1987).

8. Among nongovernmental studies concerned with the postrevolutionary economic conditions in Iran, the following are notable: Hooshang Amirahmadi and Manoucher Parvin (eds.). *Post-Revolutionary Iran* (Boulder, CO: Westview Press, 1988); Hooshang Amirahmadi, "Destruction and Reconstruction: A Strategy for the War Damaged Areas of Iran," *Disasters: The International Journal of Disaster Studies and Practice* 11, no. 2 (1987): 134–147; Hooshang Amirahmadi, "Economic Operations in Post-Revolutionary Iran: Major Impacts, Problems, and Policy Directions," paper presented at the twentieth annual meeting of the Middle East Studies Association of North America (MESA), Boston, November 20–23, 1986; Setareh Karimi, "Economic Policies and Structural Changes since the Revolution," in Nikki R. Keddie and Eric Hooglund (eds.), *The Iranian Revolution and the Islamic Republic* (Syracuse, NY: Syracuse University Press, 1986); Hooshang Amirahmadi, "The State and Territorial Social Justice in Iran," *International Journal of Urban and Regional Research* 13, no. 1 (March 1989): 92–120; Abbas Alnasrawi "Economic Consequences of the Iran-Iraq War," *Third World Quarterly* 8, no. 3 (July 1986): 869–894); Bakhash, *The Reign of the Ayatollahs;* Ebrahim Razzaqi, *Eqtesad-e Iran* [Iranian Economy] (Tehran: Nashr-e Nay, 1367); Vahe Petrossian, "Iran," *MEED, Special Report on Iran* (November 1984), pp. 1–44, and (March 1990), pp. i–xvv (centerfold pages); "Economic Warfare in the Gulf," *The Middle East* (September 1983): 12–17; Bahram Tehrani (Farboud), *Pazhuheshi Dar Eqtesad-e Iran (1354–1364)* [An Investigation into the Iranian Economy (1975–1985)], (Paris: Khavaran Publications, 1986); Mofid, *Development Planning in Iran;* Sayed Hassan Amin, *Commercial Law of Iran* (Tehran: Vahid Publications, 1986); Wolfgang Lautenschlager, "The Effects of

an Overvalued Exchange Rate on the Iranian Economy," *International Journal of Middle East Studies* 18 (1986): 31–52; Sohrab Behdad, "Foreign Exchange Gap, Structural Constraints, and the Political Economy of Exchange Rate Determination in Iran," *International Journal of Middle East Studies* 20 (1988): 1–21; Patrick Clawson, "Islamic Iran's Economic Politics and Prospects," *Middle East Journal* 42, no. 3 (Summer 1988): 371–388; Shaul Bakhash, "The Politics of Land, Law, and Social Justice in Iran," *Middle East Journal* 43, no. 2 (Spring 1989): 186–201; *Quarterly Economic Review of Iran* and its *Annual Supplement* (London: The Economic Intelligence Unit, The Economist Publications, various years); and occasional articles in *Financial Times*. On publications concerning the economy by the Iranian government, Iranian press, international agencies, and Iran press digests in English, see notes 16–20 below.

9. M. T. Naimi, *Toward a Theory of Postrevolutionary Social Change* (Boston: Office of the University Publisher, Harvard University, 1986), pp. 7–25.

10. *Official* exchange rates, rials to the U.S. dollar, have been as follows (somewhat different exchange rates are used for oil exports, see e.g., *Salnameh*, 1365, p. 715; official exchange rate for nonoil exports is also different and has varied from time to time; in 1988, it was around 300 rials to $1):

Year	1976	1977	1978	1979	1980	1981	1982
Exchange rate	70.2	70.6	70.5	70.5	70.6	78.3	83.6
Year	1983	1984	1985	1986	1987	1988	
Exchange rate	86.6	93.7	84.9	79.6	66.4	68.1	

All figures are averages of sale and purchase rates and reflect yearly averages except for 1988 for which the May figure is given. All figures are rounded. For 1976–83 period see IMF, *International Financial Statistics*, 1984, p. 334. Figures for the 1984–1988 period are taken from various issues of *Kayhan-e Hava'i* weekly newspaper. *Unofficial* (i.e., black market) exchange rates between the rial and dollar have had no relationship with the official rates particularly since the beginning of the Iran-Iraq war in September 1980. The rial has increasingly lost its value relative to the dollar. In May 1988, for example, $1 was sold for 1400 rials in the black markets throughout Iran. See also Lautenschlager, "The Effects of an Overvalued Exchange Rate."

11. Val Moghadam, "The Left and Revolution in Iran: A Critical Analysis," in Amirahmadi and Parvin (eds.), *Post-Revolutionary*

Iran, pp. 23–40; Bakhash, *Reign of the Ayatollahs;* Hiro, *Iran under the Ayatollahs;* Assef Bayat, *Workers and Revolution in Iran: A Third World Experience of Worker's Control* (London: Zed Books, 1986); Milani, *The Making of Iran's Islamic Revolution;* and Hossein Bashiriyeh, *The State and Revolution in Iran* (New York: St. Martin's Press, 1983).

12. Hooshang Amirahmadi, "Non-Capitalist Way of Development," *Review of Radical Political Economics* 19, no. 1 (Spring 1987): 22–46; Haidar Mehrgan, *October Va Zedd-e October* [October and Anti-October]. A publication of the Tudeh Party of Iran, 1360.

13. Immanuel Wallerstein, "Dependence in an Interdependent World: The Limited Possibilities of Transformation within the Capitalist World Economy," in Heraldo Munoz (ed.), *From Dependency to Development: Strategies to Overcome Underdevelopment and Inequality* (Boulder, CO: Westview Press, 1981), pp. 267–293.

14. Noam Chomsky, *Toward a New Cold War: Essays on Current Crisis and How We Got There* (New York: Pantheon Books, 1982); Theodore Geiger, *The Future of the International System: The United States and World Political Economy* (Boston: Unvin Hyman, 1988); Mikhail Gorbachev, *Perestroika: New Thinking for Our Country and the World* (London: Collins, 1987); J. Henderson and M. Castells (eds.), *Global Restructuring and Territorial Development* (Beverly Hills, CA: Sage, 1987); Michael Stewart, *The Age of Global Interdependence: Economic Policy in a Shrinking World* (Boston: MIT Press, 1984).

15. On these methods see Bruce Caldwell, *Beyond Positivism: Economic Methodology in the Twentieth Century* (London: George Allen & Unwin, 1982); E. V. Ilyenkov, *The Dialectics of the Abstract and the Concrete in Marx's Capital* (Moscow: Progress Publishers, 1982); Ernest Mandel, *Late Capitalism*, trans. J. De Bres (London: Verso, 1978), pp. 13–43; and Karl Marx, *Grundrisse*, Martin Nicolaus trans. (New York: Vintage Books, 1973), pp. 100–108.

16. The following major government reports have been consulted for this study. Short titles or abbreviations have been provided for easy reference and to save space. The majority of them are published by the Ministry of Plan and Budget (some by the Statistical Center) and the Central Bank. Other publications are also available from other ministries, particularly ministries of Economics and Finance, Labor and Social Welfare, Commerce, Industries, and Justice:

1. *Amar-e Kargaha* stands for *Amar-e Kargaha-ye Bozorg-e San'ti* [Statistics of Large-Scale Industrial Establishments] (Tehran: Statistical Center, various years).

2. *Barnameh-e Avval* stands for *Barnameh-e Avval-e Towse'h-e Eqtesadi-Ejtema'i-Farhangi-ye Jomhouri-ye Islami-ye Iran 1362–1366* [The First Economic-Social-Cultural Development Plan of the Islamic Republic of Iran, 1983–1987], 4 vols. (Tehran: Ministry of Plan and Budget, 1983). The plan has been revised several times since its inception in 1982. The latest revision came in early 1989, incorporating the postwar reconstruction strategy.

3. *Bazsazi* stands for *Bazsazi Va Barnamehrizi-ye Towse'h-e Meli Va Mantagheh'i* [Reconstruction and National and Regional Development Planning] (Tehran: Ministry of Plan and Budget, 1366). The document was prepared for presentation at the Seminar on the Role of Research in the Postwar Reconstruction, Shiraz University, 1366.

4. *Faslnameh* stands for *Faslnameh-e Amari-ye Salha-ye 1362, 1363 Va Sheshmahe-ye Sal-e 1364* [The Seasonal Book of Statistics, 1983, 1984 and the First Six Months of 1985] (Tehran: Ministry of Plan and Budget, 1986).

5. *Gozaresh* stands for *Gozaresh-e Eqtesadi* (Economic Report); published annually in two volumes (Tehran: Ministry of Plan and Budget, Office of Macro-Economics).

6. *Iran Dar A'ineh-e Amar* [Iran in the Mirror of Statistics] (Tehran: Statistical Center).

7. *Kholaseh-e Gozaresh* stands for *Kholaseh-e Gozaresh: Baravard-e Khesarat-e Eqtesadi-ye Jang-e Tahmili-ye Araq Aleyh-e Iran Ta Shahrivar Mah-e 1364* [Summary Report: An Estimate of the Economic Damage of the Imposed War of Iraq against Iran until September 1985] (Tehran: Ministry of Plan and Budget, 1986).

8. *Majaleh* stands for *Majaleh-e Bank-e Markazi* [Magazine of the Central Bank] (Tehran: Bank Markazi, 1364, third and fourth quarters, Nos. 207 and 208).

9. *Natayej-e Tafsili, Rusta* stands for *Natayej-e Tafsili-ye Amargiri Az Hazineh Va Daramad-e Khanevarha-ye Rusta'i, Sal-e 1363* [Detailed Results of the Census of Expenditures and Income of Rural Families, 1984] (Tehran: Statistical Center).

10. *Natayej-e Tafsili, Shahr* stands for *Natayej-e Tafsili-ye Amar-giri Az Hazineh Va Daramad-e Khanevarha-ye Shahri, Sal-e 1363* [Detailed Results of the Census of Expenditures and Income of Urban Families, 1984] (Tehran: Statistical Center).

11. *Olgu Va Strategi* stands for *Olgu Va Strategi-ye Towseᶜh* [Model and Strategy of Development] (Tehran: Ministry of Plan and Budget, 1985).

12. *Rouznameh-ye Rasmi* stands for *Rouznameh-ye Rasmi-ye Jomhouri-ye Islami-ye Iran: Mashrouh-e Mozakerat-e Majles-e Showra-ye Islami* [Official Gazette of the Islamic Republic of Iran: Proceedings of the Islamic Consultative Assembly] (Tehran: Ministry of Justice, several volumes).

13. *Salnameh* stands for *Salmaneh-e Amari* [Statistical Year-book] (Tehran: Statistical Center, Ministry of Plan and Budget, various years, 1986 Yearbook was published in 1988).

14. *Sarshomari-ye Omoumi* stands for *Sarshomari-ye Omoumi-ye Nofous va Maskan, Mehr Mah-e 1365: Natayej-e Tafsili, Koll-e Keshvar* [General Census of Population and Housing, Month of Mehr 1365, Detailed Results, Whole of the Country] (Tehran: Statistical Center, 1367). This is the latest ten-year census of population and housing in the country. The last census was taken in 1976.

15. *Tahavvulat* stands for *Barrasi-ye Tahavvulat-e Eqtesadi-ye Keshvar Baᶜd Az Enqelab* [Survey of Economic Changes in the Country after the Revolution] (Tehran: Bank Markazi Iran, n.d., probably 1983).

16. *Tangnaha* stands for *Negahi Be Vazᶜ-e Mujud Va Barrasi-ye Kolli-ye Tangnaha Va Moshkelat-e Eqtesadi-ye Keshvar* [A Look at the Existing Situation and General Survey of Bottle-necks and Difficulties of the Country's Economy] (Tehran: Ministry of Plan and Budget, 1985).

17. *Taraznameh* stands for *Gozaresh-e Eqtesadi Va Taraznameh* [Economic Report and Balance Sheet] (Tehran: Bank Markazi [Central Bank], various years).

18. *Tarha-ye Omrani* stands for *Natayej-e Barrasi-ye Tarha-ye Omrani, Zaman Bandi Va Ejra-ye Monaseb-e Anha* [The Results of the Survey of the Development Projects: Period-

ization and Their Suitable Implementation] (Tehran: Ministry of Plan and Budget, 1985).

19. *Tarh-e Moghadamati,* stands for *Tarh-e Moghadamati-ye Harakatha-ye Kolli-ye Eqtesad-e Keshvar Ba^cd Az Jang-e Tahmili* [A Preliminary Look at the Overall Trends in the Country's Economy after the Imposed War], an unpublished government document (Tehran: Ministry of Plan and Budget, n.d.).

20. *Zarfiyatha* stands for *Estefadeh az Zarfiyatha-ye Eqtesadi-Ejtema^ci-ye Keshvar: Tasviri az Vaz^c-e Mujud Dar Dureh-e 1361–1364* [Utilization of Capacities in Economic-Social Sectors of the Country: A Picture of Existing Situations in Period 1982–1985] (Tehran: Ministry of Plan and Budget, 1986).

17. References to *Interviews* allude to discussions, consultations, and interviews I have had with a number of Iranians, officials and nonofficials, during the four trips to Iran in March 1986, May 1988, August 1988, and November 1989, and with a member of the Ministry of Plan and Budget while he was visiting the United States, in 1986 and 1987, for participation in planning conferences.

18. A vast amount of nongovernmental sources have also been consulted, among which the following sources were particularly helpful: *The New York Times; OPEC Bulletin; Petroleum Intelligence Weekly; Quarterly Economic Review of Iran* and its *Annual Supplement* (London, The Economic Intelligence Unit, The Economist Publications, various years); *Financial Times;* and publications by international agencies. These include publications by the United Nation: *Statistical Yearbook for Asia and the Pacific,* 1981 and 1986–87; *Statistical Indicators for Asia and the Pacific* 14, no. 3 (September 1984); *1982 Yearbook of International Trade Statistics; Industrial Statistics Yearbook,* vol. 1, 1982; *Yearbook of National Accounts Statistics,* vol. 1, Part 1, 1981; *National Accounts Statistics: Main Aggregates and Detailed Tables,* 1982; *World Economic Survey,* 1988; *Handbook of International Trade and Development Statistics,* 1984 and 1985 supplements; *Handbook of International Commodity Statistics,* 1985; and *National Accounts Statistics: Compendium of Income Distribution Statistics,* 1985; publications by the International Monetary Fund, *International Financial Statistics,* 1984 and 1987; *Government Finance Statistics Yearbook,* 1984; *World Economic Outlook,* 1988; and *Direction of Trade Statistics*

(yearbook); publications by the World Bank, *World Development Report* (1979–88); *Annual Report* (1979–88); and *World Tables* (1979–88); and publications by the FAO, *Trade Yearbook*, 1980– 85; and *Production Yearbook*, 1979–87. Note that statistics in most publications of these and other similar international agencies are not updated for Iran and are limited to certain types such as demographic, production, government spending, and trade statistics.

19. The following are the most useful publications offering English translation from the Iranian press. *Economic Bulletin* was published weekly by Echo of Iran (Echo Building, Hafez Ave., Tehran, P.O. Box 11365–5551, and in London, by Leiuse Publications, 6 Horon Place, Kensington, W8 4LZ). It was then combined with Echo's other weekly, *Political Bulletin,* to create a new weekly publication called *An Economic and Political Bulletin* (first issue, vol. 35, no. 1 [November 1, 1988]). In summer of 1989, however, this latter publication was made into a monthly bulletin. In addition, Echo of Iran publishes its annual *Iran Almanac and Book of Facts and Who's Who in Iran* (most current is 18th ed., 1987). *Iran Focus* is another useful monthly bulletin of economic, financial, and political developments in Iran published in West Germany and London (the British publisher is Menas Associates, Gallipoli House, Outwell, Wisbech, Cambridgeshire PE14 8TN, England). The publisher also offers a yearbook called *Iran Yearbook* (two issues are available, 1988 and 1989).

20. *Kayhan-e Hava³i*, a Persian language weekly, which is published by the *Kayhan* daily for distribution outside Iran, publishes almost all significant official policy declarations including *fetvas* (religious decrees) by Ayatollah Khomeini, Friday Prayer sermons, interviews and major speeches by the leaders of the Islamic Republic, and minutes of open sessions of the Parliament. From time to time it also publishes reports on aspects of the country's political economy. Another useful publication on policy matters is *Ettelaᶜat-e Siasi-Eqtesadi* [Political-Economic Information], a monthly publication of *Ettelaᶜat* daily, Tehran, Iran. Occasionally it prints significant reports and analysis on aspects of the economy and interviews by the officials of the government. Other significant Persian language publications I have consulted include *Kayhan, Ettelaᶜat,* and *Resalat* (dailies); *Sanᶜt-e Haml Va Naql* [Transportation Industry], published by the Ministry of Transportation (monthly); *Barnameh Va Towseᶜh* [Plan and Development], published by the Ministry of Plan and Budget (quarterly); *Siasat-e Kharegi* [Foreign Policy], published by the Institute for Political and International Studies of the Minis-

try of Foreign Affairs (quarterly); *Majaleh-e Olum-e Ejtemaʿi Va Ensani* [Journal of Social Sciences and Humanities], published by Shiraz University (semiannual); *Hafteh Nameh* [Weekly], published by the House of Commerce and Ministry of Industries and Mines; *Keshavarz* [Farmer], an independent journal published in Tehran (monthly); and *Shahed* [Witness], the organ of the Islamic Martyer Foundation (semimonthly).

21. I agree with Lautenschlager that: "The official data are quite reliable, especially by the standards of Third World countries." See Lautenschlager, "The Effects of an Overvalued Exchange Rate on the Iranian Economy," p. 31–52. I may also add that the Islamic Republic has introduced many new publications and has expanded the coverage of many existing ones.

22. See Lance Tylor, *Varieties of Stabilization Experience* (Oxford: Clarendon Press, 1988); G. K. Helleiner, "Balance of Payments Experiences and Growth Prospects in Developing Countries: A Synthesis," *World Development* 14, pp. 877–908; E. V. K. Fitzgerald and Rob Vos (eds.), *Financing Economic Development: A Structural Approach to Monetary Policy* (London: Grower, 1989); Edmar L. Bacha, "Growth with Limited Supplies of Foreign Exchange: A Reappraisal of the Two-Gap Model," in Moshe Syrquin, Lance Taylor, and Larry Westphal (eds.), *Economic Structure and Performance: Essays in Honor of Hollis B. Chenery* (New York: Academic Press, 1984); W. R. Cline (ed.), *Policy Alternatives for a New International Economic Order* (New York, Praeger, 1979); Keith B. Griffin, "Foreign Capital, Domestic Savings, and Economic Development," *Bulletin of the Oxford University Institute of Statistics* 32, pp. 99–112; Ralph C. Bryant, et. al. (eds.), *Macroeconomic policies in an Interdependent World* (Washington DC: The Brookings Institution, 1989); Saburo Okita, Lal Jaywardena, and Arjun Sengupta, *Mobilizing International Surpluses for World Development: A WIDER plan for a Japanese Initiative* (Helsinki: World Institute for Development Economic Research, 1987); and Lance Taylor, *Stabilization and Growth in Developing Countries: A Structural Approach* (London: Harwood Academic Publishers, 1989).

CHAPTER 2. FORCES INFLUENCING THE ECONOMY

1. See references given in note 7 of the Introduction.

2. Hosain Razavi and Firouz Vakil, *The Political Environment of Economic Planning in Iran 1971–1983* (Boulder, CO: Westview

Press, 1984); and Robert Graham, *Iran: The Illusion of Power* (New York: St. Martin's Press, 1979). See also Sohrab Behdad, "The Structural Limits of Accumulation: Crisis in the Iranian Economy 1973–78," A working paper, Department of Economics, Denison University, Granville, OH, 1986.

3. Mark Hulbert, *Interlock: The Untold Story of American Banks, Oil Interests, the Shah's Money, Debts and the Astounding Connections between Them* (New York: Richardson & Snyder, 1982), pp. 105. For example, according to Hulbert, "Several American businesses had already left the country, while most of those remaining had minimized their risk." He quotes William Sullivan, then American Ambassador to Iran, as saying: "The important thing to remember" is that "by the time of the revolution" there were "very few U.S. concerns with large equity investments in Iran." See p. 105.

4. Pierre Terzian, *OPEC: The Inside Story* (London: Zed Books, 1985), pp. 258, 277.

5. On the role of the Iranian oil workers in the Revolution see Terisa Turner, "Iranian Oilworkers in 1978–79 Revolution," in Petter Nore and Terisa Turner (eds.), *Oil and Class Struggle* (London: Zed Press, 1980), pp. 272–292. For a chronology of the revolutionary movements see Charles Ismail Semkus, *The Fall of Iran, 1978–1979* (New York: Copen Press, 1979). See also Ahmad Ashraf and Ali Banuazizi, "The State, Classes, and Modes of Mobilization in the Iranian Revolution," *State, Culture, and Society* 1, no. 3 (Spring 1985): 3–40.

6. "Iran's Internal Power Struggle: No Moderates among the Mullahs," in *The Washington Report on the Middle East Affairs* (February 1988), pp. 4–6.

7. *Kayhan* daily (20 Khordad and 11 Tir 1358). For example, some $110 million was earmarked for loans to industries to meet their payrolls and raw material requirements.

8. On the policies of the PRG and the early attempts to change them see Hooshang Amirahmadi, "The State and Territorial Social Justice", *International Journal of Urban and Regional Research* 13, no. 1 (March 1989): 92–120; Shaul Bakhash, *The Reign of the Ayatollahs: Iran and the Islamic Revolution* (New York: Basic Books, 1984); Hossein Bashiriyeh, *The State and Revolution in Iran, 1962–1982* (London: Croom Helm, 1984); Dilip Hiro, *Iran under the Ayatollahs* (London: Routledge & Kegan Paul, 1985); Mansour Far-

hang, "How the Clergy Gained Power in Iran," in Barbara Freyer Stowasser (ed.), *The Islamic Impulse* (London: Croom Helm, 1987); Ashraf and Banuazizi, "The State, Classes, and Mobilization"; Val Moughadam (S. Azad), "Workers' and Peasants' Councils in Iran," *Monthly Review* 32, no. 5 (October 1980): 14–29; and Asaf Bayat, *Workers and Revolution in Iran: A Third World Experience of Worker's Control* (London: Zed Books, 1986).

9. Val Moghadam, "The Left and Revolution in Iran: A Critical Analysis," in Hooshang Amirahmadi and Manoucher Parvin (eds.), *Post-Revolutionary Iran* (Boulder, CO: Westview Press, 1988), p. 30. On the Iranian Left after the Revolution, see also Nozar Ala-olmolki, "The New Iranian Left," *Middle East Journal* 41, no. 2 (Spring 1987): 218–233; and Sepehr Zabih, *The Left in Contemporary Iran: Ideology, Organization and the Soviet Connection* (London: Croom Helm, 1986).

10. On Mojahedin, their social origin, ideology, and struggles, see Ervan Abrahamian, *The Iranian Mojahedin* (New Haven, CT: Yale University Press, 1989). See also Hiro, *Iran under the Ayatollahs*, pp. 187–268.

11. On these struggles see Bakhash, *The Reign of the Ayatollahs*; Hiro, *Iran under the Ayatollahs*; Bayat, *Workers and Revolution in Iran*; and Bashiriyeh, *The State and Revolution in Iran*.

12. Moghadam, "Workers' and Peasants' Councils," pp. 14–29; and Bayat, *Workers and Revolution in Iran*.

13. *Kayhan* daily (12 Esfand 1357).

14. The two major urban land laws enacted were the Nullification of Ownership of the Urban *Movat* Lands Law and the Urban Land Law (Tehran: Ministry of Justice, n.d.). See also the interview with two members of the Executive Board of the Urban Land Organization in *Ettelaʿat*, daily (1 Mehr 1982).

15. Amirahmadi, "The State and Territorial Social Justice"; Bakhash, *The Reign of the Ayatollahs*, Chapter 8; and Bashiriyeh, *The State and Revolution in Iran*, pp. 139–143.

16. Hooshang Amirahmadi, "A Theory of Ethnic Collective Movements and Its Application to Iran," *Ethnic and Racial Studies* 10, no. 4 (October 1987): 387–88.

17. James Bill, *The Eagle and the Lion: The Tragedy of American-Iranian Relations* (New Haven, CT: Yale University Press, 1988). p. 204.

18. Khosrow Fatemi, "The Iranian Revolution: Its Impact on Economic Relations with the United States," *International Journal of Middle East Studies* 12 (November 1980); see also Mehrdad Valibeigi, "U.S.-Iran Trade Relations after the Revolution," in Amirahmadi and Parvin, *Post-Revolutionary Iran*, p. 211.

19. *Debacle: The American Failure in Iran* (New York: Alfred A. Knopf, 1981).

20. Bill, *The Eagle and the Lion*, p. 286 (quoting Colonel Thomas E. Schaefer to USDAO Tehran personnel, "Visa Referrals," September 18, 1979 (Asnad, 1–6: 121).

21. Ibid., pp. 276–293.

22. On the hostage and Shah questions and the Iran-U.S. relations since the Revolution, see Bill, ibid.; Richard W. Cottam, *Iran and the United States: A Cold War Case Study* (Pittsburgh: University of Pittsburgh Press, 1988); Sepehr Zabih, *Iran since the Revolution* (Baltimore: Johns Hopkins University Press, 1982); R. K. Ramazani, *Revolutionary Iran: Challenge and Response* (Baltimore: Johns Hopkins University Press, 1986); J. D. Stempel, *Inside the Iranian Revolution* (Bloomington: Indiana University Press, 1981); Gary Sick, *All Fall Down: America's Fateful Encounter with Iran* (London: I. B. Tauris and Co. Ltd., 1986); and Nader Entessar, "Superpowers and Persian Gulf Security: The Iranian Perspective," *Third World Quarterly* 10, no. 4 (October 1988): 1427–1451. On why the Shah was admitted to the United States, see Trennce Smith, "Why Carter Admitted the Shah," in Robert McFardden, Joseph Treaster, and Maurice Carroll (with other colleagues), *No Hiding Place (The New York Times Inside Report on the Hostage Crisis)* (New York: New York Times Books, 1981), pp. 149–164. According to Hulbert, however, "getting the Shah into the U.S." had a lot to do with the "Chase's [i.e., the Chase Manhattan Bank's] growing need for a crisis." See Hulbert, *Interlock*, pp. 143–144.

23. *Asnad-e Laneh-e Jasousi* [Documents of the Spy Nest] (meaning American Embassy in Tehran), several vols. (Tehran: Moslem Students of the Imam's Line, n.d.).

24. On the U.S. trade embargoes against the Islamic Republic, see Mehrdad Valibeigi, "U.S.-Iran Trade Relations After the Revolution," in Amirahmadi and Parvin, *Post-Revolutionary Iran;* Hiro, *Iran under the Ayatollahs;* and Bakhash, *The Reign of the Ayatollahs.* On the cooperation of Western Europe and Japan with the American trade embargo of Iran, see Abrahim Razzaqi, *Eqtesad-e Iran* [Iranian Economy] (Tehran: Nashr-e Nay, 1367), p. 466.

25. See Bill, *The Eagle and the Lion,* p. 314 (quoting *Philadelphia Inquirer,* April 26, 1987, A01); *Iran Times* (May 1, 1987), pp. 1–2. On Nuzheh plot see Hiro, *Iran under the Ayatollahs.* On details of the CIA secret wars, see Bob Woodward, *Veil: The Secret Wars of the CIA, 1981–87* (New York: Simon and Schuster, 1987).

26. Mansour Farhang, "U.S. Policy toward the Islamic Republic of Iran: A Tale of Illusion and Incoherence," paper presented at the International Conference on the Middle East, Rutgers University, New Brunswick, NJ, 27–28 April 1987. (Forthcoming in Hooshang Amirahmadi (ed.), *The United States and the Middle East: A Search for New Perspectives.*)

27. With the Help of National Freedom Institute, Inc., the Tribal Alliance of Iran had organized a propaganda session on 16 November 1987, during the twenty-first annual meeting of the Middle East Studies Association of North America (MESA), Baltimore, November 14–17, 1987. The flyer publicizing the session was decorated with the institute's emblem.

28. See Jonathan Marshall, "Saudi Arabia and the Reagan Doctrine," *Middle East Report,* no. 155 (November–December 1988): 12–16; and Eric Hooglund, "Reagan's Iran: Factions behind US Policy in the Gulf," *Middle East Report,* no. 151 (March–April 1988): 29–31. See also Eric Hooglund and Fred Halliday, "From the Editors," *Middle East Report,* no. 144 (January–February 1987): 2–3.

29. Samuel Segev, *The Iranian Triangle: The Untold Story of Israel's Role in the Iran-Contra Affairs* (New York: The Free Press, 1988). See also *Iran Times* (13 Aban 1367), p. 16.

30. See Stuart Schaar, "Irangate: The Middle Eastern Connections." Paper presented at the International Conference on the Middle East, Rutgers University, New Brunswick, NJ, 27–28 April 1987, in Hooshang Amirahmadi (ed.), *The United States and the Middle East: A Search for New Perspectives* (forthcoming). See also *Report of the Congressional Committee Investigating the Iran-Contra Affairs with Supplemental, Minority and Additional Views* (Washington, DC: Supt. of Documents, U.S. Government Printing Office, 13 November 1987), p. 176; and "Plotting to Kill Khomeini," *Newsweek* (19 June 1989), p. 4. Schaaar cites Israel's anti-Arabism and need to sell its military exports as additional reasons for its participation in the Iran-Contra covert operation. On the Israel's need to sell its arms and act as "a corporate cutout" for empire headquarters in Washington, see Hooglund and Halliday, "From the Editors," pp. 2–3.

31. Mansour Farhang, "U.S. Policy toward the Islamic Republic of Iran: A Long Tale of Shortsightedness," in Hooshang Amirahmadi, (ed.), *The United States and the Middle East: A Search for New Perspectives* (forthcoming).

32. Shahram Chubin and Charles Tripp, *Iran and Iraq at War* (Boulder, CO.: Westview Press, 1988), p. 206. See also Hiro, *Iran under the Ayatollahs,* pp. 168, 321.

33. Banisadr's interview was given to Elaine Sciolino of *Newsweek* (6 October 1980, p. 24). See also Banisadr's interview with Eric Rouleau in *Le Monde* (8 October 1980). In the latter interview, Banisadr claimed that: "At the beginning of August we already had in our hands outlines of Saddam Hussein's [war] plans as well as a detailed account of the conversations which had taken place in France among the Iranian counter-revolutionaries, the Iraqi representatives, Americans, and Israeli military experts." Quoted in Hiro, *Iran under the Ayatollahs,* p. 168. For a translation of President Khamenei's address to the United Nations, see *Statement By H. E. Hojatolislam Mr. Ali Khamenei President of the Islamic Republic of Iran to the 42nd Session of the General Assembly of the United Nations. New York, 22nd September, 1987* (New York: Permanent Mission of the Islamic Republic of Iran to the United Nations, 1987).

34. See Bill, *The Eagle and the Lion,* p. 301, quoting Paul B. Ryan, *The Iranian Rescue Mission: Why It Failed* (Annapolis, MD: Naval Institute Press, 1985), p. 60.

35. Paul-Marie de La Gorce, "Gesticulations Militaires dans le Golfe," *Defence Nationale* (November 1980), p. 57.

36. "U.S. Policy toward the Persian Gulf," Department of State (May 1980) Publication no. 80–17087.

37. "The Political Economy of the Middle East, 1973–1978," Joint Economic Committee, U.S. Congress (21 April 1980) Publication no. 80–19391.

38. *New York Times,* 24 January 1980.

39. *New York Times,* 23 September 1980.

40. See U.S. Senate, Committee on Foreign Relations, Staff Report, *War in the Gulf,* 1984.

41. Gary Sick, "Trial by Error: Reflections on the Iran-Iraq War," *Middle East Journal* 43, no. 2 (Spring 1989): 239. See also

New York Times (3 October 1980; 4 November 1986; 15 November 1986); *Washington Post* (15 December 1986); and Bill, *The Eagle and the Lion*, p. 306. For more on the Iran-Iraq war and on the United States's involvement, see Majid Khadduri, *The Gulf War: The Origins and Implications of the Iran-Iraq Conflict* (New York: Oxford University Press, 1988); Ramazani, *Revolutionary Iran;* and Mehdi Masoud Zahrai, "The Origins and the Causes of the Iranian-Iraqi War" (Ph.D. diss., University of Idaho, 1983).

42. On the Iran-Contra fiasco and the politics behind it, see Jonathan Marshall, Peter Dale Scott, and Jane Hunter, *The Iran-Contra Connection: Secret Teams and Covered Operations in the Reagan Era* (Boston: South End Press, 1987); Bill, *The Eagle and the Lion*, Chapter 8; *The Tower Commission Report, The Full Text of the President's Special Review Board* (New York: Bantam Books, 1987); and Stuart Schaar, "Irangate: The Middle Eastern Connections," paper presented at one International Conference on the Middle East, Rutgers University, New Brunswick, NJ, 27–28 April 1987 in Hooshang Amirahmadi (ed.), *The United States and the Middle East: A Search for New Perspectives* (forthcoming).

43. Jo-Anne Hart, "Containment, Reflagging and Escalation: U.S. Policy in the Persian Gulf," paper presented at the Middle East Studies Association annual meeting, Los Angeles, 3–5 November 1988. See also Gary Sick, "Trial by Error," p. 239.

44. Jochen Hippler, "NATO Goes to the Persian Gulf," *Middle East Report*, no. 155 (November–December 1988): 18–21.

45. Gary Sick, "Trial by Error," p. 240.

46. The shooting down of the Iranian civilian plane on 3 July 1988 was widely reported in the *New York Times* over the next two months. See for example, "Errors By a Tense U.S. Crew Led to Downing of Iran Jet, Inquiry Is Reported to Find," *New York Times* (3 August 1988), p. A1; Editorial, "A Verdict on the Vincennes," *New York Times* (4 August 1988), p. A24; and John F. Burns, "World Aviation Panel Faults U.S. Navy on Downing of Iran Air Jet," *New York Times* (4 December 1988), p. A3.

47. Hart, "Containment, Reflagging and Escalation," pp. 2, 8–9.

48. See Robert Pear, "U.S. Says Tehran Will Honor Truce," *New York Times* (20 July 1988,) p. A6. On intensification of Iranian attacks on Kuwaiti targets following the reflagging, see also the Sen-

ate Foreign Relations Committee Staff Report in *New York Times* (November 1987), p. 4.

49. See Gary Sick, "Does the United States Really Want Peace in the Gulf?" *Washington Post National Weekly Edition* (2–8 May 1988), p. 21. The U.S. role in continuation of the war beyond 1987 was also acknowledged in a speech by Sir Antoni Parsons (the last British ambassador under the Shah) at the annual conference of the Arab Gulf Studies Center, University of Exeter, England. See *Iran Times* (6 Mordad 1368), p. 3.

50. "A Glimpse of Peace in the Gulf," (editorial) *New York Times* (19 July 1988), p. A30. See also "The Naval Gap in the Persian Gulf," *New York Times* (12 September 1989), p. A20.

51. According to Mansour Farhang, who served as Iran's ambassador to the United Nations during the first five months of 1980, "ʿAli-Reza Nobari, the Chairman of the Central Bank at the time, was accused of treason by Iran's clerical rulers for making the study public." Farhang also indicates that: "The freezing of the Iranian assets in U.S. banks brought so many suits against Iran that at least until the release of the hostages in January 1981, the Iranian Government had to pay an average of $500,000 a month to the lawyers defending it in its disputes with U.S. companies." According to Dr. Farhang, his position as ambassador gave him access to such information. See Mansour Farhang, "U.S. Policy toward the Islamic Republic of Iran." Farhad Simyar has estimated the total financial losses to Iran from hostage taking at over $17.5 billion. See his "Economic Consequences of the Hostage Crisis for Iran," paper presented at the fifth annual conference of the Center for Iranian Research and Analysis, Widener University, Chester, PA, April 1987.

52. Cheryl A. Rubenberg, "US Policy toward Nicaragua and Iran and the Iran-Contra Affair: Reflections on the Continuity of American Foreign Policy," *Third World Quarterly* 10, no. 4 (October 1988): 1467–1504.

53. *The U.S. Approach to Iran: Outlook for the Future*, a statement by John H. Kelly, assistant secretary for Near Eastern and South Asian Affairs, before the Subcommittee on Europe and the Middle East of the House Foreign Affairs Committee, Washington, DC, 9 November 1989. Current Policy No. 1231, United States Department of State, Bureau of Public Affairs, Washington, DC.

54. By the *Algiers Treaty,* I shall refer to both the Algiers Declaration of 6 March 1975 (joint communique between Iraq and Iran)

and the Treaty of International Boundaries and Good Neighborliness between Iraq and Iran singed on 13 June 1975. The declaration was negotiated during the OPEC meeting on 4–6 March in Algiers and at the initiative of the late President Houari Boumedienne of Ageria. The text of these documents is reproduced in Tareq Y. Ismael, *Iraq and Iran: Roots of Conflict* (Syracuse, NY: Syracuse University Press, 1982), pp. 60–68. Later, on 26 December 1975, four more complementary agreements were added to the treaty.

55. For the text of the statement see R. K. Ramazani, *Revolutionary Iran*, pp. 60–61.

56. Majid Khaduri, *The Gulf War: The Origins and Implications of the Iraq-Iran Conflict* (New York: Oxford University Press, 1988), pp. 85–87.

57. On these early anti-Baʿathism activities of the Islamic Republic and its Iraqi allies, see various issues of Iranian newspapers (*Kayhan, Ettelaʿat,* and *Jomhouri-ye Islami* dailies); Hiro, *Iran under the Ayatollahs*, pp. 166–167; Ramazani, *Revolutionary Iran*, pp. 59–60; Chubin and Tripp, *Iran and Iraq at War*, pp. 25–27; and Gary Sick, "Trial by Error," pp. 232–233.

58. The first known official communication from Iraq regarding the Iranian Revolution came on 5 April 1979 in the form of a telegraph addressed to Ayatollah Khomeini offering congratulations on the occasion of the declaration of the Islamic Republic. See "Statement of Dr. Saʿdoun Hamadi, Minister for Foreign Affairs of the Republic of Iraq, Before the Security Council of the United Nations, October 15, 1980." Printed in Ismael, *Iraq and Iran*, pp. 203–212.

59. See "Excerpts from Tareq Aziz (member of the Revolutionary Command Council and deputy prime minister) on Arab-Iranian Relations, *At-Thawrah* (Baghdad), May 1980," reprinted in Ismael, Ibid., pp. 89–100.

60. Hiro, *Iran under the Ayatollahs*, p. 166.

61. See, e.g., Khaduri, *The Gulf War*, p. 84; Eric Rouleau, "Iran: la guerre benie," *Le Monde* (6–9 January 1981); Terzian, *OPEC*, p. 281; and Hiro, *Iran under the Ayatollahs*, p. 167.

62. Chubin and Tripp, *Iran and Iraq at War*, p. 27. See also Hiro, *Iran under the Ayatollahs*, p. 167.

63. According to President Banisadr's report to UN Secretary General, on 1 October 1980, Iraq had expelled some 40,000 Iraqis

of Iranian origin between March and April of that year alone. *U.N. Monthly Chronicles* 17, no. 9 (November 1980): 6.

64. Chubin and Tripp, *Iran and Iraq at War,* p. 26. See also Ramazani, *Revolutionary Iran,* p. 60; and Terzian, *OPEC,* p. 279.

65. Chubin and Tripp, *Iran and Iraq at War,* p. 27.

66. See "Statement of Dr. Sa'doun Hamadi," in Ismael, *Iraq and Iran,* p. 211. On the *Caroline* clause see J. B. Moore, *International Adjudications, Ancient and Modern* (Washington, D.C.: Government Printing Office, 1929–1933), p. 5043.

67. Sick, "Trial by Error," p. 233.

68. Ibid., p. 234.

69. Peter Duignan and L. H. Gann, *The Middle East and North Africa: The Challenge to Western Security* (Stanford, CA: Hoover Institution Press, 1981); and Sick, "Trial by Error," p. 231.

70. "Excerpts from Tareq Aziz," in Ismael, *Iraq and Iran,* p. 94.

71. Terzian, *OPEC,* p. 281; Hiro, *Iran under the Ayatollahs,* p. 167; and *MERIP Reports* (July–August 1981): 3–4.

72. "Excerpts from Tareq Aziz," in Ismael, *Iraq and Iran,* p. 91; and "Statement of Dr. Sa'doun Hamadi," in ibid., p. 207.

73. "Excerpts from Tareq Aziz," in ibid., pp. 96, 100. See also Youssef M. Ibrahim, "A Chastened Ayatollah Calls off His Holy War," *New York Times* (24 July 1988), p. 2E.

74. On ideological differences between the Islamic Republic and Iraqi regime, see Mehdi Masoud Zahrai, "The Origins and the Causes of the Iranian-Iraqi War" (Ph.D. diss., University of Idaho, August 1983), pp. 167–177.

75. "Excerpts from Tareq Aziz," in Ismael, *Iraq and Iran,* pp. 91–92; and "Statement of Dr. Sa'doun Hamadi," in ibid., pp. 204, 207.

76. See Robert Pouliot, "Iraq's Drive for Power: Oil and Stability Fuel a Bid for Arab Supremacy," *World Press Review* (July 1980), p. 29. See also Bill, *The Eagle and the Lion,* p. 304; Chubin and Tripp, *Iran and Iraq at War,* pp. 25–28; and Ramazani, *Revolutionary Iran,* p. 65.

77. See also Fox Butterfield, "8-Year Gulf War: Victims but No Victors," *New York Times* (25 July 1988), p. A1–A10.

78. Among those who have argued that the Iran-Iraq war was rooted in "a personal feud," Mansour Farhang has offered the most comprehensive explanation thus far. See his "The Iran-Iraq War: The Feud, the Tragedy, the Spoils," *World Policy Journal* (Fall 1985), pp. 659–680. See also J. C. Hurewitz, "The Middle East: A Year Turmoil," *Foreign Affairs* 59 (1981), pp. 540–577.

79. Youssef M. Ibrahim, "A Chastened Ayatollah Calls off His Holy War," *New York Times* (24 July 1988), p. 2E.

80. Terzian, *OPEC*, p. 282 (quoting James Akins: "The Influence of Politics on Oil Pricing and Production," A speech delivered in London on 28 September 1981).

81. Abbas Alnasrawi, "The Impact of the Gulf War on the Economy of Iraq," paper presented at the International Conference on the Middle East, Rutgers University, New Brunswick, April 27–28, 1987.

82. Sick, "Trial by Error," p. 235. See also Brian Urquhart and Gary Sick (eds.), *The United Nations and the Iran-Iraq War* (New York: Ford Foundation Conference Report, August 1987), pp. 7–27. For the texts of various UN resolutions on the war, see Khadduri, *The Gulf War*, pp. 208–216.

83. See "Statement of Mohammad Ali Rajai, Prime Minister of the Islamic Republic of Iran, Before the Security Council of the United Nations, October 17, 1980," reprinted in Ismael, *Iraq and Iran*, pp. 212–219.

84. Dilip Hiro, "The Iran-Iraq War," paper presented at the International Conference on the Middle East, Rutgers University, New Brunswick, April 27–28, 1987. See also *Daily Telegraph* (12 September 1982).

85. See John F. Burns, "World Aviation Panel Faults U.S. Navy on Downing of Iran Air Jet," *New York Times* (4 December 1988), p. A3.

86. See Shahram Chubin, "The Last Phase of the Iran-Iraq War: From Stalemate to Ceasefire," *Third World Quarterly* 11, no. 2 (April 1989), pp. 1–14.

87. Gary Sick, "Does the United States Really Want Peace in the Gulf?" *Washington Post National Weekly Edition* (2–8 May 1988), pp. 21–22.

88. For the full text of Bazargan's letter see *Iran Times* (27 Khordad 1367), pp. 12, 15. The importance of the domestic opposition to war on Iran's acceptance of the cease-fire was acknowledged by President Hashemi Rafsanjani, then speaker of the Parliament, in a news conference. He was quoted by the *New York Times* as saying that: "If tomorrow it becomes clear that despite our flexibility the Iraqis still do not want to surrender to what is right, then our opponents within the country will be disarmed." See Youssef M. Ibrahim, "Iraq, Assailing Iran's Truce Terms, Says It Must Press War in the Gulf," *New York Times* (20 July 1988), pp. A1–A6. See also Robert Pear, "Iran Action Linked to Anti-War Mood," *New York Times*, 22 July 1988, p. A6. In addition to the popular antiwar mood, Pear lists a number of other factors as responsible for Iran's acceptance of the resolution, including the U.S. intervention (particularly the downing of Iranian passenger plane), difficulty of getting arms, Iraq's chemical warfare, the worsening economy, divisions between the Army and the Revolutionary Guard Corps, international isolation, and the psychological effect of the Iraqi missile attacks on the population of Tehran.

89. On Iraq calling the Iranian move *tactical* and *deceptive*, see Youssef M. Ibrahim, "Iraq Voices Strong Doubts on Iran's Good Intentions," *New York Times* (19 July 1988), p. A8; Youssef M. Ibrahim, "Iraq, Assailing Iran's Truce Terms, Says It Must Press War in the Gulf," *New York Times* (20 July 1988), pp. A1–A6; and Fox Butterfield, "U.N. Council Asks End to Hostilities in the Gulf," *New York Times* (20 July 1988), p. A6.

90. See Robert Pear, "Khomeini Accepts 'Poison' of Ending the War with Iraq, Personal Decision," *New York Times* (21 July 1988), pp. A1–A8.

91. See Sick, "Trial by Error," pp. 242–43. On Iraq's resistance to the resolution and the stepped up pressure for it to do so, see Paul Lewis, "U.N. Presses Iraq to Stop Blocking a Gulf Cease-Fire," *New York Times* (22 July 1988), pp. A1–A6; Paul Lewis, "Saudis Are Said to Step up Pressure on Iraq to Reach a Cease-Fire," *New York Times* (30 July 1988), p. 4; Paul Lewis, "Iraqi Aide Takes Hard Line at U.N.," *New York Times* (28 July 1988), p. A8; "The Gulf War Isn't Over," (editorial) *New York Times* (31 August 1988), p. A22; and Robert Pear, "U.S. Presses Iraqis to Accept Cease-Fire," *New York Times* (5 August 1988), p. A8. Iraq launched a massive chemical attack on the Iranian town of Oshnoviyeh on 2 August 1988 only a day after a UN investigative team had reported to the Secu-

rity Council that "chemical weapons continue to be used on an intensive scale" by Iraq. See also Paul Lewis, "U.N. Chief Says He Will Declare a Cease-Fire in the Iran-Iraq War," *New York Times,* (2 August 1988), pp. A1–A9; "U.N. Panel Says Iraq Used Gas on Civilian" *New York Times* (24 August 1988), p. A11; and Paul Lewis, "Iraq Is Said to Use Poison Gas Again," *New York Times* (4 August 1988), p. A8.

92. For an excerpt from Tariq Aziz's letter see *New York Times* (21 July 1988), p. A8.

93. Paul Lewis, "Iran Accepts Plan by Iraq for Truce and Direct Talk," *New York Times* (8 August 1988), pp. A1–A11; Paul Lewis, "Iran and Iraq Sharply Divided in U.N. Talks," *New York Times* (31 July 1988), p. 6; and (editorial) *New York Times,* 3 August 1988, p. 22.

94. Paul Lewis, "U.N. Chief Tries New Tack in Gulf Talk Impasse," *New York Times* (1 September 1988), p. A14; and Paul Lewis, "Iraq to Spur Talks, Says It May Develop New Port," *New York Times* (28 October 1988), p. A3.

95. See Paul Lewis, "Iraq Appears to Toughen Stance on Control of Disputed Waterway," *New York Times* (29 August 1988), p. A9; "The Gulf War Isn't Over," (editorial) *New York Times* (31 August 1988), p. A22; and Paul Lewis, "Gulf Talks Stall over a Waterway," *New York Times* (9 October 1988), p. A11.

96. See Paul Lewis, "Iraq to Spur Talks, Says It May Develop New Port," *New York Times* (28 October 1988), p. A3; and Paul Lewis, "U.N. Acts to Spur Iran-Iraq Talks," *New York Times* (January 1989).

97. On the Iranian position on the peace negotiations see the statement by the Ministry of Foreign Affairs in the occasion of the anniversary of the cease-fire in *Kayhan-e Hava²i* (4 Mordad 1368), pp. 11, 30.

98. Lewis, "U.N. Chief Tries New Tack in Gulf Talks Impasse," p. A14.

99. See Paul Lewis, "The U.N.'s Gulf War Balancing Act," *New York Times* (25 March 1989), p. A3; Paul Lewis, "Iran and Iraq Still Hold Thousands of P.O.W.'s," *New York Times* (26 March 1989), p. A6; and Alan Cowell, "With Gulf War Quiet, Foes Grapple Verbally," *New York Times* (22 August 1988), p. A6. See also "Iran Is Said to Use 'Pressure' on Iraqi Captives," *New York Times*

(1 September 1988), p. A15; "With a Dispute, Iran and Iraq Begin Exchange of P.O.W.'s," *New York Times* (25 November 1988), p. A10; "Tehran Suspends P.O.W. Trade with Baghdad," *New York Times* (28 November 1988), p. A14; and "Iran and Iraq in 2nd Exchange of Sick or Wounded Captives," *New York Times* (27 November 1988), p. A14.

100. In an editorial on 2 December, the *New York Times* wrote that "Iran and Iraq have each taken advantage of the August cease-fire in their long war to settle scores with dissenters at home. Iraq's lawless gassing of Kurdish villages has been deservedly condemned. Iran's mass killings of mainly leftist opponents have attracted less attention." See "What Iran Wants Ignored," *New York Times* (2 December 1988), p. A31. See also Paul Lewis, "Iran Says It Will Aid U.N. on Human Rights Study," *New York Times* (26 November 1988), p. A5; Paul Lewis, "Deal for U.N. Rights Inquiry in Iran Crumbles," *New York Times* (2 December 1988), p. A5; Alan Cowell, "Fleeing Assault by Iraqis, Kurds Tell of Poison Gass and Lives Lost," *New York Times* (5 September 1988), p. A1; Alan Cowell, "Iraq Asserts Its Authority in a Kurdish Stronghold," *New York Times* (6 September 1988), p. A10; Clyde Habermen, "Kurds Can't Go Home Again, Because the Homes Are Gone," *New York Times* (18 September 1988), p. A1; Julie Johnson, "U.S. Asserts Iraq Used Poison Gas Against the Kurds," *New York Times* (9 September 1988), p. A1; and "Iran Is Said to Close Its Border to Iraqi Kurds," *New York Times* (16 October 1988), p. A5.

101. See Prime Minister Mir Hosain Musavi's cicular dated 25/3/1361 to the various government offices concerning estimation of the war damage. Printed in *Raveshha va Olgouha-ye Lazem Bara-ye Baravourd-e Khesarat-e Jang-e Tahmili-ye Iraq Aleyh-e Iran* [Necessary Methods and Models for Estimation of Economic Damage of the Imposed War of Iraq Against Iran] (Tehran: Ministry of Plan and Budget, 1362).

102. Interview, 1988. Estimates of the war damage are coordinated and finalized by the Economic Commission for Estimation of Losses of the Imposed War, established within Ministry of Plan and Budget in 1982. Estimates of damage to the oil sector was, however, left totally to the Ministry of Oil and Gas. The ministry produces its estimates under strict secrecy.

103. All figures given in the paragraph are taken from Kamran Mofid, "The Economic Consequences of the Gulf War: September 1980–July 1988," paper presented at the seventh annual Conference

of the Center for Iranian Research and Analysis, Columbia University, New York City, April 7–9, 1989.

104. Hooshang Amirahmadi, "War Damage and Reconstruction in the Islamic Republic of Iran," in Amirahmadi and Parvin, *Post-Revolutionary Iran*, pp. 130–132.

105. On Iran's economic loss from the war see Hooshang Amirahmadi, "Destruction and Reconstruction: A Strategy for the War-Damaged Areas of Iran," in ibid., *Bazsazi*; and *Kholaseh-e Gozaresh*, nos. 7 and 8 (number 8 was published in 1988). See also K. Miyaji (ed.), *Proceedings of the Symposium on the Iran-Iraq War* (Tokyo: Institute of Developing Economies, August 1988).

106. Almost a month after the cease-fire, Iran announced that it had lost 123,220 soldiers (of which 80,000 belonged to the Revolutionary Guard Corps and 30,000 to the regular army) and 11,000 civilians in the war. The government also indicated that some 60,711 soldiers were missing in action, most believed to be in Iraqi prisons. The figure for POWs was reported at 30,000 but it is believed to be closer to 50,000. See *Kayhan-e Hava'i* (13 Mehr 1367), p. 23. The government's casualty figure is also believed to be an underestimate. For example, estimates by Western analysts put the number of dead at 300,000 for Iran and 120,000 for Iraq. See *New York Times* (19 September 1988), p. A8.

107. The human damage of the war was reported by the minister of Islamic Guidance as follows: number of dead—123,000 military personnel (of which 80,000 belonged to the Revolutionary Guard Corps and 30,000 to the regular army) and 11,000 civilian population; number of missing in action—61,000; and number of POWs in Iraq—30,000. See *Kayhan-e Hava'i*, (13 Mehr 1367), p. 23. These figures were released less than a month after the cease-fire and may well be underestimated. See also Amirahmadi, "War Damage and Reconstruction," p. 127.

108. Amirahmadi, "War Damage and Reconstruction," p. 127.

109. Hooshang Amirahmadi, "Iran at the Threshold of the Post-War Reconstruction," paper presented at the seventh annual Conference of the Center for Iranian Research and Analysis, Columbia University, New York City, April 1989.

110. Speech by the minister of Plan and Budget (delivered by the director of the Macroeconomic Office) at the International Confer-

ence on Aggression and Defense, Tehran, August 1988 (author was among the participants); and *Tarh-e Moghadamati.*

111. *Tarh-e Moghadamati; Kholaseh-e Gozaresh,* no. 8; and interview 1988.

112. The estimates are based on information given in *Tarh-e Moghadamati; Kholaseh-e Gozaresh,* no. 8; and interview 1988.

113. Accounting for some of the cost of elements not included in the government estimates, Kamran Mofid arrives at a grand total of some $644.3 billion for the war damage. Note that this figure includes opportunity costs. See Kamran Mofid, "The Economic Consequences of the Gulf War: September 1980–July 1988," paper presented at the seventh annual conference of the Center for Iranian Research and Analysis, Columbia University, New York City, April 7–9, 1989. See also Miyaji; and a useful study by Kiyotaki Tsuji of the Japanese Institute of Middle East Economic Studies.

114. *Tarh-e Moghadamati;* and *Kholaseh-e Gozaresh,* no. 8.

115. Speech by the Minister of Plan and Budget at the International Conference on Aggression and Defense; and *Tarh-e Moghadamati.*

116. *Iran Times* (30 Tir 1368), p. 2.

117. Mehrdad Valibeigi, "U.S.-Iranian Trade Relations after the Revolution," in Amirahmadi and Parvin, *Post-Revolutionary Iran,* pp. 210–222.

118. "Kissinger on Oil, Food, and Trade," *Business Week* (13 January 1975), p. 67. Quoted in Ed Shaffer, *The United States and Control of World Oil* (New York: St. Martin's Press, 1983), p. 223.

119. James T. Jensen, "Oil and Energy Demand: Outlook and Issues," in Robert Mabro (ed.), *The 1986 Oil Price Crisis: Economic Effects and Policy Responses* (Oxford: Oxford University Press, for the Oxford Institute for Energy Studies, 1988), p. 17.

120. Richard O'Brien, "Oil Markets and the Developing Countries," *Third World Quarterly* 8, no. 4 (October 1986): 1312–1313.

121. Peter R. Odell, *Oil and World Power,* 8th ed. (New York: Penguin Books, 1986), p. 284.

122. Cyrus Bina, "Competition, Control and Price Formation in the International Energy Industry," *Energy Economics* 11, no. 3 (July 1989), pp. 162–68; and Cyrus Bina, "Internationalization of

the Oil Industry: Simple Oil Shocks or Structural Crisis?" *Review* 11, no. 3 (Summer 1988): 329–370.

123. Terzian, *OPEC*, p. 262.

124. Introduction, in Mabro, *The 1986 Oil Price Crisis*, p. 3.

125. Ali M. Jaidah, "Producers' Policies: Past and Future," in Mabro, *The 1986 Oil Price Crisis*, pp. 71–77.

126. Mohammed E. Ahrari, *OPEC: The Failing Giant* (Lexington: University Press of Kentucky, 1986), p. 181.

127. Terzian, *OPEC*, p. 239. See also here (pp. 252–254) for the "special relations" between Saudi Arabia and the United States. Referring to the price war between Saudi Arabia and the rest of OPEC members during the December 1976 OPEC meeting in Doha, a White House spokesman commented in the *Wall Street Journal* that: "A bigger game is being played there than just oil prices. The Saudis are trying to become America's friend in the Middle East." Quoted in ibid., p. 244. And according to Ian Seymour, a British journalist and a close friend of Ahmed Zaki Yamani, then Saudi oil minister: "The Saudi plan was to administer a short sharp shock in the form of a rapid boost in production, as a consequence of which other OPEC producers would (*a*) be unable to sustain the higher price level, (*b*) lose export volume, and (*c*) be obliged to seek a compromise with Saudi Arabia." See Ian Seymour, *OPEC, Instrument of Change* (London: Macmillan Press, 1980), p. 168.

128. Mohammad Farouk Al Husseini, "Some Aspects of the Saudi Arabian Oil Supply Policy," in Mabro, *The 1986 Oil Price Crisis*, p. 110.

129. The full text of the Senate report entitled *The Future of Oil Production in Saudi Arabia* is published in a special supplement to *Petroleum Intelligence Weekly*, New York (23 April 1979). See also Terzian, *OPEC*, pp. 245–246.

130. Fereidun Fesharaki and David Isaak, *OPEC, the Gulf, and the World Petroleum Market: A Study in Government Policy and Downstream Operations* (Boulder, CO: Westview Press, 1983), p. 235.

131. Terzian, *OPEC*, p. 264. On the Saudi pricing policy following the Iranian Revolution, see also Abbas Alnasrawi, *OPEC in a Changing World Economy* (Baltimore: Johns Hopkins University Press, 1985), pp. 38–44.

132. Terzian, *OPEC,* pp. 264–265.

133. Ahrari, *OPEC,* p. 182.

134. Terzian, *OPEC,* p. 287.

135. *Middle East Economic Survey,* Supplement (1981): 1–2; and ibid. (7 September 1981), p. 2. Quoted in Abbas Alnasrawi, "The Impact of the Gulf War on the Economy of Iraq," paper presented at the International Conference on the Middle East, Rutgers University, New Brunswick, April 27–28, 1987.

136. Ralph E. Bailey, "The Impact of Low Oil Prices on US Energy Markets," in Mabro, *The 1986 Oil Price Crisis,* p. 61.

137. Odell, *Oil and World Power,* p. 284.

138. Michael Renner, "Determinants of the Islamic Republic's Oil Policies: Iranian Revenue Needs, the Gulf War, and the Transformation of the World Oil Market," in Amirahmadi and Parvin, *Post-Revolutionary Iran,* pp. 190, 193–94.

139. Terzian, *OPEC,* pp. 282–283.

140. Elizabeth Gamlen, "US Responses to the 'Tankers War' and the Implications of its Intervention," paper presented at the International Conference on Aggression and Defence, Tehran, 8–10 August 1988.

141. Bill, *The Eagle and the Lion,* pp. 311–312. Professor Bill maintains that this convergence of interests was another "strategic reason" for the U.S. overture to Iran, leading to the Irangate fiasco.

142. Youssef Ibrahim, "Saudis Call for Cut in Oil Output," *New York Times* (October 18 1988), pp. D1, D8; Youssef Ibrahim, "OPEC Studying Demand Outlook," *New York Times* (September 26 1988), pp. A1, D5; Youssef Ibrahim, "Challenge by Saudis to OPEC," *New York Times* (10 October 1988), pp. D1, D2; Matthew L. Wald, "Saudis' Plan on Oil Output Raises Prices," *New York Times* (11 October 1988), pp. D1, D19; Michael Quint, "Price War Fears Send Oil Tumbling," *New York Times* (6 October 1988), pp. D1, D16; and Youssef Ibrahim, "OPEC Price Parley Set, but Effort Seems Futile," *New York Times* (21 September 1988), p. D3.

143. Youssef Ibrahim, "OPEC Signs Accord to Lower Output for Half a Year," *New York Times* (29 November 1988), pp. A1, D7; Youssef Ibrahim, "Iran-Iraq Feuding Holds up OPEC Price

Accord," *New York Times* (20 November 1988), p. A4; Youssef Ibrahim, "OPEC Sets Quotas on Oil Production after Iran Yields," *New York Times* (25 November 1988), pp. A1, D2; and Youssef Ibrahim, "New Demands by Saudis Endangers OPEC Accord," *New York Times* (28 November 1988), pp. A1, D4.

144. Terzian, *OPEC*, p. 301. Quoting Bruno Dethomas, "La fin de la conference de l'OPEP," *Le Monde* (23 May 1982).

145. *Zarfiyatha*, various tables; and *Gozaresh*, vol. 1, pp. 108–09.

146. *Iran Times* (30 Tir 1368), p. 2.

147. *Tangnaha*, pp. 1–52; and Hosain Azimi, "Budgeh Va Towse꜀h-e Eqtesadi Dar Iran" [Budget and Economic Development in Iran], *Ettela꜀at-e Siasi-Eqtesadi* 2, no. 5 (Bahman 1366): 32.

148. See Kamran Mofid, *Development Planning in Iran: From Monarchy to Islamic Republic* (Cambridgeshire, England: Middle East and North African Press Limited, 1987), pp. 24–29; Ann K. S. Lambton, "Persia," *Journal of the Royal Central Asian Society* 31 (January 1944): 14–16; Sayyed Mohammad ꜀Ali Jamalzadeh, *Kholghiyat-e Ma Iranian* [Temperament of We Iranians] (Winter Park, FL: Kanoun Marefat Publishers, 1985); Reza Behnam, *Cultural Foundations of Iranian Politics* (Salt Lake City: University of Utah Press, 1986); and Jahangir Amuzegar, "Iran's Economic Planning Once Again," *Middle East Economic Papers* (1957): 4.

149. See "Report of the Prime Minister [Musavi] about the War and Economic and Executive Difficulties of the Country," in *Kayhan-e Hava꜀i* (15 Tir 1367), p. 24. See also "Zarorat-e Bazsazi-ye Tashkilat-e Edari" [The Need for Reconstruction of Administrative Apparatuses], in *Soroush* (21 Aban 1367); *Kayhan-e Hava꜀i* (4 Aban 1367), p. 24; (29 Tir 1367), p. 24; and (23 Azar 1367), p. 19.

150. *Kayhan-e Hava꜀i* (4 Aban 1367), p. 24; and (27 Mehr 1367), p. 14.

151. See "Report of the Prime Minister [Musavi] about the War," p. 26.

152. This was related to me during a discussion I held in 1989 with an official of the Ministry of Plan and Budget.

153. Taqi Banki, "Baznegari-ye Yek Tajrobeh" [A Look Back at an Experience], in *Barnameh Va Tous꜀ah*, nos. 4 and 5 (Spring

1365). Dr. Banki was the chief of the Plan and Budget Organization from Mordad 1360 to Esfand 1363.

154. *Kayhan-e Hava'i* (24 Esfand 1367), p. 11–12.

155. See Ahmad Zamani, Ta'sir-e Jang Dar Tahghigh Va Towse'h," [The Effect of War on Research and Development], in Gholam Vatandoust (ed.), *Proceedings of the Second Symposium at Shiraz University on the Role of Research in Reconstruction*, vol. 1: *The Social Sciences and Humanities* (Shiraz, Iran: University of Shiraz Press, 1989), pp. 8–9; *Kayhan* daily (11 Bahman 1367); and "The Drive to Lure back Specialists," in *Iran Focus* 1, no. 3 (December 1988): 12–13.

156. See, e.g., *Kayhan-e Hava'i* (13 Mehr 1367), p. 4; and (23 Azar 1367), p. 2.

157. Note that the 88.7 percent given in the paragraph for proportion of school-enrolled to education-eligible people belongs to 1985, not 1986. See *Sarshemari-ye Omoumi-ye Nefous Va Maskan 1365* [Census of Population and Housing], decennial (Tehran: Statistical Center, 1965, Total Country, #6), pp. 87–88; and *Sarshemari-ye Omoumi-ye Nefous Va Maskan 1355* [Census of Population and Housing], decennial (Tehran: Statistical Center, 1965, Total Country, #186), pp. 24, 43–44. See also *Annual Report and Balance Sheet* (Tehran: Bank Markazi Iran, 1357), pp. 131, 163–65; *Taraznameh* (1364), p. 195. *Gozideh-e Mataleb-e Amari*, no. 19 (Farvardin and Ordibehesht, 1367); *Salmameh-e Amari 1360*, p. 114; *Kayhan* daily (1 Ordibehesht 1367); and the *First Development Plan of the Islamic Republic (Social Sectors)*.

158. "Report of the Prime Minister [Musavi] about the War," pp. 24–30 and Interview, 1988.

159. Hooshang Amirahmadi and Farhad Atash, "Dynamics of Provincial Development and Disparity in Iran, 1956–1984," in *Third World Planning Review* 9, no. 2 (May 1987): pp. 155–185. The provinces of Kohkiluyeh and Boyer Ahmadi, Sistan and Baluchestan, Zanjan, Ilam, Lorestan, Hormozgan, and Kurdestan all had literacy rates below 35 percent in 1976.

160. See *Gozaresh* (1965), vol. 2, Chapter 28, pp. 16–17 and Zamani, Ta'sir-e Jang Dar Tahghigh Va Towse'h," p. 8.

161. See Paridoukht Vahidi, *Tahlili Az Hazineh-e Amouzesh-e Aali* [An Analysis of Expenditures in Higher Education] (Tehran: Ministry of Plan and Budget, 1365); Razzaqi, *Eqtesad-e Iran*, pp.

544–549; *Kayhan* daily (9 Mehr 1367), p. 5; and the *First Development Plan of the Islamic Republic (Social Sectors)*.

162. See *Kayhan* daily (16 Azar 1367), p. 5; *Iran Almanac and Book of Facts*, 18th ed. (Tehran: Echo of Iran, 1987), pp. 155–165; and *Taraznameh* (1364), p. 74.

163. *Tahavvulat* (1982), p. 604.

164. *Kayhan* daily (16 Azar, 1367), p. 5.

165. Amirahmadi and Atash, "Dynamics of Provincial Development," pp. 155–185.

166. *Sarshemari-ye Omoumi-ye Nefous Va Maskan 1365* [Total Country], p. 8.

167. *Iran Almanac and Book of Facts*, p. 155–165; and Razzaqi, *Eqtesad-e Iran*, pp. 549–552. See also *Kayhan* daily (30 Farvardin 1367), p. 15; (2 Khordad 1367); and (27 Tir 1367); Vahidi, *Tahlili Az Hazineh-e Amouzesh-e Aali; First Development Plan of the Islamic Republic, (Social Sectors)*.

168. See *Kayhan* daily (12 Ordibehesht 1367), p. 5; *Amargiri Az Gheimat-e Masaleh-e Sakhtemani, Dastmozd-e Nirou-ye Ensani Va Keraye-he Machinalat-e Moured-e Estefadeh Dar Tarha-ye Omrani* [Census of Prices of Construction Materials, Wages of Labor and Costs of Leasing Machinery Used in Development Projects] (Tehran: Statistical Center, 1365); *Amargiri Az Khanevarha-ye Ejarehneshin-e Shahr-e Tehran* [Census of Tenant Families of the City of Tehran] (Tehran: Statistical Center, 1366); *Sarshemari-ye Omoumi-ye Nefous Va Maskan;* and *Economic and Political Bulletin* (18 October 1988): 10–11.

169. Razzaqi, *Eqtesad-e Iran*, pp. 541–44; and *Iran Almanac and Book of Facts*, pp. 268–273. See also the *First Development Plan of the Islamic Republic (Social Sectors)*; and Hamid Mirzadeh, "Vazʿiyat-e Mojoud Va Khatt-e Mashi-ye Dowlat Dar Amr-e Bazsazi-ye Manategh-e Jangzadeh" [The Existing Situation and the Policy of the Government in Reconstructing the War-Damaged Areas], in Gholam Vatandoust (ed.), *Proceedings of the Second Symposium at Shiraz University*, vol. 1, pp. 15–27.

170. See *Sarshemari-ye Omoumi-ye Nefous Va Maskan 1365* [Total Country], p. 45 (Introduction); and Amirahmadi and Atash, "Dynamics of Provincial Development," pp. 155–185.

171. *Sarshemari-ye Omoumi-ye Nefous Va Maskan*, p. 278.

172. See *Gozaresh,* vol. 2 (1363 and 1365), Chapters 19 and 24, respectively; *Tahavvulat* (1982), pp. 563–569; and *Salnameh* (1365), pp. 559–580.

173. See *Gozaresh,* vol. 2, (1363 and 1365), Chapters 18 and 23, respectively; *Salnameh* (1365), pp. 630–31; and Razzaqi, *Eqtesad-e Iran,* pp. 532–33.

174. *Salnameh* (1365), p. 634.

175. See *Gozaresh,* vol. 2, (1363 and 1365), Chapters 18 and 23, respectively; and *Salnameh* (1365), pp. 635–641.

176. See *Gozaresh,* vol. 2, (1363), Chapter 18; and *Salnameh* (1365), pp. 639–641.

177. *Salnameh* (1365), pp. 656–657. Please note that the figure includes post offices, postal representatives, post office boxes, and urban post kiosks. Moreover, in calculating the number, the Urumia Lake area (4,868 sq km) has been deducted from the total land area of the country (1,648,000).

178. *Salnameh* (1365), p. 661.

179. Ibid.

180. "Law of Organization of Islamic Councils of the Country," in *Official Newspaper,* no. 11022 (7 Day 1361) (Tehran: Ministry of Justice).

181. Ibid., pp. 734–735.

182. *Summary of the Preliminary Report on Determination of the Economic-Social Policies in the Islamic Republic of Iran* (Tehran: Office of Revolutionary Projects, Mordad 1358), mimeograph.

183. Members of the Economic Council included the prime minister (chair); consulting ministers; chiefs of PBO and the Central Bank; and ministers of Economics and Finance, Agriculture, Industries, Labor and Social Affairs, Heavy Industries, Mines and Metals, Oil, Energy, Construction Crusade, and Commerce. Among the members were also the prime minister's advisor for executive affairs and a high-ranking economic expert. Over time, however, the composition of the council has changed. Please also note that PBO became a ministry in 1983.

184. Sectoralists, among them the sectoral planners working in the macroeconomic division of PBO and the ministers in the powerful Economic Council had the support of then PBO chief, Dr. Taghi

Banki. Regionalists, on the other hand, came from the relatively powerless regional planners from PBO and from the provincial planning offices. They were later joined by Prime Minister Musavi.

185. An official is quoted to have said, in a cabinet meeting, that: "We have suppressed nationalism but regionalism is suppressing us." Interviews, 1986.

186. In closing the Office of Regional Planning, the government alleged that it did not have the needed skilled personnel to back up the office's functions. See A. N. Mashayekhi, "Barrasi-ye Nezam Barnamehrizi-ye Keshvar Dar Amal Va Chand Pishnehad-e Eslahi [Investigation of the Country's (Iranian) Planning System in Practice and some corrective Proposals], *Barnameh Va Towseʿah* 1, no. 1 (Winter 1363): 9–33.

187. Provinces have followed different approaches for forming their respective councils. To prevent confusion between the Council of Provincial Planning (CPP) and the Supreme Council of Provinces, which has not yet been established in the Islamic Republic, the government has recently renamed the CPP the Provincial Planning Committee (PPC). However, the confusion, which began with the introduction of the New Planning System in 1982, continues to date even among the country's planning experts.

188. In writing the section on the procedures of formulating the first plan, I have relied primarily upon the Interviews, 1986, and Mashayekhi, "Barrasi-ye Nezam Barnamehrizi-ye Keshvar Dar Amal Va Chand Pishnehad-e Eslahi."

189. *Ahdaf-e Kammi-ye Towseʿah-e Eqtesadi-Ejtemaʿai-ye Jomhouri-ye Islami-ye Iran Dar Doureh-e 1361–1381* [Quantitative Objectives of Socioeconomic Development of the Islamic Republic of Iran in the Period of 1982–2002] (Tehran: Office of Deputy for Planning and Evaluation, Plan and Budget Organization, Esfand 1360). The report was originally sent to the Economic Council in February 1981. It took the council more than a year, until March 1982, to approve a revised version. Interviews, 1986.

190. The document was finalized and approved in April 1982.

191. *Barnameh-e Avval-e Towseʿah-e Eqtesadi, Ejtemaʿi, Farhangi-ye Jomhouri-ye Islami-ye Iran, 1362–1366* [First Economic, Social, Cultural Development Plan of the Islamic Republic of Iran, 1983–1987] (Tehran: Plan and Budget Organization, 1983). The plan includes four volumes: *Objectives and Policies, Productive*

Sectors, Infrastructural Sectors, and *Social Sectors.* It is the largest plan, in terms of both number of pages and volume of resources committed, so far made for the country. Around 6,000 people are said to have participated in its formulation at various stages, the largest number of people ever engaged in plan-making in Iran. See Mashayekhi, "Barrasi-ye Nezam Barnamehrizi-ye Keshvar Dar Amal Va Chand Pishnehad-e Eslahi," p. 17.

192. See page 1 of volume 1 of the first plan, where the role of spatial planning in national development is acknowledged. Contrary to this, also note that the plan in its four volumes does not include a single chapter on regional planning. The prerevolutionary plans had all included a section or chapter on the subject.

193. *Amayesh-e Sarzamin* was first introduced in Iran by Scetiran, a French planning firm, in 1976 and was subsequently expanded under the Center for National Spatial Planning, which was staffed by the Iranian planners. See Hooshang Amirahmadi, "Regional Planning in Iran: A Survey of Problems and Policies," in *Journal of Developing Areas* 20, no. 4 (July 1986): 501–529; *Moutalaᶜah-e Strateji-ye Derazmoddat-e Tarh-e Amayesh-e Sarzamin* [Study of Long-Term Strategy of Spatial Plan] (Tehran: Center for National Spatial Planning, Plan and Budget Organization, 1976); and Mozaffar Sarrafi and M. Baroumand Yazdi, *The Spatial Formation and Suggested Strategies for Spatial Development in Iran with Special Emphasis on the Industrial Sector* (Nagoya: United Nations Center for Regional Development, April 1986).

194. In writing the section on the Spatial Strategy Planning, I have relied primarily on Interviews 1986; and M. H. Fouladi, "Comprehensive National Spatial Planning," paper delivered at the Association of Collegiate School of Planning, Milwaukee, 1986. Mr. Fouladi presently directs the Office of Regional Planning in PBO.

195. *Motalᶜat-e Tarh-e Paye-he Amayesh-e Sarzamin-e Islami-ye Iran* [Studies of the Basic Spatial Strategy Plan of the Islamic Nation of Iran] (Tehran: Office of Regional Planning, Plan and Budget Organization, n.d.).

196. Interviews, 1986.

197. Hooshang Amirahmadi, "Middle-Class Revolutions in the Third World," in Amirahmadi and Parvin, *Post-Revolutionary Iran,* pp. 225–244; and Bakhash, *The Reign of Ayatollahs,* pp. 166–175.

198. See Ali Akbar Hashemi Rafsanjani's statement on the occasion of the Congress of the Country's Cooperatives (24 Mehr

1367) and sermon at the Friday Prayer (28 Mordad 1367) in *Kayhan-e Hava*ʾi (4 Aban 1367), p. 10, and (2 Shahrivar 1367), p. 9, respectively.

199. All references to the Constitution are taken from an English translation given in Ismael, *Iran and Iraq,* pp. 142–186.

200. Sohrab Behdad, "The Political Economy of Islamic Planning in Iran," in Amirahmadi and Parvin, *Post-Revolutionary Iran,* pp. 107–125; Amirahmadi, "Middle-Class Revolutions," pp. 225–244; and *Gozaresh* (1363), vol. 1.

201. Interviews, 1986, 1987, and 1988. See also *Kayhan-e Hava*ʾi (30 Day 1366), p. 2 and 8. See also Hooshang Amirahmadi, "The State and Territorial Social Justice"; "Imam Khomeini on Internal Affairs," *Economic and Political Bulletin* 35, no. 3 (17 November 1988): 3–4; Behdad, "The Political Economy of Islamic Planning," pp. 107–125; and Amirahmadi, "Middle-Class Revolutions," pp. 225–244.

202. *Gozaresh Az Comoucioun Khas-e Rasidegi beh Barname-he Panjsaleh beh Majles-e Showra-ye Eslami* [Report of the Special Commission to Investigate the Five-Year Plan to the Islamic Consultative Assembly], no. 1, 4/9/1364 (Tehran: Islamic Consultative Assembly, Second Period, Year Two, 1354–1365).

203. *The Summary of Views and Directives of the Economic Council on the Quantitative Goals of Economic-Social Development in the Islamic Republic of Iran for 1361–1381, Approved 30/1/1361* (Tehran: Plan and Budget Organization, 1361), mimeograph.

204. See Ayatollah Khomeini's message on the occasion of the Third Majlis' election in *Kayhan-e Hava*ʾi (24 Farvardin 1367), p. 3; and the Ayatollah's decree concerning the formation of the Collective Determining the Exegincies of the Islamic System in *Kayhan-e Hava*ʾi (28 Bahman 1366), p. 2.

205. See *Economic and Political Bulletin* 35, no. 7 (15 December 1988): 5, 6; *Iran Focus* 2, no. 1 (January 1989): 6; Ahmad Ashraf, Interview, *Middle East Report,* no. 156 (January–February 1989): 13–18; *Kayhan-e Hava*ʾi (30 Day 1366), p. 2; *Kayhan-e Hava*ʾi (1 Tir 1367); *The Washington Report on the Middle East Affairs* (February 1988), pp. 4–6.

206. For Ayatollah Khomeini's views on this see *Kayhan-e Hava*ʾi (24 Farvardin 1367), p. 3. See also *Kayhan-e Hava*ʾi (21 Bahman 1366), p. 24; "Khomeini Supporting Prime Minister," *Eco-*

nomic and Political Bulletin 35, no. 5 (1 December 1988): 3; "Radicalism in Decline," *Iran Focus* 1, no. 2 (November 1988): 5; Ahmad Ashraf, Interview, *Middle East Report;* Behdad, "The Political Economy of Islamic Planning in Iran," pp. 107–125; Amirahmadi, "Middle-Class Revolutions," pp. 225–244.

207. "Report of the Prime Minister about the War, and Economic, and Executive difficulties," *Kayhan-e Hava᾽i* (15 Tir 1367).

208. "Third Faction Takes Shape," *Iran Focus* 2, no. 1 (January 1989): 7; "Power Factions Set to Realign" and "Who Will Be the Next President and Prime Minister?" *Iran Focus* 1, no. 3 (December 1988): 6, 7–8, respectively; "Clergy Told to Live in the Present," *Iran Focus* 1, no. 2 (November 1988): 6; "Moderates Grow Stronger," *Iran Focus* 1, no. 1 (October 1988): 5; "Ayatollah Montazeri's Letter to the Prime Minister," *Economic and Political Bulletin* 35, no. 2 (10 November 1988): 3; *Kayhan-e Hava᾽i* (30 Day 1366), p. 8; and statement by Hashemi Rafsanjani in *Kayhan-e Hava᾽i* (2 Day 1366), p. 10.

209. See Hashemi Rafsanjani's Friday Sermon in *Kayhan-e Hava᾽i* (30 Day 1366), p. 8. The author is grateful to Dr. Paul Sprachman for translating the passage for this book.

210. On the recent debates between the two factions see *Kayhan-e Hava᾽i* (30 Day 1366), p. 8; (21 Bahman 1366), p. 24; (2 Day 1366). p. 10; (23 Day 1366), pp. 2 and 24; (30 Day 1366), pp. 2, 3, 4, 8; (7 Bahman 1366), p. 23; (24 Farvardin 1364), p. 3; and (12 Esfand 1366), p. 3.

211. See Claude van England, "Iran Uses Troops on Domestic Unrest," *Christian Science Monitor* (3 June 1988).

212. See, e.g., Hashemi Rafsanjani's Friday prayer sermon in *Kayhan-e Hava᾽i* (31 Farvardin 1367), pp. 8–9. See also his speech in the Parliament in *Kayhan-e Hava᾽i* (23 Day 1366), p. 24.

213. On the *fetvas* (the need for them and interpretations by the government officials and religious leaders in the country), see *Kayhan-e Hava᾽i* (23 Day 1366), pp. 2 and 24; (30 Day 1366), pp. 2, 3, 4, 8, 31; (2 Day 1366), pp. 4, 10, 30; (7 Bahman 1366), p. 23; and (28 Bahman 1366), p. 2.

214. *Kayhan-e Hava᾽i* (28 Bahman 1366), p. 2.

215. "Power Factions Set to Realign," *Iran Focus* 1, no. 3 (December 1988): 7–8; "Reconstruction Policies Clarified," *Iran Focus*

1, no. 2 (November 1988): 8–10; "Imam Khomeini on Reconstruction," *Economic and Political Bulletin* 35, no. 2 (10 November 1988): 23; and "Ansari's Letter to Imam; Imam's Answer," *Economic and Political Bulletin* 35, no. 5 (1 December 1988): 21–23.

216. The Salmon Rushdie episode was widely reported in *New York Times,* (January–March 1989). See e.g., Youssef M. Ibrahim, "Europeans Recall Envoys from Iran over Rushdie Case," *New York Times* (21 February 1989), pp. A1, A8; Thomas L. Friedman, "Bush Finds Threat to Murder Author 'Deeply Offensive'," *New York Times* (22 February 1989), pp. A1, A7; and Youssef M. Ibrahim, "Khomeini Assails Western Response to Rushdie Affairs," *New York Times* (23 February 1989), pp. A1, A15. "Khomeini Calls for Slaying of Criticized Novel's Author," *New York Times* (29 January 1989), pp. A1–A10; and Craig R. Whitney, "Britain in Talk Aimed at Iran, Calls Rushdie Book Offensive," *New York Times* (3 March 1989), pp. A1–A6.

217. See Elaine Sciolino, "Teheran Finds War Was Easier to Make Than a Stable Peace," *New York Times* (2 June 1989).

218. For the texts of Ayatollah Montazeri's letter of resignation and Ayatollah Khomeini's acceptance, see *Iran Times* (11 Farvardin 1368), p. 1. Reasons for the dismissal of Ayatollah Montazeri were outlined in a letter by Ayatollah Khomeini's son, Hojjatol Islam Ahmad Khomeini, published in *Kayhan* daily (26 Urdibehesht 1368), pp. 17–20 (repetitive pages).

219. In Iran, the most influential ideologues of the Islamic movement were Ali Shariʿti (1933–1977) and Morteza Motahhari (1920–1979). However, radical Shariʿti had died before the Revolution and centrist Motahhari was assassinated in 1 May 1979, well after he had established himself as the most influential ideologue of the Islamic Republic after Ayatollah Khomeini. Among their influential writings, see Morteza Motahhari, *Moghadameh-ʾi Bar Jehanbini-ye Islami* [An Introduction to the Islamic World Outlook] (Qum, Iran: Sadra Publications, n.d. Part of the book is also available in translation, *Fundamental of Islamic Thought,* trans. R. Campbell (Berkeley, CA: Mizan Press, 1982); Morteza Motahhari, *Elal-e Grayesh Be Maddigari* [The Causes of Attraction to Materialism] (Qum, Iran: 1357); Ali Shariʿti, *On the Sociology of Islam,* trans. Hamid Algar (Berkeley, CA: Mizan Press, 1979); Ali Shariʿti, *From Where We Shall Begin,* trans. F. Marjani (Houston: Book Distribution Press, 1980); Ali Shariʿti, *Jahatgiri-ye Tabaghati-ye Islam* [The Class Orientation of Islam] (Tehran: Office of Ali Shariʿti Press,

1980); Ali Shari'ti, *Marxism and Other Western Fallacies*, trans. R. Campbell (Berkeley, CA: Mizan Press, 1980); and Ali Shari'ti, *Che Bayad Kard* [What Is to Be Done] (Houston: Islamic Student Association Press, n.d.). On the modern Islamic movement elsewhere, see *Islam and Politics*, a special issue of *Third World Quarterly* 10, no. 2 (April 1988); and Kalim Saddiqui (ed.), *Issues in Islamic Movement* (London: The Open Press, 1983 (in several volumes).

220. For the complete text of Ayatollah Khomeini's political will, see *Kayhan-e Hava'i* (24 Khordad 1368), pp. 1–7 (centerfold). For a well-balanced description of what Ayatollah Khomeini stood for, see Shaul Bakhash, "What Khomeini Did," *New York Review of Books* 36, no. 12 (July 20, 1989), pp. 16–19. For a sample of Ayatollah Khomeini's extensive writings see *Islam and Revolution*, trans. and annotation Hamid Algar (Berkeley, CA: Mizan Press, 1981).

221. See *Kayhan-e Hava'i* (25 Aban 1367), p. 3.

222. In a press conference in 1986, Hashemi Rafsanjani pointed out that: "If these two [main] factions were in the West, they would have become two parties, but here they have not become so." See *Iran Times* (30 Khordad 1365), p. 2. The idea of a two-party system was also raised following the dissolution of the Islamic Republic Party in June 1987.

223. Reprinted in Akbar Khalili, *Gam Be Gam Ba Enghelab* [Step by Step with the Revolution] (Tehran: *Soroush*, 1360), pp. 114–116 (a publication of the Radio and Television Organization of the Islamic Republic of Iran).

224. Amirahmadi, "Middle-Class Revolutions."

225. See *Summary of the Preliminary Report on Determination of the Economic-Social Policies in the Islamic Republic of Iran.*

226. *Barnameh-e Avval.*

227. *Gozaresh* 1, p. 28.

228. Ibid., pp. 28–29.

229. *Olgu Va Strategi.*

230. *Gozaresh* 1, pp. 30–31.

231. Amirahmadi, "Middle-Class Revolutions," pp. 225–244.

232. Amirahmadi, "War Damage and Reconstruction," pp. 126–149.

233. *Kayhan-e Hava'i* (4 Tir 1365), pp. 12, 13, 18; and (16 Day 1366), pp. 17, 30 (both issues carry Prime Minister Musavi's speeches in the Parliament); *Kayhan-e Hava'i* (11 Tir 1365), p. 9 (a press release from M. Zanjani, minister of Plan and Budget).

234. Razzaqi, *Eqtesad-e Iran,* pp. 196–96.

235. Interview, 1988.

236. See *Barnameh-e Avval-e Towseʿh-e Eqtesadi, Ejtemaʿi Va Farhangi-ye Jomhouri-ye Islami-ye Iran (1368–1372)* [The First Economic, Social, and Cultural Development Plan of the Islamic Republic of Iran (1989–93)] (Tehran: Ministry of Plan and Budget, 1368). See also President Rafsanjani's revisions in this plan, which was prepared under Prime Minister Musavi and submitted to the Parliament as the Bill of the First Plan in Summer 1368 (*Layeh-e Barnameh-e Avval-e Towseʿh-e Eqtesadi, Ejtemaʿi Va Farhangi-ye Jomhouri-ye Islami-ye Iran (1368–1372)* (Tehran: Ministry of Plan and Budget, Mordad 1368). The full text of President Rafsanjani's policy statement released before his election is reprinted in *Iran Times* (17 and 24 Shahrivar, 1368), p. 11. The text of the policies and priorities of Iran's Reconstruction Plan is given in *Kayhan-e Hava'i* [27 Urdibehesht 1368], p. 19). For a general description of Iran's Postwar Five-year Development Plan, see *Kayhan-e Hava'i* (16 Khordad 1368), p. 11; and *Iran Times* (3 Khordad, 1368), p. 4.

CHAPTER 3. ECONOMIC TRENDS, PROBLEMS, AND POLICIES

1. *Gozaresh* 1 (1363): 38.

2. *Economic Bulletin* 6, no. 35 (15 September 1987), p. 5.

3. Citing G. Naadi, a Parliament representative, Echo of Iran reported a 25 percent decline. See *Economic Bulletin* 6, no. 10 (10 March 1987), p. 13; and *Economic Bulletin* 6, no. 18 (12 May 1987), p. 6.

4. Michael Renner, "Determinants of the Islamic Republic's Oil Policies: Iranian Revenue Needs, the Gulf War, and the Transformation of the World Oil Market," in Hooshang Amirahmadi and M. Parvin, (eds.), *Post-Revolutionary Iran* (Boulder, Colo.: Westview Press, 1988).

5. *Kayhan-e Hava'i* (14 Urdibehesht 1367), p. 10.

6. *Gozaresh* 1 (1363), p. 38.

7. On the growth and structure of the population, see various *Statistical Yearbooks.* On figures cited in the text see *Kayhan-e Hava'i* (2 Azar 1367), p. 8; (23 Azar 1367), p. 17; and (30 Azar 1367), p. 4. Until 1988, the Islamic Republic had determined that population control was non-Islamic. Since the end of the war, however, this has changed significantly as the more pragmatist leaders, including a number of religious authorities, have argued for population control and family planning. See, for example, *Kayhan-e Hava'i* (7 Day 1367), p. 14; and (30 Azar 1367), p. 3.

8. On debates about the role of oil, see Michael Renner, "Determinants of the Islamic Republic's Oil Policies"; *Economic Bulletin* 6, no. 39 (7 October 1987), p. 1; and *Ettela'at-e Siasi-Eqtesadi* 6, no. 1 (19 Mehr 1365). The complete issue is on various aspects of the Iranian oil production and policies; see also Ebrahim Razzaqi, "Vabastegi Dar San't-e Naft Va Raha'i Az Aan" [Dependency on Oil Industry and Liberation from It], *Ettela'at-e Siasi-Eqtesadi* 1, no. 7, pp. 31–17.

9. Feriedun Fesharaki, *Revolution and Energy Policy in Iran* (London: Economist Intelligent Unit, 1982); Michael Renner, "Determinants of the Islamic Republic's Oil Policies."

10. Ibid.

11. Ibid; *Economic Bulletin* 6, no. 39 (7 October 1987); and *Economic Bulletin* 6, no. 38 (October 1987) p. 15 (press release from minister of Oil).

12. *Economic Bulletin* 6, no. 13 (7 April 1987), pp. 4–5.

13. Ibid., p. 5.

14. *Kayhan* daily (3 Shahrivar 1366): "Amalkardha'i Keh Dast-e Dawlat Ra Dar Barnamehriziha-ye Eqtesadi Mibandad" [Operations which Prevent the Government from Undertaking Economic Planning].

15. "Laws and Regulations Governing Islamic Banking in the Islamic Republic of Iran and in Pakistan," in *The Law for Usury-Free Banking* (Tehran: Bank Markazi, 1983), pp. 31–43; Shaul Bakhash, *The Reign of the Ayatollahs* (New York: Basic Books, 1984); *Economic Bulletin* 6, no. 22 (9 June 1987), pp. 2–4; and *Economic Bulletin* 6, no. 23 (16 June 1987), pp. 9–13; and Hamid Zanganeh, "Islamic Banking: Theory and Practice in Iran," paper presented at

the Sixth Annual Conference of the Center for Iranian Research and Analysis (CIRA), University of Chicago, April 1988.

16. *Tangnaha,* pp. 12–13; *Kayhan,* 3 Mordad 1366; *Economic Bulletin* 6, no. 34 (8 September 1987), pp. 4–6; and *Economic Bulletin* 6, Nos. 22 and 23 (9 and 16 June 1987).

17. In my May 1988 trip to Iran, I visited Javid interest-free foundation established in 1969, as indicated to me by its director. Others, for example, Islamic Economic Organization, Nobouvvat Foundation, and Resalat Foundation were all established during or after the Revolution. See *Kayhan-e Hava'i* (4 Aban 1367), p. 24; and (27 Mehr 1367), p. 11.

18. *Political Bulletin* 6, no. 36 (22 September 1987), p. 4. See also statements by Ghorbanali Saleh Abadi, a Parliament representative, in the open session of the Parliament on 24 Mehr 1367, printed in *Kayhan-e Hava'i* (4 Aban 1367), p. 24.

19. *Political Bulletin* 6, no. 36 (22 September 1987), p. 4; see also *Political Bulletin* 6, no. 34 (9 September 1987) for an outline of the IEO's activities.

20. *Political Bulletin* 6, no. 38 (6 October 1987), p. 8; *Political Bulletin* 6, no. 39 (13 October 1987), p. 8; and *Political Bulletin* 6, no. 40 (20 October 1987), p. 9. Examples of such "illicit" activities include (1) the foundation's deals with associates of the former regime whose properties were controlled and administered by the government organizations: "the original proprietor would donate his property to the Foundation [which is considered charitable and non-profit] on the basis of which the Foundation would claim the property and retrieve it and would then retransfer it to the original proprietor against a payment"; (2) "a 3,000 million rial cigarettes deal between the Foundation and an individual"; and (3) "the Foundation's contracts with various factories from which the Foundation bought large amounts of products pretending they were intended for the war front." The conservative opposition to the government has cited the last two instances as examples of the government's complicity with or failure to control the foundation. (See also *Resalat* daily, 22 Mehr 1366). In my discussions with director of Javid Foundation, he rejected such "baseless accusations" and asserted that the interest-free foundations are needed because "the government has failed to improve the people's income or purchasing power" and that "many depend on these foundations for credit."

21. Interview 1989; *Kayhan* daily (27–30 Aban 1368); and *Iran Times* (24 Azar 1368).

22. Interview 1989; and *Kayhan* daily (27–30 Aban 1368).

23. Hooshang Amirahmadi, "The State and Territorial Social Justice in the Post-Revolutionary Iran," *International Journal of Urban and Regional Research* 13, no. 1 (March 1989): 92–120; Val Moghadam, "Workers' and Peasants' Councils in Iran," *Monthly Review* 32, no. 5 (October 1980): 14–29; Asaf Bayat, *Workers and Revolution in Iran: A Third World Experience of Workers' Control* (London: Zed Books, 1986); Bakhash, *The Reign of the Ayatollahs;* and Hossein Bashiriyeh, *The State and Revolution in Iran, 1962–1982* (London: Croom Helm, 1984).

24. See *Tahlili Bar Amalkard-e Sherkatha-ye Mashmoul-e Qanoun-e Hefazat Va Towseᶜh-e Sanayeᶜe Iran Taht-e Poushesh-e Sazman-e Sanayeᶜe Melli-ye Iran Va Moghayseh-e Amalkard-e Anha Az Sal-e 1356 Leqayat-e 1361* [An Analysis of Operation of the Companies Subject to the Law of Protection and Expansion of Iranian Industries under the Control of the Organization of the Nationalized Industries of Iran and a Comparison of Their Operations from the year 1976 until the End of 1982] (Tehran: Ministry of Industries, Organization of the Nationalized Industries of Iran, 1362). See also Bakhash, *The Reign of the Ayatollahs,* pp. 179–180.

25. *Statistics of Large Industrial Units under the Management of Public Sector in Iran* (Tehran: Statistical Center, 1985). See also *Tangnaha,* p. 35; and *Zarfiyatha,* p. 11.

26. In 1982, about 85 percent of value added in industries (3 million units) was produced in 6,938 large-scale establishments (units employing ten or more workers). However, these large units employed less than one-third of the industrial sector's employment. The remaining two-thirds of employment in the sector was concentrated in small-scale and rural industries producing the remaining 15 percent of industrial value added. See *Zarfiyatha,* p. 11; *Tangnaha,* p. 35.

27. *Gozaresh* 2 (1363), Chapter 13, p. 26; *Zarfiyatha,* p. 11; and *Tangnaha,* p. 34.

28. *Tangnaha,* p. 32. This source puts the extent of the dependency at $6 billion, but most experts in the country suggest $7 billion to be more accurate. Interviews 1986, 1987, and 1988.

29. Interviews 1986, 1987, and 1988. See also Alireza Shaikhattar (deputy for War Affairs of Ministry of Industries), "Nagsh-e Jang Dar Taqier-e Boniadha Va Sakhtarha-ye Toulid-e Sanᶜti" [The

Role of the War in Changing the Structures and Institutions of Industrial Production], *Ettelaᶜat-e Siasi-Eqtesadi* 1, no. 4 (22 Day 1365), pp. 8–11.

30. The claim that domestic production may have saved the government some $3 billion in reduced military imports in 1986 alone is certainly exaggerated. See *Sharif* 3, no. 25 (20 Aban 1366), p. 3 (quoting *Defense and Diplomacy* and *Economist*). On the expansion of defense industries in the postrevolutionary period, see Anoushiravan Ehteshami, "Iran's Domestic Arms Industry." paper presented at the Conference on The Iranian Revolution 10 Years Later, Chatham House, London, 19–20 January 1989 (printed in *Economic and Political Bulletin* 35, no. 16 [23 February 1989]); *Iran Almanac and Book of Facts 1987*, 18 ed. (published by Echo of Iran); *Showra*, no. 45 (Mehr–Azar 1367); *Sharif Newsletter* 3, no. 25 (20 Aban 1366) and no. 28 (30 Bahman 1366); Prime Minister M. H. Musavi's press release in *Kayhan-e Havaʾi* (16 Day 1366), pp. 16–17; and Armin Pourhamid, "Hal, Iyn Salah-e Irani Ast Keh Bar Doshman-e Motajavez Miqorrad" [Now, This Is the Iran-Made Armaments That Is Storming the Aggressive Enemy], *Kayhan-e Havaʾi* (26 Esfand, 1366, special 1367 New Year issue), pp. 6, 14.

31. *MERIP Middle East Report* (January–February 1987), p. 14.

32. Interviews 1987, 1988, and 1989; Ehteshami, "Iran's Domestic Arms Industry." See also *Kayhan* daily (27 Bahman 1362); *Ettelaᶜat* daily (29 Day 1364); *Kayhan* daily (27 Urdibehesht 1365); and *Showra*, no. 45, pp. 28–31. This last source (quoting Rafigh Doust the RGC minister speaking in the Majlis on 21 Shahrivar 1367) gives the figure of 17,500 for the number of people working in the RGC's military industries.

33. Interviews 1987, 1988 and 1989; Ehteshami, "Iran's Domestic Arms Industry." See also *Saf* magazine (Bahman 1366 and Farvardin 1367); *Kayhan* daily (4 Mehr 1363, 7 Urdibehesht 1365); and *Showra*, no. 45, pp. 29–30.

34. *Gozaresh* 2 (1363), Chapter 12, pp. 22–23.

35. Ibid., Chapter 17, pp. 4–10, 18–21.

36. See *Barrasi-ye Mahdoudeh-e 120 Kilometri-ye Tehran Va Vahedha-ye Qair-e Mojaz* [A Study of Tehran's 120-Kilometer City Limit and the Illegal (Economic) Units] (Tehran: Ministry of Plan and Budget, The Group for the Study of the Occasional Projects, 1362).

37. Interview 1986. The figure was quoted to me by an official of the Ministry of Plan and Budget.

38. Sohrab Behdad, "Foreign Exchange Gap, Structural Constraints, and the Political Economy of Exchange Rate Determination in Iran," *International Journal of Middle East Studies* 20 (1988): 15.

39. Prime Minister M. H. Musavi's speech in the Parliament, printed in *Kayhan-e Hava²i* (16 Day 1366), p. 17.

40. *Gozaresh* 1 (1363), pp. 43–44 and 2 (1363), Chapter 13; *Economic Bulletin* 6, no. 35 (15 September 1987), p. 5; and *Economic Bulletin* 6, no. 11 (17 March 1987), p. 4.

41. *Tangnaha*, p. 33.

42. For an early attempt to design a coherent industrial policy see *Ahdaf Va Siasatha-ye San²ti* [Industrial Objectives and Policies] (Tehran: Ministry of Industries, Joint Council for Planning of Industrial Sector, 1361). On the labor law, see *Majmou²he Qavanin Va Moqararat-e Kar Va Ta²min-e Ejtema²i* [A Collection of Labor and Social Security Laws and Regulations), 4th printing with revisions and additions, no. 22 (Tehran: Institute for Labor and Social Security, Shahrivar, 1367).

43. *Economic Bulletin* 6, no. 20 (26 May 1987), p. 6; and *Economic Bulletin* 6, no. 39 (7 October 1986), p. 11.

44. Prime Minister M. H. Musavi's speech in the Parliament printed in *Kayhan-e Hava²i* (16 Day 1366), p. 17.

45. On the struggle over the land tenure, see Bakhash, the *Reign of the Ayatollahs,* pp. 195–216; Bashiriyeh, *The State and Revolution in Iran,* Chapter 6.

46. On the council's reasons for rejecting the bill, see *Ettela²at* daily (25 Urdibehesht 1364), p. 15.

47. *Negareshi Bar Layeh-ye Vagozari Va Ehya²-e Arazi (Band-e Jim)* [A Look at the Bill for Land Redistribution and Reclamation (Section G)] (Muslim Student Association, United States and Canada, 1360), pp. 26–67; *Ettela²at* (28 Aban 1363); p. 14; and *Ettela²at* (19 Aban 1363), p. 16. (See also these sources on the difficulties encountered by the Seven-Person Council.)

48. For a comparison of the original and modified bills see *Ettela²at* (25 Urdibehesht 1364), p. 15 and *Ettela²at* (28 Urdibehesht 1364), p. 18. The rule of "two-third majority" was ordered by Aya-

tollah Khomeini upon the request of certain Parliament representatives, including the Speaker Hashemi Rafsanjani, to limit power of the Council of Guardians in voting against the bills considered "essential and necessary" for the Islamic Republic.

49. *Ettela^cat* (28 Urdibehesht 1364), p. 18; *Ettela^cat* (25 Urdibehesht 1364), p. 15; and *Ettela^cat* (23 Urdibehesht 1364), p. 18.

50. *Faslnameh,* p. 61; *Iran Times,* (6 June 1986), p. 12; *Kayhan-e Hava'i* (17 Day 1365), p. 24.

51. *Kayhan-e Hava'i* (16 Day 1366), p. 17. *Kayhan-e Hava'i* (18 Khordad 1367), p. 3 (on the prime minister's statements about the economy); and *Kayhan-e Hava'i* (29 Tir 1367), p. 10.

52. *Barnameh-e Avval* 1 (on objectives and strategies). See also Prime Minister Musavi's speech in the Parliament printed in *Kayhan-e Hava'i* (16 Day 1366), p. 17; *Kayhan-e Hava'i* (11 Tir 1365), p. 13; and the press release from M. Zanjani, minister of Plan and Budget, printed in *Kayhan-e Hava'i* (4 Tir 1365), p. 9.

53. Prime Minister Musavi is quoted to have expressed the statement in a meeting of planners and policy makers in the Ministry of Plan and Budget. Interview 1986.

54. It is doubtful if agriculture is *really* the "axis" of the Islamic Republic's development policy as claimed. Indeed, the tendency that defends this strategy has accused the government of making agriculture a "constitutional monarch" in a country where "industry rules" as the prime minister. Interview 1986.

55. *Tangnaha,* pp. 28–32.

56. Hosain Azimi, "Budgeh Va Towse^ch-e Eqtesadi Dar Iran" [Budget and Economic Development in Iran], *Ettela^cat-e Siasi-Eqtesadi* 2, no. 5 (Bahman 1366). See also *Ettela^cat-e Siasi-Eqtesadi* 4, no. 2 (Aban and Azar 1368), pp. 47 and 59.

57. Ibid.

58. *Salnameh-e Amari* (1363), p. 786; and *Taraznameh.*

59. *Gozaresh* 1 (1365), p. 79.

60. *Taraznameh* (1363), pp. 212–213, 50, 68, and 73.

61. *Majaleh,* p. 86.

62. On the revised plan, its short history and processes, see *Gozaresh* 1 (1363), pp. 28–33.

63. *Gozaresh* 1 (1363), p. 39. See also here Table 2 on p. 107.

64. *Economic Bulletin* 6, no. 18 (12 May 1987), p. 5.

65. Azimi, "Budgeh Va Towseᶜh-e Eqtesadi Dar Iran," p. 33.

66. Summaries of annual budgets are reported in *Kayhan* and *Ettelaᶜat* dailies. For the most recent budgets, see *Ettelaᶜat* (7 Azar 1364), pp. 7, 8, 13; *Kayhan-e Havaʾi* (14 Azar 1363), pp. 10–11; (17 Day 1365), pp. 24–25; (27 Esfand 1365), pp. 24–25; (19 Farvardin 1366), p. 24; (19 Esfand 1366), pp. 24–25; (26 Esfand 1366), pp. 24–25; and *Economic Bulletin* 6, no. 35 (15 September 1987); no. 19 (19 May 1987); no. 11 (17 March 1987); no. 20 (26 May 1987).

67. A good discussion on the evolution of the structure of the Islamic Republic's budgets is given in *Ettelaᶜat-e Siasi-Eqtesadi* 1, no. 2 (Aban 1365), pp. 3–10.

68. Prime Minister Musavi's speeches in the Parliament, printed in *Kayhan-e Havaʾi* (17 Day 1365), p. 24; and (16 Day 1366), pp. 16–17 and 30. See also the press release from the minister of Plan and Budget, printed in *Kayhan-e Havaʾi* (17 Day 1365), p. 11.

69. *Economic Bulletin* 6, no. 11 (17 March 1987), p. 4.

70. *Kayhan-e Havaʾi* (16 Day 1366), p. 17.

71. *Economic Bulletin* 6, no. 11 (17 March 1987), p. 5.

72. Note that the figure for the war refers to its share in the general budget, not to total expenditures. War expenditures are also included in current and development funds. The declining trend in the share of the war expenditures in the general budget may also be due to the fact that the government has in recent years increasingly relied on domestic military production, as a result of which substantial savings have been gained from reduced military imports. See note 30.

73. Prime Minister Musavi's speech in the Parliament, printed in *Kayhan-e Havaʾi* (16 Day 1366), p. 30.

74. *Gozaresh* 2 (1363), Chapter 5, p. 12.

75. Ibid., pp. 13–14; *Khorasan* daily (20 Azar 1367). See also *Kayhan-e Havaʾi* (28 Day 1367), p. 14.

76. *Kayhan-e Havaʾi* (17 Day 1365), p. 24. Beginning in 1987, the government has instituted new fixed taxes and raised the existing

ones, largely on industries producing motor vehicles. See *Economic Bulletin* 6, no. 15 (21 April 1987), p. 14; and no. 35 (15 September 1987), p. 8.

77. *Kayhan-e Hava'i* (16 Day 1366), p. 30.

78. M. Sa'i, "Negareshi Bar Budgeh-e Dawlat Dar Sal-e 1366" [A Look at the Government's Budget in 1987], *Ettela'at-e Siasi-Eqtesadi* 1, no. 7 (Farvardin 1366), p. 38–41.

79. Azimi, "Budgeh Va Towse'h-e Eqtesadi Dar Iran," p. 34. See also *Kayhan-e Hava'i* (28 Day 1367), p. 14.

80. The speech by S. Khalkhali, a Parliament Representative, opposing the Government's 1988 budget, printed in *Kayhan-e Hava'i*, (19 Esfand 1366), p. 25.

81. Prime Minister Musavi's speech in the Parliament at the submission of the 1987 budget, printed in *Kayhan-e Hava'i* (17 Day 1365), p. 24.

82. Azimi, "Budgeh Va Towse'h-e Eqtesadi Dar Iran," p. 34.

83. *Political Bulletin* 6, no. 10 (10 March 1987), p. 8; *Ettela'at* (14 Esfand 1364); and *Economic Bulletin* 6, no. 10 (10 March 1987), p. 13 (where G. Naadi, Parliament representative, claims that only half of the 1365 budget projections have been realized).

84. *Kayhan-e Hava'i* (19 Esfand 1366), p. 242; and *Economic and Political Bulletin* 35, no. 3 (17 November 1988), p. 4.

85. *Gozaresh* 2 (1363), Chapter 5, p. 15.

86. *Faslnameh*, no. 6 (1365), p. 189. See also *Gozaresh* (1365), Chapter 10, pp. 15, 26. *Resalat* daily (26 January 1989) revealed that the government introduced a "secret amendment" to the 1368 Budget Bill relating to "the government's new loan from the Central Bank. It appears that the government has asked the bank for a loan many times as much as it owes the bank." Such an amendment, wrote *Resalat*, never appeared during the war. The daily questions the need for the loan in the postwar when the government's expenditures supposedly should be smaller. See *Economic and Political Bulletin* 35, no. 14 (9 February 1989), p. 4.

87. The figure 19 percent is given as the growth rate of the private liquidity in 1986. See *Gozaresh* 2 (1365), Chapter 10, p. 15. See also *Economic Bulletin* 6, no. 10 (10 March 1987), p. 13; *Political Bulletin* 6, no. 36 (22 September 1987), p. 4; no. 38 (6 October

1987), p. 8; no. 39 (13 October 1987), p. 8; and no. 40 (20 October 1987), p. 9; and *Resalat* daily (20, 21, and 22 Mehr 1366).

88. Azimi, "Budgeh Va Towseᶜh-e Eqtesadi Dar Iran," p. 31.

89. The figure was reported by G. Naadi, a Parliament representative, quoting a "recent census" and was subsequently disputed by the deputy minister of Economics and Finance who put the rate of inflation for the year at 13 percent. See *Political Bulletin*, 6, no. 10 (10 March 1987), p. 8; and *Economic Bulletin* 6, no. 11 (17 March 1987), p. 4.

90. *Economic Bulletin* 6, no. 29 (28 July 1987), p. 2.

91. The author's personal observation during his visit to Iran in May 1988.

92. *Gozaresh* 2 (1363), Chapter 7; and *Iran Dar Aʾineh-e Amar,* no. 5 (1364), pp. 201–205.

93. Ibid.

94. *Gozaresh* 2 (1363), Chapter 5, pp. 13–14.

95. Saeed Moshiri, "Tajrobeh-e qeimat Gozari Va Natayej-e Eqtesadi-ye Aan Dar Iran" [The Experience of Price Control in Iran and Its Economic Consequences], *Barnameh Va Towseᶜh,* no. 10 (Summer 1366), pp. 103–131.

96. *Economic Bulletin* 6, no. 39 (13 October 1987), pp. 7–8. The black market price for a single tire in May 1988 was 250,000 rials. The author's observation during his visit to Iran.

97. "Tuziᶜe Sahih-e Niazha-ye Asasi-ye Mardom Dar Grow-e Mahar-e Naqdinegi Va Tavarroum" [The Correct Distribution of the People's Basic Needs in the Grip of Liquidity and Inflation], Interview by M. Islami Nasab, deputy for Commerce Ministry, *Ettelaᶜat-e Siasi-Eqtesadi* 1, no. 8 (Urdibehesh 1366), pp. 4–9.

98. *Gozaresh* 2 (1363), Chapter 6, p. 15.

99. Masᶜoud Nili, "Barrasi-ye Masʾleh-e Tavarroum Dar Iran" [The Study of Inflation in Iran], *Barnameh Va Towseᶜh,* no. 9 (Spring 1366), pp. 70–92.

100. *Economic Bulletin* 6, no. 29 (28 July 1987), pp. 2–3; no. 39 (13 October 1987), pp. 8–9.

101. *Political Bulletin* 6, no. 39 (13 October 1987), pp. 8–9.

102. *Economic Bulletin* 6, no. 29 (28 July 1987), p. 2; *Gozaresh* 2 (1363), Chapter 7, p. 11.

103. *Economic Bulletin* 6, no. 39 (13 October 1987), p. 5.

104. *Economic Bulletin* 6, no. 29 (July 1987), p. 2–3. See also *Kayhan-e Hava⁾i* (28 Day 1367), p. 14.

105. Ebrahim Razzaqi, *Eqtesad-e Iran,* [Iranian Economy] (Tehran: Nashr-e Nay, 1367), pp. 559–560; and Saeed Moshiri, "Tajrobeh-e Qeimat Gozari Va Natayej-e Eqtesadi-ye An Dar Iran," *Barnameh Va Towseᶜh,* no. 10 (Summer 1366), pp. 111–112.

106. *Economic Bulletin* 6, no. 29 (28 July 1987), p. 3.

107. *Gozaresh* 2 (1363), Chapter 10, p. 26.

108. Nili, "Barrasi-ye Mas⁾leh-e Tavarroum Dar Iran," pp. 77–78.

109. *Economic Bulletin* 6, no. 39 (13 October 1987), pp. 7–8; *Kayhan* daily (22–25 Shahrivar 1366).

110. Habibulah Niknam, "Naqsh-e Afzayesh-e Daramad-e Naft Dar Sheklgiri-ye Tavarroum Va Shetab-e Nerkh-e Roshd-e Aan" [The Role of Increased Oil Income in Generating Inflation and in Its Accelerated Growth Rate], *Ettelaᶜat-e Siasi-Eqtesadi* 1, no. 10 (Tir 1366), pp. 34–37.

111. *Economic Bulletin* 6, no. 33 (1 September 1987); and no. 34 (8 September 1987).

112. *Economic Bulletin* 6, no. 39 (13 October 1987), p. 5.

113. *Economic Bulletin* 6, no. 29 (28 July 1987), p. 3.

114. Nili, "Barrasi-ye Mas⁾leh-e Tavarroum Dar Iran," p. 73. See also *Economic Bulletin* 6, no. 41 (27 October 1987), p. 3; *Kayhan* daily (21 Khordad 1366); and *Political Bulletin* 6, no. 23 (16 June 1987).

115. *Economic Bulletin* 6, no. 41 (27 October 1987), p. 2.

116. Nili, "Barrasi-ye Mas⁾leh-e Tavarroum Dar Iran," p. 81.

117. *Economic Bulletin* 6, no. 39 (13 October 1987), p. 5.

118. Prime minister's press release, printed in *Kayhan-e Hava⁾i* (16 Day 1366), pp. 17, 30.

119. "System-e Sahmiyeh Bandi-ye Kalaha; Zaroratha Va Noqat-e Za⟨f⟩" [The Rationing System of Goods; Necessities and the Weak Points], *Ettela⟨at-e Siasi-Eqtesadi* 1, no. 10 (Tir 1366), pp. 21–25.

120. *Economic Bulletin* 6, no. 31 (18 August 1987), pp. 5–6 (tables).

121. *Iran Focus* quotes Deputy Prime Minister Hamid Mirzadeh, reporting the achievements of the Price and Inflation Control Central Commission at a press conference on 14 September 1988, as saying that: (1) "Out of 2.7 million economic units inspected, 1.1 million had been offenders, of which 130,000 were punished"; and (2) "Nineteen cases of major embezzlement and illegal profiteering involved Government or Government-affiliated institutions." According to *Iran Focus*, however, the cases of embezzlement were discovered by the Intelligence Ministry, not the commission. See *Iran Focus* 1, no. 1 (October 1988), p. 7.

122. *Ettela⟨at* daily (14 Esfand 1365); and *Economic Bulletin* 6, no. 31 (18 August 1987), pp. 5–6 (tables).

123. Prime minister's speech in the Parliament, printed in *Kayhan-e Hava⟩i* (16 Day 1366), p. 30.

124. *Political Bulletin* 6, no. 30 (4 August 1987), p. 11.

125. *Economic Bulletin* 6, no. 29 (28 July 1987), p. 3.

126. *Economic Bulletin* 6, no. 39 (13 October 1987), p. 5.

127. *Economic Bulletin* 6, no. 29 (28 July 1987), p. 3.

128. *Economic Bulletin* 6, no. 32 (25 August 1987), p. 5.

129. *Economic Bulletin* 6, no. 39 (13 October 1987), p. 8.

130. On writing this section on unemployment and sectoral employment shifts, I have consulted the following publications: Mohammad Alizadeh, *Vizhegiha-ye Rahbordi-ye Bazaar-e Kar-e Iran (Kar Va Bikari) Dar Dahe-ye 1355–65* [Specificity Trends of Labor Market in Iran (Employment and Unemployment) in the Decade of 1976–86] (Tehran: Ministry of Plan and Budget, Office of Population and Human Resources, 1367); *Tazehha-ye Amari* [New in Statistics] (Tehran: Statistical Center, 1366); *Sarshemari-ye Nefous Va Maskan 1355* [Census of Population and Housing] and *Sarshemari-ye Nefous Va Maskan 1365* (Tehran: Statistical Center); *Gozideh-e Masa⟩l-e Eqtesadi-Ejtema⟨i* [A Selection of Economic-Social Issues],

nos. 65, 66, 71, 73 (Tehran: Statistical Center); *Natayej-e Tarh-e Amari-ye Barrasi-ye Masaʾl-e Kolli-ye Nirou-ye Ensani Va Eshteghal-e Porseshnameh-e Khanevar-e Sal-e 1361, Manateq-e Shahri-ye Keshvar* [Results of the Statistical Project Investigating the General Issues of Human Resources and Employment of the Household Survey 1982, Country's Urban Places] (Tehran: Office of Human Resources Statistics, Ministry of Labor and Social Affairs, 1362); *Fehrest-e Kargaha-ye Shahri-ye 1364 Keshvar* [List of Country's Urban Workshops] (Tehran: Office of Human Resources Statistics, Ministry of Labor and Social Affairs, 1365); Mohammad Alizadeh, *Jamʿiyat, Manabeʿ, Va Towseʿh Dar Iran* [Population, Resources, and Development in Iran] (Tehran: Office of Population and Human Resources, Ministry of Plan and Budget, 1365); and *Barrasi-ye Eshteghal Dar Bakhsh-e Sanayʿ Sangin (Grouh-e Khoudrou)* [Survey of Employment in Heavy Industry Sector (Vehicles Group)] (Tehran: Office of Population and Human Resources, Ministry of Plan and Budget, 1365).

131. *Gozideh-e Mataleb-e Amari*, no. 13 (Day–Bahman 1365); *Political Bulletin* 6, no. 10 (10 March 1987), p. 8; *Economic Bulletin* 6, no. 11 (17 March 1987), p. 4; and *Sarshemari-ye Nefous Va Maskan* (1355 and 1365).

132. *Political Bulletin* 6, no. 10 (10 March 1987), p. 8.

133. For slightly different figures see *Gozaresh* 1 (1363), pp. 50–51.

134. Alizadeh, *Vizhegiha-ye Rahbordi-ye Bazaar-e Kar-e Iran*, pp. 5, 10, 15; and *Gozideh-e Masaʾl-e Eqtesadi-Ejtemaʿi* (1365).

135. Alizadeh, *Vizhegiha-ye Rahbordi-ye Bazaar-e Kar-e Iran*, pp. 10–13, 47–50.

136. *Tangnaha*, pp. 16–17. For a somewhat different figure and a detailed study of labor market in 1976–86 period, see Alizadeh, *Vizhegiha-ye Rahbordi-ye Bazaar-e Kar-e Iran*. On women's employment see Val Moghadam, "Women, Work, and Ideology in the Islamic Republic," *International Journal of Middle East Studies* 20, no. 2 (May 1988), pp. 221–243.

137. Alizadeh, *Vizhegiha-ye Rahbordi-ye Bazaar-e Kar-e Iran*, pp. 5–6, 15, 20.

138. *Sarshemari-ye Nefous Va Maskan* (1355 and 1365); Alizadeh, *Vizhegiha-ye Rahbordi-ye Bazaar-e Kar-e Iran*, pp. 20–26; *Barrasi-ye Eshteghal Dar Bakhsh-e Sanayʿ Sangin (Grouh-e Khoudrou)*; and *Gozideh-e Masaʾl-e Eqtesadi-Ejtemaʿi*.

139. Alizadeh, *Vizhegiha-ye Rahbordi-ye Bazaar-e Kar-e Iran*, pp. 27–30; and *Salnameh* (various issues).

140. *Sarshemari-ye Omoumi-ye Keshavarzi, 1367* [General Census of Agriculture, 1988] (Tehran: Statistical Center, 1367). See also *Gozideh-e Mataleb-e Amari* [Selected Statistical Subject] (Tehran: Statistical Center, no. 20, Shahrivar 1367).

141. *Tazehha-ye Amari* (1366); *Fehrest-e Kargaha-ye Shahri-ye 1364 Keshvar* (1365); *Natayej-e Tarh-e Amari-ye Barrasi-ye Masaᶜl-e Kolli-ye Nirou-ye Ensani Va Eshteghal-e Porseshnameh-e Khanevar-e Sal-e 1361, Manateq-e Shahri-ye Keshvar;* and *Barrasi-ye Eshteghal Dar Bakhsh-e Sanayᶜ Sangin (Grouh-e Khoudrou).*

142. *Political Bulletin* 6, no. 11 (17 March 1987), p. 5.

143. Alizadeh, *Vizhegiha-ye Rahbordi-ye Bazaar-e Kar-e Iran*, p. 8.

144. Ibid., p. 7.

145. Hosain Asimi, "Budgeh Va Towseᶜh-e Eqtesadi Dar Iran," p. 36.

146. Sohrab Behdad, "Winners and Losers of the Iranian Revolution: A Study in Income Distribution," in *International Journal of Middle East Studies* 1, no. 3 (August 1989), p. 330.

147. *Political Bulletin* 6, no. 11 (17 March 1987), p. 3. Quoting *Resalat* daily (14 Esfand 1987).

148. Ibid.

149. *Kayhan* daily (28 Esfand 1364), p. 18.

150. Quoted in *Political Bulletin* 6, no. 23 (16 June 1987). See also *Kayhan* daily (21 Khordad 1366); and *Economic Bulletin* 6, no. 41 (27 October 1987).

151. *Economic Bulletin* 6, no. 41 (27 October 1987), p. 2. On decline in purchasing power of workers, also see *Economic Bulletin* 6, no. 39 (13 October 1987), p. 5. In my May 1988 trip to Iran, I asked a university professor in Tehran how, given the generally low-level of wages and salaries, the people could afford to pay for the exorbitantly priced commodities. His reply may be summarized as follows: (1) many middle- and lower-class people increasingly have been selling their home appliances and furniture; (2) many have reduced their consumption level and others have changed their diets toward commodities offered in rationed markets and at official

prices; (3) many have used the last rials of their savings and others have incurred debts at alarming rates; and (4) most such debts are owed to interest-free Islamic financial institutions (*sanduqha-ye gharzulhasaneh*) such as Islamic Economic Organization and Javid and Nobouvvat Foundations. Private debt to banks have also increased.

152. *Gozaresh* 2 (1363), Chapter 13, p. 28. The figures for 1984 used in calculations were for the first six months of the year.

153. *Economic Bulletin* 6, no. 39 (13 October 1987), p. 5 and *Political Bulletin* 6, no. 9 (3 March 1987), pp. 14–15.

154. *Kayhan-e Hava²i* (Day 1367), p. 14.

155. Personal observations and interview 1988.

156. *Gozaresh* 1 (1363), pp. 56, 58.

157. Azimi, "Budgeh Va Towseᶜh-e Eqtesadi Dar Iran," p. 32.

158. *Gozaresh* 1 (1363), pp. 7. On income distribution under the Shah's regime, see Ahmad Jabbari, "Economic Factors in Iran's Revolution: Poverty, Inequality, and Inflation," in A. Jabbari and R. Olson (eds.), *Iran: Essays on a Revolution in the Making* (Lexington, Ky.: Mazda Publishers, 1981); and M. H. Pesaran, "Income Distribution and Its Major Determinants in Iran," in J. W. Jacqz (ed.), *Iran: Past, Present, and Future* (Aspen, Colo.: Aspen Institute for Humanistic Studies, 1976).

159. *Gozaresh* 1 (1363), p. 55; and *Tangnaha*, p. 20. A coefficient below 0.25 is considered "normal" but one between 0.25 and 0.40 indicates very unequal distribution.

160. *Tangnaha*, p. 21.

161. Ibid. This source gives 2.8 and 4.7 as ratios of urban to rural consumption expenditures for 1971 and 1977, respectively. The figures seem to be misstated.

162. Ibid.; see also Azimi, "Budgeh Va Towseᶜh-e Eqtesadi Dar Iran," p. 36.

163. *Gozaresh* 1 (1363), p. 55; see also Prime Minister Musavi's speech in the Parliament, printed in *Kayhan-e Hava²i* (15 Aban 1364), p. 15.

164. See Editorial in *Ettelaᶜat-e Siasi-Eqtesadi* 1, no. 8 (Urdibehesht 1366), p. 3.

165. *Tarh-e Moghadamati-ye Harakatha-ye Kolli-ye Eqtesad-e Keshvar Ba^cd Az Jang-e Tahmili* [A Preliminary Look at the Overall Trends in the Country's Economy after the Imposed War] (Tehran: Ministry of Plan and Budget, n.d.).

166. Azimi, "Budgeh Va Towse^ch-e Eqtesadi Dar Iran," p. 32.

167. "Amalkardha'i Keh Dast-e Dawlat Ra Dar Barnameh-riziha-ye Eqtesadi Mibandad" [Practices that Handicap the Government in Planning the Economy], *Kayhan* daily (3 Shahrivar 1366).

168. Reported in *Iran Times* (7 Aban 1367), p. 5. See also *Iran Times* (10 Tir 1367).

169. *Political Bulletin* 6, no. 10 (10 March 1987), p. 8; *Economic Bulletin* 6, no. 41 (27 October 1987), p. 5; *Political Bulletin* 6, no. 11 (17 March 1987), p. 3.

170. *Economic Bulletin* 6, no. 41 (27 October 1987), p. 5; *Economic Bulletin* 6, no. 39 (October 1987), p. 5.

171. *Gozaresh* 1 (1363), pp. 57–58.

172. Ibid., p. 58.

173. Hooshang Amirahmadi, "Popular Movements, Incidental Factors, and the State Measures for Regional Development in the Islamic Republic of Iran," *Review of Urban and Regional Development Studies* 1, no. 1 (January 1989), pp. 47–64.

174. *Political Bulletin* 6, no. 11 (17 March 1987), p. 5.

175. *Kayhan-e Hava'i* (30 Day 1366), p. 2; (24 Farvardin 1367), p. 3; (28 Bahman 1366), p. 2; and (30 Day 1366), p. 8.

176. Amirahmadi, "The State and Territorial Social Justice."

177. Hooshang Amirahmadi and Farhad Atash, "Dynamics of Provincial Development and Disparity in Iran: 1956–1984," in *Third World Planning Review* 9, no. 2 (May 1987), pp. 167–177.

178. Amirahmadi, "The State and Territorial Social Justice."

179. Plan and Budget Organization, *Barnameh-e Avval*, Op. cit.; M. Kamiar, "Changes in Spatial Patterns of Development in Iran: An Example of Regional Inequality, 1966–1976" (Ph.D. diss., Michigan State University, 1985); I. Imam-Jomeh, "Petroleum-Based Accumulation and the State Form in Iran: Aspects of Social and Geographic Variations, 1953–1979" (Ph.D. diss., University of Cal-

ifornia at Los Angeles, 1985); N. Nattagh, "Consideration of Some Aspects of Regional Development in Iran in the Third, Fourth, and Fifth Plan Periods" (Ph.D. diss., University of London [SOAS], 1984); F. Atash, "Spatial Disparity in Iran: 1949–78" (Ph.D. diss., Rutgers University, New Brunswick, N.J., 1986); F. Nourbakhsh, "Tabaqehbandi-ye Ostanha-ye Iran Va Modeli Baray-e Taʾain-e Arjaᶜaiyatha Baray-e Kahesh-e Tafavoutha-ye Mantaqehei" [Classification of the Iranian Provinces and a Model for the Determination of Priorities to Reduce Regional Differences] (Tehran: Plan and Budget Organization, 1977); G. E. Wright, Jr., "Regional Inequality in Economic Development of Iran, 1962–1970" (Ph.D. diss., University of Michigan, 1977); and B. Renaud, *National Urbanization Policy in Developing Countries* (New York: Oxford University Press, 1982).

180. Battelle Engineering Corporation, *Battelle Regional Development Project, Unified Report* (Tehran: Plan and Budget Organization, 1972); Scetiran Corporation, *National Spatial Strategy Plan* (Tehran: Plan and Budget Organization, 1976); Ital Consult, *Report on the Southeastern Iran* (Tehran: Plan and Budget Organization, 1957).

181. Hooshang Amirahmadi, "A Theory of Ethnic Collective Movements and Its Application to Iran," *Ethnic and Racial Studies* 10, no. 4 (October 1987), pp. 363–391; A. Aghajanian, "Ethnic Inequality in Iran: An Overview," in *International Journal of Middle East Studies* 15 (May 1983); A. R. Ghassemlou, "Kurdistan in Iran," in G. Chalian, ed., *People without a Country: The Kurds and Kurdestan* (London: Zed Press, 1980), pp. 107–34; J. Saddigh, *Masʾleh-e Melli Va Enghelab Dar Iran* [The National Question and Revolution in Iran] (New York: Fanos Press, 1973); H. Muʾmeni, *Dar Bareh-e Mobarezat-e Kordestan* [About the Struggles of Kurdistan] (Tehran: Shabahang Press, 1979); L. Beck, "Revolutionary Iran and Its Tribal Peoples," in T. Asad and R. Owen, (eds.), *The Middle East* (New York: MR Press, 1983); R. Olivier, "Regional Problems and Decentralization," *Employment and Income Policies for Iran*, Mission Working Paper No. 11, International Labor Organization, 1973; and *Ayandegan* daily, "Balouchestan: Yak Arziabi-ye Siasi, joghrafiaʾi, Tarikhi" [Baluchestan: Political, Geographic, Historical Appraisal] (22–24 July 1979).

182. Richards, H., "Land Reform and Agribusiness in Iran," *MERIP Reports*, no. 43 (December 1975); H. Safari, *Enhesarat-e Bainol Mellali Dar Iran* [International Monopolies in Iran] (Tehran: Publication of the Tudeh Party of Iran, 1980); F. Daftari and M.

Borghey, *Multinational Enterprises and Employment in Iran* (Geneva: ILO World Employment Program, Research Paper no. 14, 1976).

183. Imam-Jomeh, "Petroleum-Based Accumulation and the State Form in Iran"; Nattagh, "Consideration of Some Aspects of Regional Development in Iran"; Atash, "Spatial Disparity in Iran"; Hooshang Amirahmadi, "Regional Planning in Iran: A Survey of Problems and Policies," *The Journal of Developing Areas* 20, no. 4 (July 1986), pp. 501–529; and Amirahmadi, "Theory of Ethnic Collective Movements."

184. Bashiriyeh, *The State and Revolution in Iran;* and Amirahmadi, "The State and Territorial Social Justice."

185. *Gozideh-e Mataleb-e Amari* [Selected Statistics] (Tehran: Statistical Center, Ministry of Plan and Budget, nos. 10–15, 1987); and Hooshang Amirahmadi, "Middle Class Revolutions in the Third World," in Amirahmadi and Parvin, *Post-Revolutionary Iran.*

186. *Salnameh-e Amari, 1363,* p. 59.

187. Amirahmadi and Atash, "Dynamics of Provincial Development and Disparity in Iran."

188. Amirahmadi, "Regional Planning in Iran."

189. *Ettelaᶜat* daily (26 Esfand 1363).

190. "Law of Organization of Islamic Councils of the Country," in *Official Newspaper,* no. 11022 (7 Day 1361) (Tehran: Ministry of Justice).

191. Amirahmadi, "Middle Class Revolutions in the Third World."

192. A. R. Shaikh Attar, "Naghsh-e Jang Dar Taqier-e Boniadha Va Sakhtarha-ye Toulid-e Sanᶜti" [The Role of the War in Changing the Foundations and Structures of Industrial Production], in *Ettalaᶜat-e Siasi-Eqtesadi* 1, no. 4 (January 1987).

193. *Kayhan-e Havaʾi* (21 Esfand 1364, 19 Farvardin 1365).

194. *Motalaʾat-e Strateji-ye Derazmouddat-e Tarh-e Amayesh-e Sarzamin* [Study of Long-Term Strategy of Spatial Plan] (Tehran: Plan and Budget Organization, Center for National Spatial Planning, 1976).

195. *Kayhan-e Havaʾi* (19 & 26 Esfand 1366).

196. *Kayhan-e Hava'i* (19 Esfand 1366, 21 Esfand 1364).

197. *Kayhan-e Hava'i* (21 Esfand 1364).

198. *Kayhan-e Hava'i* (19 Esfand 1366).

199. *Kayhan-e Hava'i* (19 Esfand 1366).

200. *Kayhan-e Hava'i* (19 Esfand 1366).

201. *Economic Bulletin* 6, no. 45 (November 1987).

202. *Kayhan-e Hava'i* (26 Esfand 1366).

203. Hooshang Amirahmadi, "Destruction and Reconstruction: A Strategy for the War-Damaged Areas of Iran," in *Disasters: The International Journal of Disasters Studies and Practice* 11, no. 2 (1987), pp. 134–147.

204. Amirahmadi and Atash, "Dynamics of Provincial Development and Disparity in Iran."

205. Ibid.

206. *Economic Bulletin* 6, no. 28 (21 July 1987), p. 7.

207. M. Ashrafi, "Foqdan-e Barnameh, Vizhehgi-ye Omdeh-e Bazargani-ye Keshvar Dar Salha-ye Jang" [Lack of Plan, the Principal Character of the Country's Commerce in the War Years], *Ettela'at-e Siasi-Eqtesadi* 1, no. 4 (Day 1365), pp. 3–7; and M. Khosrow Taj, "Bazargani-ye Kharegi, Sakhtar-e Ista, Tekrar-e Khata" [Foreign Trade, Static Structure, Repetition of Mistake], *Ettela'at-e Siasi-Eqtesadi* 1, no. 9 (Khordad 1366), pp. 10–13.

208. *Salnameh-e Amari, 1363*, p. 393 and *Taraznameh*.

209. *Kayhan-e Hava'i* (17 Day 1365), p. 24; (4 Tir 1365), p. 9; (11 Tir 1365), pp. 12–13, 18; and *Economic Bulletin* 6, no. 30 (4 August 1987), p. 8.

210. This was related to me during a discussion with a member of the Ministry of Plan and Budget in Tehran in 1989.

211. *Kayhan-e Hava'i* (18 Khordad 1367), p. 3.

212. Prime Minister Musavi's speech in the Parliament, printed in *Kayhan-e Hava'i* (16 Day 1366), p. 17.

213. *Economic Bulletin* 6, no. 17 (5 May 1987).

214. *Economic Bulletin* 6, no. 17 (5 May 1987); no. 14 (14 April 1987); no. 10 (10 March 1987); no. 18 (12 May 1987); no. 34

(8 September 1987); no. 9 (3 March 1987); no. 4 (20 October 1987); no. 28 (21 July 1987); and no. 27 (14 July 1987).

215. For an account of Iran's postrevolutionary nonoil exports and the state's policies see *Ettelaʿat-e Siasi-Eqtesadi* 1, no. 3 (Azar 1365), pp. 14–23. See also Fereshteh Imamian, "Saderat-e Qair-e Nafti, Shenakht-e Tanghnaha" [Nonoil Exports, Recognition of Obstacles], *Ettelaʿat-e Siasi-Eqtesadi* 2, no. 2 (Aban 1366), pp. 44–51, 66; Said Dadkhah, "Afzayesh-e Saderat-e Qair Nafti Va Zarorat-e Taqier-e Sakhtar-e Eqtesadi" [Increase in Nonoil Exports and the Need for Changes in Economic Structure], *Ettelaʿat-e Siasi-Eqtesadi* 1, no. 7 (Farvardin 1366), pp. 26–30; and Ebrahim Razzaqi, "Olgu-ye Tejarat-e Kharegi-ye Iran" [Iran's Foreign Trade Model], *Ettelaʿat-e Siasi-Eqtesadi* 1, no. 9 (Khordad 1366), pp. 4–9, 13.

216. *Kayhan-e Havaʾi* (12 Azar 1365), p. 31.

217. *Economic Bulletin* 6, no. 31 (18 August 1987), p. 13.

218. *Economic Bulletin* 6, no. 32 (25 August 1987), p. 13.

219. *Economic Bulletin* 6, no. 18 (12 May 1987), pp. 2–3; and *Economic Bulletin* 6, no. 35 (15 September 1987), p. 17.

220. Mehrdad Valibeigi, "U.S.-Iranian Trade Relations After the Revolution," in Amirahmadi and Parvin, *Post-Revolutionary Iran*.

221. *Gozaresh* 2 (1363), Chapter 8, pp. 12–14; and *Taraznameh* (1363), p. 225.

222. *Economic Bulletin* 6, no. 17 (5 May 1987), p. 11 (quoting the minister of Commerce's press release on 29 April 1987).

223. *Gozaresh* 2 (1363), Chapter 8, pp. 12, 14; and *Taraznameh* (1363), p. 220.

224. *Economic Bulletin* 6, no. 17 (5 May 1987), p. 11 (quoting the minister of Commerce's press release on 29 April 1987).

225. *Taraznameh* (1355 and 1363), various pages.

226. *Economic Bulletin* 6, no. 28 (21 July 1987), p. 9.

227. Ibid.

228. *Sharif*, no. 20 (Aban 1366) (quoting the minister of Defense); *Iran Times* (15 April 1988), pp. 6, 12. On savings on other major import-substitution production, see *Kayhan-e Havaʾi* (16 Day 1366), p. 17 (Prime Minister Musavi's speech in the Parliament).

229. *Kayhan-e Hava'i* (14 Urdibehesht 1367), p. 10; and (12 Esfand 1366), p. 7.

230. *Kayhan-e Hava'i* (25 Khordad 1367), p. 1.

231. In Youssef M. Ibrahim, "Tehran Said to Reassess the Future of Its Dream," *New York Times* (6 June 1988), pp. A1, A10. On the possibility of "default," Ibrahim quotes Heino Kopietz, a senior defense analyst at the London International Institute of Strategic Studies. Ibrahim also quotes Iran's former president, Aboul Hasan Banisadr, as saying that: "Iran's short-term debt to suppliers is about $10 billion." This figure seems too large to be reliable; but whatever the exact amount, Iran's short-term debt is on the increase. *Kayhan-e Hava'i* (18 Khordad 1367), p. 3 (on the prime minister's statements about the economy).

232. Youssef M. Ibrahim, "Iran May Borrow at Banks Abroad to Revive Economy," in *New York Times* (3 February 1989), pp. A1, A6; and Ibrahim, "Tehran Said to Reassess the Future of Its Dream."

CHAPTER 4. THE POSTWAR RECONSTRUCTION

1. President Ali Akbar Hashemi Rafsanjani has repeatedly warned about the unstable situation that exists between Iran and Iraq. See *Kayhan-e Hava'i* (13 Mehr 1367), p. 4; and (2 Azar 1367), p. 4. The negative impact of the no-peace no-war situation on the postwar reconstruction is also acknowledged by the officials of the state. See, for example, *Economic and Political Bulletin* 35, no. 7 (15 December 1988), p. 21.

2. On the postdisaster reconstruction, see Hooshang Amirahmadi, "Destruction and Reconstruction: A Strategy for the War-Damaged Areas of Iran," in *Disasters: International Journal of Disaster Studies and Practice* 11, no. 2 (1987), pp. 134–147; E. J. Haas, R. W. Kates, and M. J. Bowden, *Reconstruction Following Disaster* (Cambridge, Mass.: MIT Press, 1977); Thomas E. Drabek, *Human System Responses to Disaster: An Inventory of Sociological Findings* (New York: Springer-Verlag, 1986); W. K. Hancock and M. M. Gowing, *British War Economy* (London: Her Majesty's Stationary Office, Longman, Green and Co., 1949); Ian Davis, *Shelter After Disaster* (Oxford: Oxford Polytechnic Press, 1978); James Lewis, "Risk, Vulnerability and Survival," *Local Government Studies* (July–August 1987); Gholamreza Vatandoust (ed.), *Proceedings of the First Symposium at Shiraz University for the Reconstruction*

of War-Damaged Areas (Shiraz, Iran: University of Shiraz Press, 1987); *Planning for Human Settlements in Disaster Prone Areas* (Nairobi: United Nations Center for Human Settlements, 1983); Victor Ramos Salinas, *Housing Reconstruction Program: A Memoir* (Mexico City: Ministry of Urban Development and Ecology, Housing Development Program, 1988); Anders Wijlkman and Lloyd Timberlake, *Natural Disasters, Acts of God or Acts of Man* (Philadelphia: Earthscan, 1988); *Shelter after Disaster*, (New York, United Nations, 1982); "Settlement Reconstruction (PostWar)," proceedings of a two-day workshop at the of Advanced Architectural Studies, University of York, 1988; *The U.S.S.R. in Reconstruction: A Collection of Essays* (New York: American Russian Institute for Cultural Relations with the Soviet Union, 1944); B. Jones and M. Tomazevic, *Social and Economic Aspects of Earthquakes* (Skopje, Yugoslavia: Institute of Earthquake Engineering and Engineering Seismology, 1981); and *Germany 1945–1954* (Cologne: Boas International Publishing, n.d.).

3. *The U.S.S.R. in Reconstruction.*

4. *Germany 1945–1954.*

5. Mikhail Gorbachev, *Perestroika* (London: Colins, 1987).

6. See Hooshang Amirahmadi, "Economic Reconstruction of Iran: Costing the War Damage," *Third World Quarterly* 12, no. 1 (January 1990), pp. 26–47; and Hashemi Rafsanjani's sermon at the Friday Prayer on 28 Mordad 1367, printed in *Kayhan-e Havaʾi* (2 Shahrivar 1367), p. 9.

7. *Tarh-e Moghadamati-ye Harakatha-ye Kolli-ye Eqtesad-e Keshvar Baʿd Az Jang-e Tahmili* [An Overall Look at the Trends in the Country's Economy after the Imposed War] (Tehran: Ministry of Plan and Budget, n.d.); and *Kayhan-e Havaʾi* (4 Aban 1367), p. 3. See Ayatollah Ali Khamanei's sermon at Friday Prayer on 4 Shahrivar, 1367, printed in *Kayhan-e Havaʾi* (9 Shahrivar 1367), p. 9.

8. See Rafsanjani's sermon on 28 Mordad 1367.

9. *Kayhan-e Havaʾi* (9 Shahrivar 1367), p. 9; and (20 Mehr 1367), p. 9.

10. See Mir Hosain Musavi, in *Kayhan-e Havaʾi* (27 Mehr 1367), p. 11; Ayatollah Ardabili, in *Kayhan-e Havaʾi* (19 Mordad 1367), p. 8; and Ali Akbar Mohtashemi, in *Kayhan-e Havaʾi* (23 Azar 1367), p. 2.

11. See *Kayhan-e Hava'i* (3 Khordad 1368), p. 11 (gives a press release from the minister of Plan and Budget on the main goals and priorities of the first plan revised in the postwar period with an eye on the reconstruction).

12. See Hashemi Rafsanjani's sermon at the Friday Prayer on 28 Mordad 1367, printed in *Kayhan-e Hava'i* (2 Shahrivar 1367), p. 9.

13. *Kayhan-e Hava'i* (4 Aban 1367), p. 10.

14. *Kayhan-e Hava'i* (13 Mehr 1367), p. 4; and (9 Shahrivar 1367), p. 10.

15. See Hashemi Rafsanjani's statement on the Seminar for Cultural Elevation of the Reconstruction in *Kayhan-e Hava'i* (30 Azar 1367), p. 3.

16. See *Iran Times* (9 Tir 1368), pp. 1, 14.

17. See *Iran Times* (19 Aban 1368), pp. 1, 12; and (9 Tir 1368), pp. 1, 14.

18. See Eliane Sciolino, "Bush Hopes to Settle Iranian Assets Issue," *New York Times* (8 November 1989), p. A14. See also *Iran Times* (19 Aban 1368), pp. 1, 12, 15; and Thomas L. Friedman, "U.S. and Iran in Accord on 2,500 Small Claims," *New York Times* (10 May 1990), p. A6.

19. See "Reconstruction Policies Clarified," *Iran Focus* 1, no. 2 (November 1988), pp. 8–10; and "The First Economic Development Plan," *Economic and Political Bulletin* 35, no. 1 (1 November 1988), pp. 5–6. For the detail on the 10-Year Plan for Expansion of the Oil and Petrochemical Industries, see *Kayhan-e Hava'i* (20 Mehr 1367), p. 11.

20. *Kayhan-e Hava'i* (20 Mehr 1367), p. 3.

21. See *Barnameh Avval-e Towse'h Eqtesadi, Ejtema'i Va Farhangi-ye Jomhouri-ye Islami-ye Iran (1368–1372)* [The First Economic, Social and Cultural Development Plan of the Islamic Republic of Iran, 1989–1993] (Tehran: Ministry of Plan and Budget, 1368).

22. See *Layhe-e Barnameh-e Avval-e Towse'h Eqtesadi, Ejtema'i Va Farhangi-ye Jomhouri-ye Islami-ye Iran (1368–1372)* [The Bill of the First Economic, Social and Cultural Development Plan of the Islamic Republic of Iran, 1989–1993] (Tehran: Ministry of Plan and Budget, Mordad, 1368). See also President Rafsanjani's press inter-

view on 17 Mehr 1368, printed in *Iran Times* (21 Mehr 1368), pp. 1, 12. Further, see *Iran Times* (28 Mehr 1368), pp. 1, 12. The president's election platform is also printed in *Iran Times* (17 and 24 Shahrivar 1368), pp. 11 and 11. On policy changes in the post-Khomeini era, see "New Leaders Break with Khomeini," *Iran Times* (30 Tir 1368), p. 16 (first English page). The report is based on a speech by the new leader of the Republic, Ayatollah Khamanei.

23. See *Kayhan-e Hava²i* (3 Aban 1368), pp. 1, 11.

24. *Iran Focus* 3, no. 1 (January 1990), p. 10.

25. For the text of the corrected articles and of the new amendments to the Constitution, see *Kayhan-e Hava²i* (28 Tir 1368), pp. 11, 28.

26. See Youssef M. Abrahim, "Divided Iranians Seem Unable to Settle on Firm Policy Course," *New York Times* (10 October 1989), pp. 1A, 14A.

27. *Kayhan-e Hava²i* (7 Day 1367), p. 25.

28. For details on the National Cooperation Tax for Reconstruction, see *Kayhan-e Hava²i* (10 Esfand 1368), p. 25; and (17 Esfand 1368), p. 10; and *Iran Times* (4 Farvardin 1368), p. 2.

29. See Sarajaldin Kazrouni, "Negareshi Bar Siasatha-ye Qabel-e Bahregiri Dar Erteqa⁵ Harakat-e Bazsazi-ye Manateq-e Jang-zadeh" [A Look at the Usable Policies in Promoting the Movement for Reconstruction of the War-damaged Areas], pp. 29–35; "Tarh-e Jameᶜh Bazsazi Va Towseᶜh Va Omran-e Sharha" [The Comprehensive Plan for Development Reconstruction and Urban Development], all in Gholamreza, Hamdolah Asafi, and Ahmad Broujerdi (eds.), *Majmouᶜh Maqalat-e Dovvoumin Gerd-e Hama²-ye Daneshgah-e Shiraz Piramoun-e Naghsh-e Pazhouhesh Dar Bazsazi, Jeld-e Avval (Maqalat-e Oloum-e Ejtemaᶜi Va Ensani* [Proceedings of the Second Symposium at Shiraz University on the Role of Research in Reconstruction, vol. 1 (Papers on Social Sciences and Humanities)] (Shiraz: University of Shiraz Press, 1989), pp. 36–38; and Masᶜoud Roughani Zanjani, "Motalᶜat-e Bazsazi Dar Qaleb-e Tarh-e Jameᶜh-e Towseᶜh-e Panj Ostan-e Gharb-e Keshvar" [Reconstruction Studies within the Framework of the Comprehensive Development Plan of the Five Western Provinces of the Country], pp. 39–70, See also Directive (in the text of this chapter) and Hooshang Amirahmadi, "Iran: At the Threshold of Reconstruction" (interview), *The Urban Edge: Issues and Innovations* 12, no. 10 (December 1988), pp. 4–5

(published by the World Bank). Further, see Akbar Zargar, "Development and Reconstruction," *Open House International* 13, no. 2, pp. 22–36; and Ali Madanipour, "Design and Change: The Case of Rural Settlements in Iran," *Open House International* 13, no. 4, pp. 29–35.

30. *Bazsazi Va Barnamehrizi-ye Towseᶜh-e Meli Va Mantagheh'i* [Reconstruction and National and Regional Development Planning] (Tehran: Ministry of Plan and Budget, 1366); and Hooshang Amirahmadi, "The State and Territorial Social Justice in Post-Revolutionary Iran," *International Journal of Urban and Regional Research* 13, no. 1 (March 1989), pp. 92–120.

31. *Tarh-e Moghadamati.*

32. Haas, Kates, and Bowden, *Reconstruction Following Disaster.*

33. B. Jones and M. Tomazevic, *Social and Economic Aspects of Earthquakes* (Skopje, Yogoslavia: Institute of Earthquake Engineering and Engineering Seismology, 1981).

34. Hooshang Amirahmadi, "War Damage and Reconstruction in the Islamic Republic of Iran," in Hooshang Amirahmadi and Manoucher Parvin (eds.), *Post-Revolutionary Iran* (Boulder, Colo.: Westview Press, 1988), pp. 126–149.

35. *Jomhouri-ye Islami* daily (7 Shahrivar 1367), p. 5.

36. See President Khamanei's sermon at the Friday Prayer on 15 Mehr 1367, printed in *Kayhan-e Hava'i* (20 Mehr 1367). See also *Kayhan-e Hava'i* (4 Aban 1367), p. 9.

37. "Changes in the Constitutional Law," *Economic and Political Bulletin* 35, no. 7 (15 December 1988), pp. 5–6; and "Constitutional Amendments on the Way," *Iran Focus* 2, no. 1 (January 1989), p. 6–7.

38. See *Kayhan-e Hava'i* (30 Azar 1367), p. 10.

39. See *Kayhan-e Hava'i* (29 Day 1367), p. 8; and (23 Farvardin 1367), p. 10.

40. *The U.S.S.R. in Reconstruction.*

41. See *Proceedings of International Conference on Reconstruction of the War-Damaged Areas* (Tehran: Tehran University Press, 1367); and Amirahmadi, "War Damage and Reconstruction," pp. 126–149.

42. See Hamid Mirzadeh, "Vazⁱiyt-e Mojoud va Khatt-e Mash-ye Dowlat Dar Amr-e Bazsazi-ye Manateq-e Jangzadeh" [The Existing Situation and the Government's Reconstruction Policy in the War-Damaged Areas], in Vatandoust, Asafi, and Broujerdi, *Proceedings of the Second Symposium,* pp. 15–27; *Proceedings of International Conference on Reconstruction of the War-Damaged Areas;* Amirahmadi, "War Damage and Reconstruction," pp. 126–149; and *Kayhan-e Havaʾi* (19 Tir 1364), p. 9.

43. See Gholamreza Vatandoust (ed.), *Majmouᶜh Maqalat-e Avvalin Gerd-e Hamaʾ-ye Daneshgahe Shiraz Piramoun-e Naghsh-e Pazhouhesh Dar Bazsazi* [Proceedings of the First Symposium at Shiraz University for the Reconstruction of War-Damaged Areas] (Shiraz: University of Shiraz Press, 1987); Aboulhasan Vafaʾi, "Sokhani Piramoun-e Markaz-e Pazhouhesh-ye Bazsazi" [Some Words about the Center for Reconstruction Research], in Vatandoust, Asafi, and Broujerdi, *Proceedings of the Second Symposium,* pp. 11–13; and Amirahmadi, "War Damage and Reconstruction," pp. 126–149; and Amirahmadi, "Destruction and Reconstruction."

44. Amirahmadi, "War Damage and Reconstruction," pp. 126–149; and Amirahmadi, "Destruction and Reconstruction." See also Haas, Kates, and Bowden, *Reconstruction Following Disaster.*

45. See Mirzadeh, "Vazⁱiyt-e Mojoud va Khatt-e Mash-ye Dowlat Dar Amr-e Bazsazi-ye Manateq-e Jangzadeh"; and *Kayhan-e Havaʾi* (16 Aban 1362), p. 3.

46. Ayatollah Khomeini, *Iran Times* (25 Shahrivar 1367), p. 7.

47. See Hashemi Rafsanjani's statement on the occasion of the Seminar for Cultural Elevation of the Reconstruction in *Kayhan-e Havaʾi* (30 Azar 1367), p. 3. See also the Directives in the text of this chapter.

48. See the statement by Aboul Hasan Haerizadeh, Parliament representative, in the open session of the Parliament published in *Kayhan-e Havaʾi* (14 Day 1367), p. 24.

49. "Santa Satan: The Changing Iran," an interview with Hooshang Amirahmadi, Richard Bulliet, and James Bill in *Barron's: National Business Weekly* 69, no. 3 (January 16, 1989), pp. 10–11, 17–21; see also *Kayhan-e Havaʾi* (2 Shahrivar 1367), p. 3 (carries an statement from Dr. Mohammad Javad Larijani, deputy foreign minister concerning the good prospects for Germany's involvement in

the postwar reconstruction); *Kayhan-e Hava'i* (9 Shahrivar 1367), p. 13; and *Economic and Political Bulletin* 35, no. 6 (8 December 1988), p. 5.

50. Youssef M. Ibrahim, "Iran May Borrow at Banks to Revive Economy," *New York Times* (3 February 1989), p. A1. On discussions with IMF and IBRD, see *Kayhan-e Hava'i* (26 Urdibehesht 1369), p. 10.

51. *Kayhan-e Hava'i* (2 Azar 1367), p. 6; and (27 Mehr 1367), p. 9.

52. "Making up with Gulf States," *Iran Focus* 2, no. 1 (January 1989), pp. 4–5. See also *Economic and Political Bulletin* 35, no. 9 (5 January 1989), pp. 23–24.

53. "Reconstruction: The Financing Problem," *Iran Focus* 1, no. 3 (December 1988), p. 11.

54. Ibrahim, "Iran May Borrow at Banks to Revive Economy," pp. A1, A6.

55. Echo of Iran quotes Mr. Majidi, the managing director of the Islamic Republic Airlines (originally published in *Kayhan* daily, 23/11) as reporting that on 16 November 1988 "A Memorandum of Understanding has been signed between Iran and France, on the basis of which, Iran will purchase three airbus planes within two years. Preliminary arrangements have been made for the purchase of five additional aircrafts." He is then quoted to have said that: "An airbus can carry 280 passengers on domestic flights. It costs $US 60 to 70 million." See *Economic and Political Bulletin* 35, no. 1 (1 December 1988), p. 4. See also *Kayhan-e Hava'i* (2 Azar 1367), p. 11.

56. See Sohrab Shahabi, "Iran's Reconstruction and the Persian Gulf States," paper presented at the International Conference on the Persian Gulf, Tehran, 20–22 November 1989.

57. "The Drive to Lure Back Specialists," *Iran Focus* 1, no. 3 (December 1988), pp. 12–13.

58. *Kayhan-e Hava'i* (5 Bahman 1367), p. 13.

59. See President Khamanei's sermon at the Friday Prayer on 4 Shahrivar printed in *Kayhan-e Hava'i* (9 Shahrivar 1367), p. 9. See also *Kayhan-e Hava'i* (19 Day 1367), p. 8.

60. On 15 Azar 1367, Iran and the Federal Republic of Germany signed a Memorandum of Understanding concerning construction projects. See *Kayhan-e Hava'i* (23 Azar 1367), p. 11.

61. *Kayhan-e Hava³i* (23 Azar 1367), p. 2; and (12 Mordad 1367), p. 10.

62. "Zarorat-e Bazsazi-ye Tashkilat-e Edari" [The Need for Reconstruction of Administrative Apparatuses] *Soroush* (21 Aban 1367). See also *Kayhan-e Hava³i* (4 Aban 1367), p. 24; (29 Tir 1367), p. 24; and (23 Azar 1367), p. 19.

63. *Kayhan-e Hava³i* (4 Aban 1367), p. 24; and (27 Mehr 1367), p. 14.

64. "IRGC Merger Postponed," *Iran Focus* 1, no. 1 (October 1988), p. 7.

65. See *Majmouᶜh-e Qavanin Va Moqarrat-e Kar Va Ta³min-e Ejtemaᶜi* [A Collection of Laws and Regulations of Labor and Social Security], 4th ed. with revisions and editions (Tehran: Institute for Labor and Social Security, no. 22, 1367); *Majmouᶜh-e Qavanin-e Avvalin Doureh-e Majlis-e Showra-ye Islami, 7 Khordad 1359 Ta 6 Khordad 1363* [A Collection of Laws Passed by the First Parliament, 28 May 1980 to 27 May 1984] (Tehran: Islamic Consultative Assembly, 1366); *Majmouᶜh-e Qavanin-e Dovvomin Doureh-e Majlis-e Showra-ye Islami, 7 Khordad 1363 Ta 6 Khordad 1367* [A Collection of Laws Passed by the Second Parliament, 28 May 1984 to 27 May 1988] (Tehran: Islamic Consultative Assembly, n.d., most probably 1368); and Hooshang Amirahmadi, "Middle-Class Revolutions in the Third World," in Amirahmadi and Parvin, *Post-Revolutionary Iran*, pp. 225–244.

66. Reports of the executions were carried by most of the Western press including the *New York Times*. The United Nations passed a Resolution on human rights in Iran and the Amnesty International published several statements. See "Statement of Amnesty International about the Recent Executions in Iran," *Economic and Political Bulletin* 35, no. 8 (22 December 1988), pp. 19–20; and "Amnesty International's Statement to the 45th Session of the UN Commission on Human Rights," *Economic and Political Bulletin* 35, no. 14 (9 February 1989), pp. 23–24. See also Mohamad Javad Larijani, deputy minister of Foreign Affairs, on the execution of Tudeh leaders in *Economic and Political Bulletin* 35, no. 9 (5 January 1989), p. 4. See further "UN Human Rights Resolution Stings," *Iran Focus* 2, no. 1 (January 1989), p. 7. On the government responses to these charges, see "Rafsanjani Attacks Western Records on Human Rights," *Economic and Political Bulletin* 35, no. 8 (22 December 1988), pp. 20–22; and "UN Human Rights Resolution Stings," *Iran Focus* 2, no. 1 (January 1989), p. 7.

67. In my two summer 1988 trips to Iran, I learned that the most frequent complaint voiced by the crowds in the streets was about the lack of social security (*amniyat-e ejtema⁶i*) in the country, and when I asked them to define what they meant by the phrase, most people listed a variety of problems ranging from physical abuse by members of the Revolutionary Committees, to socioeconomic poverty and concerns, to lack of political and individual freedom.

68. On the Iranian culture in general, and political culture in particular, see Seyyed Mohammad Ali Jamalzadeh, *Kholghiyat-e Ma Iranian* [Temperaments of We Iranians] (Winter Park, Fla.: Kanoun Marefat Publishers, 1985); Roy Mottahedeh, *The Mantle of the Prophet* (New York: Pantheon Books, 1985); Reza Behnam, *Cultural Foundations of Iranian Politics* (Salt Lake City: University of Utah Press, 1986); Ann K. S. Lambton, "Persia," *Journal of the Royal Central Asian Society* 31 (January 1944), pp. 14–16; and Jahangir Amuzegar, "Iran's Economic Planning Once Again," *Middle East Economic Papers* (1957), p. 4.

69. See for example Jamalzadeh, *Kholghiyat-e Ma Iranian.*

70. See Hooshang Amirahmadi, "Development Paradigms at a Crossroad and the Korean Experience," *Journal of Contemporary Asia* 19, no. 2 (1989), pp. 167–185; and Hooshang Amirahmadi, "Global Restructuring and Implications for Use of Force," paper presented at the Conference on the Persian Gulf, Institute of Political and International Studies, Tehran, May 1988.

71. "No Breakthrough in Peace Talks," *Iran Focus* 1, no. 3 (December 1988), pp. 2–3; and "Impasse in Peace Process," *Iran Focus* 2, no. 1 (January 1989), p. 2.

72. Warren Richey, "Iraq and Iran Use Truce for Massive Arms Buildups," *Christian Science Monitor* 81, no. 31 (January 10, 1989).

73. *Kayhan-e Hava²i* (2 Azar 1367), p. 4.

CHAPTER 5. CONCLUSIONS: EMPIRICAL AND THEORETICAL

1. See especially the following publications: *Barnameh-e Avval-e Towse⁶h-e Eqtesadi, Ejtema⁶i Va Farhangi-ye Jomhouri-ye Islami-ye Iran (1368–1372)* [The First Economic, Social and Cultural Development Plan of the Islamic Republic of Iran, 1989–1993] (Tehran: Ministry of Plan and Budget, 1368) (this is a revised version of the revised First Plan prepared after the cease-fire, undertaken by the Prime Minister Musavi's government and submitted to the Parlia-

ment as the Reconstruction Plan); *Layeh-e Barnameh-e Avval-e Towseᶜh-e Eqtesadi, Ejtemaᶜi Va Farhangi-ye Jomhouri-ye Islami-ye Iran (1368–1372)* [The Law of the First Economic, Social and Cultural Development Plan of the Islamic Republic of Iran, 1989–1993] (Tehran: Ministry of and Budget, Mordad 1368) (this is the revised version of the Musavi Plan prepared under the President Hashemi Rafsanjani's government); *Salnameh-e Amari-ye 1366* [The Statistical Yearbook of 1987] (Tehran: Statistical Center, 1367); Hosain Azimi, "Negahi Be Naqsh-e Dowlat dar Towseᶜh-e Eqtesadi" [A Look at the Role of the State in Economic Development], *Ettelaᶜat-e Siasi-Eqtesadi* 4, no. 1 (Mehr 1368); and Victor Mallet, "The Harder Tasks of Building the Peace," *Financial Times* (17 November 1989), p. 24.

2. On the economic conditions of the Third World in the 1980s, see, for example, *World Development Report, 1988; International Financial Statistics, 1987;* and *Statistical Yearbook for Asia and the Pacific, 1986–1987.* On the Iranian external debt at the end of 1989, see *Iran Focus* 3, no. 1 (January 1990), p. 10 (quoting President Hashemi Rafsanjani, responding to the radical critics of his plan bill in a 4 December 1989 unofficial session of the Majlis).

3. See *Soroush* (21 Aban 1367); and *Kayhan-e Havaᵓi* (23 Azar 1367), p. 19.

4. Amirahmadi, "Middle-Class Revolutions in the Third World," pp. 225–244.

5. Ibid., pp. 225–244.

6. See, For example, Jean Leca, "Algerian Socialism: Nationalism and Industrialization and State Building," in Helen Defosses and Jacques Levesque (eds.), *Socialism in the Third World* (New York: Praeger, 1975); T. A. Kofi, "Prospects and Problems of the Transition from Agrarianism to Socialism: The Case of Angola, Guinea Bissau, and Mozambique," *World Development* 9, nos. 9–10 (1981); A. F. Lowenthal (ed.), *The Peruvian Experiment* (Princeton, N.J.: Princeton University Press, 1975); A. Fenichel and A. Khan, "The Burmese Way to Socialism," *World Development Report* 9, nos. 9–10 (1981); Fuad Ajami, "Egypt Retreat from Economic Nationalism," in G. Abdel Khalek and R. Tignor (eds.), *The Political Economy of Income Distribution in Egypt* (New York: Holmes & Meier, 1982); Alfred Stepan, *Peru in a Comparative Perspective* (Princeton, N.J.: Princeton University Press, 1978); M. Ata Alla, *The Arab Struggle for Economic Independence* (Moscow: Progress Pub-

lishers, 1974); Hooshang Amirahmadi, "The Non-Capitalist Way of Development," *Review of Radical Political Economics* 19, no. 1 (Spring 1987), pp. 24–46; Mahmoud Abdel Fadil, *The Political Economy of Nasserism* (Cambridge: Cambridge University Press, 1980); and Edmund W. Clark, *Socialist Development and Public Investment in Tanzania* (Toronto: University of Toronto Press, 1978).

7. In the specific case of Iran, the war, oil, and domestic politics seem to have caused the most damage and changes in certain economic and social sectors (for example, banking and education) have been more extensive than in other areas. What, however, distinguishes the Iranian Revolution is its cultural impact, a subject that has not been investigated in this book.

Bibliography

The following selected list includes the most important sources used or consulted in writing this book. The sources are organized into the following five categories: (1) publications and reports by the Iranian government; (2) published books, monographs, and reports or documents by international agencies; (3) published articles, interviews, speeches, and miscellaneous documents; (4) unpublished dissertations and papers; and (5) newspapers, magazines, and journals cited.

PUBLICATIONS AND REPORTS BY THE IRANIAN GOVERNMENT

Ahdaf-e Kammi-ye Towse^ch-e Eqtesadi-Ejtema^ci-ye Jomhouri-ye Islami-ye Iran Dar Doureh-e 1361–1381 [Quantitative Objectives of Socioeconomic Development of the Islamic Republic of Iran in the Period of 1982–2002]. Tehran: Office of Deputy for Planning and Evaluation, Plan and Budget Organization, Esfand 1360.

Ahdaf Va Siasatha-ye San^cti [Industrial Objectives and Policies]. Tehran: Ministry of Industries, Joint Council for Planning of Industrial Sector, 1361.

Alizadeh, Mohamad. *Vizhegiha-ye Rahbordi-ye Bazaar-e Kar-e Iran (Kar Va Bikari) Dar Dahheh-e 1355–1365* [The Specific Trends of Labor Market in Iran (Employment and Unemployment) in the Decade of 1979–1986]. Tehran: Ministry of Plan and Budget, Office of Population and Manpower, Tir, 1367.

Amar-e Kargaha-ye Bozorg-e San^cti [Statistics of Large-Scale Industrial Establishments]. Tehran: Statistical Center, various years.

Amargiri Az Gheimat-e Masaleh-e Sakhtemani, Dastmozd-e Nirou-ye Ensani Va Keraye-he Machinalat-e Moured-e Estefadeh Dar Tarha-ye Omrani [Census of Prices of Construction Materials, Wages of Labor and Costs of Leasing Machineries Used in Development Projects]. Tehran: Statistical Center, 1365.

Amargiri Az Khanevarha-ye Ejarehneshin-e Shahr-e Tehran [Census of Tenant Families of the City of Tehran]. Tehran: Statistical Center, 1366.

Barnameh-e Avval-e Towseᶜah-e Eqtesadi, Ejtemaʾai, Farhangi-ye Jomhouri-ye Islami-ye Iran, 1362–1366 [First Economic, Social, Cultural Development Plan of the Islamic Republic of Iran, 1983–1987], 4 vol. Tehran: Plan and Budget Organization, 1362.

Barnameh-e Avval-e Towseᶜh-e Eqtesadi-Ejtemaᶜi-Farhangi-ye Jomhouri-ye Islami-ye Iran 1368–1372 [The First Economic-Social-Cultural Development Plan of the Islamic Republic of Iran, 1989–1993], revised First Plan (under Prime Minister Musavi) for Reconstruction. Tehran: Ministry of Plan and Budget, 1368.

Barrasi-ye Mahdoudeh-e 120 Kilometri-ye Tehran Va Vahedha-ye Qair-e Mojaz [A Study of Tehran's 120-Kilometer City Limit and the Illegal (Economic) Units]. Tehran: Ministry of Plan and Budget, The Group for the Study of the Occasional Projects, 1362.

Barrasi-ye Tahavvulat-e Eqtesadi-ye Keshvar Baᶜd Az Engelab [Survey of Economic Changes in the Country After the Revolution]. Tehran: Bank Markazi Iran, n.d., probably 1362.

Battelle Engineering Corporation. Battelle Regional Development Project, Unified Report. Tehran: Plan and Budget Organization, 1972.

Bazsazi Va Barnamehrizi-ye Towseᶜh-e Meli Va Mantaghehʾi [Reconstruction and National and Regional Development Planning]. Tehran: Ministry of Plan and Budget, 1366.

Estefadeh az Zarfiyatha-ye Eqtesadi-Ejtemaᶜi-ye Keshvar: Tasviri az Vazᶜ-e Mujud Dar Dureh-e 1361–1364 [Utilization of Capacities in Economic-Social Sectors of the Country: A Picture of Existing Situations in Period 1982–1985]. Tehran: Ministry of Plan and Budget, 1365.

Faslnameh-e Amari-ye Salha-ye 1362, 1363 Va Sheshmahe-ye Sal-e 1364 [The Seasonal Book of Statistics, 1983, 1984, and the First Six Months of 1985]. Tehran: Ministry of Plan and Budget, 1365.

Gozareshi Az Comicioun-e Khas-e Rasidegi Beh Barname-he Panjsaleh Beh Majles-e Shoura-ye Eslami [Report of the Special

Commission Investigating the Five-Year Plan to the Islamic Consultative Assembly], No. 1, 4/9/1364. Tehran: Islamic Consultative Assembly, Second Period, Year Two, 1354–65.

Gozaresh-e Eqtesadi [Economic Report]. Published annually in two volumes, Tehran: Ministry of Plan and Budget, Office of Macro-Economics.

Gozaresh-e Eqtesadi Va Taraznameh [Economic Report and Balance Sheet]. Tehran: Bank Markazi, various years.

Gozideh-e Mataleb-e Amari, monthly, various issues and years.

Iran Dar Aʾineh-e Amar [Iran in the Mirror of Statistics]. Tehran: Statistical Center, 1363–65.

Ital Consult. Report on the Southeastern Iran. Tehran: Plan and Budget Organization, 1957.

Khalili, Akbar. Gam Be Gam Ba Enghelab [Step by Step with the Revolution]. Tehran: Soroush, 1360, a publication of the Radio and Television Organization of the Islamic Republic of Iran.

Kholaseh-e Gozaresh: Baravard-e Khesarat-e Eqtesadi-ye Jang-e Tahmili-ye Araq Aleyh-e Iran Ta Shahrivar Mah-e 1364 [Summary Report: An Estimate of the Economic Damage of the Imposed War of Iraq Against Iran until September 1985]. Tehran: Ministry of Plan and Budget, 1365.

Kholase-he Nazarat Va Dastourolamalha-ye Showra-ye Eqtesad Dar Bareh-e Ahdaf-e Kammi-ye Towseᶜh-e Eqtesadi-Ejtemaᶜi Dar Jomhouri-ye Islami-ye Iran Bara-ye salha-ye 1361–1381, Mosavvab-e 30/1/1361 [Summary of Views and Directives of the Economic Council on the Quantitative Goals of Economic-Social Development in the Islamic Republic of Iran for 1361–81, Approved 30/1/1361]. Tehran: Plan and Budget Organization, 1361, mimeograph.

"Laws and Regulations Governing Islamic Banking in the Islamic Republic of Iran and in Pakistan," in The Law for Usury-Free Banking. Tehran: Bank Markazi, 1362, pp. 31–43.

Layhe-e Barnameh-e Avval-e Towseᶜh Eqtesadi, Ejtemaᶜi Va Farhangi-ye Jomhouri-ye Islami-ye Iran (1368–1372) [The Bill of the First Economic, Social and Cultural Development Plan of the Islamic Republic of Iran, 1989–1993]. Tehran: Ministry of Plan and Budget, Mordad, 1368, prepared under President Hashemi Rafsanjani.

Majaleh-e Bank-e Markazi [Magazine of the Central Bank]. Tehran: Bank Markazi, various issues, 1360–64.

Majmouᶜh-e Maghalat-e Seminar-e "Barrasi-ye Masaʾl-e Khalij-e Fars" [Proceedings of the Seminar on the Persian Gulf Issues]. Tehran: Institute for Political and International Studies, 1368.

Majmouᶜh-e Qavanin-e Avvalin Doureh-e Majlis-e Showra-ye Islami, 7 Khordad 1359 Ta 6 Khordad 1363 [A Collection of Laws Passed by the First Parliament, 28 May 1980 to 27 May 1984]. Tehran: Islamic Consultative Assembly, 1366.

Majmouᶜh-e Qavanin-e Dovvomin Doureh-e Majlis-e Showra-ye Islami, 7 Khordad 1363 Ta 6 Khordad 1367 [A Collection of Laws Passed by the Second Parliament, 28 May 1984 to 27 May 1988]. Tehran: Islamic Consultative Assembly, n.d., most probably 1368.

Majmouᶜh-e Qavanin Va Moqarrat-e Kar Va Taʾmin-e Ejtemaᶜi [A Collection of Laws and Regulations of Labor and Social Security], 4th ed. with revisions and additions. Tehran: Institute for Labor and Social Security, no. 22, 1367.

Motaleᶜh-e Strateji-ye Derazmoddat-e Tarh-e Amayesh-e Sarzamin [Study of Long-Term Strategy of Spatial Plan]. Tehran: Center for National Spatial Planning, Plan and Budget Organization, 1355.

Natayej-e Barrasi-ye Tarha-ye Omrani, Zaman Bandi Va Ejra-ye Monaseb-e Anha [The Results of the Survey of the Development Projects: Periodization and Their Suitable Implementation]. Tehran: Ministry of Plan and Budget, 1364.

Natayej-e Tafsili-ye Amargiri Az Hazineh Va Daramad-e Khanevarha-ye Roustaʾi, Sal-e 1363 [Detailed Results of the Census of Expenditures and Income of Rural Families, 1984]. Tehran: Statistical Center, 1364.

Natayej-e Tafsili-ye Amargiri Az Hazineh Va Daramad-e Khanevarha-ye Shahri, Sal-e 1363 [Detailed Results of the Census of Expenditures and Income of Urban Families, 1984]. Tehran: Statistical Center, 1364.

Negahi Be Vazᶜ-e Mujud Va Barrasi-ye Kolli-ye Tangnaha Va Moshkelat-e Eqtesadi-ye Keshvar [A Look at the Existing Situation and General Survey of Bottlenecks and Difficulties of the Country's Economy]. Tehran: Ministry of Plan and Budget, 1364.

Olgu Va Strategi-ye Towse^{c}h [Model and Strategy of Development]. Tehran: Ministry of Plan and Budget, 1364.

Proceedings of the International Conference on Reconstruction of the War-Damaged Areas. Tehran: Tehran University Press, 1367.

Raveshha va Olgouha-ye Lazem Bara-ye Baravord-e Khesarat-e Jang-e Tahmili-ye Iraq Aleyh-e Iran [Necessary Methods and Models for Estimation of Economic Damage of the Imposed War of Iraq against Iran]. Tehran: Ministry of Plan and Budget, 1362.

Rouznameh-ye Rasmi-ye Jomhouri-ye Islami-ye Iran: Mashrouh-e Mozakerat-e Majles-e Showra-ye Islami [Official Gazette of the Islamic Republic of Iran: Proceedings of the Islamic Consultative Assembly]. Tehran: Ministry of Justice, several volumes and years, 1358–66.

Salmaneh-e Amari [Statistical Yearbook]. Tehran: Statistical Center, Ministry of Plan and Budget, various years, 1355–67.

Sarshomari-ye Omoumi-ye Nofous va Maskan, Mehr Mah-e 1365: Natayej-e Tafsili, Koll-e Keshvar [General Census of Population and Housing, Month of Mehr 1365, Detailed Results, Whole of the Country]. Tehran: Statistical Center, 1367.

Scetiran Corporation. *National Spatial Strategy Plan.* Tehran: Plan and Budget Organization, 1976.

Statement By H. E. Hojatolislam Mr. Ali Khamenei President of the Islamic Republic of Iran to the 42nd Session of the General Assembly of the United Nations. New York, 22nd September, 1987. New York: Permanent Mission of the Islamic Republic of Iran to the United Nations, 1987.

Tahlili Bar Amalkard-e Sherkatha-ye Mashmoul-e Qanoun-e Hefazat Va Towse^{c}h-e Sanaye^{c}e Iran Taht-e Poushesh-e Sazman-e Sanaye^{c}e Melli-ye Iran va Moghayeseh-e Amalkard-e Anha Az Sal-e 1356 Legayat-e 1361 [An Analysis of Operations of the Companies Subject to the Laws for Protection and Expansion of the Nationalized Industries of Iran and a Comparison of Their Operations from the Year 1976 until the End of 1982]. Tehran: Ministry of Industries, Organization of the Nationalized Industries of Iran, 1362.

"Tarh-e Jame^{c}h Bazsazi-ye Towse^{c}h Va Omran-e Sharha" [The Comprehensive Plan for Development Reconstruction and Urban Development]. in Gholamreza Vatandoust, Hamdolah Asafi, and

Ahmad Broujerdi (eds.). *Majmouᶜh Maqalat-e Dovvoumin Gerd-e Hamaʾ-ye Daneshgaha Shiraz Piramoun-e Naghsh-e Pazhouhesh Dar Bazsazi, Jeld-e Avval (Maqalat-e Oloum-e Ejtemaᶜi Va Ensani)* [Proceedings of the Second Symposium at Shiraz University on the Role of Research in Reconstruction, Volume 1 (Papers on Social Sciences and Humanities)]. Shiraz: University of Shiraz Press, 1989, pp. 36–38.

Tarh-e Moghadamati-ye Harakatha-ye Kolli-ye Eqtesad-e Keshvar Baᶜd Az Jang-e Tahmili [A Preliminary Look at the Overall Trends in the Country's Economy after the Imposed War]. Tehran: Ministry of Plan and Budget, n.d. probably 1367.

Vahidi, Paridoukhti. *Tahlili Az Hazineh-e Amouzesh-e Aali* [An Analysis of Expenditures in Higher Education]. Tehran: Ministry of Plan and Budget, 1365.

PUBLISHED BOOKS, MONOGRAPHS, AND REPORTS OR DOCUMENTS BY INTERNATIONAL AGENCIES

Abrahamian, Ervand. *Iran between Two Revolutions.* Princeton: Princeton University Press, 1982.

Abrahamian, Ervand. *The Iranian Mojahedin.* New Haven, Conn.: Yale University Press, 1989.

Afkhami, Gholam. *The Iranian Revolution: Thanatos on a National Scale.* Washington, D.C.: The Middle East Institute, 1985.

Ahrari, Mohammed E. *OPEC: The Failing Giant.* Lexington: University Press of Kentucky, 1986.

Akhavi, Shahrough. *Religion and Politics in Contemporary Iran: Clergy-State Relations in the Pahlavi Period.* Albany: State University of New York Press, 1980.

Algar, Hamid. *The Roots of the Islamic Revolution.* London, The Open Press, 1983.

Alla, M. Ata. *The Arab Struggle for Economic Independence.* Moscow: Progress Publishers, 1974.

Alnasrawi, Abbas. *OPEC in a Changing World Economy.* Baltimore: Johns Hopkins University Press, 1985.

Al-Sadr, Ayatollah Baqer. *Islam and Schools of Economics.* New York: Islamic Seminary, 1982.

Amin, Sayed Hassan. *Commercial Law of Iran.* Tehran: Vahid Publications, 1986.

Amirahmadi, Hooshang, and Manoucher Parvin (eds.). *Post-Revolutionary Iran.* Boulder, Colo.: Westview Press, 1988.

Amsden, Alice H. *Asia's Next Giant: South Korea and Late Industrialization.* New York: Oxford University Press, 1989.

Arjomand, Said Amir. *The Turban for the Crown: The Islamic Revolution in Iran.* New York: Oxford University Press, 1988.

Arjomand, Said Amir. *Authority and Political Culture in Shi'ism.* Albany: State University of New Press, 1988.

Asad, T., and R. Owen (eds.). *The Middle East.* New York: MR Press, 1983.

Asnad-e Laneh-e Jasousi [Documents of the Spy Nest (meaning American Embassy in Tehran)], several volumes. Tehran: Moslem Students of the Imam Line, n.d.

Bakhash, Shaul. *The Reign of the Ayatollahs: Iran and the Islamic Revolution.* New York: Basic Books, 1984.

Banisadr, Aboulhasan. *The Fundamental Principles and Precepts of Islamic Government,* trans. Mohammad R. Ghanoonparvar. Lexington, Ky.: Mazda Publishers, 1981.

Bashiriyeh, Hossein. *The State and Revolution in Iran, 1962–1982.* London: Croom Helm, 1984.

Bayat, Asadoulah. *Manabe'e Mali-ye Dawlat-e Islami* [The Financial Sources of the Islamic Government]. Tehran: Kayhan Publications, 1365.

Bayat, Asaf. *Workers and Revolution in Iran: A Third World Experience of Workers' Control.* London: Zed Books, 1986.

Bazargan, Mehdi. *Enghelab-e Iran dar Dou Harakat* [Iranian Revolution in Two Movements]. Tehran: Nehzat-e Azadi-ye Iran, 1363.

Behnam, Reza. *Cultural Foundations of Iranian Politics.* Salt Lake City: University of Utah Press, 1986.

Bill, James, and W. M. Rogers (eds.). *Musaddiq, Iranian Nationalism and Oil.* Austin: University of Texas Press, 1988.

Bill, James. *The Eagle and the Lion: The Tragedy of American-Iranian Relations.* New Haven, Conn.: Yale University Press, 1988.

Bina, Cyrus. *The Economics of the Oil Crisis.* New York: St. Martin's Press, 1985.

Bryant, Ralph C., et. al. (eds.). *Macroeconomic Policies in an Interdependent World.* Washington D.C.: The Brookings Institution, 1989.

Caldwell, Bruce. *Beyond Positivism: Economic Methodology in the Twentieth Century.* London: George Allen & Unwin, 1982.

Cattom, Richard W. *Iran and the United States: A Cold War Case Study.* Pittsburgh: University of Pittsburgh Press, 1988.

Chalian, G., (ed.). *People without a Country: The Kurds and Kurdestan.* London: Zed Press, 1980, pp. 107–34.

Chamsky, Noam. *Toward a New Cold War: Essays on Current Crisis and How We Got There.* New York: Pantheon Books, 1982.

Chubin, Shahram, and Charles Tripp. *Iran and Iraq at War.* Boulder, CO.: Westview Press, 1988.

Clark, Edmund W. *Socialist Development and Public Investment in Tanzania.* Toronto: University of Toronto Press, 1978.

Cline, W. R. (ed.). *Policy Alternatives for a New International Economic Order.* New York: Praeger, 1979).

Daftari, F., and M. Borghey. *Multinational Enterprises and Employment in Iran.* Geneva: ILO World Employment Program, Research Paper no. 14, 1976.

Davis, Ian. *Shelter after Disaster.* Oxford: Oxford Polytechnic Press, 1978.

Debacle: The American Failure in Iran. New York: Alfred Knopf, 1981.

Drabek, Thomas E. *Human System Responses to Disaster: An Inventory of Sociological Findings.* New York: Springer-Verlag, 1986.

Duignan, Peter, and L. H. Gann. *The Middle East and North Africa: The Challenge to Western Security.* Stanford: Hoover Institution Press, 1981.

Enayat, Hamid. *Modern Islamic Political Thought*. Austin: University of Texas Press, 1982.

Esposito, John L. *Islam and Development: Religion and Sociopolitical Change*. Syracuse: Syracuse University Press, 1980.

Fadil, Mahmoud Abdel. *The Political Economy of Nasserism*. Cambridge: Cambridge University Press, 1980.

FAO. *Production Yearbook*, 1979–87.

FAO. *Trade Yearbook*, 1980–85.

Fesharaki, Fereidun, and David Isaak. *OPEC, the Gulf, and the World Petroleum Market: A Study in Government Policy and Downstream Operations*. Boulder, Colo.: Westview Press, 1983.

Fesharaki, Feriedun. *Revolution and Energy Policy in Iran*. London: Economist Intelligent Unit, 1982.

Fischer, Michael M. J. *Iran: From Religious Dispute to Revolution*. Cambridge, Mass.: Harvard University Press, 1980.

Fitzgerald, E. V. K. and Rob Vos (eds.). *Financing Economic Development: A Structural Approach to Monetary Policy*. London: Grower, 1989.

Geiger, Theodore. *The Future of the International System: The United States and World Political Economy*. Boston: Unwin Hyman, 1988.

Germany 1945–1954. Cologne: Boas International Publishing, n.d.

Gorbachev, Mikhail. *Perestroika: New Thinking for Our Country and the World*. London: Collins, 1987.

Graham, Robert. *Iran: The Illusion of Power*. New York: St. Martin's Press, 1979.

Green, Jerrold D. *Revolution in Iran: The Politics of Countermobilization*. New York: Praeger, 1982.

Haas, E. J, R. W. Kates, and M. J. Bowden. *Reconstruction following Disaster*. Cambridge, Mass.: MIT Press, 1977.

Halliday, Fred. *Iran: Dictatorship and Development*. New York: Penguin Books, 1979.

Hancock, W. K., and M. M. Gowing. *British War Economy*. London: Her Majesty's Stationary Office, Longman, Green and Co., 1949.

Henderson, J., and M. Castells (eds.). *Global Restructuring and Territorial Development*. Beverly Hills, CA: Sage, 1987.

Hiro, Dilip. *Iran under the Ayatollahs*. London: Routledge & Kegan Paul, 1985.

Hojjati Ashrafi, Gholamreza (ed.). *Majmou^{c}h-e Qavanin Va Moqarrat-e Bazargani Va Tejarati ba Akharin eslahat Va El-haqat, 1363* [A Collection of Trade and Commercial Laws and Regulations with the Latest Corrections and Additions, 1984]. Tehran: Ketabkhaneh-e Ganj-e Danesh, 1363.

Hooglund, Eric. *Land and Revolution in Iran, 1960–1980*. Austin: University of Texas Press, 1982.

Hulbert, Mark. *Interlock: The Untold Story of American Banks, Oil Interests, the Shah's Money, Debts and the Astounding Connections Between Them*. New York: Richardson & Snyder, 1982.

Hussain, Asaf. *Islamic Iran*. New York: St. Martin's Press, 1985.

Ilyenkov, E. V. *The Dialectics of the Abstract and the Concrete in Marx's Capital*. Moscow: Progress Publishers, 1982.

International Monetary Fund. *Government Finance Statistics Yearbook, 1984*.

International Monetary Fund. *International Financial Statistics, 1984 and 1987*.

International Monetary Fund. *World Economic Outlook, 1988*.

Iran Almanec and Book of Facts and Who's Who of Iran, 18th ed. Tehran & London: Echo of Iran, 1987.

Iran Yearbook (London: MENAS Press, 1988).

Jabbari, A., and R. Olson, (eds.). *Iran: Essays on a Revolution in the Making*. Lexington, Ky.: Mazda Publishers, 1981.

Jacqz, Jane W. (ed.). *Iran: Past, Present, and Future*. New York: Aspen Institute for Humanistic Studies, 1975.

Jamalzadeh, Sayyed Mohammad Ali. *Kholghiyat-e Ma Iranian* [Temperaments of We Iranians]. Winter Park, Fla.: Kanoun Marefat Publishers, 1985.

Jazani, Bizhan. *Capitalism and Revolution in Iran*. London: Zed Press, 1980.

Jones, B., and M. Tomazevic. *Social and Economic Aspects of Earthquakes*. Skopje, Yogoslavia: Institute of Earthquake Engineering and Engineering Seismology, 1981.

Katouzian, Homa. *Political Economy of Modern Iran, 1926–1979*. New York: New York University Press, 1981.

Kazemi, Farhad. *Poverty and Revolution in Iran*. New York: New York University Press, 1980.

Keddie, Nikki. *Roots of Revolution*. New Haven, Conn.: Yale University Press, 1981.

Khaddauri, Majid. *The Gulf War: The Origins and Implications of the Iran-Iraq Conflict*. New York: Oxford University Press, 1988.

Khomeini, Imam (Ayatollah Rouholla). *Islam and Revolution: Writings and Declarations*, trans. and annotated by Hamid Algar. London: KPI, 1985.

Lenczowski, George. *Iran under the Pahlavis*. Stanford, Calif.: Hoover Institution Press, 1978.

Looney, Robert E. *Economic Origins of the Iranian Revolution*. New York: Pergamon Press, 1982.

Lowenthal, A. F. (ed.). *The Peruvian Experiment*. Princeton, N.J.: Princeton University Press, 1975.

Malek, M. M. H. *The Political Economy of Iran under the Shah*. London: Croom Helms, 1986.

Mandel, Ernest. *Late Capitalism*, trans. J. De Bres. London: Veso, 1978.

Marshall, Jonathan, Peter Scott, and Jane Hunter. *The Iran-Contra Connection: Secret Teams and Covered Operations in the Reagan Era*. Boston: South End Press, 1987.

Marx, Karl. *Grundrisse*, trans. Martin Nicolaus New York: Vintage Books, 1973.

McFardden, Robert, Joseph Treaster, and Maurice Carroll (with other colleagues). *No Hiding Place* (The New York Times Inside Report on the Hostage Crisis). New York: Times Books, 1981, pp. 149–164.

Mehrgan, Haidar. *October Va Zedd-e October* [October and Anti-October]. A publication of the Tudeh Party of Iran, 1360.

Milani, Mohsen. *The Making of Iran's Islamic Revolution: From Monarchy to Islamic Republic.* Boulder, Colo.: Westview Press, 1988.

Mofid, Kamran. *Development Planning in Iran: From Monarchy to Islamic Republic.* Cambridgeshire, U.K.: Middle East and North African Press Limited, 1987.

Motahhari, Morteza. *Fundamental of Islamic Thought.* R. Campbell. Berkely, Calif.: Mizan Press, 1982.

Mottahedeh, Roy, *The Mantle of the Prophet.* New York: Pantheon Books, 1985.

Muʾmeni, H., *Dar Bareh-e Mobarezat-e Kordestan* [About the Struggles of Kurdistan]. Tehran: Shabahang Press, 1979.

Naimi, M. T. *Toward a Theory of Postrevolutionary Social Change.* Boston: Office of the University Publisher, Harvard University, 1986.

Najmabadi, Afsaneh. *Land Reform and Social Change in Iran.* Salt Lake City: University of Utah Press, 1987.

Nasr, Seyyed Hossein, Hamid Dabashi, and Seyyed Vali Reza Nasr (eds.). *Shiʿism: Doctrines, Thoughts, and Spirituality.* Albany: State University of New York Press, 1988.

Negareshi Bar Layeh-ye Vagozari Va Ehyaʾ-ye Arazi (Band-e Jim) [A Look at the Bill for Land Redistribution and Reclamation (Section G)]. Muslim Student Association, U.S., and Canada, 1360.

Okita, Saburo, Lal Jaywardena, and Arjun Sengupta. *Mobilizing International Surpluses for World Development: A WIDER Plan for a Japanese Initiative.* Helsinki: World Institute for Development Economic Research, 1987.

Planning for Human Settlements in Disaster Prone Areas. Nairobi: United Nations Center for Human Settlements, 1983.

Political Economy of the Middle East, 1973–1978. The Joint Economic Committee, U.S. Congress (April 21, 1980). Publication no. 80–19391.

Quarterly Economic Review of Iran and its *Annual Supplement.* London: The Economic Intelligence Unit, The Economist Publications, various years.

Rajaee, Farhang. *Islamic Values and World View: Khomeini on Man, the State and International Politics.* Lanham, Md.: University Press of America, 1983.

Ramazani, R. K., *Revolutionary Iran: Challenge and Response.* Baltimore: Johns Hopkins University Press, 1986.

Razavi, Hosain, and Firouz Vakil. *The Political Environment of Economic Planning in Iran 1971–1983.* Boulder Colo.: Westview Press, 1984.

Razzaqi, Ebrahim. *Eqtesad-e Iran* [Iranian Economy]. Tehran: Nashr-e Nay, 1367.

Renaud, B. *National Urbanization Policy in Developing Countries.* New York: Oxford University Press, 1982.

Rodinson, Maxime. *Islam and Capitalism,* Brian Pearce trans. Austin: University of Texas Press, 1978.

Ryan, Paul B. *The Iranian Rescue Mission: Why It Failed.* Annapolis, Md.: Naval Institute Press, 1985.

Saddigh, J. *Mas'leh-e Melli Va Enghelab Dar Iran* [The National Question and Revolution in Iran]. New York: Fanos Press, 1973.

Safari, H. *Enhesarat-e Beinol Mellali Dar Iran* [International Monopolies in Iran]. Tehran: Publication of the Tudeh Party of Iran, 1980.

Sarrafi, Mozzafar, and M. Baroumand Yazdi. *The Spatial Formation and Suggested Strategies for Spatial Development in Iran with Special Emphasis on the Industrial Sector.* Nagoya, Japan: United Nations Center for Regional Development, April 1986.

Salinas, Victor. *Housing Reconstruction Program: A Memoir.* Mexico City: Ministry of Urban Development and Ecology, Housing Development Program, 1988.

Segev, Samuel. *The Iranian Triangle: the Untold Story of Israel's Role in the Iran-Contra Affairs.* New York: Free Press, 1988.

Semkus, Charles Ismail. *The Fall of Iran, 1978–1979.* New York: Copen Press, 1979.

Seymour, Ian. *OPEC, Instrument of Change.* London: Macmillan Press, 1980.

Shaffer, Ed. *The United States and Control of World Oil.* New York: St. Martin's Press, 1983.

Shelter after Disaster. New York: United Nations, 1982.

Sick, Gary. *All Fall Down: America's Fateful Encounter with Iran.* London: I. B. Tauris and Co. Ltd., 1986.

Stempel, J. D. *Inside the Iranian Revolution.* Bloomington: Indiana University Press, 1981.

Stepan, Alfred. *Peru in a Comparative Perspective.* Princeton, N.J.: Princeton University Press, 1978.

Stewart, Michael. *The Age of Global Interdependence: Economic Policy in a Shrinking World.* Boston: MIT Press, 1984.

Taleqani, Seyyed Mahmood. *Islam and Ownership,* trans. Ahmad Jabbari and Farhang Rajaee, Lexington, Ky.: Mazda Publishers, 1983.

Taleghani, Ayatullah Sayyid Mahmud. *Society and Economics in Islam,* trans. R. Campbell. Berkeley: Mizan Press, 1982.

Tareq, Y. Ismael. *Iraq and Iran: Roots of Conflict.* Syracuse: Syracuse University Press, 1982.

Taylor, Lance. *Stabilization and Growth in Developing Countries: A Structural Approach.* London: Harwood Academic Publishers, 1989.

Taylor, Lance. *Varieties of Stabilization Experience.* Oxford: Clarendon Press, 1988.

Tehrani, Bahram (Farboud). *Pazhuheshi Dar Eqtesad-e Iran (1354–1364)* [An Investigation into the Iranian Economy (1975–1985)], 2 vols. Paris: Khavaran Publications, 1986.

Terzian, Pierre. *OPEC: The Inside Story.* London: Zed Books, 1985.

Tower Commission Report. The Full Text of the President's Special Review Board. New York: Bantam Books, 1987.

United Nations. *Handbook of International Commodity Statistics,* 1985.

United Nations. *Handbook of International Trade and Development Statistics,* 1984 and 1985 supplements.

United Nations. *Industrial Statistics Yearbook,* vol. 1, 1982.

United Nations. *National Accounts Statistics: Compendium of Income Distribution Statistics*, 1985.

United Nations. *National Accounts Statistics: Main Aggregates and Detailed Tables*, 1982.

United Nations. *Statistical Indicators for Asia and the Pacific*, 14, no. 3 (September 1984).

United Nations. *Statistical Yearbook for Asia and the Pacific*, 1981 and 1986–1987.

United Nations. *World Economic Survey*, 1988.

United Nations. *Yearbook of International Trade Statistics*, 1982.

United Nations. *Yearbook of National Accounts Statistics*, vol. 1, Part 1, 1981.

Urquhart, Brian, and Gary Sick (eds.). *The United Nations and the Iran-Iraq War*. New York: Ford Foundation Conference Report, August 1987, pp. 7–27.

U.S. Policy toward the Persian Gulf. Washington, D.C.: Department of State, May 1980, Publication no. 80–17087.

U.S.S.R. in Reconstruction: A Collection of Essays. New York: American Russian Institute for Cultural Relations with the Soviet Union, 1944.

Vatandoust, Gholamreza (ed.). *Majmouʿh Maqalat-e Avvalin Gerd-e Hamaʾ-ye Daneshgahe Shiraz Piramoun-e Naghsh-e Pazhouhesh Dar Bazsazi* [Proceedings of the First Symposium at Shiraz University for the Reconstruction of War-Damaged Areas]. Shiraz, Iran: University of Shiraz Press, 1987.

Vatandoust, Gholamreza, Hamdolah Asafi, and Ahmad Broujerdi (eds.). *Majmouʿh Maqalat-e Dovvoumin Gerd-e Hamaʾ-ye Daneshgahe Shiraz Piramoun-e Naghsh-e Pazhouhesh Dar Bazsazi, Jeld-e Avval (Maqalat-e Oloum-e Ejtemaʿi Va Ensani)* [Proceedings of the Second Symposium at Shiraz University on the Role of Research in Reconstruction, Volume 1 (Papers on Social Sciences and Humanities)]. Shiraz, Iran: University of Shiraz Press, 1989.

Wallerstein, Immanuel. *The Modern World-System*. New York: Academic Press, 1976.

War in the Gulf. Washington, D.C.: Committee on Foreign Relations, U.S. Senate Staff Report, 1984.

Wijlkman, Anders, and Lloyd Timberlake. *Natural Disasters, Acts of God or Acts of Man.* Philadelphia: Earthscan, 1988.

Woodward, Bob. *Veil: The Secret Wars of the CIA, 1981–87.* New York: Simon and Schuster, 1987.

World Bank. *Annual Report* (1979–88).

World Bank. *World Development Report* (1979–88).

World Bank. *World Tables* (1979–88).

Zabih, Sepehr. *Iran since the Revolution.* Baltimore: Johns Hopkins University Press, 1982.

Zabih, Sepehr. *The Left in Contemporary Iran: Ideology, Organization and the Soviet Connection.* London: Croom Helm, 1986.

PUBLISHED ARTICLES, INTERVIEWS, SPEECHES, AND DOCUMENTS

Ajami, Fuad. "Egypt Retreat From Economic Nationalism." In G. Abdel Khalek and R. Tignor (eds.), *The Political Economy of Income Distribution in Egypt.* New York: Holmes & Meier, 1982.

Alaolmolki, Nozar. "The New Iranian Left." *The Middle East Journal* 41, no. 2 (Spring 1987), pp. 218–233.

Alnasrawi, Abbas. "Economic Consequences of the Iran-Iraq War," *Third World Quarterly* 8, no. 3 (July 1986), pp. 869–894).

Amirahmadi, Hooshang. "Economic Reconstruction of Iran: Costing the War Damage." *Third World Quarterly,* vol. 12, no. 1 (January 1990), pp. 26–47.

Amirahmadi, Hooshang. "A Theory of Ethnic Collective Movements and Its Application to Iran." *Ethnic and Racial Studies* 10, no. 4 (October 1987), pp. 363–391.

Amirahmadi, Hooshang. "Destruction and Reconstruction: A Strategy for the War-Damaged Areas of Iran." *Disasters: The International Journal of Disaster Studies and Practice* 11, no. 2 (1987), pp. 134–147.

Amirahmadi, Hooshang. "Iran: At the Threshold of Reconstruction" (interview). *The Urban Edge: Issues and Innovations* 12, no. 10 (December 1988), published by the World Bank.

Amirahmadi, Hooshang. "Middle-Class Revolutions in the Third World." In Hooshang Amirahmadi and Manoucher Parvin (eds.). *Post-Revolutionary Iran.* Boulder, Colo.: Westview Press, 1988, pp. 225–244.

Amirahmadi, Hooshang. "Popular Movements, Incidental Factors, and the State Measures for Regional Development in the Islamic Republic of Iran." *Review of Urban and Regional Development Studies* 1, no. 1 (January 1989), pp. 47–64.

Amirahmadi, Hooshang. "Regional Planning in Iran: A Survey of Problems and Policies." *The Journal of Developing Areas* 20, no. 4 (July 1986), pp. 501–529.

Amirahmadi, Hooshang. "The Non-Capitalist Way of Development." *Review of Radical Political Economics* 19, no. 1 (Spring 1987), pp. 24–46.

Amirahmadi, Hooshang. "The State and Territorial Social Justice in Post Revolutionary Iran." *International Journal of Urban and Regional Research* 13, no. 1 (March 1989), pp. 92–120.

Amirahmadi, Hooshang. "War Damage and Reconstruction in the Islamic Republic of Iran." In Hooshang Amirahmadi and Manoucher Parvin (eds.). *Post-Revolutionary Iran.* Boulder, Colo.: Westview Press, 1988, pp. 126–149.

Amirahmadi, Hooshang. "Finalizing the Development Strategy," *MEED* 34, no. 8 (2 March 1990), pp. viii–xiv.

Amirahmadi, Hooshang, and Farhad Atash. "Dynamics of Provincial Development and Disparity in Iran, 1956–1984." *Third World Planning Review* 9, no. 2 (May 1987), pp. 155–185.

Amirahmadi, Hooshang, and Ali Kiafar. "Tehran: Growth and Contradictions." *Journal of Planning Education and Research* 6, no. 3 (Spring 1987), pp. 167–177.

"Amnesty International's Statement to the 45th Session of the UN Commission on Human Rights." *Economic and Political Bulletin* 35, no. 14 (9 February 1989), pp. 23–24.

Amuzegar, Jahangir. "Iran's Economic Planning Once Again." *Middle East Economic Papers* (1957).

"Ansari's Letter to Imam; Imam's Answer." *Economic and Political Bulletin* 35, no. 5 (1 December 1988), p. 21–23.

Ashraf, Ahmad, and Ali Banuazizi. "The State, Classes and Modes of Mobilization in the Iranian Revolution." *State, Culture and Society* 1, no. 3 (Spring 1985), pp. 3–40.

Ashraf, Ahmad. "Interview." *Middle East Report*, no. 156 (January–February 1989), pp. 13–18.

Ashraf, Ahmad. "Peasants, Land and Revolution." In *Ketab-e Agah*. Tehran: Agah Publishers, 1982, pp. 6–49.

Ashrafi, M. "Foqdan-e Barnameh, Vizhehgi-ye Omdeh-e Bazargani-ye Keshvar Dar Salha-ye Jang" [Lack of Plan, the Principal Character of the Country's Commerce in the War Years]. *Ettelaʿat-e Siasi-Eqtesadi* 1, no. 4 (Day 1365), pp. 3–7.

Athari, Kamal. "Eqtesad-e Iran: Goriz Az Tangnaha." [The Iranian Economy: Escape from the Bottlenecks]. *Ettelaʿat-e Siasi-Eqtesadi* 4, no. 2 (Aban and Azar 1368), pp. 38–47.

"Ayatollah Montazeri's Letter to the Prime Minister." *Economic and Political Bulletin* 35, no. 2 (10 November 1988), p. 3.

Azimi, Hosain. "Budgeh Va Towseʿh-e Eqtesadi Dar Iran" [Budget and Economic Development in Iran]. *Ettelaʿat-e Siasi-Eqtesadi* 2, no. 5 (Bahman 1366).

Bacha, Edmar L. "Growth with Limited Supplies of Foreign Exchange: A Reappraisal of the Two-Gap Model." In Moshe Syrquin, Lance Taylor, and Larry Westphal (eds.). *Economic Structure and Performance: Essays in Honor of Hollis B. Chenery.* New York: Academic Press, 1984.

Bakhash, Shaul. "The Politics of Land, Law, and Social Justice in Iran." *The Middle East Journal* 43, no. 2 (Spring 1989), pp. 186–201.

Bakhash, Shaul. "What Khomeini Did." *The New York Review of Books* 36, no. 12 (20 July 1989).

Beck, L. "Revolutionary Iran and Its Tribal Peoples." In T. Asad and R. Owen (eds.), *The Middle East*. New York: MR Press, 1983.

Behdad, Sohrab. "Foreign Exchange Gap, Structural Constraints, and the Political Economy of Exchange Rate Determination in Iran." *International Journal of Middle East Studies* 20 (1988), pp. 1–21.

Behdad, Sohrab. "The Political Economy of Islamic Planning in Iran." In Hooshang Amirahmadi and Manoucher Parvin (eds.).

Post-Revolutionary Iran. Boulder, Colo.: Westview Press, 1988, pp. 107–125.

Bina, Cyrus. "Competition, Control and Price Formation in the International Energy Industry." *Energy Economics* 11, no. 3 (July 1989), pp. 162–168.

Bina, Cyrus. "Internationalization of the Oil Industry: Simple Oil Shocks or Structural Crisis?" *Review* 9, no. 3 (Summer 1988), pp. 329–370.

Chubin, Shahram. "The Last Phase of the Iran-Iraq War: From Stalemate to Ceasefire." *Third World Quarterly* 11, no. 2 (April 1989), pp. 1–14.

Clawson, Patrick. "Islamic Iran's Economic Politics and Prospects." *The Middle East Journal* 42, no. 3 (Summer 1988), pp. 371–388.

Dabashi, Hamid. " 'Islamic Ideology': The Perils and Promises of a Neologism," In Hooshang Amirahmadi and Manoucher Parvin (eds.). *Post-Revolutionary Iran.* Boulder, Colo.: Westview Press, 1988, pp. 11–22.

Dadkhah, Said. "Afzayesh-e Saderat-e Qair Nafti Va Zarorat-e Taqier-e Sakhtar-e Eqtesadi" [Increase in non-Oil Exports and the Need for Changes in Economic Structure]. *Ettela^cat-e Siasi-Eqtesadi* 1, no. 7 (Farvardin 1366), pp. 26–30.

Entessar, Nader. "Superpowers and Persian Gulf Security: The Iranian Perspective." *Third World Quarterly* 10, no. 4 (October 1988), pp. 1427–1451.

Farhang, Mansour. "How the Clergy Gained Power in Iran." In Barbara Freyer Stowasser (ed.), *The Islamic Impulse.* London: Croom Helm, 1987.

Farhang, Mansour. "The Iran-Iraq War: The Feud, the Tragedy, the Spoils." *World Policy Journal* (Fall 1985), pp. 659–680.

Farhang, Mansour. "U.S. Policy toward the Islamic Republic of Iran: A Long Tale of Shortsightedness." In Hooshang Amirahmadi (ed.). *The United States and the Middle East: A Search for New Perspectives.* Albany, N.Y.: SUNY Press (forthcoming).

Fatemi, Khosrow. "The Iranian Revolution: Its Impact on Economic Relations with the United States." *International Journal of Middle East Studies* 12 (November 1980).

Fenichel, A., and A. Khan. "The Burmese Way to Socialism." *World Development* 9, no. 9–10 (1981), pp. 813–824.

Friedman, Thomas L. "Bush Finds Threat to Murder Author 'Deeply Offensive'." *New York Times* (22 February 1989), pp. A1, A7.

Ghassemlou, A. R. "Kurdistan in Iran," In Chalian G. (ed.), *People without a Country: The Kurds and Kurdestan* (London: Zed Press, 1980), pp. 107–134.

Gorce, Paul-Marie de La. "Gesticulations Militaires dans le Golfe." *Defence Nationale* (November 1980).

Griffin, Keith B. "Foreign Capital, Domestic Savings, and Economic Development." *Bulletin of the Oxford University Institute of Statistics*. 32, pp. 99–112.

Habibulah Niknam, "Naqsh-e Afzayesh-e Daramad-e Naft Dar Sheklgiri-ye Tavarrom Va Shetab-e Nerkh-e Roshd-e Aan" [The Role of Increased Oil Income in Generating Inflation and in Its Accelerated Growth Rate], *Ettela'at-e Siasi-Eqtesadi* 1, no. 10 (Tir 1366), pp. 34–37.

Hashemi Rafsanjani, Ali Akbar. "Statement on the Occasion of the Congress of the Country's Cooperatives" (24 Mehr 1367) and "Sermon at the Friday Prayer" (28 Mordad 1367). *Kayhan-e Hava'i* (4 Aban 1367), p. 10, and (2 Shahrivar, 1367), p. 9.

Helleiner, G. H. "Balance of Payments Experiences and Growth Prospects in Developing Countries: A Synthesis." *World Development*, 14, pp. 877–908.

Hippler, Jochen. "NATO Goes to the Persian Gulf." *Middle East Report*, no. 155 (November–December 1988), pp. 18–21.

Hooglund, Eric, and Fred Halliday. "From the Editors." *Middle East Report*, no. 144 (January–February 1987), pp. 2–3.

Hooglund, Eric. "Reagan's Iran: Factions Behind US Policy in the Gulf." *Middle East Report*, no. 151 (March–April 1988), pp. 29–31.

Hurewitz, J. C. "The Middle East: A Year Turmoil." *Foreign Affairs* 59 (1981), pp. 540–577.

Ibrahim, Youssef M. "Challenge by Saudis to OPEC." *New York Times* (10 October 1988), pp. D1, D2.

Ibrahim, Youssef M. "Europeans Recall Envoys from Iran over Rushdie Case." *New York Times* (21 February 1989), pp. A1, A8.

Ibrahim, Youssef M. "Iran-Iraq Feuding Holds up OPEC Price Accord." *New York Times* (20 November 1988), p. A4.

Ibrahim, Youssef M. "Iran May Borrow at Banks Abroad to Revive Economy." *New York Times* (3 February 1989), pp. A1 and A6.

Ibrahim, Youssef M. "Khomeini Assails Western Response to Rushdie Affairs." *New York Times* (23 February 1989), pp. A1, A15.

Ibrahim, Youssef M. "New Demands by Saudis Endangers OPEC Accord." *New York Times* (28 November 1988), pp. A1, D4.

Ibrahim, Youssef M. "OPEC Price Parley Set, but Effort Seems Futile." *New York Times* (21 September 1988), p. D3.

Ibrahim, Youssef M. "OPEC Sets Quotas on Oil Production after Iran Yields." *New York Times* (25 November 1988), pp. A1, D2.

Ibrahim, Youssef M. "OPEC Signs Accord to Lower Output for Half a Year." *New York Times* (29 November 1988), pp. A1, D7.

Ibrahim, Youssef M. "OPEC Studying Demand Outlook." *New York Times* (26 September 1988), pp. A1, D5.

Ibrahim, Youssef M. "Saudis Call for Cut in Oil Output." *New York Times* (18 October 1988), pp. D1, D8.

Ibrahim, Youssef M. "Tehran Said to Reassess the Future of Its Dream." *New York Times* (6 June 1988), pp. A1, A10.

Imamian, Fereshteh. "Saderat-e Qair-e Nafti, Shenakht-e Tanghnaha" [Nonoil Exports, Recognition of Obstacles]. *Ettelaᶜat-e Siasi-Eqtesadi* 2, no. 2 (Aban 1366), pp. 44–51, 66.

"Imam Khomeini on Internal Affairs." *Economic and Political Bulletin* 35, no. 3 (17 November 1988), pp. 3–4.

"Imam Khomeini on Reconstruction." *Economic and Political Bulletin* 35, no. 2 (10 November 1988), p. 23.

"Iran's Internal Power Struggle: No Moderates among the Mullahs." *The Washington Report on the Middle East Affairs* (February 1988), pp. 4–6.

Jensen, James T. "Oil and Energy Demand: Outlook and Issues." In Robert Mabro (ed.), *The 1986 Oil Price Crisis: Economic Effects and Policy Responses.* Oxford: Oxford University Press, for the Oxford Institute for Energy Studies, 1988.

Karimi, Setareh. "Economic Policies and Structural Changes since the Revolution." In Nikki R. Keddie and Eric Hooglund (eds.), *The Iranian Revolution and the Islamic Republic.* Syracuse, N.Y.: Syracuse University Press, 1986.

Kazrouni, Sarajaldin. "Negareshi Bar Siasathay-e Qabel-e Bahregiri Dar Erteqaʾ Harakat-e Bazsazi-ye Manateq-e Jang-zadeh" [A Look at the Usable Policies in Promoting the Movement for Reconstruction of the War-Damaged Areas]. In Gholamreza Vatandoust, Hamdolah Asafi, and Ahmad Broujerdi (eds.), *Majmouʿh Maqalat-e Avvalin Gerd-e Hamav-ye Daneshgahe Shiraz Piramoun-e Naghsh-e Pazhouhesh Dar Bazsazi, Jeld-e Avval (Maqalat-e Oloum-e Ejtemaʿi Va Ensani)* [Proceedings of the Second Symposium at Shiraz University on the Role of Research in Reconstruction, Volume 1 (Papers on Social Sciences and Humanities)]. Shiraz: University of Siraz Press, 1989, pp. 29–35.

Kofi, T. A. "Prospects and Problems of the Transition from Agrarianism to Socialism: The Case of Angola, Guinea Bissau, and Mozambique." *World Development* 9, no. 9–10 (1981).

Lambton, Ann K. S. "Persia." *Journal of the Royal Central Asian Society* 31 (January 1944).

Lautenschlager, Wolfgang. "The Effects of an Overvalued Exchange Rate on the Iranian Economy." *International Journal of Middle East Studies* 18 (1986), pp. 31–52.

Leca, Jean. "Algerian Socialism: Nationalism and Industrialization and State Building." In Helen Defosses and Jacques Levesque (eds.), *Socialism in the Third World.* New York: Praeger, 1975.

Marshall, Jonathan. "Saudi Arabia and the Reagan Doctrine." *Middle East Report,* no. 155 (November–December 1988), pp. 12–16.

Mashayekhi, A. N. "Barrasi-ye Nezam Barnamehrizi-ye Keshvar Dar Amal Va Chand Pishnehad-e Eslahi" [Investigation of the Country's (Iranian) Planning System in Practice and Some Corrective Proposals]. *Barnameh Va Towseʿah* 1, no. 1 (Winter 1363), pp. 9–33.

Masʿoud Nili, "Barrasi-ye Masʿleh-e Tavvroum Dar Iran" [The Study of Inflation in Iran], *Barnameh Va Towseʿh,* no. 9 (Spring 1366), pp. 70–92.

Mirzadeh, Hamid. "Vazʿiyat-e Mojoud va Khatt-e Mash-ye Dowlat Dar Amr-e Bazsazi-ye Manateq-e Jangzadeh" [The Existing Situation and the Government's Reconstruction Policy in the War-Damaged Areas]. In Gholamreza Vatandoust, Hamdolah Asafi, and Ahmad Broujerdi (eds.), *Majmouʿh Maqalat-e Avvalin Gerd-e Hamav-ye Daneshgahe Shiraz Piramoun-e Naghsh-e Pazhouhesh Dar Bazsazi, Jeld-e Avval (Maqalat-e Oloum-e Ejtemaʿi Va Ensani)* [Proceedings of the Second Symposium at Shiraz University on the Role of Research in Reconstruction, Volume 1 (Papers on Social Sciences and Humanities)]. Shiraz: University of Shiraz Press, 1989, pp. 15–27.

Moghadam, Val. "The Left and Revolution in Iran: A Critical Analysis." In Hooshang Amirahmadi and Manoucher Parvin (eds.), *Post-Revolutionary Iran.* Boulder, Colo.: Westview Press, 1988, pp. 23–40.

Moghadam, Val. "Women, Work, and Ideology in the Islamic Republic." *International Journal of Middle East Studies* 20, no. 2 (May 1988), pp. 221–243.

Moghadam, Val. (S. Azad). "Workers' and Peasants' Councils in Iran." *Monthly Review* 32, no. 5 (October 1980), pp. 14–29.

Moshiri, Saeed. "Tajrobeh-e Qeimat Gozari Va Natayej-e Eqtesadi-ye Aan Dar Iran" [The Experience of Price Control in Iran and Its Economic Consequences]. *Barnameh Va Towseʿh,* no. 10 (Summer 1366), pp. 103–131.

O'Brien, Richard, "Oil Markets and the Developing Countries." *Third World Quarterly* 8, no. 4 (October 1986).

Olivier, R. "Regional Problems and Decentralization." *Employment and Income Policies for Iran,* Mission Working Paper No. 11, International Labor Organization, 1973.

Parvin, M. and M. Taghavi, "A Comparison of Land Tenure in Iran Under Monarchy and Under the Islamic Republic" In Hooshang Amirahmadi and Manoucher Parvin (eds.). *Post-Revolutionary Iran.* Boulder, Colo.: Westview Press, 1988, pp. 168–182.

Pesaran, M. H. "Income Distribution and Its Major Determinants in Iran." In J. W. Jacqz (ed). *Iran: Past, Present, and Future.* Aspen: Aspen Institute for Humanistic Studies, 1976.

Petrossian, Vahe. "Iran." *MEED*, Special Report on Iran (November 1984), pp. 1–44.

Pourhamid, Armin. "Hal, Iyn Salah-e Irani Ast Keh Bar Doshman-e Motajavez Miqorrad" [Now, This is the Iran-Made Armaments That Is Storming the Aggressive Enemy]. *Kayhan-e Hava'i* (26 Esfand, 1366), pp. 6, 14.

Quint, Michael. "Price War Fears Send Oil Tumbling." *New York Times* (6 October 1988), pp. D1, D16.

Razzaqi, Ebrahim. "Olgu-ye Tejarat-e Kharegi-ye Iran" [Iran's Foreign Trade Model]. *Ettela'at-e Siasi-Eqtesadi* 1, no. 9 (Khordad 1366), pp. 4–9, 13.

Razzaqi, Ebrahim. "Vabastegi Dar San't-e Naft Va Raha'i Az Aan" [Dependency on Oil Industry and Liberation from It]. *Ettela'at-e Siasi-Eqtesadi* 1, no. 7, pp. 31–17.

Renner, Michael. "Determinants of the Islamic Republic's Oil Policies: Iranian Revenue Needs, the Gulf War, and the Transformation of the World Oil Market." In Hooshang Amirahmadi and Manoucher Parvin (eds.), *Post-Revolutionary Iran*. Boulder, Colo.: Westview Press, 1988, pp. 183–209.

Richards, H. "Land Reform and Agribusiness in Iran." *MERIP Reports*, no. 43 (December 1975).

Richey, Warren. "Iraq and Iran Use Truce for Massive Arms Buildups." *Christian Science Monitor* 81, no. 31 (January 10, 1989).

Rubenberg, Cheryl A. "US Policy toward Nicaragua and Iran and the Iran-Contra Affair: Reflections on the Continuity of American Foreign Policy." *Third World Quarterly* 10, no. 4 (October 1988), pp. 1467–1504.

Sa'i, M. "Negareshi Bar Budgeh-e Dawlat Dar Sal-e 1366" [A Look at the Government's Budget in 1987]. *Ettela'at-e Siasi-Eqtesadi* 1, no. 7 (Farvardin 1366), pp. 38–41.

"Santa Satan: The Changing Iran." An interview with Hooshang Amirahmadi, Richard Bulliet, and James Bill in *Barron's: National Business Weekly* 69, no. 3 (16 January 1989), pp. 10–11, 17–21.

Schaar, Stuart. "Irangate: The Middle Eastern Connections." in Hooshang Amirahmadi (ed.), *The United States and the Middle East: A Search for New Perspectives*. Albany, N.Y.: SUNY Press (forthcoming).

Shaikhattar, Alireza (deputy for War Affairs of Ministry of Industries). "Nagsh-e Jang Dar Taqier-e Boniadha Va Sakhtarha-ye Toulid-e San'ti" [The Role of the War in Changing the Structures and Institutions of Industrial Production]. *Ettela'at-e Siasi-Eqtesadi* 1, no. 4 (22 Day 1365), pp. 8–11.

Sick, Gary. "Trial by Error: Reflections on the Iran-Iraq War." *Middle East Journal* 43, no. 2 (Spring 1989).

Skocpol, Theda, "Rentier State and the Shi'a Islam in the Iranian Revolution." *Theory and Society,* 11, no. 3 (May 1982), pp. 265–283.

Taj, M. Khosrow. "Bazargani-ye Kharegi, Sakhtar-e Ista, Tekrar-e Khata" [Foreign Trade, Static Structure, Repetition of Mistake]. *Ettela'at-e Siasi-Eqtesadi* 1, no. 9 (1366), pp. 10–13.

Turner, Terisa. "Iranian Oil Workers in 1978–79 Revolution." In Petter Nore and Terisa Turner (eds.), *Oil and Class Struggle.* London: Zed Press, 1980, pp. 272–292.

Vafa'i, Aboulhasan. "Sokhani Piramoun-e Markaz-e Pazhouhesh-ye Bazsazi" [Some words about the Center for Reconstruction Research]. In Gholareza Vatandoust, Hamdolah Asafi, and Ahmad Broujerdi (eds.), *Majmou'h Maqalat-e Avvalin Gerd-e Hama'-ye Daneshgahe Shiraz Piramoun-e Naghsh-e Pazhouhesh Dar Bazsazi, Jeld-e Avval (Maqalat-e Oloum-e Ejtema'i Va Ensani)* [Proceedings of the Second Symposium at Shiraz University on the Role of Research in Reconstruction, Volume 1 (Papers on Social Sciences and Humanities)]. Shiraz: University of Shiraz, 1989, pp. 11–13.

Valibeigi, Mehrdad. "U.S.-Iranian Trade Relations after the Revolution." In Hooshang Amirahmadi and M. Parvin (eds.), *Post-Revolutionary Iran.* Boulder, Colo.: Westview Press, 1988, pp. 210–222.

Wald, Matthew L. "Saudis' Plan on Oil Output Raises Prices." *New York Times* (11 October 1988), pp. D1, D19.

Wallerstein, Immanuel. "Dependence in an Interdependent World: The Limited Possibilities of Transformation within the Capitalist World Economy." In Heraldo Munoz (ed.), *From Dependency to Development: Strategies to Overcome Underdevelopment and Inequality* (Boulder, Colo.: Westview Press, 1981), pp. 267–293.

Wallerstein, Immanuel. "Patterns and Prospectives of Capitalist World-Economy." *Contemporary Marxism,* no. 9 (Fall 1984), pp. 59–70.

Zanjani Roughani, Masʿoud. "Motalʿat-e Bazsazi Dar Qaleb-e Tarh-e Jameʿh-e Towseʿh-e Panj Ostan-e Gharb-e Keshvar" [Reconstruction Studies within the Framework of the Comprehensive Development Plan of the Five Western Provinces of the Country], In Gholareza Vatandoust, Hamdolah Asafi, and Ahmad Broujerdi (eds.), *Majmouʿh Maqalat-e Avvalin Gerd-e Hamaʾ-ye Daneshgahe Shiraz Piramoun-e Naghsh-e Pazhouhesh Dar Bazsazi, Jeld-e Avval (Maqalat-e Oloum-e Ejtemaʿi Va Ensani)* [Proceedings of the Second Symposium at Shiraz University on the Role of Research in Reconstruction, Volume 1 (Papers on Social Sciences and Humanities)]. Shiraz: University of Shiraz, 1989, pp. 39–70.

UNPUBLISHED DISSERTATIONS AND PAPERS

Alnasrawi, Abbas. "The Impact of the Gulf War on the Economy of Iraq." Paper presented at the International Conference on the Middle East, Rutgers University, New Brunswick, N.J., 27–28 April 1987.

Amirahmadi, Hooshang. "Economic Operations in Post-Revolutionary Iran: Major Impacts, Problems, and Policy Directions." Paper presented at the 20th Annual Meeting of the Middle East Studies Association of North America (MESA), Boston, 20–23 November 1986.

Amirahmadi, Hooshang. "From Feudalism to Capitalist Manufacturing and the Origins of Dependency and Underdevelopment in Iran, 1796–1921." Ph.D. Diss. Cornell University, Ithaca, N.Y., 1982.

Amirahmadi, Hooshang. "Iran at the Threshold of the Post-War Reconstruction." Paper presented at the 7th Annual Conference of the Center for Iranian Research and Analysis, Columbia University, New York City, 7–9 April 1989.

Atash, F. "Spatial Disparity in Iran: 1949–78." Ph.D. Diss., Rutgers University, New Brunswick, N.J., 1986.

Behdad, Sohrab. "The Structural Limits of Accumulation: Crisis in the Iranian Economy 1973–78." Working Paper, Department of Economics, Denison University, 1986.

Ehteshami, Anoushirvan, "Iran's Domestic Arms Industry." Paper Presented at the Conference on the Iranian Revolution 10 Years Later, Chatham House, London, 19–20 January 1989.

Gamlen, Elizabeth. "US Response to the 'Tankers War' and the Implications of Its Intervention." Paper presented at the International Conference on Aggression and Defense, Tehran, 8–10 August 1988.

Hart, Jo-Anne. "Containment, Reflagging and Escalation: U.S. Policy in the Persian Gulf." Paper presented at the Middle East Studies Association Annual Meeting, Los Angeles, 3–5 November 1988.

Dilip Hiro, "The Iran-Iraq War," paper presented at the International Conference on the Middle East, Rutgers University, New Brunswick, April 27–28, 1987.

Imam-Jomeh, I., "Petroleum-Based Accumulation and the State Form in Iran: Aspects of Social and Geographic Variations 1953–1979." Ph.D. Diss. University of California at Los Angeles, 1985.

Kamiar, M. "Changes in Spatial Patterns of Development in Iran: An Example of Regional Inequality, 1966–1976." Ph.D. Diss. Michigan State University, East Lansing, 1985.

Mofid, Kamran. "The Economic Consequences of the Gulf War: September 1980–July 1988." Paper presented at the 7th Annual Conference of the Center for Iranian Research and Analysis, Columbia University, New York City, 7–9 April 1989.

Nattagh, N. "Consideration of Some Aspects of Regional Development in Iran in the Third, Fourth, and Fifth Plan Periods." Ph.D. Diss. University of London (SOAS), 1984.

"Settlement Reconstruction (Post-War)." Proceedings of a two-day workshop at the of Advanced Architectural Studies, University of York, 1988.

Shahabi, Sohrab. "Iran's Reconstruction and the Persian Gulf States." Paper presented at the International Conference on the Persian Gulf, Tehran, 20–22 November 1989.

Simyar, Farhad. "Economic Consequences of the Hostage Crisis for Iran." Paper presented at the 5th Annual Conference of the Center for Iranian Research and Analysis, Widener University, Chester, Pa., April 1987.

Wright, Jr., G. E. "Regional Inequality in Economic Development of Iran, 1962–1970." Ph.D. Diss. University of Michigan, Ann Arbor, 1977.

Zahrai, Mehdi Masoud. "The Origins and the Causes of the Iranian–Iraqi War." Ph.D. Diss. Graduate School, University of Idaho, 1983.

Zangeneh, Hamid. "Islamic Banking: Theory and Practice in Iran." Paper presented at the 6th Annual Conference of the Center for Iranian Research and Analysis (CIRA), University of Chicago, April 1988.

NEWSAGENCIES, NEWSPAPERS AND PERIODICALS

Arabia: The Islamic World Review (Slough, U.K.)

Barnameh Va Towseᶜh (Tehran)

Barron's: National Business Weekly (New York)

BBC Summary of World Broadcasts (Reading, U.K.)

British Society for Middle Eastern Studies Bulletin (U.K.)

Christian Science Monitor (Boston)

CIRA Newsletter (New Brunswick, N.J.)

Contemporary Marxism (U.S.)

Daily Telegraph (London)

Disaster: The International Journal of Disaster Studies and Practice (England)

Economist (London)

Economic and Political Bulletin (Echo of Iran)

Economic Bulletin (Echo of Iran)

Energy Economics (U.S.)

Engelab-e Islami (Tehran)

Ethnic and Racial Studies (England)

Ettelaᶜat (daily, Tehran)

Ettelaᶜat-e Siasi-Eqtesadi (published by *Ettelaᶜat* daily, Tehran)

Financial Times (London)

Foreign Affairs (U.S.)

Foreign Broadcast Information Service (Washington, D.C.)

Guardian (London)

International Journal of Middle East Studies (Tucson, Ariz.)

International Journal of Urban and Regional Research (U.K.)

Iran Focus (MENAS Press)

Iranian Studies (U.S.)

Iran Times (weekly, Washington, D.C.)

Islamic Republic News Agency (Tehran)

Jomhouri-ye Islami (daily, Iran)

Journal of Developing Areas (U.S.)

Journal of Planning Education and Research (U.S.)

Journal of the Royal Central asian Studies (U.K.)

Kayhan Daily (Iran)

Kayhan-e Hava'i (published by *Kayhan* daily and distributed outside Iran)

Keshavarz (Iran)

Ketab-e Agah (Tehran)

Khorasan Daily (Iran)

Le Monde (Paris)

Majaleh-e oloum-e Ejtema'i Va Ensani (Shiraz, Iran)

MERIP Middle East Report (Washington)

Middle East Economic Digest (London)

Middle East Economic Papers (U.S.)

Middle East Economic Survey (Nicosia)

Middle East Executive Report (Washington, D.C.)

Middle East Journal (Washington)

Monthly Review (New York)

Newsweek (New York)

New York Times

New York Review of Books (New York)

Observer (London)

OPEC Bulletin

Petroleum Intelligence Weekly (U.K.)

Political Bulletin (Echo of Iran)

Quarterly Economic Review and its *Annual Supplement* (published by *Economist*, London)

Resalat Daily (Iran)

Review (U.S.)

Review of Radical Political Economics (U.S.)

Review of Urban and Regional Development Studies (Tokyo)

San⁽t-e Haml Va Nagl (Tehran)

Shahed (Iran)

Sharif newsletter (Iran)

Shawra (Paris)

Siasat-e Kharegi (Tehran)

Soroush (Iran)

State, Culture and Society (U.S.)

Tehran Times (Tehran)

Third World Planning Review (England)

Third World Quarterly (London)

Time (New York)

Urban Edge, The: Issues and Innovations (World Bank, Washington, D.C.)

Washington Post (Washington, D.C.)

Washington Report on the Middle East Affairs (Washington, D.C.)

World Development (U.S.)

World Policy Journal (U.S.)

Index